An Iron
Wind

An Iron Wind

Europe Under Hitler

Peter Fritzsche

BASIC BOOKS

New York

Basic Books
Hachette Book Group
1290 Avenue of the Americas, New York, NY 10104
www.basicbooks.com

Printed in the United States of America

First Trade Paperback Edition: April 2018

Published by Basic Books, an imprint of Perseus Books, LLC, a subsidiary of Hachette Book Group, Inc. The Basic Books name and logo is a trademark of the Hachette Book Group.

The Hachette Speakers Bureau provides a wide range of authors for speaking events. To find out more, go to www.hachettespeakersbureau.com or call (866) 376-6591.

The publisher is not responsible for websites (or their content) that are not owned by the publisher.

Designed by Amy Quinn

The Library of Congress has cataloged the hardcover edition as follows:
Names: Fritzsche, Peter, 1959– author.
Title: An iron wind : Europe under Hitler / Peter Fritzsche.
Description: New York : Basic Books, [2016] | Includes bibliographical references and index.
Identifiers: LCCN 2016018828 (print) | LCCN 2016025604 (ebook) | ISBN 9780465057740 (hardcover) | ISBN 9780465096558 (ebook)
Subjects: LCSH: World War, 1939–1945—Occupied territories. | World War, 1939–1945—Europe. | World War, 1939–1945—Personal narratives, European. | World War, 1939–1945—Social aspects—Europe. | Civilians in war—Europe—History—20th century. | Violence—Social aspects—Europe—History—20th century. | War and society—Europe—History—20th century. | Hitler, Adolf, 1889–1945—Influence. | Europe—Social conditions—20th century. | BISAC: HISTORY / Modern / 20th Century.
Classification: LCC D802.A2 F77 2016 (print) | LCC D802.A2 (ebook) | DDC 940.53/4—dc23
LC record available at https://lccn.loc.gov/2016018828

ISBNs: 978-0-465-05774-0 (hardcover); 978-0-465-09655-8 (ebook); 978-1-5416-9882-6 (paperback)

LSC-C

10 9 8 7 6 5 4 3 2 1

For Franziska, my love

CONTENTS

PREFACE

After I completed my book *Life and Death in the Third Reich* and corrected the galleys, I left for Germany with my children for a semester-long sabbatical. When I got to Berlin in January 2008, I simply kept on going, researching the book I had just finished, prowling the archives, looking for stories, trying to find more voices to help me understand the calamity of World War II and the Holocaust. At the same time, I became increasingly aware of how contemporaries themselves recorded events and established archives in order to make sure that a history of the war could be written. Some of this activity was undertaken by Germans, usually as they looked forward to a great victory; much of it was undertaken by Jews as they contemplated the destruction of their families in the ghettos into which they had been shoved. Slowly, I organized my thoughts and conceived of a book that would explore how people in World War II struggled to make sense of the murderous events occurring around them. I wanted to understand what people thought they were seeing in German-occupied Europe. Civilians constituted the great majority of the victims in the war, but they also deliberately refused to see or they misunderstood what they did see. Ordinary men and women thereby contributed to the horror that engulfed Europe. Even patriotic narratives of anti-German resistance mirrored Nazi views of the world in crucial ways. This book is about the wartime experience of civilians, the often dubious parts they played in the war, and the ways they approached their neighbors and the groups persecuted by the Germans. The violence of the war was so extensive that people tried to contain it by separating themselves from the fate of others. World War II revealed the broad collapse of structures of empathy and solidarity in a way that World War I never did. People helped each other, but they also betrayed each other. They were blinded by myopia, but they were also brutally frank and occasionally startlingly incisive. *An Iron Wind* tells the story of how people struggled to find meaning in World War II. It tries to listen in—to the talk in wartime.

This book has been a long time in the making, and I finally began writing in 2014. I would not have completed this book without the love and support of my wife, Franziska, to whom it is dedicated. She is my great love. I have always been nourished by my children, Lauren, Eric, Elisabeth, Joshua, and now Matteo, whom I neglected but with whom I also sometimes, hopefully often enough, played hooky. I am deeply grateful to my colleague Harry Liebersohn and my mother, Sybille Fritzsche, for reading and commenting on the manuscript. Many thanks to my agent, Andrew Wylie, for his consistent support and to Brian Distelberg at Basic Books for his extraordinary suggestions on how to improve my argument. Many years ago, Matti Bunzl and the Jewish Studies reading group at the University of Illinois provided an early and hugely welcome forum for what were still my hugely rough ideas. My thanks also to Geoff Eley, Anne Fuchs, and Michael Geyer. Many people, most of whom I know only through their words, were in my thoughts as I wrote this book; I want to name one of them: my father, Hellmut, himself a World War II veteran. I have become a better scholar and writer thanks to these collaborations, but the errors and problems that remain are all mine. Ultimately, no book on World War II can ever be finished or be adequate in any meaningful way, which is both the origin and the conclusion of *An Iron Wind*.

Urbana

March 23, 2016

INTRODUCTION

Stalingrad's World War II memorial is inscribed with the words "An iron wind beat into their faces," followed by "but they all kept marching on." For German-occupied Europe, the first part is true; the second part is not. The war was an "iron wind," massively and unrelentingly destructive on the home front as well as the battlefield. But not everyone marched. People were deported, enslaved, and massacred. Others crouched down to find shelter from the wind of war, or they turned with the wind to collaborate or somehow make do. Those who did fight did not always do so from the war's beginning or find themselves alive at its end. This book is about how people scattered by the iron wind of Germany's war in Europe in the years 1939–1945 came to intellectual grips with the most terrible conflict in modern history.

When World War II came, it smashed through the expectations about battle that had been formed during the Great War that preceded it. The war marched into civilian lives in an unprecedented way. Not only were cities bombed but homes invaded, neighbors arrested, and Jews deported. The iron wind also unsettled and then blew apart notions of empathy and solidarity. In no previous modern war was the casualty rate among civilians so high and suspicion about neighbors so acute. In dramatic contrast to the fallen uniformed soldiers mourned after World War I, the vast majority of the dead in World War II were noncombatant men, women, and children, some 20 million in all. Nearly 1 million civilians died in aerial bombardments, with tens of millions more left homeless, but the air war's casualties were not nearly as high as Europeans anticipated at the outbreak of the war. Instead, thousands upon thousands of civilians were slaughtered as hostages, as Germany retaliated against partisan attacks on its soldiers, or were killed simply for being Polish or Jewish. Nearly 1 out of every 5 Poles perished during the conflict, in contrast to 1 in 50 who did so in France. Three-quarters of Europe's Jews, a total of 6 million people, did not survive; they were the neighbors most likely to be deported and murdered. The war turned military barracks such as those in Theresienstadt and Auschwitz into civilian concentration camps. It is imperative to reconsider World War II not simply as a military conflict but as an extraordinary assault on civilians.

World War II's "home front" was the setting for what was new and most shocking about the war. Trouble in the streets, noises in the stairwell, and wartime curfews meant that people stayed at home for longer periods of time, at least until they were forced to leave. It was in their rooms that observers tried to figure out what was going on, where they looked out of windows, explored labyrinths of the heart, and pieced thoughts into philosophy. People sought to make sense of the war and the new circumstances it imposed. Words gained new meanings in the violence, even as they lost much of their ability to communicate events. Speakers and listeners, texts and contexts, were torn from familiar moorings by the iron wind. The words people spoke and wrote reveal the labor of comprehension and the struggle for meaning in World War II.

War in the twentieth century ripped apart assumptions about progress and civilization. The "Great War" in 1914–1918—a war that was great because it was so murderous and long—exposed basic failings in major social institutions, which often proved themselves to be inept, inflexible, and unaccountable. In contrast, individual men and women emerged from the war abused, victimized, but still very much human. The cynicism of the interwar years thus targeted parliamentary leaders and their patriotic speeches, business executives and their profiteering, and military strategists and their misguided directives, but not the soldiers who had fought and sacrificed in the trenches.

World War II exposed something else. The drama of the war was found not in a contemptible betrayal of the front by the rear but in the betrayals that characterized civilians at home. In Europe the war was first and foremost a regime of German occupation, bracketed by often quite rapid military engagements at the beginning and the end. During the occupation, neighbors often divided on basic political issues regarding Germany's war aims and the durability of the new order it sought to impose on the Continent. Some people collaborated, others resisted, but most wavered in a moral no-man's-land between the two positions. Opportunism and greed motivated civilians, fear paralyzed them, and disregard for others blinded them. The war erased whole horizons of empathy as people crouched within their own little worlds of tenuous security. Neighbors failed one another. The terms *Jew* and *Aryan* quickly became part of everyday speech, widening the gulf between the two groups, who experienced very different wars. Patriots and resistors did rally against the Germans, but the patriotic narratives they embraced became much more ethnically and religiously homogenous. In sum, the war made men and women look smaller: they were easily misled, apt to be envious, mistrustful, and indifferent to the fate of others, particularly Jews, and more often than not accommodated themselves with surprising ease to circumstances in which they simply struggled to survive.

At the heart of the war was the experience of civilians who suffered and who aggravated suffering in extraordinary ways. War has often been compared to a plague that sweeps through a population, a natural catastrophe that suddenly destroys everyday routines, or a weather front that darkens the skies. These images aptly convey how war affected everything in daily life. But they fail to account for the part that civilians played in the disaster and the far-reaching consequences of their interpretations and responses. *An Iron Wind* explores the lessons civilians learned as they learned the war. It follows the conversations by which people comprehended the war as it unfolded and the sight lines by which they witnessed the depredations occurring around them. While most accounts of German-occupied Europe examine German policies and the pathways people took to collaboration and resistance, this book expands the focus to investigate what people thought about themselves, about the violence the Germans meted out, and the indifference the violence prompted as well as the explanations proffered to understand its proliferation into all the corners of daily life. The chapters that follow are ultimately about how neighbors, people who were likely to meet and to share common spaces, looked at themselves in conditions of extreme violence. The self-examination demanded by the war revealed new creatures, some of them sympathetic, many of them loathsome. Because the Nazi assault on Europe's Jews occurred in plain view of millions of people, but was not properly seen or understood at the time, the Holocaust is central to appreciating how the home front responded to and was marked by extreme violence. Examining how occupied Europe made sense of World War II is essential to understanding what became of men and women in a war that was very much directed at civilians and civilian society.

The "iron wind" dispersed people, uprooted them, and forced them to rally to new lines of defense. It also rearranged the words they used to make sense of the turbulence going on around them. Words consoled, but they also misled, and they often proved insufficient to provide a full understanding of the German assault. This inadequacy was part of the devastation of the war. These words in destruction often misrepresented the horrors of war, justified them, yet ultimately, in however insufficient a way, they also witnessed and narrated them. If read carefully, the incomplete and inadequate descriptions of the war that survive offer unparalleled insights into the everyday experience of the war, conveying the mixture of illusion, hope, anguish, and indifference that it prompted. The inscription at Stalingrad describing "an iron wind" is a perfect example of how words—in this case, composed in 1967—could both distort the record of the war, which did not provide evidence for massive collective resistance, and contribute to that record by offering a rallying myth for those who did resist. Words like *an iron wind* tell us something about the frightening nature of the conflict, the problems inherent in fully and accurately understanding it, and people's great eagerness to find narrative forms that would create meaning and enable the remembrance of suffering and sacrifice.

Ordinary people undertook a great deal of intellectual work to understand the war. Mostly, they talked. There was endless talk about the war, the aims of the Nazis and their relationship to the German people as a whole, the possibility of the war expanding over time and through space, and, of course, the prospects for a final victory. It consumed families

over the rationed courses of dinner, it preoccupied shoppers standing in
long lines curling out of the butcher's or baker's, and it furnished rumors
and jokes to travelers on railway journeys. At home people took up ambitious reading programs that gave books such as Tolstoy's *War and Peace*
unprecedented popularity, even as the large shelf of volumes on soldiers
fighting World War I remained largely untouched. Victorious German
soldiers pasted together commemorative photo albums right up until
the point when they started to retreat. Indeed, much of the documentary evidence about the Holocaust comes from amateur photographers
in the ranks of the German military. Millions and millions of pieces of
mail were sent to and from the military fronts; battlefields were littered
with the letters and notebooks that fallen soldiers had stuffed into their
gear. Along the railroad tracks carrying the freight cars of deported Jews,
passersby sometimes picked up and even posted crumpled letters that
had been thrown through the cracks. Across Europe diarists recorded
the conversations and rumors they heard and the impressions they gathered; especially in the Polish ghettos into which the Germans herded local Jews, everyone seemed to keep a diary. An astonishing number of
these survived, since great care was taken not only to bear witness but
also to preserve the text of witnessing. Indeed, many of the diaries that
cover the years 1939 to 1945 were begun with the explicit intention to
leave a record of wartime experience. War generated copy. Most of these
personal papers have not previously been used in a critical or central way
to tell the story of the war.

   Witnesses wrote with a mixture of confusion and confidence, and
both attitudes shaped ordinary people's wartime experience and contributed to their ability to understand and act. In Jewish ghettos, for
example, diarists trembled as they set pen to paper, they anguished over
whether words existed to convey the terrifying realities unfolding around
them, and they worried about the capacity of readers after the war to
believe or comprehend the narratives they left behind. Sometimes they
stopped writing because they were paralyzed or dispirited. At the same
time, they could write only because they had some confidence that they
were communicating with future readers. Diarists who recorded Germany's implementation of the "final solution" contemplated the possibility

that their experience would be forgotten entirely. But they nevertheless turned the page, because they believed there was a reasonable chance that their lives and their sufferings might be recognized and incorporated into a different kind of postwar history. Confusion created insight regarding the power and frailty of words and provided a glimpse into despair and fright. Confidence depended in large measure on worn clichés, consoling precedents, and conventional narratives that generated hope but did not always shed light.

Germans often wrote with great confidence about the epic nature of the victories they had achieved, but the stories they told also betrayed confusion and bewilderment about the losses those victories required. Likewise, in France and Poland, witnesses watched the actions of their neighbors and had to guess at their motives and weigh their own. They asked themselves about the extent of collaboration with or resistance to the German occupiers and the depth of even their own anti-Semitism. Yet the citizens of the occupied nations also consoled themselves with tight patriotic narratives that obscured unwelcome or confusing evidence of complicity in German policies. It is precisely the everyday work of mulling over, but also denying, unwelcome truths about collaboration and anti-Semitism in conversations, diaries, and letters that makes wartime talk such a rich source for understanding people's experience in German-occupied Europe.

An Iron Wind is organized around a series of contrasting perspectives. At every step I analyze how different perspectives influenced the choices civilians made, showing both how the experience of war shaped the record of war and how the record shaped the experience. I begin with Europeans contemplating war in 1938, the year when most everybody expected the outbreak of a high-tech air war, contrasting the "great debate" about intervention and Hitler's intentions with the actual racial war that ultimately unfolded. This picture of before and after indicates how thoroughly Europeans could misunderstand German intentions in World War II and how they could mistake Hitler's principal victims, European Jews, for intemperate warmongers. I use Paris and Warsaw, the two largest cities occupied by the Germans, to provide different perspectives on the occupation and civilian responses to it. Paris became more like Warsaw over time, but the Germans consistently acted with more thorough brutality in Warsaw, which was basically leveled at the end of the war, than in Paris, which was not. I also compare how Jews in Paris and Warsaw and elsewhere perceived the war and were perceived in the war by their fellow citizens. It becomes very clear that across Europe, there was both a Jewish and a non-Jewish war zone, which were separate in crucial ways despite overlapping in time and space. The erection of this mental border was one grim achievement of the German occupation. It cleared the path to genocide, but also had the deleterious effect of forcing Jews themselves to make distinctions between those they believed could be saved and those who could not. Living with these borders, people across Europe accepted the proposition that their own survival depended in large part on the death sentences meted out to others. Finally, I have used the somewhat unusual example of Switzerland to draw out discussions about the promise and the limits of the new order that the victorious Third Reich represented and the startling frankness with which Germans justified the violence that the new order entailed. In many ways, the Swiss were "cousins" to the Germans, at once intimate and distant enough to consider seriously the appeal of Nazism and to prod the Nazis to explain themselves. Swiss witnesses thereby recorded the voices of German perpetrators. While *An Iron Wind* spotlights civilians, it also examines the uniformed German soldiers who menaced them.

Focusing on French, Polish, Jewish, German, and Swiss witnesses leaves a great deal out, since the Germans occupied much more of Europe, creating extraordinary devastation in the Soviet Union and relying on client states such as Hungary, Italy, and Croatia to pursue their ambitious continental policies. But Paris and Warsaw provide illuminating perspectives on the overall contours of civilian experience during World War II and on the effort to comprehend the war, from the most basic outlines of the conflict to its deepest implications regarding the nature of God, divine justice, the scope of humanity, and the adequacy of testimony. Using the ordinary documents that observers created for themselves, I have tried to listen and to analyze how people made sense of the deadliest war in modern times. The dilemmas of choice, responsibility, and witnessing that World War II exposed still structure the intellectual world we live in today. In the most dramatic way, the war posed existential questions about the solidarities among men and women, the human capacity to accept evil, the existence of God, and the shortcomings of witnessing, many of the elements that make up our own postmodern sensibility. Whenever we return to the terrible years 1939–1945, we are forced to wonder about what it is that makes us human and frail.

1

Talk in Wartime

ENGLISH WRITER LEONARD WOOLF DESCRIBED THE EXPERIENCE OF the new war as something like "endlessly waiting in a dirty, grey railway station waiting-room, with nothing to do but wait endlessly for the next catastrophe." Woolf's repetition—"waiting . . . waiting . . . wait"—suggests his sense of complete arrest. Woolf's anticipation and apprehension were rooted in his keen understanding of the "terrible difference" between August 1914, when ideas of armed conflict remained wrongly scaled to events that had occurred at Austerlitz and Waterloo one hundred years earlier, and September 1939, when, as a result of the war of 1914–1918, people now knew "exactly" the "horrors of death and destruction, wounds and pain and bereavement and brutality." Across Europe when war was declared in 1939 for the second time in a lifetime, there was no sign of the lighthearted, celebratory mood that had rushed over the capital cities twenty-five years earlier. Families still grieved for sons and brothers and fathers who had fallen in the Great War. You could see men missing legs or arms walk across all scenes of everyday life. Now the next trainload of events was rolling into the station. Woolf's "exactly" bespoke his expectation of terrible things oncoming: call-up orders, memorized song, pale lies, casualty lists, tear-streaked faces. But in fact the Great War did not furnish exact knowledge about the next much greater war that was on its way.[1]

The difference between August 1914 and September 1939 was not just better knowledge of the costs of war. The new conflict appeared more omnivorous because it was poised to destroy homes and neighborhoods, not just soldiers on the front. In September 1939, civilians thought not only about loved ones in uniform, but also about themselves. Writer Virginia Woolf, Leonard's wife, remarked on the domestic state of the emergency, describing "heaps of sandbags in the streets," "men digging trenches" in the parks, "lorries delivering planks" on corners. Indeed, in the fall of 1940 the Woolfs lost their home in London in an aerial bombardment, and they continued to be menaced by the "wail of the sirens" and the "drone of the German planes flying in from the sea" after they had retreated to the country in Sussex. Not least because she feared that German soldiers would follow German airplanes, Virginia Woolf committed suicide at the end of March 1941. What was different about World War II was that war came in "from the sea," across the borders that separated the battlefront from the home front, that it swept into domestic lives, and that it kept coming as one danger waved in the next.[2]

The sense of being assaulted but not knowing when "the next catastrophe" would come or from where created the feeling of being stuck in a "railway station waiting-room." The wait was not only endless but all-enveloping. It was a new sort of self-consciousness: the war threatened to "become all you know." Virginia Woolf herself had for a long time tried to stay clear of the waiting room, remaining an outsider to the war. Who could "care one straw," she asked in 1938, about a future war? "We know winning means nothing." But when air war did come from across the Channel, it spread like a "terrible disease." Suddenly, the outsider was inside. Woolf wrote about "our wounded," "our men," "our majestic city." She soon felt trapped inside: after the defeat of France in June 1940, she wrote, "We're fighting alone with our back to the wall."[3]

In the uncertain wait for the "next catastrophe," wartime stretched out the present moment so very far that it felt like an eternity. "Time since the armistice" between France and Germany in June 1940, remarked writer Léon Werth, this time from Lyons in 1941, "has not been real time"; it has simply been a "time of waiting." Using the same metaphor as Leonard Woolf, he wrote, "We can classify it as the category of time which one spends in a train station waiting for a train."[4] It was a time that both annihilated and stayed, cutting away the past, postponing the future, and elongating the present amid an unceasing barrage of events. And as in any "railway station waiting-room," the stranded travelers read timetables, they reread bulletins, they peered down the tracks, and they talked constantly among themselves about the next train. They waited for the wail of the siren, anticipated the drone of the bomber, and wondered when soldiers would invade. In World War II, the waiting and waiting-room chatter went on and on.

The stretched-out present was time without a frame, terrain without a horizon. Normal timetables no longer applied. In Dresden Victor Klemperer, a professor of literature and a German Jew, who was protected by his marriage to a Catholic, waited for some sort of conclusion—not so much a sign on the horizon as a sign of the horizon. Surely, the terrible laws in September 1941 requiring Jews to wear yellow stars represented "the final act," his friend Missy Meyerhof, writing from Berlin, argued: "I too believe it is the fifth act." Klemperer agreed. But unlike Shakespeare's plays, he noted, "some plays in world literature, e.g., Hugo's *Cromwell*, have *six* acts." Would there be another catastrophe after the star decree? In Paris, a year later, in July 1942, another student of literature, Hélène Berr, herself already wearing the yellow Jewish star, suspected that "something is brewing." She figured that the "next catastrophe" would certainly be "a tragedy" for fellow Jews, but she did not know whether it would it be "*the* tragedy."[5] Would the fifth act be the final act? And would the final act bring an end to the war, or would it bring an end to the travelers in the railway station waiting room? This confusion was the condition of end-lessly waiting for the next catastrophe.

Contemporaries such as Leonard Woolf, Léon Werth, Victor Klemperer, and Hélène Berr talked without end about the end of the war, and they searched for signs—the "vox populi," in Klemperer's words—that might help them reach some sort of conclusion. However, what they found were often "voces populi," a confusing array of contradictory data. Very little was predictable or certain. The first season of the war in the autumn of 1939 was quickly designated as the "phony war" because the expected air bombardments of London, Paris, and Berlin failed to materialize. The fall of France to Germany in June 1940 was supposed by many to end in a scenario in which Britain would be knocked out of the war, but this did not happen either. Germany's "Blitzkrieg" offensives against the Soviet Union in the summer of 1941 and again a year later ended neither in defeat nor in victory. The dramatic events of the year 1943, after Germany suffered huge losses at Stalingrad and Italy turned against its coalition partner, did not bring about Germany's capitulation, as many observers had assumed. What is more, the Allies did not open a second front in 1942 or 1943, as promised. And when it did come at last, in June 1944 with the invasion of Normandy, predictions by military commanders that Germany would surrender by Christmas proved to be wrong. "Logistical planning in the Second World War was a nightmare," concludes one historian.[6] This nightmare had the effect of making talk in wartime more animated, more obsessive, and more inconclusive.

Woolf's "railway station" image is especially apt because opinions about the "next catastrophe" were frequently expressed in actual train stations and on trains. Trains and stations were places where one was likely to have time on one's hands, to meet strangers who might have heard something new, and to pick up threads of wartime talk. One could literally take a train between 1939 to 1945, whether it was an express from Warsaw, a local out of Bourg, a German army transport to Dnipropetrovsk in Ukraine, or a tram around Amsterdam, and hear constant chatter about the war: the summer offensive, the second front, and the end of the war; food shortages, the black market, and the cold of winter; the depredations of soldiers and the deportation of Jews. Trains, train stations, and waiting rooms were garrulous spaces, and diarists often read the signs of the war by reporting on conversations among travelers. Other public spaces such as food lines and air-raid shelters similarly conferred anonymity and stopped time, making the people in their confines more approachable to one another.

The Gestapo went precisely to these places—"the streetcar, railway station waiting rooms, taverns, cafes, cinemas, markets, swimming pools, factory courtyards, canteens," and air-raid shelters—to report on morale. Occupation authorities in Paris supposedly recruited local agents to stand undercover in food lines where they might hear anti-German remarks.[7] French satirical novelist Marcel Aymé, a great skeptic of loyalty to anything but the foibles of ordinary people, placed talkative, complaining countrymen in a food line in order to capture in short story form the degraded condition of France during the war ("Do you think the war will go on long?")—though the fourteenth person in line ended up saying nothing, "for she had just died all of a sudden" of "poverty, fear, and exhaustion." Across the frontier, Swiss officials focused their concerns about loose talk that might offend German visitors on dangerous places, including "restaurants, trains, etc." In such locations, authorities hung posters with statements warning citizens to hold their tongues: "Keep your mouth shut, or else you'll hurt the homeland." Less concerned about offending German feelings than bolstering Swiss morale, exiled theologian Karl Barth believed that it made a great difference to public order whether the "grumbling, muttering, and gossiping" one could hear everywhere, "in the tavern, on the tramway, in the stores," was expressed in a "resolute or a worn out manner." His written admonition, however, was censored.[8] The war's waiting room was oppressive, not least because it was so noisy and redundant—and a bit rebellious.

The railway station waiting room was a place for talk, but it also was a way station for millions of Europeans who found themselves on the move during the war, displaced from home, separated from family, and often unable to return to the places they had come from. War made the extraordinary scale of dislocation plain to see. Wilm Hosenfeld, an observant Catholic and one of the few Wehrmacht officers to come to the aid of Polish Jews—including pianist Wladyslaw Szpilman, later the subject of the film *The Pianist*—reckoned quite accurately that "since the earth has existed, there has not been such a movement of masses as in this war." Writing in 1944, he actually knew where to begin:

> Beginning with the Poles fleeing and flooding back to the border regions, the resettled ethnic Germans, the refugees in France, and now in Italy and Russia, where people have been chased out two or three times. What Russ. civilians have endured is excruciating. Then the extermination of several million Jews, the destruction of German cities and the dispersion of their inhabitants, in addition to millions of foreigners who have forced to come to Germany and work. Everywhere, millions of troops

of the warring nations face off to destroy each other—a revolution and catastrophe of unprecedented proportions.[9]

Stationed in Poland since the beginning of the war, Hosenfeld was well placed to construct a clear picture, giving a complete summary of the extraordinary racial ambitions of Germany's empire builders. His account is noteworthy because it was not seen solely through the self-centered perspective of mounting German losses: after January 1945, millions more German civilians would join the exodus of refugees that had begun in Polish towns and villages in September 1939. What he saw, which most contemporaries did not, was more turbulence from beginning to end.

Most refugees had no real destination, which intensified the nervous dislocations of the waiting-room war. Once families set on the road, they frequently forfeited the ability to return home. German and Soviet annexations made former homes off-limits to thousands of Poles. Already in 1939, Zygmunt Klukowski, a good-hearted small-town doctor called up as a reserve officer in the Polish army and himself on the road without a plan, remarked that masses of "people, seized with panic, were going ahead, without knowing where or why, and without any knowledge of where the exodus would end." Polish civilians commandeered city buses from Lodz, Kraków, and Warsaw or set out on "all types of motorized vehicles" or "horse-drawn wagons"; "people on foot and on bicycles added to the confusion."[10] Some went east, others west. Baggage was quickly abandoned because it was too heavy. Bundles of possessions grew smaller and smaller. Nine months later, refugees from Belgium and France sought to escape the advancing German armies, moving south and west along the main roads that they shared with mobilized military units until they were overtaken either by the victorious Wehrmacht or by the fact of the armistice. Jews, as well as French Africans and Algerians, who had fled to the unoccupied zone in southern France were not allowed to return to the German occupied zone. And even though most other French citizens were able to return home in a few months, families remained broken apart. The majority of French soldiers taken prisoner by the Germans, nearly 2 million, did not come home until 1945. Dislocation as much as waiting defined the experience of occupation.

When the Germans restarted the war of movement with the invasion of Yugoslavia, Greece, and then the Soviet Union in the spring and summer of 1941, roads were overrun with exhausted refugees who filed past the corpses of starved Russian soldiers taken prisoner or simply shot as stragglers. Charkov, the second-largest city in Ukraine, was captured and recaptured three times by the Germans between 1941 and 1943 before the Red Army finally liberated the almost deserted city in August 1943. The Germans transported millions of conscript workers from across Europe into the Reich and threw Jews, Poles, and others out of the territories they annexed. At the other end of the war, German civilians fleeing the Russian advance in the winter of 1945 crowded into Berlin, where psychologist Matthais Menzel saw them waiting "for trains which don't depart, headed for destinations which no longer make sense." As refugees waited to move on, farther westward, "the howling and whining of the air-raid sirens drive them with kit and caboodle into bunkers and basements." Only a few lucky refugees escaped Europe's war altogether, some of them reaching Lisbon, "this last open port," in engagé novelist Arthur Koestler's description, "Europe's gaping mouth, vomiting the contents of her poisoned stomach."[11]

The massive, involuntary movement of so many people jumbled travelers in the corridors of trains. Within the Third Reich, one Swiss journalist came across a strikingly polyglot scene, a din of "Italian and French"—"the Balkans are also abundantly represented"—that contradicted the picture of racial homogeneity that the Nazis had so carefully arranged. A French prisoner assigned to a farm or a serving girl recruited from a concentration camp could be easily folded into familiar domestic routines. But Germans who watched workers impressed from Poland and Ukraine standing "in clumps" outside train stations, "dirty, freezing, almost all of them without coats," found the sight disturbing, a sign of general squalor. For Lisa de Boor, a journalist from Marburg, the presence of so many people stranded by war caught her by surprise: it was "something I had not seen before." For the most part, however, travelers in the Reich saw the movement around them in an exclusively German frame. But what appeared to de Boor at first to be terribly exciting, as German soldiers journeyed "for days" across "enormous distances" that used to exist only in Russia (to which, she left unsaid, Germany's fate had now been yoked), looked very different in 1943.

In March 1943, de Boor found herself once traveling by train. She described "the difficult lives of all these people around me!" but contemplated only German tragedies:

> The couple evacuated from Cologne with kids, the husband on leave from Africa waiting on the platform in Kassel. Next to him, a blinded soldier, on his way to the School for the Blind in Marburg, greedily smoking the cigarette that his companion has stuck in his mouth. Then a big, fat soldier on crutches, without shoes, his feet wrapped in bandages, the frozen toes having been amputated. Next to him, two soldiers from around Vjasma; they have been on the road for seven days, their homes in Cologne are burned out, their families don't have a roof over their heads. Children from cities in the West evacuated to the countryside. Hitler Youth, called up to a military training camp, pore over guidebooks on the proper use of a submachine gun. An SS officer dozing next to his very beloved bride. A Ukrainian who has been traveling for twelve days to locate relatives in his homeland but is unable to get there.[12]

Although de Boor noticed the Ukrainian, who was one among millions of foreign workers conscripted into the Third Reich, her sightseeing was basically in German.

This partial view, which made some things visible and obscured others, was typical of train travel. Not being able to see was part of the overall feeling of dislocation. As soldiers, refugees, and other travelers journeyed across the greater German Empire, they saw supply trains rumbling to the eastern front; coal cars in which only the heads of Russian prisoners of war were visible in the frigid winter air; trains to the camps at Westerbork, at Treblinka, at Auschwitz; wagonloads of ethnic Germans resettled to and then evacuated from White Russia; the "humming and rolling of trains" with "tired, war-weary soldiers"; the arrival in Warsaw of hospital trains full of Wehrmacht with "crumpled-up overcoats and dead-faced expressions"—"*rabanka*," or chopped meat, the Poles said. It was not uncommon to see work details of Jewish forced laborers shoveling snow along the main streets or concentration camp inmates in tattered uniforms and wooden shoes repairing infrastructure. Yet most diarists did not mention these sights. There are far more references to the departure of French men rounded up to work in Germany, leaving the stations at Dijon and Montluçon in carriages chalked with slogans like "Down with the unjust Relève! Down with Laval!" and singing "The Internationale," than there are to the deportation trains carrying French Jews to the assembly camp at Drancy, outside Paris. Shoveling snow at Bucharest's Grivita Station, Romanian writer Mihail Sebastian felt himself "becoming a railway worker—worse, a platform sweeper and track clearer." At one point, he could see "the Constanta train passing a few hundred meters away" and thought, "Two years back I could have been one of its passengers, one of those looking from a carriage window at men on the line with pick and shovel." But would he have seen them? As a Jew, perhaps. Did others see him on his snow-clearing day in March 1942? Probably not. Hitler actually had the blinds pulled down when his train stopped alongside a transport of wounded German soldiers.[13] There was much to see from the railway station waiting room, but not everyone looked.

Likewise, there were many people who heard only what they wanted to hear. Any consideration of wartime talk has to take note of the hush that fell when Hitler spoke. Broadcast over the radio and even over loudspeakers set up in train stations, Hitler's speeches were national occasions, and Germans knew quite well that their far-flung friends and relatives had also tuned in. "All of Germany hears the Führer" was the official watchword. "Mother just telephoned to say that the Führer will speak in 5 minutes," one German wrote, explaining why her letter had to be completed quickly. Another mother wrote the last lines of her letter right on time as well: "Tonight Hitler addresses the 'foreign press.' I *definitely* have to hear that." The next day impressions would be shared; it was "totally enthralling and overwhelming," "very confident and completely overwhelming," or simply "grand."[14] The words suggested the desire to stand firm and be enrolled in the nation.

To a Swiss observer, a driver working for a team of Swiss doctors on the eastern front who found himself among German soldiers in Warsaw,

the "call-and-response" that characterized Hitler's addresses displayed
a certain mindlessness. Writing under the pseudonym Franz Blättler, he
recorded his impressions of experiencing Hitler talk as an outsider:

> When we entered the canteen, it was already completely full. . . . With
> the first notes of the national anthem, everyone stands up, takes up
> position with the right hand stretched out, and sings. . . . Then the
> Führer speaks. Quiet as a mouse, everyone sits on their chair so they can
> catch every word. I think that Hitler's words are a religion for them. . . .
> He lists off the latest victories. You can actually see how every single
> breast swells up. Once in a while someone throws a knowing glance
> at us or at the three places we have left demonstratively unoccupied.
> The meaning is clear: Watch yourselves, you little shepherd boys, your
> time will come soon enough. The Führer then moves on to the topic of
> Churchill and you can hear loud laughter through the loudspeaker. All
> at once, the whole canteen is laughing. If the radio broadcasts a "boo,"
> a loud "boo" echoes to my left and my right as well as behind and in
> front of me. It gets really dramatic when the choir on radio starts up
> with "Sieg Heil." Then there are no bounds to the enthusiasm of the
> audience. Everyone stands up and adds their "Siegs" and their "Heils."

Blättler was glad to be "little shepherd boy and not a member of this
herd here."[15] And indeed, German soldiers and civilians routinely let the
Führer talk through them, expressing their opinions by quoting what
Hitler said and consulting his pronouncements for guidance.

The blaring German loudspeaker serves as a reminder of how
uncomfortable many citizens were speaking their own minds in the midst
of so much simulated unanimity. Given that he was surrounded by people who appeared to be completely "beclouded, befogged," "blinded and
seduced," small-town German bureaucrat Friedrich Kellner, an old Social
Democrat, believed he had to exercise "extreme caution" when talking
to acquaintances. Police even brought him in for questioning at the end
of January 1940. Loose talk was probably less tolerated by friends and
neighbors at the beginning of the war than at the end, when doubts about
victory and even the Führer's speeches had accumulated. But by that time,

the police and the Gestapo were also much more vigilant about defeatist attitudes, so an "objective" point of view or simply words of "caution" could be construed by the authorities as the "first step toward treason," as Kellner put it. He, in any case, became more rather than less outspoken, despite the risks.[16]

Hitler's loud and long speeches, the authority and banality of the radio, the allegedly ever-present Gestapo, the exercise of self-caution among strangers with divided political loyalties—all this deformed and diminished speech. In contrast to the revolutionary years after 1789 when the "flood of French speech" Thomas Carlyle described could hardly be stanched, or the years after 1917 when "The Talk" in Petrograd never stopped "spurting up," in John Reed's words, people in the years 1939–1945 did not feel at liberty to frankly debate the issues swirling around them.[17] But self-absorption with one's own fate was just as important as circumspection in shaping wartime conversations. Although civilians were in fact arrested for telling barbed jokes, the rapid and smooth circulation of the same series of wartime jokes indicates that the trouble with wartime talk was not simply how dangerous it was. As people talked incessantly about the war, the cold winters, and food; exchanged rumors, predictions, and jokes; and passed on the latest news, they created a nexus of communication "between ourselves" that often ignored the suffering of others. Talk could express shock, but it could also serve as a shock absorber.

Civilians bore the brunt of Germany's occupation regimes, with their food rationing, labor impressments, political purges, and racial selections. One of the characteristics of this brutal war against civilians was that the worse the situation got, the more unlikely it seemed that it would last. The model was very simple: what goes up must come down, and the higher the war stacked up its tower of difficulties, the sooner it seemed it must tumble down of its own accord. The notion that "it can't go on like this" measured the gap between the awful expansion of the conflict and the assumption that the war had to come to an end. Rumors created an alternative reality in which this gap might be closed. News bulletins announced the successes of the German war machine, while rumors cut it back down to size. Wartime talk was ultimately about the life and death of war.

In an extraordinary collection of the "myths of war," psychoanalyst Marie Bonaparte analyzed the stories that were frequently told and retold by people in the war's figurative railway station waiting rooms. Often, they involved actual train travelers. Bonaparte was the great-granddaughter of Lucien Bonaparte, one of Napoleon's younger brothers who remained more committed to the revolutionary (and Corsican) cause, to the emperor's irritation. Although mistrusted by Napoleon and later by the restored Bourbon monarchs, the family retained enough money across the revolutions of nineteenth-century France to make Marie a plausible match to one of the younger sons of Greece's King George I. So it was Princess Marie Bonaparte who studied psychoanalysis, and though not an accredited professional, she undertook serious research into sexual frigidity in order to find a cure for her own. She even sought out Sigmund Freud and paid the "exit tax" that allowed him to leave Vienna for London after the Anschluss in 1938.[18] Thereafter, she took up the study of wartime rumors.

Soon after the Munich agreements had averted war in September 1938, Bonaparte recorded stories predicting the death of Hitler that had begun to circulate around France. The elaborate quality of these stories' plots served to authenticate the otherwise unadorned prediction that Hitler would die or be killed within six months. The stories featured young lovers on the eve of their separation by the order of mobilization or soldiers traveling between postings who encountered a mysterious stranger, usually a gypsy. In one version, the stranger predicts two things: a terrible accident in which the young people will find themselves face-to-face with a corpse and the death of Hitler. The unfortunate appearance of the corpse at the end of the story (in the backseat of a car on the way to Paris—or was it Zurich?) lent credibility to the happier announcement of Hitler's demise. In the other version, a gypsy haggles with travelers in a subway or train compartment and accurately guesses the amount of money in that lady's purse (sixty francs, which "wouldn't be worthwhile" stealing) or this gentleman's wallet (two thousand francs, worth the while, if the gypsy were a thief). Once the purse is opened and the wallet retrieved, the crowd that has gathered asks for further displays of the gypsy's clairvoyant powers. These involve predictions about the end of the war. Once the gypsy provides the forecast—"Hitler will be murdered before the end of the year"—the wealthy gentleman replies, "If it's true, I'll give you the two thousand francs!" In the first case, the corpse in the car represented a "propitiation sacrifice," Bonaparte concluded, in the second, the bundle of francs a "thank offering," but both registered exchange rates for peace.[19] Both stories made the deliverance that was unlikely but greatly desired seem credible and near at hand, which is why they were told and retold.

More pious travelers in the waiting room told tales of divine intervention. In Poland these stories featured the prophecy attributed to seventeenth-century Catholic martyr Andrew Bobola, who had been canonized in 1938, that "our slavery will be over after 101 days, which would mean December 8," a date in close agreement with the one that had appeared "on the miraculous picture of Our Lady, the so-called Black Madonna" of Czestochowa, namely, December 12, 1939. In France stories circulated about Odile, the patron saint of Alsace, who prophesied "an abrupt end" to the war, often as early as the sixth month of the second year, so early 1941, through either the bankruptcy of the Italians or a decimating epidemic among the Germans.[20] Other tall tales similarly denied the hold of the present situation by reference to new facts that would change everything. Not long after the fall of France, rumors suddenly had the English setting fire to the Channel or littering the beaches of France with dead Germans. Hitler and "Old Fatty" Göring died thousands of deaths in the rumor mills of World War II, usually in the aftermath of German military setbacks in 1942 and 1943, but also earlier on, when German power seemed unassailable. For instance, news of Rudolf Hess's bizarre parachute landing in Scotland on May 10, 1941, metamorphosed into the rumor, which "spread like lightning" through the Warsaw Ghetto by May 16, that "Göring had been shot and had died of his wounds."[21]

Of course, Germans told the same stories, including the one about the clairvoyant gypsy who, this time in a Berlin streetcar, predicted a rapid end to the war and final victory for the Third Reich. As the war stretched out and things looked bleaker, Germans also hoped for miracles, like the one Zarah Leander sang about in her 1942 hit, "I know that someday a miracle will happen," and put their faith in "wonder weapons," which, as

Friedrich Kellner overheard as he sat around in railway station waiting rooms in Hungen and Stockheim at the end of 1943, were sure to turn the tide of German fortunes.[22]

"What news?" "Now what news?" "What news abroad?" "What's the news?" "What news, what news, in this our tottering state?" Wartime conversations, like the speeches of Shakespeare, were full of questions about the latest news. News and rumors about changing fortunes, shifting tides, surprising turns, untimely deaths, and wonder weapons created an unconventional network of information that constantly replenished itself. Bits and pieces of information moved about continuously, undeterred by borders of nationality or social standing and undeterred as well by standards of credibility or probability. Like Shakespeare's description of Rumor in *Henry IV*, wartime rumors pulled together an indiscriminate, nondiscriminating "wavering multitude" in the railway station waiting rooms, a "blunt monster with uncounted heads," who once having entered the theater "painted full of tongues" effortlessly stuffed "the ears of men" in "every language." "When loud Rumor speaks," no one stopped "the vent of hearing." And no one, for that matter, put aside official tracts or propaganda: regardless of their politics, most Parisians read collaborationist newspapers such as *Le Petit Parisien* or *Le Matin* in the Metro and listened to Radio Paris. In Poland Jews scrupulously pieced together news from both official and clandestine sources, reading between the lines, panning for gold, trying to figure out German intentions and international realities. That occupation authorities banned Poles from owning or listening to radios, and even prohibited the Polish- and German-language newspapers they themselves published from circulating in the Jewish ghettos, indicates the political value that could be extracted from news of any kind.[23]

Rumors functioned because people did not believe official sources, and what made the market in rumors valuable was not the factual or fictional quality of the information exchanged but its clandestine nature. It laid the foundations of "us" against "'them,' 'the collabos,' the enemy." According to one scholar, "This was vital to the process of rediscovering unity." Indeed, the French rumor mill, "l'agence DNB," or "derniers nouveaux bobards" (our latest fibs), became known much more familiarly as "diffusez nos bobard" (spread our latest fibs). Rumors expressed "deeply felt desires," which is why they were necessarily mad and "out of joint with reality," but they were "ours," so in line with civilian hopes. "More than ever," noted Liliane Schroeder, a Parisian schoolgirl, about the first seasons of the German occupation of France, "the 'I've heard,' or 'I've been told,' the 'it seems that' are taken seriously."[24]

Gossip mattered. A ride on the streetcar became one of the most popular pastimes in wartime Warsaw because that was "the point of origins of the rumors and jokes that later spread across the entire city." "The streetcar sympathized with us and shared our hate and disdain," one resident recalled. To fabricate and indulge in rumors was "irrational Jewish optimism," admitted Jacob Gerstenfeld, who escaped the ghetto in Lwów and passed as a German. They were muddleheaded because they were fashioned in the "belief, blind, stupid, baseless, contradicting reality, that perhaps someone would, in spite of all, do something for us." Nonetheless, in the dark days of the ghettos, the news agency Gerstenfeld mocked as "AJW (as Jews want)" was actually a "priceless gift." Not to indulge in rumor threatened the solidarity of the beleaguered community, as "one wise Jew" discovered when "the group wanted to tear him to shreds" after he expressed his pessimistic opinion about the Allies.[25]

For all the solidarity and endurance that rumors fortified, and for all the shock they sometimes triggered, information during wartime ultimately proved to be flimsy and unsatisfying, especially as questions about "what news" continued to be posed without indications that much had really changed. If anything, day-to-day life got worse, with food increasingly scarce and Nazi terror more prevalent. The year 1943 was perhaps "the most psychologically debilitating and demoralizing" one in German-occupied Europe. With news about Stalingrad, "Tunisgrad," and Italy's declaration of war on Germany, the year "offered hope that the war might end soon" without resolving "the mystery of *how* the war would end," one historian has written. (By late in that year, Germans might not yet have conceded that "we have lost the war," but, at the same time, they increasingly realized that "it can still last a long time.")[26] This state of endless waiting and repeated deferral diminished the cathartic effect of rumor and storytelling. As the conflict persisted, war news persisted but could not easily be inserted into meaningful or conclusive narratives. Hopes that blossomed in the morning withered by afternoon. That was the way DNB or AJW operated in wartime. For all the dreams of release and the laughter of a good joke ("Well, boys," Soviet soldiers are said to have jested as they pried open donated American food cans, "here is the opening of the Second Front"), people fell "back into reality, or even into excessive pessimism." As one historian of occupied France summarized, "Rumor creates an atmosphere which is both credulous and cynical, making people eager to believe anything they hear, however fantastic, but at the same time reluctant to believe anything, however well authenticated."[27] Credulity and cynicism constituted the two-stroke momentum of wartime news gathering.

And so the conversations went on, but with the effect that they went around and around. In a third-class compartment on a train to Bordeaux at the end of 1943, as imagined by Jean-Louis Curtis in his wartime novel *The Forests of the Night*, "all the passengers" talked about nothing but "rations, war, bombs, the advance in Italy—the advance in Italy, bombs, war, rations." A few weeks later, Anne Frank complained to her diary: "All day long that's all I hear. Invasion, invasion, nothing but invasion. Arguments about going hungry, dying, bombs, fire extinguishers, sleeping bags, identity cards, poison gas, etc., etc. Not exactly cheerful." Friends and family had been invited for dinner at Jeanne Oudot's home in the small French village of Mancenans, tucked into the hills north of Switzerland. Oudot, a schoolgirl, wrote that the conversation was "agitated": "the war, always the war. We talk about it from morning to night. If someone comes in the door, we start back from the beginning. Everyone has their opinions, their ideas, their doubts, their fears."[28]

This perpetual back-and-forth had an incapacitating effect, leading nowhere, even as it divided participants into pessimists and optimists, or "lengtheners" of the war versus the smaller number of "shorteners." Over a "wretched" lunch of mashed potatoes and pickled kale, pieces of conversation were picked up again by the residents of Anne Frank's Secret Annex on Amsterdam's Prinsengracht. Mrs. van Daan remained convinced that "the Germans will win at the end," her husband remarked that he could better stand his wife's moods if he was just able to "smoke and smoke and smoke," while Mr. Dussel considered the "political situation" to be "outschtänding," declaring that "it is 'eempossible' that we'll be caught." Anne found the talk nerve-racking: the optimists and pessimists all believed they had a "monopoly on the truth"; each side enjoyed goading the other into endless "quarrels" pursued with "unflagging energy." "All it takes is a single question, a word or a sentence, and before you know it, the entire family is involved!" The wartime division between pessimists and optimists was fundamental, appearing again and again in the records left behind. But it was not always clear-cut, since each individual also wavered. In the Lodz Ghetto, Dawid Sierakowiak at first greeted the news that Germany had declared war on the Soviet Union on June 22, 1941, as "wonderful, incredible," but reprimanded himself a week later when he realized the Germans kept "moving ahead, pushing on as though nothing can stop them."[29]

That there were so many parties to rumors undermined the fortitude of hope and the astuteness of insight. The circulation of rumors underscored the inability to see and predict the course of the war and the incapacity to intervene in events. Although the war intervened much more dramatically in domestic life than World War I had, it did not turn observers into protagonists. The war required civilians to try to figure out what was going on, but the blows of war did not make them into self-assured actors. If war has been described as a "condition of eventfulness," it also prompted a recognition of powerlessness. For Léon Werth, writing after the French armistice with the Germans, "History will be the same for us as it will be for the others, but we will not have made it. Events come to the French, the French do not go out to the events." Werth felt trapped, at the mercy of events to which he could only inadequately respond. Werth found this feeling of immobility, which he compared to imprisonment, profoundly isolating. In the past, the legibility of the world around him had allowed him to make connections, find analogies, and reach conclusions, but in the circumstances of illegibility created by the war's unpredictable events, words simply drifted away. All Werth felt he had left was the memory of past authorship, the mirage of meaning.[30]

For Werth, as for other Jews in France and elsewhere in Europe, rumors also produced a heightened state of alertness to the danger of arrest and deportation. To be "confronted constantly," day after day, by the "Radio-Rue–des Rosiers" (a reference to one of the main streets in the "Jewish quarter" of Paris), as one resident described it, created a burden of fear that non-Jews simply did not have to bear. Rumor highlighted the narrowing confines of a captive population contemplating its fate over the course of the long evenings of confinement at home. (Beginning in February 1942, the curfew for Jews in France ran from 8:00 p.m. to 6:00 a.m.) Rumor marked out Jews as much as the yellow star.[31]

Rumors and other wartime talk proliferated because men and women spent an inordinate amount of time waiting in line. Paris journalist Jacques Bielinky noted that food lines were so long that they chopped themselves up into "sections, to let pedestrians pass." Already in September 1940, one woman stood in line for five hours to buy a quarter pound of butter. On the Rue Mouffetard, Bielinky waited for three hours to buy five and a half pounds of potatoes. A few weeks later, he lined up on Rue Drouot at 2:00 in the afternoon, and it was not until 7:00 in the evening that he was able to purchase some sausage. These were the lines in which Parisians passed along the joke about the Germans who had delivered ashes to the French (a reference to the repatriation in December 1940 of the remains of Napoleon's son) when what they needed was coal. The lines themselves were the subject of bitter humor. Do you know the one about three people who recounted their small victories in line? one joke went. The first one had waited for eight days to get a half pound of butter; the second waited for only four days, but managed to get a bar of Persil soap; and the third waited even longer, this to get ten minutes of electricity that allowed him to turn on the radio only to hear the British broadcast, "Patience, we're coming."[32]

Especially during the cold winters—and they all seemed particularly harsh during the occupation—people grumbled constantly about shortages. The most basic items such as potatoes and bread were on everyone's mind, but also tobacco, wine, and shoes. As the lines inched forward, shared resentments against shopkeepers, bureaucrats, and German occupiers developed. Perhaps that is why Bielinky, who as a Jew carefully watched for signs, concluded that "there is not evidence of anti-Semitism in the lines." The sympathy was guarded, however, in his telling, extending to the poor Jews who had been arrested but not to the rich ones—the "big bankers and speculators"—whose sins apparently always went unpunished. There was so much talk against the Jews who had been "the masters during the Republic" that one Parisian, upset by the accusations, tartly observed that under the Jews, "no one declared war, there was no rationing, we had neither coupons nor tickets and could buy whatever we wanted, eat to our heart's content." Even "the bread was white."[33]

Conversations in line about "fat cats" and "little guys," and about varieties of rich and poor Jews, indicated how quickly the camaraderie of the line could dissolve into social resentment. Solidarity typically had an edge that expressed the particular and often difficult situations in which men and women found themselves. A reliable guide is Marcel Aymé, who assembled a line of misery in his short story "While Waiting." In his story, people talk about themselves while waiting together, but they remain fundamentally alone. Things are so bad that no one wants to return home. Home is empty without the widower's wife, is filled with guilty pleasures now that the husband is a prisoner of war in Germany, or is where "the four little ones" wait ("the fifth one died in 1941"). One boy is scared to go back to his mother because he has lost the family's bread-ration cards. Another is "always hungry." Near the end of the line on the Rue Caulaincourt, a voice cries out a simple truth: "I'm a Jew." The line where everyone prefers to stay rather than go home is an imaginary space of solace, setting off in a humorous way the particular difficulties that Parisians endured, often by themselves.[34] The line epitomizes the misery, passivity, and resignation that in 1941 and 1942 threatened to seize the spirit of the French.

The long, stretched-out present in which so many French civilians waited during those years caught up with German soldiers in 1943 or 1944 when the story line of victorious Germany began to falter. Wehrmacht soldiers too spent a long time in railway station waiting rooms and up to four days on the transport trains that took them to the eastern front or back home. Official policy attempted to give soldiers at least one home leave each year, although these opportunities became more irregular after the summer of 1942. Soldiers had plenty of time to talk to men from other divisions in the overfilled compartments and to make sense of the

war news. It was on trains that soldiers were able to gradually piece together the parts they had played in the systematic murder of Jewish civilians. Especially toward the end of the war, soldiers spoke quite frankly
about Germany's war against the Jews, but most of the time they talked
about girls, drinking, and vacation; debated the virtues and deficiencies of
military technology; or groused about Nazi bigwigs.[35]

What must have been boisterous trips home in 1939 from Poland and
in 1940 from France, places from which soldiers took as many goodies as
they could carry, became more somber in 1942 and 1943. More and more
soldiers left the front on hospital trains and returned to the front after a
period of convalescence. They also passed through or changed trains in
bombed-out railway stations after they crossed the German border, and
they milled around with evacuated citizens seeking some sort of roof
over their heads. In March 1942, writer Gerhard Nebel engaged in lively
conversations with his fellow soldiers, and he did so without any fear of
denunciation. Opinions about the war varied, but Nebel noted that soldiers who had served in the Soviet Union "assure us that we have to win
the war under all circumstances. Because if we lose and are treated any-
where near to how we have treated the populations in the East, it will be
our certain downfall." This view was quite widespread, but victory seemed
within reach, at least as good as a "fifty-fifty" proposition. Two years later,
the odds were judged to be longer. The emphasis was on a victory that
could *still* be attained because of wonder weapons or Japan's invasion of
the Soviet Union—"what ifs," ersatz rumors with which Germans had to
make do at the end of the war. Hitler's argument to his generals held that
if the Russians had turned their situation around in 1941, it was possible
for the Germans to do so as well.[36]

"Daily and nightly debates" became more "furious" among German
soldiers in 1944, along with the growing realization about what was lost
forever: "a frighteningly large part of my life and my youth" was the way
Heinrich Böll, the future novelist, put it to his wife, Annemarie, "summer
after summer, fall after fall and 6 hard winters and 6 glorious springs."
After the war Böll reworked these thoughts into a short story, "Reunion
on the Avenue," in which soldiers began to talk after "the fourth or fifth
glass," usually about the past, because the wartime present, which they

"loathed," no longer had "the virtues of a 'mission,'" and because by 1944 the future appeared like "a black tunnel full of sharp corners that we were going to bump into." Yet the past was also unsatisfying because it was about what the young soldiers had never really possessed, "meager rudiments of what our fathers might have called life," perhaps because it was about the "girl who lived at the end of the avenue," "that girl, you know," "and the last time I was on leave . . . "[37] Ultimately, Böll's comrades, too, found themselves stuck in the railway station waiting room as the war went on and on.

A VETERAN OF THE FRENCH RESISTANCE, ALBAN VISTEL RECALLED that at the beginning, opponents of the German occupation had nothing but words with which to attack their enemies. "Whether it was whispered or written, the single verb was the birth of the act," he wrote. Strong convictions could be expressed in simple words, in lines of poetry, in songs, in cries of distress. It is certainly true that words such as *liberty*, *patriotism*, and *the Republic*, whose meanings had faded before the war, acquired new vigor in intimate conversations and clandestine writings as the Resistance gradually gathered confidence. Whether a *V* scrawled on a wall meant "victory" or "freedom," the sight of "nothing but Vs and still more Vs everywhere" across France, Holland, Belgium, and Poland at the end of March 1941 created a sense of encouragement and a "feeling of conspiracy."[38]

But letters and words could also be misleading. Repeated attempts to describe or anticipate the direction of the war made very clear that the Germans had the power to direct the scene. The unending circulation of wartime rumors produced solidarity but also feelings of helplessness and imprisonment. And the word *Jew* emblazoned on yellow stars distinguished the very different fates of Jews and non-Jews; it left its Jewish wearers exposed and was more likely to disable rather than enable resistance. Talk in the railway station waiting room and along the lines expressed sympathy for those who were persecuted by the Germans. Yet many stories were completely self-centered since the war acted on everyone, though in different ways. Contemporaries were aware of some of the things that were happening to the Jews, but they often focused on their own problems, whether a bombed-out apartment or scarcities of food. Moreover, the news about the Jews that was communicated often came prefaced by the French *on dit* or the German *man sagt* (it is said), a construction that was like watching action through a closed window. Observation was a step toward bearing witness, but the grammar also created distance, a prerequisite for indifference and for not telling the stories at all. *On dit* marked the horrible information passed on in all the talk about the Jews as somewhat dubious, not quite known, possible but not certain—news out there but not ours.

Wartime talk, haunted by the recent past and frightened of the uncertain future, was a constant in the long present of the years 1939–1945. But talk of war began years earlier, starting in earnest when Adolf Hitler started to speak over the world's radio waves after becoming Germany's chancellor in 1933. That was when Europe's "railway station waiting-room" took on its dispiriting contours.

2

Hitler Means War!

"HITLER, THAT MEANS WAR." THIS WAS THE IMMEDIATE REACTION OF Heinrich Böll's mother when she heard the news that Germany's president, the old war hero Paul von Hindenburg, had appointed Adolf Hitler as chancellor on January 30, 1933. Böll, who, after the war, would become one of Germany's great novelists, was fifteen years old at the time, and he happened to be in bed with the flu, reading and smoking a forbidden cigarette. (He later half jestingly wondered whether the flu epidemic that winter had not been neglected by historians as a key factor to explain the delirium accompanying Hitler's seizure of power.) Böll was miserable. His family had just moved into an ugly apartment on Cologne's Maternusstrasse. The Rhein River was nearby, as was a large park that had been spruced up in 1927 with a soaring column crowned with the German eagle to honor the "heroes" who had fallen in World War I. "Numero oppressis menti invictis" read the defiant inscription—Germany's soldiers had been conquered by "superior numbers," but they had not been "vanquished in spirit." Named after Hindenburg, the park had, by 1933, become a melancholy place where unemployed men sat around, smoked, and waited. Would there really be a new war? In the conversation around the stove, Mother's contention was "hotly denied": "The fellow wouldn't last long enough to be able to start a war." Maybe so. Although she detested Hitler, she also could not quite take the "turnip head" seriously.[1]

Households across Germany debated the implications of Hitler's rise to power in the weeks following his appointment by Hindenburg. In the previous year, 1932, there had been two presidential elections pitting

Hitler against Hindenburg, and two parliamentary elections, one in July in which the Nazis emerged as the largest party, and one in November in which they suffered setbacks. At the same time, local and regional elections continued to remind Germans of how divided they were over the issue of Hitler and the future of the Weimar Republic. When a reluctant Hindenburg finally agreed to Hitler's chancellorship, Germans did not know whether they faced civil war, revolution from the nationalist right, or a new offensive against their old enemies in the Great War. The great debates of the 1930s had begun. They were shaped by the growing might of Hitler and his Nazi supporters who, using the carrot of economic growth and the stick of political terror, rapidly established the most popular dictatorship in the twentieth century.

Discussions continued over the kitchen table at the Dürkefäldens home, a working-class family in Peine, near Hanover. One Sunday in May 1933, Emma brought "her latest beau" over for coffee. The talk turned to Hitler and to war. The boyfriend had been temporarily blinded after being shot in the head in the last war. "He doesn't want to take part in any war again," Emma's brother Karl reported. "He suffered enough." But his resolve was not shared by Emma's other brother, Willi, who as a result of the new political developments "appeared to take more interest in tradition," that is, in Germany's imperial past. He rummaged around for his wartime diary, which, as Karl disdainfully remarked, he had never cared about before. To Willi's consternation, his mother had long ago thrown out the letters he had written during the war. Willi was one among millions of Germans who suddenly discovered their soldierly patriotism and hurried to join the Nazi Party or enlist in its brown-shirted paramilitary wing, the SA (Sturmabteilung). There were so many who overcame their scruples regarding the Nazis that new recruits were called "casualties of March." A dispirited Karl later looked out of the kitchen window to see Willi and many other neighbors, marching the streets in new uniforms, singing the tunes of the new National Socialist era. Karl stood aside, but "father, mother, and Emma"—they had all become "fanatical Hitler supporters."[2]

The new martial spirit was visible, and audible, everywhere in Germany. On a visit to Weimar in July 1933, playwright Erich Ebermayer found the city unbearable: "You hear the uninterrupted smack of SA boots on the pavement, and 'Heil Hitler' cries echo through the quiet streets." The only boys visible seemed to be Hitler Youth; "young people don't walk anymore; they march." And in between, "a few old people shuffle along, lonesome, intimidated remnants of another era." Nazi Party strongholds had the hustle and bustle of military fortresses. One after the other, Germans bought new outfits: brown shirts, belts and buckles, caps and visors, ties and party pins, and boots—"high marching boots," "a good pair" to be acquired for "a decent price."[3] Less than twenty years after the start of World War I, the country looked like August 1914 again, more disciplined, perhaps, but just as ready for military engagement. And just as in 1914, the enemy, at least as far as the Nazis were concerned, was French: Versailles, where the hated peace treaty had been signed in 1919; Paris, where so many statesmen had thwarted Germany's initiatives over the course of the 1920s; Geneva, in French-speaking Switzerland, the site of the League of Nations from which Hitler, to the world's alarm, withdrew in November 1933 in a move to advance Germany's national interests. Observers could be forgiven if they had the suspicion that the marching that had begun in the Great War and continued under the aegis of a dozen or so paramilitary associations right through the Weimar Republic was now, with the ranks of Hitler's uniformed supporters ever growing, pointed straight toward a new war. Sometime around 1933 the line between postwar and prewar was crossed. Years in which there had been much talk about "the war to end all wars," "the end of the war," and "after the war" gave way with a sudden lurch to a new period threatened by the "next catastrophe," the "next war."

The debate about whether "Hitler means war" inevitably spilled over Germany's borders to France, Britain, and the United States, the powers that had dictated the peace of Versailles and also the destination for thousands of refugees fleeing Germany to escape the political and anti-Jewish persecution that began almost immediately after the Nazis assumed power. Photographs of newly constructed concentration camps splashed across the pages of illustrated magazines advertised the resolve of Germany's new rulers to enforce their political revolution. Refugees therefore had few illusions about Hitler's willingness to use force. But they also found themselves considered, by many, unwelcome messengers of war. For some Europeans, Jews were evidence of the ferocity of Hitler's violence. Many on the Left soon cast off their pacifist convictions in order to take up the fight against fascism. For many others, however, Jews threatened Europe with an unnecessary and destructive war that in the end could only benefit themselves and the Communists. Nationalists accused Jews of being warmongers, anticipating the ugly propaganda of the Nazis who held Jewry, whether in the form of "Jewish plutocracy" or "Judeao-Communism," to be the main cause of global conflict. *Warmongers*, or *bellicistes*, was the collective term of opprobrium in the 1930s—not *appeasers*. War was the extremist position, and both in Europe and in the United States politicians believed they had to mollify or persuade a public that was basically pacifist. The question was at what point the price to avert war with Germany became too high.

"Hear ye! hear ye! hear ye!" the debate in the United States had begun. "All those who have business before this court of civilization give your attention and ye shall be heard." Preceded by taps blown by a bugler from the American Legion Post 39 and then a moment of silence in honor of those murdered by the Nazis, this cry marked the start of a mock trial of Hitler's government held before 20,000 spectators on the evening of March 7, 1934, at New York City's Madison Square Garden. The indictment accused the government of "compelling the German people to turn back from civilization to an antiquated and barbarous despotism which menaces the progress of mankind toward peace and freedom." Twenty witnesses representing trade unions, Jewish organizations, and city and state government presented "The Case of Civilization Against Hitlerism." Speakers detailed the violation of human rights in the Third Reich, the persecution of minorities, the imprisonment of labor leaders, and infringements on free intellectual inquiry. Former New York governor Alfred E. Smith described the revival of "cave-man law, the law of the sharpest tooth, the angriest growl, and the greediest maw." The "deification of force" not only terrorized the German people but also falsified Hitler's numerous pledges of peace. Samuel Seabury of the New York Bar Association summed up "the case for civilization" by quoting Hitler against Hitler. With references to the "final conflict," the "extermination" of France, and the superior rights and imperial mission of Europe's 80 million Germans, Seabury caught the spirit if not the letter of Hitler's 1925 book, *Mein Kampf*. Seabury concluded with the confident assertion that "public opinion" provided the force and economic boycott the "weapon" to break the "power of Hitlerism" and preserve "world peace." The resolution in favor of civilization and against Hitler was passed with a "great swelling roar" of unanimous approval.

A rebuttal followed two months later when "20,000 Nazi Friends" filled Madison Square Garden on May 17, 1934. Standing between German and American flags, speakers representing the "German-American Business Committee" denounced the "Jewish boycott" of Germany as an incitement to racial hatred. Boycotts were bad for business, but also rested on a misunderstanding of Hitler's actions. There "was no alternative for Germany except Hitler—or chaos," "whatever our attitude toward Hitler may be," explained George Viereck, one of the "Friends of the New Germany." Hitler had "emancipated Germany from the bondage of Versailles" and erected a bulwark against "the red sea of bolshevism." The troublemakers, Walter Kappe, publisher of the *Deutsche Zeitung*, pointed out, were not Nazis but Jews. Jews constituted "a State within a State" in New York to wage their own "private war against Germany." The meeting adjourned with the crowd singing the "Horst Wessel Song" and shouting "Heil Hitler."[4]

Speeches and rallies addressed the converted, as the unanimous resolutions, roaring cheers, and collective singing in Madison Square Garden confirmed. But the question of whether Hitler meant war engaged millions more people. Many confronted the issue mostly through sounds broadcast over the radio. It was during the 1930s, precisely when the issues of war and peace were hotly debated in Europe and in the United States, that radio audiences expanded dramatically. Radio ownership was highest in the United States, where nearly 90 percent of households could tune in, but in the 1930s rates doubled and tripled in western Europe so that a radio could be found in more or less every second home in Germany, Britain, and France. In Czechoslovakia, the focus of world attention in September 1938, 1 in 10 people listened to the radio at home; in Greece only 23,000 could. Like all media—such as newspapers, books, and magazines—radio programming infiltrated enclosed spaces, the living room and kitchen, of course, but also invisible walls of custom surrounding towns and villages. It pulled together national audiences around common repertoires of music, entertainment, and news. With the latest popular hits and news bulletins, broadcasting also allowed people to feel "up-to-date." Radio was the sound of the present becoming the future.[5]

Listening to the radio was very different from reading a newspaper. On the radio, settings could be rendered more realistic through "variations of tempo and pitch" but also more dramatic. Without radio, listeners would never have described Hitler as "confident and enthralling," or "dynamic" and "spellbinding," or as someone who "ranted and snarled." Without the radio, it would not have been possible for "Hitler's bellowing" to convince "hundreds of thousands of Frenchmen of Hitler's evil intentions."[6] These are just a few examples of the diverse reviews that Hitler's speeches received, but they all indicate ways in which radio intensified impressions of Hitler. Radio broadcasts enabled listeners to hear intonations of reassurance, resolution, or intimidation. It was these same attributes of intimacy and directness that made radio such an excellent way to convey or simulate emergency, as was the case in the fever-pitched broadcasts of the *Hindenburg* zeppelin disaster in Lakehurst, New Jersey, in May 1937 or Orson Welles's adaptation of *The War of the Worlds* on Halloween eve in 1938. Radio hyped the enticements and assaults of the modern world.

Hitler generally spoke in front of an audience—workers assembled on the Berlin shop floor of Siemens's Dynamowerk, where the Führer stepped onto the top of a cable drum to urge voters to approve Germany's withdrawal from the League of Nations on November 10, 1933; party faithful gathered on Nuremberg's grandiose Zeppelinfeld, where he pitched his demands regarding Czechoslovakia on September 12, 1938; or Reichstag deputies meeting in the Kroll Opera House in Berlin, where Hitler to great applause threatened the extermination of the Jews on January 30, 1939. Part of the effect of a broadcast of a Hitler speech was the interaction of speaker and audience. Even when they understood that the setting was carefully choreographed, listeners around the world never failed to appreciate the "huge cheering," the "tumultuous cheers," the "frenzied cheers" that "reechoed" across the borders of the Reich.[7] The response of the crowd to the declarations of the Führer heightened the impression of German national unity and strength.

The fact that Nazi authorities encouraged group listening, installed loud speakers in public places such as markets and subway stations, and made listening to Hitler's speeches mandatory in factories, schools, and government offices made the loud pulse of speech and cheer, Führer and *Volk*, a pervasive part of the soundscape of the Third Reich. Victor Klemperer found himself on Bismarckplatz in Dresden one day in March 1936 when he "ran into the middle of Hitler's Reichstag speech" announcing the remilitarization of the Rhineland: "I could not get away from it for an hour. First from an open shop, then in the bank, then from a shop again." And so it was across Europe, where listeners routinely fiddled with the radio dial to tune in a variety of international stations, and newspapers regularly published foreign radio programs. The BBC and big-city American radio stations—WABC, WEAF, WJZ, and later corporations such as CBS and NBC, which each had dozens of local affiliates—routinely broadcast the second high-spirited half of Hitler's speeches with English summaries at the end or quick voice-over digests during fade-outs of the cheering (which is an indication of how long the applause lasted).[8] Even outside Germany, Hitler quickly became part of the sights and sounds of everyday life. At London's Madame Tussaud's Wax Museum, he mingled with the great cricketer Don Bradman ("the Don"); Greta Garbo, film star of *Mata Hari* and the *Grand Hotel*; and the king and queen (Hitler's was the only figure to be defaced). On the airwaves, he mixed with Gracie Fields, Tino Rossi, and Jack Hylton. No wonder Adolf Hitler is one of the most well-known names in the twentieth century.

"Heil, Heil, Heil"—radio noise made urgent the question of war and peace, but those strange voices drifting over from Germany in the night seemed to confirm the existence of new kinds of energy similar to radio waves or airpower. It stirred up the imagination in terrifying new ways. The notorious French fascist Robert Brasillach, a gifted novelist, explained the ways in which radio collaborated with Hitler. In his estimation, the year 1933 was a key date when postwar became prewar. The radio, the young writer observed, "had virtually waited for this year in order to spread itself everywhere." In the preceding years, he explained, "it was squeaky and temperamental": "collected, around unreliable sets," only the most patient listeners were "engrossed in searching for a concert amid frightening gurgling noises." But after 1933, "all was ready for us to tune into German stations in the evenings to hear that extraordinary National-Socialist election campaign, with its torrent of bells, drums and violins." The elections set "all the demons of music" loose. Brasillach accurately captured the dynamic of the Nazis' rise when he noted the enormous energy with which "Hitler moved forward, eating up the Nationalists, eating up the Monarchists, eating up the Stahlhelm [a nationalist veterans' group], eating up the [Catholic] Center, then, without stopping at the sight of a Marxist bloc that was still solid, he suddenly established his dark and devouring power in Germany, and turning to the world, his voice still gentle, said to it: 'Now it's between the two of us.'" After the efforts at international cooperation in the mid-1920s, in Brasillach's account, after the spirit of Locarno and "the day-dreams of Geneva" and the League of Nations, after "the doves of Lac Leman" and all "the frolics and follies of the postwar period," the "enormous planet" of Germany suddenly "took up a position in the very center of the heavens with the radiating glow of a conflagration." In any case, Brasillach wrote, "this is what we kept telling ourselves, as we followed the initiatory ceremonies of the new cult on the wireless sets, listening to the bells ringing, every few minutes, to punctuate the speeches and to bow the heads of crowds."[9] It was as if the familiar structures of everyday life had been smashed apart by great storms of spiritual energy.

Most Europeans hesitated, not sure what to make of the new places and new sounds. This is why Brasillach called fascism the "mal du siècle," a symptom of "world weariness," a temptation rather than a resolution. Ultimately, Brasillach claimed that Germany remained a "profoundly *strange* country," although he would later admit that he wanted to sleep with her. What Brasillach wanted to possess "in our own country, in our own way," were "the virtues of nation, race, and history" and, behind those, the carnal experiences of "faith," "suffering, blood, and death" that he had discovered in Germany. "Why not us?" he asked.[10]

The "Great Debate" in the interwar years was not really about whether "Hitler means war," and it was not about whether and to what extent American interests were at stake in the war in Europe once it began in earnest in 1940–1941.[11] It cut much deeper, posing fundamental questions about the legacy of the past war, the consequences of a new war, and the role of aggression and détente in contemporary international affairs. It was also about the virtue of the martial spirit, the decadence of democracy, and the search for new sources of political energy. Radio noise scored much of the debate.

Postwar

ONE AND A HALF MILLION FRENCHMEN LOST THEIR LIVES OVER THE course of the war in 1914–1918; another 2 million returned to their homes wounded or maimed. "Never again!" was the deep yearning that emerged from the slaughter of the war—the first "never again" that anticipated the "never again" of Holocaust remembrance. In France pacifism was the broadest common denominator to be found in the fractious politics of the postwar Third Republic.[12] Pacifist tendencies ran deep in Britain as well. Statesmen on both sides of the Channel took seriously the 1928 "Kellogg-Briand Pact," officially known as the "General Treaty for Renunciation of War as an Instrument of National Policy." Pacifism was not so much a true creed as porous disposition or favored inclination, although important pacifist organizations were active, and vague antiwar notions often firmed up into something quite new: an absolute opposition to war and its carnage under any circumstances.

Pacifism in the 1930s had a neighborhood feel about it, with poster parades, street-corner meetings, and peace pledges. When hundreds of citizens came out to pacifist meetings in small towns, they were responding to the admonishment of the ghosts of the dead from the Great War. "The dead remained strangely present," recalled historian Raoul Girardet. "Almost every day you could hear references to the names of the dead in conversation." And if "you entered a neighbor's house," "the faces," and they were "such young faces," stared back from photographs on the walls and mantels. Everyday life reflected the long "shadow of the war": in "the black outlines of the women, in the sometimes unbearable likeness of the mutilated, the commemorations on November 11, the powerful associations of veterans." Novelist Irène Némirovsky tucked the last war throughout the pages of her novel *Suite Française*, about France's new war in 1940: "The golden letters of the names of people who had died in 1914 shimmered on a marble tablet" in the town's church; the tax inspector who "rubbed the hand that had been lacerated by a shell explosion in 1915"; and the scene when the invading soldiers asked for a cigarette, the news agent on the main street replied in "bad German" because "he had been among the occupying forces in Mainz in '18."[13] Veterans of the war made up 40 percent of the male population in France.

Memory of the war was a living force that nourished an "immense longing for peace." "The horror of the war aroused the men of my generation"—that was the verdict of French journalist Robert Lazurick explaining the mood of 1939.[14] The Great War in its common devotions and profound futilities shaped the memories of the French and the British in the twentieth century, as had the French Revolution and Napoleon in the nineteenth century. The center of gravity of France's soul shifted from the Champ de Mars (site of the Eiffel Tower), the Arc de Triomphe, and the Place de la Revolution (Place de la Concorde) in Paris to the monuments to the dead in the small towns of Provence ("AUX NOS MORTS," "AUX ENFANTS")—thirty-six thousand in all. It was ordinary places and ordinary soldiers—the French *poilu* (the hairy one) or the British "Tommy"—that shaped the legacy of the war; the poignancy of the war was expressed in neighborhood portraits.

This local frame encouraged people's pacifist inclinations. The prevailing approach to commemoration tended to focus on the ordinary soldiers who had died and suffered. It was as family members and neighbors that the bereaved cradled their lost loved ones, withholding *nos morts* and *enfants* from the nation. This sort of reckoning added to the distance between the dead and the bereaved, on the one hand, and the generals and statesmen, on the other. Locals regarded elites with suspicion, questioning grand narratives about national interests. That neighbors controlled so much of the memory of the war also meant it was easier for

French townspeople to imagine their German counterparts as not so very different. Of course, many veterans nursed bitter resentments against the enemy, but, even so, local perspectives on the war tended to tamp down differences among the belligerents. If there was one single piece of art in postwar Europe that managed to incorporate these quietist perspectives on the war most fully, it was German author Erich Maria Remarque's 1929 novel, *All Quiet on the Western Front*.

Whether the young writer from Osnabrück—his international debut and the fame and riches that followed came when he was only thirty-one years old—intended to write an antiwar novel, *All Quiet on the Western Front* became such a book because of its close focus on only a few characters. In the opening pages, the protagonist's Second Company returns from the front with only 80 out of 150 men alive. A few chapters later, only 32 remain. Of the 20 classmates who signed up along with Paul Bäumer, "seven are dead, four wounded, one in a madhouse." By the fall of 1918, only Paul remains alive, and he too is killed in the last lines of the novel. The war's high casualty rates cut the cast down to a workable size, 4 or 5 main characters whom Remarque moves along the stations of the cross: the arrival of new recruits ("infants"), the first experience of being shelled, the attack, the retreat, the chow line, the hospital, the return home, the renewed offensive, and death. Moreover, Remarque makes the war familiar, down-to-earth, even vulgar. He admits the higher-ups into the novel only as caricatures and denigrates the "phrases" of the war, which would give it a higher meaning. Instead, he shows how the men become "burnt up by hard facts": the ability to light a cigarette in the rain, to make a fire in the forest, to requisition a pair of boots or steal a goose. Remarque zooms in to search for truth and pans out (following Paul on his leave home, for example) to expose falseness and hypocrisy. The narrow precincts of the front are made more familiar by the inclusion of a cobbler, a locksmith, and a peat digger among the student volunteers. Not only do soldiers from different social backgrounds understand each other, but the German men also find companionship among French women, and, in the novel's most poignant scene, Paul Bäumer recognizes the Frenchman he has killed as a comrade, for whom Remarque provides a name (Gérard Duval), profession (printer), and family (wife and daughter). The novel creates bonds across no-man's-land, which contrast with the failed lines of communication between the front and the rear and between the battlefront and the home front.[15]

The achievement of *All Quiet on the Western Front* was to write "from the gut," as one young reader put it, and thereby to reorient the focus of the experience of the war to the individual and collective bodies of soldiers: the book's premise was that to tell it like it was meant denying the use value of war. This sense of waste frustrated Remarque's critics, who disputed Remarque's war record, but resonated with the readers who made *All Quiet on the Western Front* an instant international success. By the end of 1929, the novel had sold 1 million copies in Germany and another million in France, Britain, and the United States, where the Book-of-the-Month Club had made the book its main selection for June 1929. With his story of battered Second Company, Remarque enjoyed, the journal *Nouvelles Littéraires* guessed, "the largest audience in the world."[16] Many of the pacifist declarations in the years that followed read as if they were adaptations of key scenes in *All Quiet on the Western Front*.

Paul Bäumer's disillusionment with the "words, words, words" in his high school books, the "collected works" bound in "blue cloth" from which schoolteacher Kantorek lifted his phrases about "Iron Youth" to convince the 20 boys in the class to enlist, resonates with the famous "King and Country" debate at the Oxford Union on February 9, 1933. At that event, students voted 275 to 153 in favor of the motion "that this House will in no circumstances fight for its King and Country." It was an unprecedented statement of absolute pacifism and a rebuke to what one historian refers to as the presumed lies of "the recruiting posters, patriotic propaganda, and war hysteria of 1914." The Oxford Union vote should be understood as a "backward looking protest at what had happened in August 1914," when Europeans publicly celebrated the declaration of war.[17]

If war left formerly enthusiastic middle-class boys like Bäumer disenchanted, it menaced peasant boys from the very beginning. For novelist Jean Giono, who had fought at Verdun and Chemin-des-Dames, and who had been gassed and nearly blinded, the Great War constituted "the massacre of paysans from all countries." "War Spells Ruin for Your

Rams, Your Ewe-Lambs and Your Crops," he wrote. If peasants embodied the very ideal of life—Giono was someone able to describe a woman who "peeled off her stockings as though skinning a rabbit"—then the state, the city, industrial civilization, and, most of all, war represented threats to the ability to "live each and every day." When life "moves in complete harmony with the condition of the earth," it does so without "abrupt shocks." "I do not want to sacrifice myself," Giono admitted. "To be alive is a far grander thing than to be a dead hero."[18] In his view, the bakers, shoemakers, and shepherds of the village of Manosque, nestled in the mountains above the Côte d'Azur, where he was born in 1895 and where he died in 1970, did not want war. International conflicts had their origins in regimes external to the lives of ordinary men. In *All Quiet on the Western Front*, Tjaden, the locksmith, came to a similar conclusion: "'State, State'—Tjaden snaps his fingers contemptuously, 'Gendarmes, police, taxes, that's your State;—if that's what you are talking about, no, thank you.'" So did Kat, the cobbler: "Now just why would a French blacksmith or a French shoemaker want to attack us? No, it is merely the rulers," the kaiser, the generals. For Giono, as for Tjaden and Kat, the local neighborhood provided the perspective by which to judge the war and its losses. Bäumer and the Oxford students rebelled against middle-class settings furnished with libraries, books, and patriotic and imperial sentiments. These great things no longer counted. Giono and Kat, on the other hand, spoke up in favor of the small life of the village; they wanted to go home and stay home.[19]

The middle-class pacifism of Bäumer and the Oxford Union would ultimately crumble because German aggression restored patriotic qualities to both king and country. Giono's brand of pacifism, however, was more resistant because it was so rooted in the soil of home. It was basically defensive, a radical disengagement from national foreign policy that imagined that villages such as Manosque would survive undisturbed, no matter what came. Nothing was worth the destruction of battle. Not even the rise of Hitler and the aggressive policies of Germany moved Giono to redefine his pacifist stance, which he reasserted in increasingly inflexible terms as the "Great Debate" heated up. "For my part I prefer to be a living German than a dead Frenchman," Giono insisted, regarding the prospect of a German invasion. Many others in the postwar period agreed with Giono that war was worse than occupation. "Modern war is practically certain to have worse consequences than even the most unjust peace," philosopher Bertrand Russell asserted in 1936. The logic of this counsel was inflexibility in military and strategic policy. It did not make differentiations between who might be invading France (or Czechoslovakia or Poland) and for what purpose. Ultimately, in the face of war, Giono proposed a policy of indifference, even blindness. During the occupation itself, nothing the Germans did induced Giono to look beyond the defensive perimeter he had drawn around Manosque. When asked about "the Jewish problem," Giono would not be bothered: "I don't give a damn," he replied. "There are better things to do on this earth than worry about the Jews."[20] Humanitarianism was simply the name of another regime of complicity to force Manosque out of its tranquillity.

In many ways, Giono simply adopted on a small scale the same policy France pursued on a national scale with the construction of the defensive Maginot Line on its eastern frontier. André Maginot, who served on and off as minister of war from 1922 to 1932, lamented the fate of France with words strikingly similar to Giono's. "We are always the invaded, we are always the ones who suffer, we are always the ones to be sacrificed," he said, and so France would remake itself in the image of Manosque. The French constructed immense fortifications to avert more suffering and sacrifice. Right up until the German offensive, military strategists such as Marshal Philippe Pétain and Commander in Chief Maurice Gamelin not only considered the Maginot Line impenetrable but even celebrated the safety of the "island" status that France had finally achieved for itself. Rural leaders themselves considered the peasantry a Maginot Line protecting France's national vitality, and this in October 1939. Maginot offered France the possibility of security, virtue, and happiness: according to one deputy, "we will be undisturbed [*tranquille*] behind the Maginot Line," precisely the state of being left alone that Giono craved.[21]

Given the huge international success of *All Quiet on the Western Front*, French and British readers could be forgiven if they believed that characters Paul and Tjaden spoke for Fritz, the German everyman. Each of the belligerents had suffered horrendous casualties. At Verdun the French lost

377,000 men; in the same place, the Germans lost 337,000. Remarque's success seemed to confirm that Europeans thought about the war in basically similar terms, as a horror that must not be repeated. This was the premise of Giono's appeal to "paysans" who populated "all countries." The regime was French or German; the paysan was universal. The assumption that nobody really wanted war persisted as late as spring 1940; things would somehow sort themselves out ("Qu'ils se débrouiller" was the turn of phrase in France).[22] French premier Edouard Daladier was sure that his fellow veteran Adolf Hitler no more wanted war than he.

In Germany, however, other writers aspired to rebut rather than concur with Remarque. But, these contrarian "second-wave" (and second-rate) novelists, such as Josef Magnus Wehner, Hans Zöberlein, and Franz Schauwecker, were not translated into French or English. In the end, *All Quiet on the Western Front* misled its international readers. Germans read Remarque, but not only Remarque.

In some ways, the anti-Remarque books were not so different from *All Quiet on the Western Front*. Wehner kills off his "seven at Verdun" just as Remarque destroyed Second Company. There was no disputing the horrendous casualty rates. Moreover, nationalist authors shared Remarque's mistrust of Germany's old military leaders. The comradeship between men from different backgrounds, a "more complete communion" than "even lovers have," that Remarque cherished was completely consistent with the virtues prized by nationalists and National Socialists.[23]

However, the energetic German dissenters from Remarque aimed to resurrect the dead for the life of the nation. As a thirteen-year-old, Georg Hensel attended a "training course" in Darmstadt in July 1936 in his capacity as a leader in the "Jungvolk," which prepared children for the adolescent Hitler Youth. Two texts were read side by side: "a few pages from the prohibited novel, 'All Quiet on the Western Front,' in which soldiers, following an inspection by the kaiser, speak soberly and skeptically about the kaiser, the war, and the fatherland. Then we read a corresponding scene from a novel by Franz Schauwecker in which the soldiers burn with enthusiasm for the kaiser and willingness to die for the fatherland." "We were told that this was a truthful portrayal," Hensel wrote, while Remarque had "dragged the idealism of German soldiers through the mud." Hensel found Schauwecker to be "patriotic kitsch" and resigned his leadership post, but the lessons stuck. Heinrich Böll, who affirmed many times that he "hated war, really," dismissed Remarque when he comforted his wife, Annemarie, after her brother had been killed in April 1943: "Let me tell you, completely sober and clear, with all the sobriety and imagination of my being, that there is no higher, more noble way to die than to die as a soldier in the face of the enemy, somehow, somewhere. Really, I believe it." To belabor the "incompetent officer" or "tactical mistake," which had cost the brother his life, "is actually terrible"; it was "the dreadful side of the book, *All Quiet on the Western Front*, which is based on those realities." Böll insisted, desperately, perhaps, on a higher redemptive meaning to war. During World War II, millions of soldiers, who, as boys, sometimes as young as Georg Hensel, had been socialized in paramilitary organizations and in Nazi Party institutions since the early 1920s, agreed. War letters reveal that some German soldiers went into battle with scenes of *All Quiet on the Western Front* in their heads; most did not.[24] Tjaden did not speak for Fritz. In this regard, Giono and Daladier miscalculated. In the "Great Debate," *All Quiet on the Western Front* reinforced pacifist inclinations outside Germany, while it ultimately served as a foil to bolster the nobility and even the necessity of war inside Hitler's Germany.

Prewar

IN 1930 THE *REVUE HEBDOMADAIRE*, AN INFLUENTIAL PARIS WEEKLY, suggested that the year "marked the end of the postwar period." Versailles no longer provided a railhead into the future; instead, the way forward was obscured by the uncertainties of international conflict, ideological polarity, and economic hardship. All around him, concurred novelist Julien Green, an American writer based in France, people talked about the next war. If the last war cast a long shadow across the everyday life of small towns such as Manosque, the next war came to loom equally as large. British war correspondent John Langdon-Davies wrote in 1938, mindful of his experiences in the civil war in Spain, of "the forces of darkness stealing up in the obscurity of an uncertain future." Mathieu, the central character in Jean-Paul Sartre's novel about the interwar years, *The Reprieve*, spoke for contemporaries when he expressed feeling "compressed between two high, hopeless walls."[25]

The specter of the "next war" appeared much more menacing to Europeans at the end of the 1920s—the decade of progress when most apartments were electrified and switched on to municipal gas and water lines—because modern war became widely associated with a high-tech "aerochemical" war in which civilians would be primary victims. The extreme vulnerability of European cities to an air attack made war not only more frightening but also more likely. Already in 1920, in his *Outline of History*, H. G. Wells predicted that a future conflict would leave Europe ravaged by air attacks, making the "'bombing of those 'prentice days'" of 1914–1918 look like "child's play." In 1935 he opened his screenplay to Alexander Korda's popular film *Things to Come* with an air war that annihilated civilization. Airpower theorists such as Giulio Douhet in Italy, Lord Trenchard in Britain, and Billy Mitchell in the United States gained considerable authority in the 1920s, as they detailed grim scenarios of whole cities destroyed by fearsome bomber attacks, biological and chemical agents released to disfigure the species, and the unfortunate survivors driven to panic and flight. When British prime minister Stanley Baldwin declared in the House of Commons in November 1932 that "no power on earth can protect [the man in the street] from being bombed. . . . [T]he bomber will always get through," he expressed a broad European consensus.[26] The fear of ferociously destructive air raids sat as deeply in the bones of Europeans in the 1930s as the fear of nuclear attack would during the Cold War a generation later. Readers flipped through the pages of the *Illustrated London News*, the *Berliner Illustrirte Zeitung*, or *L'Illustration*. Week by week, page by page, they encountered images of the strong-armed technologies of future war. They browsed technological capacity and carnage.

The outline of the imagined future war was very different from the remembered last war. Instead of a massacre of peasant soldiers, there would be a massacre of metropolitan women and children. "The Most Dangerous of All Places" would be the home. It must be made "unequivocally clear to civilians of every age and sex," wrote novelist Aldous

Huxley in 1932, "that the next war is meant for them." "There will be no soldiers to suffer vicariously for them," he explained. "All the bleeding and choking, all the groaning and dying will have to be done personally, even by the most respectable bankers and archdeacons and Dames of the British Empire."[27] What artillery shells had been to the last war, long-range bombers would be to the next. The public was confronted with the wildest predictions. One French general estimated that Germany's commercial aircraft, which were "barely disguised instruments of war," could drop 685 tons of bombs on French targets every day; other commentators figured the daily tonnage of the bombardier at 2,500. At the Disarmament Conference in Geneva, representatives spoke of 1,000 bombers paralyzing entire nations with 30,000 tons of bombs in just twenty-four hours. (As it actually happened, Germany deployed an average of 163 bombers every night to drop some 200 tons of bombs on London during the Blitz in the fall of 1940.)[28] In 1937 official British estimates put the number of civilian casualties during a sixty-day air campaign at 2 million. Two years later, the number of dead in a three-week campaign was put at 250,000, with ten times as many panicked citizens fleeing cities such as London; it was assumed that a new war would leave half of the world's largest cities in ruins. Bertrand Russell even asserted that a future war on the scale of the Great War would kill off 50 to 90 percent of all men and women living in Europe.[29]

Moreover, in a well-planned surprise attack, the feared and anticipated *guerre brusquée*, the work of annihilation would proceed with extraordinary speed, a complete departure from the monthlong slow-motion battles at Verdun and the Somme in 1916. According to an article in the authoritative *Revue des Deux Mondes* in August 1934, 100 planes could smother Paris with a deadly cloud of gas in a single hour. Other observers feared that civilization could be "wiped out, in a few moments." There was an "extravagant provision for the *dead*" in all these scenarios: "One hour" or just "a few moments" to do the killing, 685, 30,000, or 2 million, or simply 90 percent killed. This guesswork was all gross miscalculation, but a sign nonetheless of how hard it was to get a sober grip on the threat posed by air warfare and also how inclined contemporaries were to apply a catastrophic scale.[30] Description was persistently short-circuited by fear and uncertainty. Extravagance signaled the lack of right words, the muddle of anticipation.

Authorities on air war always stressed the superiority of the offense and the ineffectiveness of the defense. Air-raid shelters, gas masks, and counteroffensive fighter squadrons did not much matter. Baldwin's assertion echoed from capital to capital: "If the enemy wants to get through, he will get through." Airpower promised to mark a dramatic departure from the superiority of the defense that had prevailed in the trench warfare of the Great War. And fears of air war created the precise opposite of the sense of security the Maginot Line produced; instead of a postwar island fortress impenetrable to infantry attack, the prewar nation in the "shadow of the bomber" lay completely exposed.[31] The most basic defensive accessories such as gas masks intended for civilians in the "next war," not just for poor soldiers on the front lines such as those depicted in John Singer Sargent's emblematic 1919 painting Gassed, came with vexing problems. When equipping millions of citizens with gas masks, British air-defense officials did not know what to do about babies; the prototypes of gas-proof prams and "baby bags" they designed proved unworkable. In any case, experts believed that women and children "will certainly not be able to make full use of protective apparatus; every gas attack would cause a panic." Trained soldiers themselves had experienced considerable difficulty putting on gas masks and maintaining discipline during gas attacks.[32] Who didn't know Wilfred Owen's poem "Dulce et Decorum Est" from the Great War? "Gas. Quick, boys!" read the line. "Fumbling" with "clumsy helmets," "stumbling," then "flound'ring," read the next; "guttering, choking, drowning"—the following lines told about boys not quick enough.

Although citizens in countries across Europe shared a fear of an air war, a wrenching anxiety concerning bombs and gas, each nation dramatized its own particular vulnerability. In Britain voices prophesying war described the total destruction of London. French literature on the subject detailed threats to "Tours, or Dijon, or Reims, or, especially, Paris." Elsewhere, "Nice, Toulon, Alger, Tunis" constituted the "fields of slaughter and death." In German propaganda, huge arcs superimposed on maps of the Reich showed that French, Czech, and Polish bombers could strike every, any, town in Germany. *"Germany!! Are You Sleeping?? Air Danger Threatens! In 1 Hour! Fliers! Bombs! Poison Gas! Over Berlin! Your Cities! Your Industrial Areas!"* screamed the long-winded alarm of one 1932 publication.[33] One analyst explains that the self-centered concern with "our town" was partially the result of authors working to keep their particular strategic cause alive. National spokesmen were also reluctant to imagine themselves unleashing horrific bomber raids on others; it was easier to see oneself as target and victim of the bestial conduct. Thus, readers, especially in France and Britain, received the "subliminal message that the bomber flew only one way."[34]

Fearful Europeans regarded themselves as completely defenseless. They walked along the streets of their neighborhoods imagining their own demise. At the height of the Czechoslovak crisis in September 1938, when Germany's threat to annex the Sudetenland made war an imminent possibility, an American couple visiting London described the uncanny feeling: "We go out and walk in the drizzle, going down Piccadilly—buses and cars, policemen, bicycles, women with hair 'brushed up.' . . . I feel as though I were watching the dead, seeing the doomed. Impossible to think it might all be interrupted with bomb holes and shattered buildings in another week." Observers contemplated the next war at extremely close quarters. Gas masks lay about the kitchen "floor like a growth of black fungus" after "Mrs. Miniver," the stalwart character of Jan Struther's popular column in the *Times* of London, stood in line with "two young children, their nanny, cook and parlor maid" to pick up her family's consignment. "It was for this," Mrs. Miniver reflected, "that one had boiled the milk for their bottles, and washed their hands before lunch."[35] Beloved but endangered homes such as Miniver's were the urban counterpart to Giono's merry village. The metropolitan's helplessness matched the paysan's refusal. Both nourished horror at the prospect of war. They reinforced deep pacifist inclinations and added to an overall sense of paralysis. As a result, people's horizons of understanding and responsibility narrowed. "Compressed between two high, hopeless walls," as Sartre put it, people had a tendency to bunker down to protect *ville* and *vie*.

In the late 1930s, there seemed to be only two sorts of people, as one critic writes, the lords in the air and the victims of the lords in the air. But in Nazi Germany, a third type emerged, the well-prepared civilian who was neither lord nor victim. Whereas in France and Britain government officials were slow to organize air-defense preparations, their counterparts in the Third Reich built an elaborate, nationwide air-defense effort that enrolled more than 8 million volunteers in seven thousand branches of the Reich Civil Defense League. The popular scope of air-defense work was impressive. In 1934 and 1935, air-defense shows were visited by a remarkable 28 percent of the population in twenty-one selected cities; the rates increased considerably in border areas, to 40 percent in Heidelberg, 46.7 percent in Frankfurt an der Oder, and 48 percent in Düsseldorf. To drive home the urgency of self-mobilization, organizers of the 1933 air show "Kiel in Flames" brought the event to an end by spraying unsuspecting spectators with tear gas: "a sea of handkerchiefs was suddenly in motion." Tear gas, party organization, and authoritarian government drove home the lesson that the Nazis could manage the extraordinary dangers of the air age as others could not. As far as the Nazis were concerned, the appropriate answer to the apocalyptic quality of these modern times was renewed vigilance and more discipline. German painter Barthel Gilles's striking portrait of himself pulling on a gas mask against a dark, exploding horizon indicated that there was not going to be "fumbling" "stumbling," and "flound'ring" in the Third Reich. Germany's air-defense officials hoped to mold air-minded survivors, willing collaborators in the disciplinary regime of the state of emergency (Gilles himself had been gassed in World War I). Against a background of searchlights licking the black sky, Gilles presents himself as competent and alert, knowledgeable about the next war rather than obsessed with injuries sustained in the last war, ready and able to live in the prewar. The Nazi air-defense slogan summed up the ethos: "One People, One Danger, One Defense."[36]

The rise of Hitler in 1933 intensified fears of war, which in turn both undermined and strengthened pacifist inclinations. On the one hand, Hitler's withdrawal from the League of Nations, the extraordinary investments Germany directed toward rearmament, and the introduction of universal conscription in the Wehrmacht signaled the end of the peace of Versailles. All this made the ability of France and Britain to check German aggression much less effective. Growing international instability in the 1930s made the possibility of a new war with Germany more likely, and both France and Britain reoriented their strategic planning accordingly. On the other hand, the martial spirit of the Nazi revolution, the expansion of the Wehrmacht, and the new might of Germany's Luftwaffe intensified the general European commitment to avoid modern war and all it implied. Ultimately, the new dictatorship in Germany strengthened rather than weakened pacifist inclinations. "The desire for peace with Hitler, rather than war with Germany, was an overriding concern," concludes one historian about France in this period.[37] "Never again!" seemed to make even more sense after 1933, a strange fact that suggests the complicated ways Hitler, war, and peace interacted in the 1930s. Since more French and British statesmen came to acknowledge the injustices of Versailles, and even disputed that Germany bore the lion's share of the guilt for the outbreak of war in 1914, it seemed increasingly possible to finally realize a "brotherhood of the trenches" that could honor without contradiction the deep attachments the former belligerents had to both the nation and the peace. As public opinion gradually moved against Versailles, Germany's grievances appeared more understandable.

What vexed this spirit of accommodation, however, were Nazi Germany's claims, based on the principle of national self-determination, on the sovereign countries of Austria, Czechoslovakia, and later Poland. Strategic and balance-of-power considerations, in addition to the constraints of sovereignty, prevented an easy, straightforward application of self-determination to endorse the right of ethnic German communities to become part of a Greater Germany. But it was difficult to counter on principle the "ethnical argument," especially if the alternative was all-out aerochemical war. Of course, it was Germany itself that posed the alternatives in such stark terms; the recklessness of its foreign policy continuously undermined efforts to accommodate peacefully Germany's acknowledged grievances. The recklessness also fed suspicions that Nazi foreign policy was driven by the desire for empire, not ethnic consolidation. Hitler's ferocious violence against Jews and political opponents had already turned many pacifists into antifascists. As a dictatorship, Germany appeared to such converts to be extremely dangerous both at home and abroad. Yet on the Right, anticommunist tendencies tended to trump anti-Nazi ones; if the Soviet Union constituted the primary danger to domestic peace and labor tranquillity, it made sense to appease the staunchly anticommunist Third Reich.

Thus, in the years after Hitler's assumption to power, Europe's Left and Right each found themselves reorienting their attitudes toward Germany. In the "prewar" years of the 1930s, leftists in Britain and France pushed for a firmer line against Germany, which had generally been the position of rightists in the "postwar" years of the 1920s. The Left was now more apt to consider Germany a menace because of Hitler, and the Right largely dropped its firm line against traditional German militarism to seek appeasement. This remarkable exchange of political views was especially pronounced in France. Ultimately, the mainstream popularity of pacifism ended up helping the Right more than the Left; pacifists believed that Hitler's belligerence required more rather than less accommodation precisely in order to avoid war. Strangely enough, the establishment of the Third Reich marginalized anti-German attitudes in the 1930s.

Pacifism, antifascism, anticommunism, and revised attitudes about Versailles and the principle of self-determination—these strands were all twisted tightly together in September 1938 when the European powers confronted Hitler's demands regarding Czechoslovakia's German-speaking Sudetenland. There was still the postwar talk about the horrible losses in the Great War but also new nightmarish prewar fears of the aerial bomber. As people attentively tuned in to current events, they heard the broadcast of Hitler's speeches over the airwaves and noted the frightful roar of the crowds. They expressed the loquacious, open-handed, but never boundless spirit of accommodation and rapprochement, and they felt the nasty prick of guilty conscience about the cost of the maxim "Never again."

"The Child Is Dead in Europe"

THE CRISIS IN SEPTEMBER 1938 WAS ONE OF THE MOST FRIGHTENING intervals in modern European history. Between Hitler's bellicose speech threatening Czechoslovakia at the Nuremberg rally on September 14 and the final agreement on Germany's annexation of the Sudetenland on September 30, radio broadcasts, news bulletins, and newspaper headlines brought the specter of an all-out war closer and closer. Diarists across the Continent telegraphed fright in their entries: "The awful tension weighs on everyone. It has made me completely sick," wrote one housewife in Amerfoort, Holland, on September 28.[38]

Europeans watched events tumble over each other in an increasingly agitated state of collective anxiety as Neville Chamberlain, the British prime minister, made three trips to Germany, the first on September 15, another exactly one week later, and a third on September 29, a day when many observers believed that bombs were about to fall on their neighborhoods. Chamberlain expressed the anguish of his contemporaries when he repeatedly accounted the price of war with the most intimate domestic scenes. Throughout the crisis, he invoked the families who had lost young men during the last war, the homes that would be destroyed by long-range bombers in a new war, and the precious gift of being able to "sleep quietly in your beds" once he had secured "peace for our time."[39] For the first time, Europeans across the Continent envisaged the next war from the vantage point of bedrooms, which made it much easier to bend on principles in order to preserve domestic peace.

Charles and Anne Lindbergh provide a poignant example of the ways in which the looming war was conjured up as a home invasion that threatened quiet sleep. During the crisis, the couple mingled with some of the most important decision makers in Europe, adding their counsel about the cost of war, the power of Germany, and the capacity of technology. And like so many other people around them, they had recurrent nightmares of dead family and friends. But thinking of bombs and babies, the Lindberghs also exemplified the general failure to consider the centrality of racial thinking to Germany's great-power ambitions. They extrapolated from the Great War while ignoring the new ideas that the Nazis had about war for living space and empire and war against the Jews.

At the end of 1935, more than three years after the kidnapping and murder of their first child, Charles and Anne Lindbergh arrived in Europe for a period of indefinite self-imposed exile. They left their home in Hopewell, New Jersey, to escape the disruptive glare of notoriety and what they considered to be tawdry aspects of American life: the "false high-pressuring newspapers," "flashy and cheap magazines," "racy and material advertising," "sex-appeal movies," and "blustering politicians." The Lindberghs found solitude in two "remarkable homes," first Long Barn in Kent, England, which they rented from diplomat Harold Nicholson and his wife, writer Vita Sackville-West, and then a castle on the island of Illiec, off the cost of Britanny in France, which the couple purchased outright. Yet after years of "no comment," Charles gradually recovered his voice. The Lindberghs had arrived in England just as Europeans were beginning to pay attention to Hitler, and, as an expert in aviation and the hero who was the first person to fly alone across the Atlantic in 1927, Charles became increasingly involved in the debates about Germany's intentions and military capacities. He shuttled back and forth to London and Paris and made three semiofficial trips to Berlin and another to Moscow on behalf of the United States. He filed pessimistic reports outlining Germany's lead in airpower, and as war approached in April 1939, after the Lindberghs returned to the United States, he summarized his findings in influential articles written for *Reader's Digest*. Once war did break out in Europe in September 1939, Lindbergh turned his confidential assessment that neither Britain nor France was ready for war into public appeals against American intervention. He "could not stop talking." He wrote for the *Atlantic*, lectured on NBC radio broadcasts, addressed an August 1940 rally organized in Chicago by "Citizens to Keep-America-Out-of-War," and finally campaigned on behalf of the isolationist America First Committee, drawing huge antiwar crowds to events held in the Hollywood Bowl and in Des Moines. There, in September 1941, he blamed the talk in favor of war not just on the Roosevelt administration but also on the British, whom he had come to believe were decadent, and on Jews, "other peoples" who would "lead our country to destruction." Lindbergh made himself the center of scandalous attention, with the price of a final silencing and departure from public life once the United States entered the war in December 1941.[40]

Years later, Anne Morrow Lindbergh reproached herself and her husband for naïveté. She described his new and insistent voice as a throwback to the language of his father and grandfather. Charles spoke in "the

cadence of the old West," a virtuous place and spirit Lindbergh believed
to be under attack by mass democracy, big-city life, and intervention in
the war in Europe. For Anne, meanwhile, the war in Europe seemed to
repeat the kidnapping of her child, on a much vaster scale. Both were
home invasions.

"I thought of the people I loved," she wrote on September 3, 1939, the
day Britain and France declared war on Germany, two days after its invasion of Poland; "I saw them tortured, torn, dead, cut off before their time
(or even if not killed or tortured—embittered, turned to ashes inside),
before their work, their dreams are finished—wasted, spilled out for nothing." She thought of the places where she had found security: Paris, Illiec,
Chartres, Mont–St. Michel, Long Barn, "our old life, our old happiness."
"We will never see peace again, even after 'war' ceases," she concluded.
"My husband and my friends will go in the beginning of this long struggle
and my children in the end of it." Anne made the connection between the
kidnapping of her oldest child from his bedroom in Hopewell and the war
that threatened "my husband" and "my children" explicit:

> I look at the newspapers piled up on our table, fruitless words, fruitless
> telegrams, letters, meetings, negotiations, airplane trips of diplomatists,
> words of pleading, of hope, prayers. All useless. It makes me think of
> Hopewell—that tremendous machine set going: state troopers, hand-
> writing experts, ticker tapes, telephone services, detectives, specialists,
> politicians, friends, reporters, letters . . . for what use, for what purpose?
>   The child is dead.
>   The child is dead in Europe.

Given the "concrete scale of war," the Lindberghs did not believe war
against Germany could be justified, certainly not American intervention.[41]
War amounted to a huge violation of home and family, happiness and
security. It is strange that, in 1939, Anne did not see the murderer of her
child, Bruno Hauptmann, himself an (illegal) German immigrant, in Hitler's madness. Instead, she blamed the Allies for insisting that Hitler had to
be stopped. What the Allies considered a righteous "Crusade" on behalf
of Europe, she considered a prelude to "turmoil, revolution, terror."[42]

If the Lindberghs had abandoned America in disgust in 1935, they quickly grew disillusioned with Britain and France in the years that followed. England was old-fashioned and decrepit: "The people of that nation had never adjusted themselves to the tempo of this modern era," Charles concluded. "Their minds were still attuned to the speed of sail rather than to that of aircraft." "A great tradition can be inherited, but greatness itself must be won." Matters were even worse in France. "Her politics were corrupt," he wrote, "her financial situation serious, her people divided, her workmen dissatisfied."[43] By contrast, the great new thing on the Continent was the Third Reich, which the Lindberghs first encountered in July and August 1936, as the Olympic Games were under way in Berlin. Charles considered Germany "the most interesting nation in the world today." For Anne, it resembled nothing so much as the treasured airplane. "There is no question of the power, unity, and purposefulness of Germany," she wrote to her mother after returning from Berlin. "It is terrific. I have never in my life been so conscious of such a *directed* force. It is thrilling when seen manifested in the energy, pride, and morale of the people." Germans had "a spirit of hope, pride, and self-sacrifice. We haven't got it—or France or England." To be sure, Germany was a dictatorship, and Anne disliked the "brute-force manner" and "regimentation" of the regime, but Hitler had to be given credit for the country's spiritual renewal. The "strictly puritanical view at home that dictatorships are of necessity wrong, evil, unstable" made no sense to the Lindberghs, who gave serious consideration to moving the family to Berlin in October 1938.[44]

For the Lindberghs, aviation was a key sign of national vigor and virility. Air forces registered the state's war-making capacity. In discussions with diplomat Nicholson, Charles guessed that the Germans possessed "the most powerful air-force in the world, with which they could do terrible damage to any other country." A year later, Lindbergh returned from Germany and prepared a more detailed report, "General Estimate as of November 1, 1937." Germany's "air force and her air industry have emerged from the kindergarten stage," he concluded. "Germany is once more a world power in the air," with the industrial capacity to manufacture six thousand planes annually. He estimated that the standing air force totaled twenty-four hundred planes.[45]

This state of affairs led Lindbergh to two conclusions. First, because Germany "has more than her share of the elements which make strength and greatness among nations," it needed to be afforded the room for action commensurate to its status. Lindbergh believed that the Third Reich should be allowed to expand into eastern Europe. Such an accommodation was consistent with his view of natural history, in which might created its own right and adjustments to the balance of power had to be continually made. Moreover, Germany's strength relative to Britain and France had drastically curtailed the Allies' room for maneuver. While "Germany has developed a huge Air Force," England had "slept," unaware of "the change aviation has made." The English "have always before had a fleet between themselves and their enemy," Lindbergh explained.[46] Without a sufficient counteroffensive bombing force, or fast fighter planes, Britain and France were simply not in a position to check Germany, regardless of where their statesmen stood on the matter of Hitler's claims on Czechoslovakia in 1938 or Poland in 1939. Given his fame as an aviation pioneer and the expertise he had acquired on his fact-finding missions to Germany, Lindbergh was sought out during the jittery crisis in September 1938. He spoke with great authority. He was hardly the only observer to raise alarm, but he enjoyed unusually good access to government officials in London and Paris.

Lindbergh returned to Paris at the beginning of September 1938 after a three-week trip to inspect aviation facilities in the Soviet Union, by which time international tensions around the question of the German-speaking Sudetenland in Czechoslovakia preoccupied European leaders. A series of compromise plans (a conciliatory "Third Plan," an acquiescent "Fourth Plan") had had little effect except to rapidly move the discussion from autonomy to plebiscite to outright annexation. The issue of Czechoslovakia's sovereignty and thus France's treaty obligations to the democratic state moved to the center of debate. At the same time, despite the powerful "ethnical argument," Hitler's demands appeared to be increasingly rushed and unreasonable, raising the specter of a European war in the absence of a workable solution. And the threat of war sharpened fears of aerial bombardment, the destruction of cities, and the end of civilization. In the foreground was the weeklong Nazi Party rally at Nuremberg, which featured vicious assaults on the Czech state and concluded with Hitler's much-anticipated speech on September 14. Around the world, larger and larger audiences gathered around radio news broadcasts. For the first time since the end of the Great War, it seemed possible that the European powers would find themselves at war, which everybody knew would be more terrible than the last.

On his first day back in Paris, on September 9, Lindbergh had dinner with Guy la Chambre, France's minister of aviation and a veteran of the Great War. According to Lindbergh, "The French situation is desperate. Impossible to catch up to Germany for years, if at all. France is producing about forty-five or fifty airplanes per month. Germany is building from 500 to 800 per month, according to the best estimates. England is building in the vicinity of seventy per month." Moreover, in his view, German bombers were faster than any French fighter plane. Because "the German air fleet is stronger than that of all other European countries combined," an assessment that Lindbergh repeated again and again, an "attack on the old Western front" would be "suicide" because it would trigger massive air raids on Paris against which there was "no known defense."[47] The next day, Georges Bonnet, the foreign minister, picked up on Lindbergh's gloomy assessment and concluded that in the event of war, "French and British towns would be wiped out and little or no retaliation would be possible."

At the request of the American ambassador to Great Britain, Joseph Kennedy, Lindbergh flew to London a little more than a week later. The talk of the town focused on "air warfare" that could "level" Paris or London. Lindbergh repeated his estimation about Germany's production rates: "500–800 planes per month." War would "easily result in the loss of European civilization." With respect to Czechoslovakia, France and Britain, unprepared as they were, had no choice but "to permit Germany's eastward expansion." Lindbergh had no patience with the interventionist "spirit of the 'Light Brigade'"; the sentiments of Tennyson were "too high," as 1914 had shown. Lindbergh prepared a written summary that Kennedy handed to the prime minister, Neville Chamberlain, just before he flew to Bad Godesberg on September 22 to meet with Hitler for a second time.[48]

In the negotiations, Hitler raised the stakes, and Chamberlain returned home disappointed. For many, war seemed inevitable, but also unthinkable. Horrific images of mass destruction unnerved statesmen and ordinary citizens alike. Bonnet thought about air raids all the time: "Do you know what war is like?" he badgered Genevieve Tabouis, the prointerventionist journalist at *L'Oeuvre*. "War with bombs?" As Chamberlain flew back from Bad Godesberg on September 24, "he saw spread out like on a map beneath him the mile upon mile of flimsy houses which constituted the East End of London, [and] he could not bear to think of their inmates lying a prey to bombardment from the air." And the next catastrophe recalled the last, which Chamberlain's prolix, repetitious words reveal had left deep marks. Already in July 1938, he had concluded that "in war, whichever side may call itself the victor, there are no winners"; "all are losers." He started to count casualties: "I think of the 7,000,000 young men who were cut off in their prime, the 13,000,000 who were maimed and mutilated, the misery and the suffering of the mothers and the fathers, the sons and the daughters, and the relatives and the friends of those who were killed, and the wounded." As far as Chamberlain was concerned, any "war postponed may be a war averted."[49] When measured up against the consequences of modern war, the causes did not seem very important. Wasn't this the lesson of 1914?

London and Paris busied themselves with the practical intelligence that "the bomber will always get through." Anne Morrow Lindbergh looked out the window of Brown's Hotel onto the "large gas-mask center on Piccadilly, and into the ground floor of one of those huge motorcar showrooms where volunteers sit showing people how to fit and wear gas masks." "This Was 'Gas Mask' Sunday," the headline in the *Daily Express* announced on September 26, 1938. "Advice flashed on cinema screens, messages blared from loud-speakers on cars in the streets," and "leaflets displayed in cafes, restaurants and hotels" all urged people to make their way to the "Air Raid Precaution" centers that had been set up across the city in order to be fitted with gas masks. Lady Diana Cooper spent the day volunteering at a local Air Raid Precaution station, "clamping snouts and schnozzles on to rubber masks, parceling them and distributing them to queues of men and women." Everyone from "titled people" to "telephone girls" gathered for their "first face-to-face meeting with gas masks." It was a little like a "church social," commented the *Daily Express*. The streets were crowded, and people talked loudly about the war, noted Virginia Woolf. On the whole they showed themselves capable: "no excitement," "no fuss." Nonetheless, photographs in the newspapers "underscored exactly whom this new war threatened," women and children, Long Barn and Hopewell. Not being able to purchase their own masks, the Lindberghs, as expatriates, had to wait all week until a shipment of gas masks arrived at the American Embassy. Then, finally after lunch, "Anne and I practiced putting on and packing away the gas masks. Packing takes longest. Putting them on is quite simple after the original adjustments are made."[50]

Officials in Paris could put their hands on far fewer gas masks and sought to empty the capital of as many of its 3 million inhabitants as possible; about 1 in 3 did leave. "It started on Sunday," September 25, 1938: one thousand buses and thousands more taxis and automobiles sped out of the danger zone, to the west and the south. The train stations bustled: "We are off to grandmother's in the Creuse" or "to my sister-in-law's outside Rouen." "The opening of schools was postponed from October 1 to October 10. . . . [I]mmense crowds were assembled at the railway stations. . . . There were long queues outside the savings banks. . . . Trenches were being dug in the Parc Montsouris . . . and at the Louvre pictures were being packed up." The *Daily Mail* reported that cities on the German frontier such as Strasbourg, Belfort, and Nancy "have been almost entirely evacuated."[51]

The next day, Monday, September 26, Hitler was scheduled to speak from Berlin, and on both sides of the Atlantic people gathered anxiously around radios, half expecting Germany's declaration of war. *Time* positioned Europe "on the verge." Two weeks earlier, Hitler had spoken from Nuremberg on what the newspapers had dubbed "Hitler Night." Across the United States, 70 NBC stations and 112 CBS stations carried his speech live from 3:00 to 3:30 in the afternoon to what *Variety* described as "the greatest and most profoundly interested listening audience in radio history." On September 26, the audience was even bigger. Wall Street came to a full stop as "throngs surrounded taxicabs with radios. In board rooms of commission houses customers and staff members alike clustered about loudspeakers." In France, "Hitler's torrent of words poured in over just about every radio."[52]

That night the Lindberghs attended a dinner party hosted by at the Astors, a prominent family in business and politics (originally from Walldorf, Germany—hence New York City's Waldorf Astoria Hotel) at their estate in Cliveden, outside London. As Anne recorded in her diary,

> They turn the radio on. You hear the mob shouting in Germany. It is terrifying.
>
> Lord Astor and Thomas Jones are on the floor at the feet of the radio and C. near them listening tensely. They are quite prepared for what is tantamount to a declaration of war from Hitler. . . . The German boys are taking down what he says. Lady Astor, the women, and a few of the men go in to dinner. Conversation is almost impossible. . . . All one can do is wait for each scrap of news—listen whenever anyone says something new.
>
> The men come in. There has been no declaration of war. . . .
>
> One gets scraps of the speech. Hitler traced the whole of the postwar history, his attempts toward peace and settling of the European situation. How he was forced to use force, to give up diplomatic means and establish a strong Army, Air Force, etc, which is equal to none, with which Germany can stand up to the world. He says he is still ready for peace, that his peace plan, or offers, are the same as the English-French ones except in the matter of execution—which he will have no delay on. Beneš [the Czech president] cannot squeeze out, this time. Saturday they will occupy the Sudetenland. . . .
>
> Around the table people snatch at straws. . . . It is interesting how they fall. The older people follow the old line of rather romantic idealism, without really thinking it out. . . . "There are some things that are worth more than life." Yes—but what are they? The issues are not clear, as they used to be in war. They are fighting because of a series of entanglements, a series of blunders, and because, it seems, they are committed to abide by the blunders, right or wrong. . . . The young generation see no reason to make a final blunder in order to get out of

all the previous blunders. They see quite plainly and face their complete unpreparedness, and probably failure in case of war—mass suicide. . . . [T]hey do not see anything gained for the world after this sacrifice.

The entry is an extraordinary transcript of fear and anticipation.

Lady Astor was with the young people: "'Fight for what— Czechoslovakia? For Beneš? For the word of a Frenchman?' she rails. And then she has Germany and the 'scrap of paper' and the last war thrown at her." No one knew with certainty; everyone guessed. Just before they tucked themselves into bed at Cliveden, Anne and Charles heard the latest radio bulletin. Germany had announced mobilization in anticipation of the October 1 deadline. All night long, Anne thought of war, "of Florrie and Lady Astor and their sons, of hundreds more like them, wiped out, England going under, air raids, gas, misery year after year." "Thinking about England being bombed," Charles also had trouble sleeping.[53] Across Europe fear of war and bombardment crept into the body.

The door left open, the armies mobilized, the deadline looming, September 27, 1938, turned into a "frightful afternoon—the worst I have ever spent," remembered Sir Alexander Cadogan, permanent undersecretary at the Foreign Office. There were "four days in which to rescue the world"; as London's *Daily Mail* presented the urgent stakes, "Britain can perhaps do more yet by perseverance." The paper provided readers sample prayers for peace from which to choose. On his way to confer with Lloyd George, Britain's prime minister during the Great War, who blamed Beneš for "a lot of the trouble" in Czechoslovakia, Lindbergh saw trenches being "dug in most of the parks and open spaces we passed." The intention was to "dig all night" in the "light of flares." Up to seven feet deep and outfitted with seats, the zigzag of trenches recalled those in the Great War, but this time they were designed to protect civilians from bombs, not trained soldiers on the western front. The sights all over London drove Chamberlain to distraction. He spoke to the nation over the BBC at eight o'clock that evening: "How horrible, fantastic, incredible it is that we should be digging trenches and trying on gas masks here because of a quarrel in a far-away country between people of whom we know nothing." The ultimate consequences of war completely overwhelmed the immediate cause, which, by comparison, seemed puny and distant.[54]

In the end, after Chamberlain and Daladier conceded to Hitler's demands, a four-power agreement signed in Munich on the night of September 29 averted war. Germany annexed the Sudetenland. As an afterthought, a supplementary document, signed by Hitler and Chamberlain the next day, promised what Chamberlain offered to the public as "peace for our time" between Britain and Germany. There was tremendous emotional and physical relief. The *Daily Express* in London, and also the *Tribune* in Chicago, headlined the message: "PEACE!"—"the three-inch-high letters set in the largest typescript ever seen on the front of a British newspaper."[55] That a "terrible oppression has been lifted" well described the mood of the day, in Britain, in France, in the United States, and in Germany as well. (Hitler was a bit flummoxed at the relief the Germans expressed and the cheers they reserved for Chamberlain.) While Czechoslovakia's strategic and political interests were entirely ignored, most people at the time agreed that Germany, Britain, France, and Italy, the "four great powers," as Chamberlain explained, could by discussion, rather than force of arms, resolve their differences and thereby avoid "a catastrophe that would have ended civilization as we have known it."

With the "foundations of lasting peace" laid, trumpeted the *Daily Mail*, "the watchword for the future is 'Never Again!'" That autumn, in 1938, Chamberlain, whose "reception in England was such as no man has received before," found himself the most celebrated man on the Continent. In France umbrellas became known as *mon Chamberlain*, as popular in the spirit of thanksgiving as they would be reviled as symbols of weakness two years later. *Paris-soir* launched a subscription to buy the prime minister "a corner of French soil," preferably one "beside a river, since he likes to fish." Large majorities in the British Parliament (366 to 144) and the French National Assembly (537 to 75) endorsed the Munich Agreement; French radicals and socialists voted for peace in the name of the ordinary farmers and workers they represented, constituents of *la France profonde* who resided in towns like Manosque and deserved to be spared the horrors of war. Surprisingly, public opinion was more divided. A French opinion poll found that 57 percent favored the accords, less than the majority voting in the National Assembly, and 37 percent opposed them—a far greater share than the reviled 73 anti-Munich Communists; "a striking majority (70 per cent)" asserted their refusal to go any further in making concessions to the Germans.[56]

Once Germany invaded what remained of Czechoslovakia in March 1939 and raised new demands against Poland, all the while accompanying its threats with radio broadcasts of bawling crowds, most Europeans came around to the harsh verdict that Winston Churchill had delivered on Munich the previous fall: "a defeat without a war." Whether in London or Paris, citizens no longer accepted a state of affairs in which "the periods of European history" were "determined by the intervals between Herr Hitler's speeches"—in the trenchant words of Duff Cooper, who as First Lord of the Admiralty had resigned from Chamberlain's cabinet over the issue of appeasement. The public was no longer willing "to scramble for the crumbs of comfort that fall from the table."[57] Nonetheless, it is probably also true that Britain and France were better prepared for war in September 1939 both psychologically and materially than they had been in September 1938.[58] The trenches dug in the parks were never filled back in; air-raid personnel stayed on call; hotels continued to place discreet notices informing guests what to do in the event of an attack. The desired "foundations of peace" did not change the anticipated foundations of the next war.

When war did come on September 3, 1939, Chamberlain addressed the British nation over radio just after eleven o'clock in the morning about the "evil things" the nation was fighting against. Instructions about what to do in the event of an air attack followed. "Hardly have these finished than the sirens begin to sound," as one Londoner chronicled the onset of wartime. "We scatter about the building in small groups. I go to the basement . . . with about four others. Some of us try on our gas masks and adjust straps. Somebody puts up the shutters. We sit there keeping perhaps rather self-consciously calm and cheerful." Civilians had begun to perform the unfamiliar routines of seeking shelter from endangered homes in the "trenches" of basements and subways. They would continue to do so for more than five years. On September 3 it was a false alarm, but Mass Observation, the study of everyday life in England, nevertheless reported that "planes had been *seen* by hundreds of eye-witnesses falling in flames." War swept over the body and the senses.[59]

On London streets, girls appeared in "very scanty shorts, with gas masks slung over their shoulders"; businessmen walked about "solemnly with cardboard boxes strung around their necks." You couldn't get into a movie theater without a gas mask. Some people were "confirmed gas mask carriers," others not. "'One of the first things that struck me was my husband's preoccupation with his gas mask,' reported one woman to Mass Observation—'mine lies more or less forgotten in the bottom of my wardrobe.'" According to one journalist, in Paris's "elegant neighborhoods, leather or satin cases camouflage these reminders of the dangers of being asphyxiated by gas with a distinguished optimism." The windows of shops were x-ed with strips of paper to diminish the impact of shattered glass. But the bombing of Paris and London, or Berlin, never took place that fall. It was the "world's weirdest war," confirmed one person interviewed by Mass Observation, who anticipated by a few weeks the idea of the *drôle de guerre*, the phony war of 1939–1940.[60]

In Warsaw, where the war was actually taking place on September 3, 1939, circumstances were different. There Poles watched German bombers fly "in triangle formations, seven or nine planes to each triangle, very, very high." The planes reappeared in the sky: "I could see that there were scores and scores of them." Suddenly, the world "caught fire." The result: "tumult, fear, commotion."[61] But despite the thousands of civilians killed in Warsaw, and later in London and Coventry, the salient feature of the next new war was not air attacks from the sky. In the end, the new war would be very different from the Great War, but not on account of the destruction of kitchens and parlors in Warsaw or London. Despite Germany's deliberate policy of *coventryisieren*, it would be German civilians, not British, who would be slaughtered in the greatest numbers by the air raids of the Second World War: six hundred thousand versus sixty thousand when the totals were summed in 1945. And even so, until Hiroshima, in no country were cities "leveled" in hours, nor were quarter-millions killed in "moments." More important, despite the horrific 1939 bombardment of Warsaw, in which fifty thousand Poles lost their lives, civilians in Poland, and in France and elsewhere in German-occupied Europe, would find themselves far more threatened by Germany's racial policemen than by its air raiders. This reality was not seen at the time, and news from occupied Poland did not easily reach France and Britain.

After the fall of France, in October 1940, Charles Lindbergh congratulated himself on his prescience: "I thought Germany would expand eastward—she did. I thought the French Army could not break through the West Wall—they failed. I felt there was no way to give effective aid to Poland—none was given. . . . I knew the German Air Force was vastly superior to all other air forces in Europe combined—that is now a well-established fact. In every technical estimate I was right. . . . Nevertheless, war was declared—declared by the weak and not the strong, by those who would lose, not by those who would win." In fact, what Lindbergh's reports failed to note, as his biographer explains, was that "Nazi Germany was building a powerful tactical ground-support air force well suited for Hitler's blitzkrieg operations on the European mainland, but was not building the strategic heavy bomber force needed if Hitler intended decisive operations against England."[62] More to the point: the Germans were up to something far more sinister in Poland and France than Lindbergh and other airpower strategists ever considered. Preoccupied with the bomber's "home invasion," the imperial ambitions and genocidal intentions of German occupying forces in Europe escaped the notice of observers who sweated through the "frightful afternoon" of September 27, 1938.

THE "GREAT DEBATE" SHOWED HOW PROFOUNDLY AMBIVALENT Europeans were about engaging Germany in a new war even as late as September 1939. They were deeply afraid of war even as they falsely characterized its dangers, and they were accordingly more willing to accommodate the Third Reich, not least because they imagined ordinary Germans to be as peace loving as they themselves were. Europeans lacked an understanding both of Hitler's imperial intentions and of the deep support he enjoyed among his fellow citizens. Misunderstandings ran even deeper in Poland, a country that helped itself to the spoils of Czechoslovakia in 1938 without imagining it was next on Germany's list of territories to conquer and subjugate. In the face of the growing power of the Third Reich, the fear of a new war as expressed in the "Great Debate" had the effect of discounting anti-German views. Similarly, the rapid victories of German armies in 1939 and 1940 raised the question of whether a new pro-German order in Europe was inevitable, even desirable and, if so, how it would have to be accommodated in far-reaching ways.

What the Nazis proposed to do in the new war was not simply add territory to build Germany's empire or reap the economic and political advantages of hegemony here or there, but to swing the arc of history so that the thousand-year Reich eclipsed the liberal epoch of European history that had begun with the French Revolution in 1789. They introduced themselves as the "wave of the future," as Anne Morrow Lindbergh presciently put it. National Socialism was profoundly aware of times and dates, and it anticipated replacing the progressive forward movement of modern time with the scientifically ordained idea that races and peoples were locked in timeless struggle. Seeking to stop the clock and reset time, the Nazis would shock the world by showing that the civilization of the twentieth century provided no protection from merciless killing.

3

A New Authoritarian Age?

WORLD WAR II BEGAN WITH GERMANY'S INVASION OF POLAND ON September 1, 1939, but the idea that German power might install a sinister new world order took hold only after its victories over Holland, Belgium, and France in May and June 1940. Spring 1940, not fall 1939, marked the shatter point of twentieth-century European history.

As the armies of the German Wehrmacht advanced across France in May and June 1940, they literally imposed German time. Because Germany had reintroduced Middle European summer time on April 1, 1940, as a wartime savings measure, this meant that the French had to set their clocks one hour ahead. In Sedan on May 14, in Amiens on May 21, in Lille on May 31, in Rouen on June 9, in Reims on June 11, and in Paris at 11:00 at night on June 14, French authorities "invited" inhabitants to reset their clocks and watches. The armistice itself was signed on "22 June 1940 à 18 h 50 heure d'été allemande," that is, 6:50 in the evening, German summer time. When the German government abruptly decided to remain on summer time on October 2, four days before winter time was supposed to resume, the French in the occupied zone suddenly jumped two hours ahead of prewar winter time. This ordinance remained in effect for more than two years. For two winters, 6:00 in the morning actually felt like 4:00. And in the summer, the 10:00 nighttime curfew imposed in many places fell at what had been 8:00 before the war, an hour when the sun had not yet set. Whether curfews began at 10:00 and ended at 6:00 or, once relaxed, cleared the streets from 11:00 to 5:00, they had the effect of throwing people out onto the streets in total darkness on winter mornings, when the sun rose as late as 9:00, and penning them up before the long sunny days had ended on summer evenings. Punitive curfews lengthened periods of incarceration. Beginning in February 1942, authorities banned Jews from the streets from 8:00 in the evening until 6:00 in the morning. "Too bad for those who go to the movies or plays," quipped journalist Jacques Bielinky. For days in December 1941, all of Paris was locked down at 6:00, following attacks on German military personnel. Employees quit work around 3:30 p.m., and department stores closed at 4:30. Just before 6:00 (so 4:00 old time), "papas and mamas" would take their "doggy-darling" out for a quick walk, but then "there was no one out anymore, no one at l'Etoile . . . at Bastille . . . at Villette"; "Paris was abandoned, dead."[1]

GMT+2: the French in the occupied zone had to adjust to German time and the German regimen. They saw their movements severely restricted, municipal services such as gas and electricity rationed and cut back drastically, the franc devalued to their terrible disadvantage, and food and coal stocks plundered. The title of Jean-Louis Bory's 1945 novel, *My Village on German Time*, not only referred to the enforced timetable of daily life under the occupation but also served as a general metaphor for the new future the Germans intended to install in France.[2] To set the clock an hour or two later appeared to be the first step to recalibrate the French to the new order in Europe. In the summer of 1940, Generalissimo Franco switched Spain from Greenwich mean to German new time (where it has remained ever since) to indicate which side he was taking in the European war. But even as Germans portrayed themselves as the representatives of the modern, for many French citizens "German time" was not so much a step forward as it was a step back into an antique or archaic past or simply a step into the dark. Genuine French proponents of Germany's new European order were few in number, and with its celebration of rural virtues, the collaborationist regime in Vichy that governed the nonoccupied portion of the country appeared at best a restoration of old authority and at worst a parody of the Third Reich. The future remained unclear. "What time is it?" was a question the French asked after Germany's victory in 1940, one that remained unresolved for many years.

Colette, the fabled, aged performer and author of the novels *Cheri* and *Gigi*, watched wintry Paris from the windows of her apartments in the Palais-Royal. Writing "at the dark break of dawn," she checked the time: "It is seven, if I am to believe my clock, which I don't." And she looked out her window. The streets had begun to fill with pedestrians who, in the complete darkness, made their way with flashlights. The crisscross of beams illuminated their feet, which caught Colette's attention: "Look at all the transparent stockings, the lightly cut shoes! The tulle stocking, the thin shoe reveal the determination of women to stay in fashion, common sense and the weather notwithstanding." The darting movements of pale pools of light on the city pavement suggested an out-of-kilter time. She couldn't believe it was seven; it was so dark and so cold outside that Colette's advice was simply to "go back to bed." But the self-reliance of the women of wartime Paris reminded her of the making do and the patchwork in the darkened hours of her own childhood. For Colette, the German occupation was a little like turning clocks back to the late nineteenth century in the Burgundy countryside.[3] It was not so different from what Vichy was trying to do in its valorization of France's agrarian past.

In fact, millions of French families fled to the countryside at the beginning of the war, not to Colette's ancient Burgundy, but to points farther west and south in order to escape quickly advancing German troops. Along the way, they lost many of the things they had collected since the end of the nineteenth century. The exodus began on the first day of the German invasion, on May 10, 1940, when refugees from Luxembourg crowded the roads on which French military vehicles were operating. Memories of German atrocities against Belgian civilians in the Great War were long; Maxence van der Meersch's 1935 best-selling recapitulation of Roubaix under German occupation, *Invasion 14*, or even Margaret Mitchell's scenes of Atlanta at the end of the American Civil War in *Autant en emporte le vent*, translated by Gallimard in 1938 and on everyone's lap in 1939, may have brought these memories to the fore. Within a few weeks, one in three Belgians, about 2 million people in all, had abandoned their homes and made their way toward Paris. Thousands of French civilians followed, pushed along by fear and bewilderment. "Beneath my windows," the police chief of Paris could see "an

uninterrupted and infinitely sad procession of horse-drawn vehicles, oxen
pulling wagons, baby carriages, as well as people on bicycles and on foot,"
along with dogs and farm animals.[4] By the middle of June, 8 million
Luxembourgians, Belgians, and French were on the road, among them
2 million Parisians. Only 800 out of Chartres's 23,000 inhabitants stayed
behind. The "exode" had taken on an almost biblical scale to become the
"Exodus."

   To the aviator in the sky, to whom scorn came easily, it looked as if
"somewhere in the north of France," a giant's "boot had scattered an
anthill." It was precisely this general civilian demoralization that experts
had, in the past decade, predicted in the event of massive air raids. From
the ground, however, the exodus was an endlessly varied tragedy. Colette
caught the scene in "Fin juin 1940": "The cattle trucks, the hay carts,
the large motor-cars wreathed in dust, the wheelbarrows and the open
wagons stretched on . . . the fields of ripe grass in which every blade
was covered by a cluster of people asleep, a car decked with mattresses, a
sleeping child rolled up in a towelling dressing gown, a pair of doves in a
cage, a fox terrier tied to a tree." Many observers commented almost glee-
fully on the "spring cleaning" of bourgeois attics that occurred during the
escape, the "Sèvres porcelain," the "three fur coats," "the gold-fringed
satin cushions from the drawing room," and "hat boxes full of men's
and women's hats," but "to whom will they take these hats off?"[5] Most
refugees did not have a destination in mind; a few followed rough maps
printed on the backs of calendars that the post office had once distributed, but most travelers had no real plan other than to "adapt oneself to
this new way of life: move on." Maps didn't matter in the end because
automobiles ran out of gas and fell into newly strung lines of abandoned
vehicles, "their doors open, baggage still tied to the roof." As an observer
recorded, "there was sometimes a dog howling, pulling on his lead, or a
cat miaowing frantically, locked in its basket." "Against this background,"
writes one historian, "it is easy to understand why many people would
greet the news of an armistice with such relief."[6] Civilians rallied around
"le Maréchal Pétain," the beloved general of the Great War who had been
appointed premier at the last minute, trusting that he and his new government in Vichy would help them find their way back home. "Knocked out

by the breadth of the catastrophe," the French demonstrated "a quasi-biological need to recover and withdraw."[7]

Prewar time had given way to wartime, and it had hit civilians the hardest. One hundred thousand civilians lost their lives in the exodus, more than the number of French military casualties in the Battle of France. In addition, the victorious Germans transferred nearly 2 million French prisoners of war, about 1 in 3 soldiers who had mobilized in the war, to camps in Germany, where the great majority would languish for the duration of the conflict. Dispersed along the roads, rounded up behind barbed wire, family members were not reunited until the end of the war. Abandoned houses dotted the countryside, while shuttered shops notched city streets, evidence of proprietors who had died or not come home. Many more French shared the tragedy of the exodus than participated subsequently in either the collaboration or the Resistance. It was as decisive in shaping French attitudes for the rest of the war as the blitzkrieg victory of the Wehrmacht was for the Germans, who, with the memory of when "miracles are now on our side," as "each milepost gives witness: (Paris, 70 km, Paris 60 km, Paris 58 km)," thought they were unbeatable until the end. A sense of dislocation unsettled French hearts and minds. "An entire people of stragglers" seemed to be thrown back to the Middle Ages. "I bow my way out," singer Jean Sablon had sung when he closed out his prewar performances with the hit "Je tire ma révérence," saying good-bye to lost love, "I am off to who knows where / Along the roads of France." Now the showstopper made more sense. After the exodus, life in France was like living in Old Testament scenes of devastation, metaphors now as real as life.[8]

The time was not set accurately at GMT+2. "Along the roads of France," the hour and minute hands were wobbly. There were those who accepted the defeat as the judgment of history, who were prepared to go down the path of repentance as urged by Pétain, and who were determined to divest themselves of the decadence of the Third Republic. Already on June 9, after she had arrived safely in Concareau, in Brittany, having fled Paris with her daughters, "Mamma" had to endure "court hearings" set up by sisters-in-law: "She has a job," as her daughter Benoîte Groult transcribed the charges. "She does not go to mass, wears beach pajamas, and has never concealed from us how children are made." "These accusations were all gathered into a single bouquet" that they "handed her with jubilation."[9] But this path of purgation ran through places like the rural village of Manosque, not the German capital of Berlin, a place where women also had jobs and wore beach pajamas. Pétain's collaborationist government appealed to those French who had been frightened by the socialist Popular Front a few years earlier or were just fed up with thirty-three prime ministers who had led the governments since the end of the war (Britain had had nine). Vichy stirred the hearts of those who had never reconciled themselves to the Republic, who stood with the anti-Dreyfusards against the Dreyfusards, with the black against the red. The origins of collaboration and resistance after the armistice have to be understood in this basically nineteenth-century framework of France's domestic politics, and if there was a new order to French politics, it was far more visible among the patriotic Catholics who eventually rallied to the Resistance than among the few socialists who initially made peace with Vichy. Support of the Vichy regime did not imply a full calibration with German time, as genuine fascists in Paris such as Robert Brasillach knew, to their regret, very well. There was no shared sense of the future in the retreat of Pétain's government into the spa hotels of Vichy.

Even so, the idea of adjusting to new circumstances seemed compelling enough. Demand for German lessons shot up, and German replaced English as the most popular foreign language at Paris's Berlitz School. "French bourgeois vituperate against collaboration, but," noted journalist Albert Fabre-Luce in 1941, "they are learning German: so they must believe it has a long future." On the streets of "Zone libre," uniformed paramilitary formations and youth groups brought France into step with Germany. It was not unusual for Vichy officials to greet each other with the Hitler salute. There were plenty of people ready to adopt a more appropriately authoritarian style. Not surprisingly, loyal republicans felt out of place and out of joint immediately after the fall of France. Léon Werth wondered if France and Europe would be "Germanized" for "twenty years, for fifty years, for a century." Perhaps republicans would have to hide out like the monks of the Middle Ages who kept alive "the flame of the ancient world" until the time of the Renaissance.[10]

As Colette observed from her windows, people had to set their clocks to German time, but when they woke up it was dark and they needed flashlights. They remained disoriented. Vichy itself stayed on French winter time, an hour behind both Paris and Berlin, suggesting the limits to recalibration in the new Europe. And at home, some individuals resolved not to live on German time, even though this left a "deadly gap" between "the end of Mass and the beginning of Sunday lunch." In France the answer to the question "What time is it?" depended on how contemporaries read events. For Vichy, the fall of France was the judgment of history. A new authoritarian age had foreclosed the time of liberalism. But others saw the defeat as just another turn in the violent cycles of history, a disaster that would be evened out over time. One schoolgirl imagined herself in a history lesson five hundred years in the future: "During the second half of the 19th and the first half of the 20th centuries, for vague and sometimes incomprehensible reasons, intermittent struggles divided the people of western and central Europe."[11] In time, she thought, the war would resemble the Hundred Years' War. Responses in the summer of 1940 also depended on the chances of Britain falling down alongside France and on judgments of whether Germany had bitten off more than it could chew. Most French waited, venturing out in the morning darkness and rushing to catch "the last metro" home in the evening. They reset their clocks but wondered how long German time would last.

Swiss Watch

GERMANY'S BLITZKRIEG VICTORY OVER FRANCE COMPLETELY confounded the expectations regarding a future war that Europeans had harbored before 1939. At least in western Europe, the frightening prospect of aerial bombardment and the complete destruction of cities, the nightmare scenarios that so disturbed civilians in 1938 and 1939, did not unfold. Nor was there a resumption of the costly battles of attrition along the western front. Instead, what loomed on the horizon was the German occupation—for twenty years, one hundred years, one thousand years? It did not seem foolish to contemplate the occupation in epochal terms, and contemporaries repeatedly spoke about the "end of civilization," that is, the end of the liberal era that had dawned in 1789. The Germans had smashed the traditional European balance of power that had guaranteed the existence of sovereign states and guarded against empire and tyranny. In the summer of Germany's triumph, the year 1940 was frequently cited as the beginning of a modern authoritarian age, a new order in Europe. Across Europe people had to fit the events of the year 1940 into larger historical contexts and to adjust themselves accordingly.

The Germans themselves were surprised by their rapid breakthrough, but the speed of victory also became a strong argument for its inevitability. It was more than the "impenetrable" Ardennes that had come crashing down. At once actual historical developments seemed to bear out the clutter of ideas the Nazis had postulated and theorized over the years—about old "system time," the end of the nineteenth century, the obsolescence of liberalism, and the onset of "new time" in a "new order." ("The nervous nineteenth century has reached its end. There will not be another revolution in Germany for the next 1000 years" was Hitler's claim in 1934.) Germans celebrated their triumphs as "truly grand history." They described their joy to be able to live "in these times."[12]

German rulers had a great incentive in convincing Europeans of the definitiveness of the break in 1940 because the new baseline provided a forceful historical justification for German empire. Again and again, they replayed the summer of 1940 and the events that had led up to it, the "eighteen days" in which Poland was conquered in September 1939, the "six weeks" in which France collapsed in May and June 1940. They tried hard to yoke Europeans to movie theater seats to watch German newsreels and propaganda movies about the "baptism" of German arms in Poland (*Feuertaufe,* released on April 5, 1940) and the march into France (*Sieg im Westen,* released in January 1941). These films were intended as "documentaries of intimidation." The sequences hit hard, as marching columns and motorized vehicles filled up the screen over and over again. The continuous motion of the camera allied itself to the invincible military machine it depicted to create the effect of the complete conquest of time and space. "Every camera trick was used to enhance the drama of the German machines reaping the cities as they passed," remembered

Olivia Manning, watching newsreels in Bucharest in the spring of 1940. "The tanks, made monstrous by the camera's tilt, passed in thousands— or, so it seemed." Catching the roaring fires of Rotterdam, "the camera backed, barely evading a shower of masonry as tall facades, every window aflame, crashed towards the audience." Watching the same newsreels in Paris, writer Ernst Jünger remarked on the devouring nature of the images: "Propaganda was becoming terror." German embassies in Copenhagen, Bern, and elsewhere arranged special screenings for politicians, military personnel, and other influential figures.[13]

At Berlin's university, the Deutsches Auslandswissenschaftliches Institut invited scholars, military officers, and journalists to special "vacation seminars" to survey Germany's power. The Wehrmacht, Foreign Ministry, and Nazi Party all played leading parts in the two-week course, Germany at War, in October 1940. At the tank school in Wünsdorf, outside the capital, 266 participants from thirty-seven countries (including 16 Americans) witnessed a full demonstration of a tank attack: "The wreckage of a blown-up bunker suddenly spun high as a tower into the air," one of the observers wrote. The display of military prowess was just the prelude to introduce the "task of the Reich to establish order in Europe." Instructors deliberately avoided topics such as Jews and concentration camps, focusing instead on the new European order. They emphasized the "uniqueness and sovereignty" of each country, but declared that the parts had to become integrated into a new whole, "under the guidance of the strongest nation and state." A united Europe's ability to act as a "great power" depended on authoritarian principles of governance, they argued. Representatives of the army emphasized that Germany was able to act resolutely because decisions were not obstructed or delayed by parliamentary debates. The lasting impression, wrote one visitor from Switzerland, a country that Germany very much wanted to bring into line, was one of "very exceptional power." This power was evident in two ways: "remarkable will" and "superior achievement." Germany's military might represented the strong arm of political and economic modernization, the organization of European states in a German empire, and the regulation of European statecraft along authoritarian lines.[14] Films of bombed-out cities, demonstrations of tank attacks, and lessons on streamlined political authority were all designed to indicate the inevitability of the new German time.

Fifteen Swiss took part in the course Deutschland im Kriege in 1940. What time did the Swiss—who enjoyed a world reputation for manufacturing excellent watches—think it was? Switzerland lay in the middle of Europe, intensely aware of the destruction of small neutral states such as Norway, Holland, and Belgium and of its own vulnerability. During the spring 1940 campaign, anyone who wanted to could climb up a hill on the outskirts of Basel and see "German arms twinkling in the sunshine across the border." The radio echoed with the chants of German soldiers: "We'll settle up with Switzerland, that little porcupine, on our way back." With the fall of France, Switzerland was, for the first time in its history, completely surrounded by a single warring party (Nazi Germany, fascist Italy, and Vichy France). In little more than two years, Austria, Czechoslovakia, Poland, Denmark, Norway, Luxembourg, Belgium, and France had all fallen, and the geography of Europe itself, its nations with their distinct colors on the map, had been wiped away. Newspaper editor Ernst Schürch compared Switzerland's predicament to that of "an egg in an armored fist."[15] After Germany's annexation of Alsace and Lorraine in 1940, the only German speakers in Europe who had not "returned" home were those who lived in Switzerland. And although Switzerland had been spared the war, Germany's ability to defeat France without having to cross the Swiss border was taken as a sign of the Wehrmacht's towering strength. Under threat as it was, however, Switzerland was not occupied by the Germans, so it was not absorbed with the life-and-death issues of occupation that the Poles and French faced. Freedom of speech and freedom of the press made possible an extremely lively discussion about the state of Europe and the future of Switzerland in the summer of 1940. The Swiss conversation was unique, but it also reflected the key dynamics that shaped the broader European debate on resistance, collaboration, and history.

In Switzerland, as in the rest of Europe, pro-Nazi and fascist "fronts, leagues, and militias erupted from the ground like mushrooms" during the *Frontenfrühling*, the "front spring," in 1933, but their impact waned after Swiss voters decisively rejected the right-wing proposal for a total revision of the federal constitution two years later. There were business elites who, after Switzerland's own brush with revolutionary unrest in 1918, admired the restoration of order in the Third Reich. Some also mistrusted neutral Switzerland's membership in the League of Nations, which had been constructed exclusively by Allied hands after World War I. But the Swiss affinity for "Berlin theater directors, Hessian professors, Schwabian chamber maids, Ullstein Publishers, the big Brockhaus Encyclopedia, Darmstädter toys and Frankenthaler sugar," as novelist Kurt Guggenheim described Germany's exports, had long passed.[16] Most Swiss felt attached to a European political order that guaranteed the continued existence of small states, something the Third Reich had been in the process of wrecking since 1938. Residents let the some one hundred thousand Germans who lived in Switzerland know that they thought of them as tiresome "Schwabens," or, worse, obnoxious Nazis, and they knew themselves the wiser when Swiss soccer players bested their German counterparts, 2–1, on Hitler's birthday in 1941. More important in determining Swiss attitudes was the movement toward "concordance" in Swiss politics; since the mid-1930s, political tensions between the Left and Right and over the issue of military service had diminished. Socialists, reversing their old position, now supported the army and its role in protecting democracy.

But if the Germans in the Reich were not beloved, they were certainly recognized as powerful. The unexpected German victory over the French and British armies demanded that the Swiss confront Germany's military threat and deal with its political demands. This meant confronting the deeper meaning of the events of the summer of 1940. If Germany's victories were more than just fleeting luck, was it the case that one era had given way to another? How tied to world history was Switzerland? Was it time for the Swiss to accommodate themselves to a world where Germany set the clocks? Questions regarding the could and should and must of democracy, modern authoritarianism, and social solidarity were expressed in terms of "Adapt," which meant embarking on an effort to renew the nation in the spirit of the new authoritarian age, or "Resist," which presumed that Switzerland could and should retain its unique political traditions. But in practice, the positions described with these freighted labels overlapped in many ways. The terms of the debate were set in the summer of 1940 after President Maurice Pilet-Golaz called for the nation to recognize the "power of facts" in a radio address on June 25, 1940, and when General Henri Guisan, exactly one month later, assembled the entire officer corps at the Rütli, the site of the famous "Companions of the Oath" establishing Swiss sovereignty in 1291, to express the national will to repel attacks from the outside at any price.

President Pilet-Golaz and General Guisan were unlikely interlocutors. Switzerland's political system discouraged strong, charismatic, or opportunistic leadership, with the president of the seven-member Federal Council elected to a single-year term and lacking any special powers. Pilet-Golaz was a conservative and, as the former head of the Department of Posts and Railways, Switzerland's largest employer, someone who knew a balance sheet. He had been elected vice president for 1939 and thus assumed the presidency in 1940. Fifty-one years old, he was born the same year as Hitler, in 1889. The defeat of France just happened to fall on his presidential watch. But after March 1940, Pilet-Golaz also headed the Political Department, which oversaw foreign affairs, a powerful position he retained until his resignation over the issue of diplomatic relations with the Soviet Union in 1944.

As for Guisan, he was an untroubled estate owner and career military officer whose genial personality and fluency in German and French led to rapid promotions; at the age of fifty-eight, in 1932, he was appointed three-star Oberstkorpskommandant, or lieutenant general, the highest rank in the Swiss Army. In time of war, however, Switzerland's constitution empowered the Federal Assembly to elect a four-star general, and Guisan easily won election as the fourth (and last) general in Switzerland's history on August 30, 1939. Well liked by his troops, whose outposts he visited regularly, and credited in Bern by socialists as well as liberals for upholding Swiss honor and neutrality during the war, Guisan ended up a hugely popular figure, big enough for critics to take note of an emerging Swiss-flagged "Führer" cult. For decades afterward, visitors could see framed photographs of *le Général* under the wooden timbers of the Swissman's *Stube*.[17] Three hundred thousand citizens lined the route of Guisan's funeral procession in Pully, outside Lausanne on the shore of Lake Geneva, on April 12, 1960.

Historians have made clear that Pilet-Golaz and Guisan were far from stick figures representing diametrically opposed positions of "Adapt" and "Resist." Nonetheless, in the summer of 1940, contemporaries saw the two speeches, the first one by the president on the radio and then the general's extemporaneous inspirational address to his senior officers, as call-and-response; both declarations provide insight into the talk of a new, more authoritarian, and social-minded Switzerland at the moment of unexpected and overwhelming German power. Switzerland had adapted to the French Revolution and adopted many of its liberal ideas over the course of the nineteenth century. Now the critical question was posed: Was 1940 another 1789, a moment requiring the Swiss to recalibrate their political, economic, and social life to the outside world?

After weeks of silence, as German tanks rolled across France, President Pilet-Golaz, as the representative of the Federal Council, addressed the nation just twelve hours after the armistice between Germany and France went into effect on June 25, 1940. The timing of the address underscored Switzerland's dire political circumstances as a small island in an expanding fascist lake. Pilet-Golaz spoke in French at 12:45 p.m., immediately following the midday news bulletin on Swiss radio. Later, two of his fellow councillors provided translations in German and Italian. Pilet-Golaz understood that he had two audiences: Swiss citizens, shocked at the course of events (most people had assumed the Germans would lose), and the impatient Germans abroad. By the end of June, Axis troops loitered along the borders of Switzerland, Berlin pressed the issue of German airmen who had been shot down and captured by the Swiss, and Germans made clear their resentment of anti-Nazi declarations in the Swiss press. Pilet-Golaz later reminded lawmakers that victorious Germany and its ally Italy controlled the train traffic delivering winter coal to Switzerland and transporting Switzerland's exports across Europe. In Bern the Political Department dealt with repeated German threats to make Switzerland "pay for the window panes" that its scandalous press had "smashed in" at its neighbor's house with anti-Nazi attacks—"We haven't forgotten anything."[18] Germany's strategic leverage was the point of *Baptism of Fire* in the cinemas and the study-abroad courses for Switzerland's journalists.

Pilet-Golaz reminded his listeners that the "continent remained in a state of alarm," that the armistice that had been signed was not the same as peace, but his speech was premised on clarity rather than confusion, consequence rather than irresolution, action rather than hesitancy. "Our commerce," "our industry," and "our agriculture" demanded that Switzerland make the "difficult adjustment" to "new conditions," he declared. According to Pilet-Golaz, his "confédérés" had become too "cozy," too "easy-going," and too "old-fashioned." Everyone had the obligation to "discard the old person," to avoid taking "worn-down paths" for the sake of "tradition," and to recognize that the time for "inner rebirth" had arrived. "Events are marching rapidly"; it was necessary to "adapt to their rhythm." Pilet-Golaz used the concept of new time to prod his fellow citizens out of "cozy" homes and off old paths, to lead them from the mountains to the plains, where there were tempo, rhythm, manufacturing, and marching. Small worlds had to integrate themselves into larger wholes, an easygoing life had to become a more disciplined one, and idle chatter and endless debate had to give way to resolution and obedience to federal authority. Without explicitly saying so, Pilet-Golaz implied that the Swiss needed to step out into the new Europe and work with the Germans as partners. Toward the end of the speech, Pilet-Golaz committed the government to provide employment to "Swiss folk," "cost what it may."[19] The speech had an unmistakable authoritarian edge to it not only because of Pilet-Golaz's defense of federal power but also because he portrayed events as compelling action. But he also sounded the notes of reform, acknowledging the social responsibilities of government, praising the virtues of social solidarity, and warning against the dangers of special interests and partisan factions.

As Pilet-Golaz described it, the fall of France, the triumph of Germany, and the problems of Switzerland were all symptoms of larger epochal trends and were all related to each another. "Developments were culminating in epochs without regard to human fate," noted the Social Democratic *Berner Tagewacht*. The "revolution" was "speaking to us," wrote one reader in Zurich, and would not stop at the Swiss border.[20] In this sense, the speech was capitulation in the form of recalibration.

In a confidential weekly report prepared for the Federal Council, one official described reactions to the speech as "extraordinarily divergent." It found favor among young people and those impatient with party strife and supportive of more powerful and capable government. With his emphasis on authority, rather than deliberation, Pilet-Golaz provided a "salutary warning announcing difficult times." "Finally a new language," wrote one businessman. Another correspondent spoke for the younger generation that found it "obvious that we will in large part have to adapt to the 'new world.'" There could be no hesitation, as "so much is alarmingly rotten in our State." The French-speaking press generally liked the speech, given its emphasis on "order and work," its disdain for materialism and the "power of money," and its recognition that Switzerland must reconnect with the rest of Europe.[21]

For others, however, the "speech of adjustment" was a betrayal of Swiss traditions that were left unmentioned: the diversity of Switzerland's people, its democratic tradition, and its spirit of independence. Alfred Ernst remembered that he and his fellow army officers "threw our helmets on the ground because we felt cheated and betrayed." Writer Denis de Rougemont bumped into an officer who exclaimed that "for the first time in my life, I was ashamed to be Swiss." In Bern liberal newspaper editor Markus Feldmann considered the "strange" speech to be a "revival" of the discredited "paramilitary racket of 1933 and 1934." Given Pilet-Golaz's vocabulary, the *Basler Nachrichten* felt "already relocated in advance to a different era." The words "could not be found in a Swiss dictionary," agreed the Social Democratic *Tagewacht*.[22] Reactions were more negative in German-speaking Switzerland, where the point of reference was Hitler and Germany rather than Pétain and Vichy.

Historians have generally found the speech weak, confused, and accommodating. Some parts were lost in translation so that the French *guide* became *Führer* and *disloqué*, or *dislocated*, *Umbruch*, German words with a Nazi ring to them. Pilet-Golaz himself continued to act very much in the spirit of the speech, assuring the German ambassador some weeks later that Switzerland was in the process of renewing itself with the aim of reorienting itself inside the new European order. As late as 1942,

Pilet-Golaz believed that the Germans would win the war; the democracies had come and gone, he felt. He resigned himself to the reality that Switzerland was surrounded and had no choice but to cooperate with the Axis powers.[23] His position and vocabulary were widely shared, at least at the beginning, but his speech inaugurated a tumultuous debate about where Switzerland stood in Europe and where 1940 sat in the sweep of history.

It may well be true that General Guisan was "disappointed," even "furious," after hearing the president's speech, as his biographer indicates. But in their assessments of Switzerland's precarious circumstances, the two men had no great differences. Guisan had frequently updated Pilet-Golaz about the course of the war in France. If, in his deliberations, Pilet-Golaz repeated and underscored the basic fact that "Switzerland is hemmed in," Guisan performed his duties with images of German tanks smashing through the first line of defense at the Swiss border in his mind. With a view to events in France, military trainers became obsessed with antitank tactics. Answering the questions of anxious soldiers, the general was very sober and very clear. "The garrisons at the forts and pillboxes at the border and between the border and the defense line shall resist to the last shell," he wrote, "even if they have been bypassed and are totally isolated." The units at the border "know their mission and are aware of the sacrifice that it entails." On inspection tours, Bernard Barbey, Guisan's chief of staff, looked at the deserted fields across the Rhine and wondered how long the Germans would postpone their invasion of Switzerland. When would it be Switzerland's turn?[24]

The difference between Pilet-Golaz and Guisan lay in the president's typically maudlin assessment of the inadequacy of "courage and patriotism," which he later compared to "Yugoslavian illusions," a reference to the anti-German Yugoslavs whom the Germans had easily overrun in April 1941. In contrast, the general retained confidence in a strong-willed army and revised strategic plans that shifted the secondary and primary lines of defense farther into the interior, around the mountainous center of the country, the national Réduit. It was a bold plan, abandoning the long-held strategy of defending the vast majority of Swiss territory from positions parallel to the border. It also required new fortifications. In effect, two-thirds of the army would withdraw from three-quarters of the country. This was Switzerland's military response to tank warfare. The Réduit would at once decrease the vulnerability of the exposed Swiss line to tank attacks by dramatically contracting its circumference and increase the advantage of a counterattack by conducting artillery fire from the mountains rather than the plains. To bolster morale and outline the Réduit strategy, Guisan wanted to personally address the officer corps; with the spirit of the Swiss fight for independence very much on the general's mind, his aides hit upon the idea of assembling on the meadow of the Rütli, the "sacred ground" where the federation's original oath of independence had been sworn in 1291. After a flurry of new rumors about German reconnaissance along the border, increased espionage activity, and plans to divide Switzerland between Germany, Italy, and France, the date for the assembly was quickly set for July 25.[25]

Invitations went out to active commissioned officers down to the level of battalion commander. With about 420 officers present, the Rütli gathering was the largest such assembly in Swiss history. To save money, Guisan and most officers took trains to Lucerne, where they boarded the pleasure steamer *Stadt Lucern*, which took them across the lake to the Rütli. By three o'clock everyone was back in the city with time enough to return to their command posts before the end of the day. Guisan had prepared a typescript speech, but, because of time pressure, he spoke extemporaneously. The short remarks deliberately put emphasis on the idea of "resistance" rather than "defense," a word choice designed to heighten the historical drama and to strengthen morale. He referred to the symbolic importance of this ancient spot for Swiss independence; hearing the "mystical renown" of the Rütli, the army would draw strength from "the spirit of the past" and rely on "the cunning of time" rather than superior numbers to master the challenges that Swiss commoners in the federation had encountered since its inception in 1291. Four days later a press release reported that the officer corps had sworn to "resist any attack from the outside." "We still hold our own fate in our own hands," Guisan declared.[26]

On Switzerland's National Day celebrations on August 1, patriotic speakers made references to Guisan and the Rütli. On August 7, on an inspection tour, Guisan's Buick came to a full stop in the center in Balsthal on account of the cheering crowds. Women and children crowded around and threw "gladiolas, dahlias, and zinnias into the car." The pastor ordered church bells rung. Guisan's chief of staff could "barely recognize" the Swiss people who usually appeared so restrained. "Guisan's words provided a secular revelation," concluded Edgar Bonjour in his sprawling history of Swiss neutrality. "Switzerland remembered itself as it was. A wave of good old Swiss spirit rushed over the country." But there were critical reactions as well. The Réduit strategy never sat well with all military commanders, some of whom were uncomfortable with the "hedgehog position at the Gotthard": Why, asked one of Guisan's corps commanders, "defend mountain tops and glaciers if the plains," where most of the soldiers lived, were surrendered? More serious was Guisan's stress on "resistance." Ulrich Wille, the son of Switzerland's general during World War I, and himself keen on assuming Guisan's position, found the "saber rattling" at the Rütli completely wrongheaded. It threatened improved relations with Nazi Germany. Another critic, Gustav Däniker, who like Wille allied himself to the Prussian traditions once favored in the Swiss army and thought of himself as a grand strategist with the big picture in mind, found the word *resistance* provocatively anti-German. He preferred Pilet-Golaz's speech, which had promised an end to Switzerland's "small town" mentality.[27] Wherever observers stood on the issue of resistance and the Réduit, however, they took the Rütli oath to be the rejoinder to Pilet-Golaz's radio address.

In fact, Guisan's written text echoed many of Pilet-Golaz's themes. The draft immediately created consternation when it was finally published in 1984 because it was so at odds with the general's carefully cultivated reputation. What Guisan did not say at the Rütli, but what he had written down in notes, was that Switzerland would have to "adapt to the conditions of the new Europe." He expressed his conviction that "the old parties have lost their meaning," and he warned against "red enemies," whom Guisan continued to mistrust for undermining the martial spirit of the Swiss army with their pacifist calls "Never Again War!" To keep the press from provoking Germany, and as a general salutary disciplinary measure, Guisan also favored censorship, a measure Pilet-Golaz rejected. The long-lost draft of the Rütli speech is a reminder that political choices were not presented in black and white. "Adaptation" and "Resistance" were not simply opposite positions. Most citizens certainly prized Switzerland's independence. Nonetheless, when the two speeches are compared, the choice of words and the contrasting conceptions of the state of Switzerland offered in the summer of 1940 are telling. If Pilet-Golaz wanted to bring his "confédérés" down from the mountains and away from small towns, that is exactly where Guisan took them back, to the historic Rütli. Pilet-Golaz emphasized the challenges imposed by a vastly altered future, whereas Guisan repeatedly invoked the inspirational spirit of 1291 and employed a familiar vocabulary of independence and resistance. For Pilet-Golaz, time compelled the Swiss to give up their old habits, while Guisan took comfort in the "cunning of time." Indeed, the whole Réduit strategy sought to counter the "rapid march" of events by using the mountains and seasons to "divide up time" and "delimit the stages" of an assault.[28] Pilet-Golaz wanted to speed up time, while Guisan was looking for ways to slow it down.

Weighing the fall of France, the example of Germany, the challenge to Switzerland, the *Neue Zürcher Zeitung*, Switzerland's leading daily commented that "once again, our country has fallen into incessant discussions;" "young and old are reading the newspapers." Newspapers opened their columns to readers to facilitate what was called a "Discussion About the Questions of the Moment." Huge pamphlet wars ensued during the summer and fall of 1940: *The Switzerland of Tomorrow*, *Federal Socialism*, *What Will Happen to Switzerland?* The time had long since passed when politicians could conduct their business without interference while everyone else paid attention only to "sports and movies." The boisterous, unguarded talk of renewal in the summer of 1940 was based on ideas about time and about the changing European climate and the Swiss microclimate. Pilet-Golaz's vocabulary of "new time" was widely invoked if not always deeply rooted. "New time" implied an encompassing "spirit of the times," in which transformations possessed a universal character and registered self-evidently across space. It also presupposed that history constituted a sequence of dramatic revolutionary breaks signaled by markers such as 1789 or 1914, which made it possible to judge people and practices as "old-fashioned" or "up-to-date." To refer to "new times" was to embrace those willing to disdain the reactionary and to laugh at the nostalgic. There was something remarkably self-evident in references to "new time." One did not argue for "new time"; one announced it. It was like taking out a pocket watch and showing contemporaries what time it was. "It behooves particularly us, who manufacture the most precise watches in the world," wrote one professor in the *Neue Zürcher Zeitung* in July 1940, "to know at any time the hour that history has struck."[29]

Most Swiss observers who advocated fundamental renewal regarded the course of events that led to the fall of France in terms of changes in climate that required adjustments from all and applied to everyone. The specific issues that Switzerland needed to address were familiar pre-war concerns about social justice, crass materialism, and federal authority, but they now acquired a new dynamic and vitality and were presented as necessary elements of historical development. For the most part, Nazi Germany showed the basic way forward in 1940, just as revolutionary France had in 1789. It was not a question of scrupulously copying Germany's national revolution in Swiss letters. What the example of National Socialism provided was the spirit of renewal. In a letter to the editor, one businessman put forward the proposition that "revolutionary forces . . . portend the beginning of a new spirit of the age for our entire conti-nent." New state-building forces were at work, suggested one soldier; "no national border" could hold them back. Another reader used a mix of metaphors to establish the absolute validity to the new times. "The horse-men of the apocalypse are on the hunt across the world," he began; all of Europe and indeed the "entire world trembles." The forces were of such magnitude, whether they were biblical, "elemental" (*Urgewalt*), or geological—literally like an "earthquake"—that they would not allow for a Swiss exception. The French Revolution was frequently cited both to affirm the universal character of revolutions and to announce the end of the liberal era it had commenced: with the "present-day revolution," "the age of liberalism" had come to an end. "Reorganization" had foreclosed on "the age of individualism."[30]

Many youth, asserting the claims of generation over the traditions of heritage and place, advocated recognizing "new time." With their "unspoiled spiritual and physical power" and their "fervent belief in the possibility of reshaping man and his world," only the young could "quickly create the values" consonant with the revolutionary spirit of the times, averred one white-collar clerk; what was necessary was to *vivere pericolosamente*, to live dangerously, rather than live "comfortably in security" and rely on "the timetables of long-range planning." In this case, it was not so much a matter of resetting Swiss watches but of putting them aside. Young people, with their affinity for unprecedented, radical, and fast-moving elements, found it easier to think about new epochs. Moreover, the mobilization of hundreds of thousands of soldiers since the end of August 1939 had created for many contemporaries a binding "front experience" in which a "spirit of splendid comradeship" had been cultivated irrespective of party politics or social origin. Soldiers serving on the borders and on the Réduit believed that newly shared military values would renew the "earthbound" ways of civilians.[31]

Some socialists, accustomed to thinking in global terms, saw the fall of the "capitalist form of democracy" in France as a crucial sign. Without endorsing Nazism as such, they interpreted the political realignment in Europe as part of larger processes of social collectivization validating new duties and social responsibilities. In the opposition in Bern, Social Democrats considered calibrating themselves to the "dynamic" of the "new time." But it was figures on the political Right who were most comfortable with the winds of change. The end of liberalism and individualism set the stage for a new society "based on values, rather than numerals and numbers," wrote Catholic historian Gonzague de Reynold. His fear was not Switzerland's "encirclement," but its "encapsulation." "Our clock stopped at the end of the nineteenth century," he explained; Switzerland could not defy the logic of world history by "preserving democracy by locking it in a glass cabinet." The Germans themselves frequently mocked Switzerland for being a museum relic.[32]

Nothing announced the new era so much as the imperatives of war. Swiss authorities acceded to German demands and imposed nightly blackouts so that British bombers would have more difficulty orienting themselves. (Ireland refused a similar British request regarding German bombers.) With black-out regulations taking effect at 10:00 p.m., ration cards that came out on Mondays, and the "field gray" composition of its streets, Switzerland had become, as the wartime phrase put it, a "besieged fortress." The restlessness of the population "kept pace" with the bureaucratic decrees coming out of Bern. Given the dangers and scarcities of wartime, government regulations called upon citizens to educate themselves about "the rationing of food and heating materials, the construction of air-raid shelters, the collection of scrap, the use of warming ovens for more efficient cooking, the planting of vegetables, the reuse of worn clothing, how to store potatoes in the basement, the hygienic preservation of supplies, the appropriate storage of soap and flour, the best way to avoid colds," and "exercising caution in conversations." The administration of civilian life made Switzerland look increasingly like the belligerents that surrounded it. "New time" was even visible when people cleared out their attics to make them more flame resistant in the event of air raids. Old and old-fashioned things were thrown onto big nineteenth-century garbage heaps: "worn-out shoes," "moldy quilts, table lamps, dresses, and umbrellas that had gone out-of-fashion, empty bottles, busted dishware, rusty scissors, shelves and consoles, flower pots and vases, ice skates and tennis balls and iron bed frames."[33] In this respect, people did "discard the old person," as Pilet-Golaz had urged.

The common denominators in conceptions of "new time" were social virtue rather than individual egotism and greater state power, greater centralization, and greater deference to authority. *Einordnen*, getting into line, as the Germans had done since 1933, was both the means and the aim of the new social organization. Why had "pre-Hitler Germany" perished? asked one proponent of "New Order." The reason was the "amoral individualism of 60 million tiny me's." Whether because it had not fully integrated workers into the national whole, or because it had left the energies of young people undeveloped, or because it permitted too many party and class interests to mismanage the state, Switzerland had become immobilized in tradition and "routines." Birthrates had fallen by 50 percent so that there were eleven deaths to every eight births, while the divorce rate soared.[34] A new order was a matter of national survival, in this view.

Ultimately, however, support of renewal and the new order reflected a wide range of basically irreconcilable views—Nazis and Communists both called themselves "socialists" without finding common ground. What remained was broad political support for an expansion of social welfare policies, but such a commitment did not require investing in "new time," lining up in a "new order," recognizing "the age of authority," or cooperating in continental partnerships with Nazi Germany.[35]

If the professor took out his fine Swiss watch to see that "the hour of history had struck," novelist Kurt Guggenheim also took out his. For him, Switzerland was "a very precise mechanical instrument," but it was "extremely complicated and nuanced," something that people from the outside with "their simple, brutal, and definitive recipes" could not understand. He saw no reason to reset his watch. The liberal press made the same argument with a slightly different metaphor. Writing in the *Neue Zürcher Zeitung*, Ernst von Schenk summarized the state of Switzerland with the expressive words, "There is the dust of age, but little that is foul." Editorials warned readers to distinguish between "resetting" or "re-learning," something required of every generation, and "falling or knocking down," which would be a complete capitulation to mechanical forces: "That is something that neither wise men nor good Swiss do."[36]

"Falling down" was certainly not something to be seen on the wonderful Sunday of August 4, 1940, when the country's trains, excursion steamers, and swimming pools reported traffic in record-breaking numbers. Every week in the summer and fall of 1940, moviegoers could enjoy a new roster of Hollywood stars: Jimmy Stewart, Ginger Rogers, Mickey Rooney, Spencer Tracy, Cary Grant, Bette Davis. *Ninotchka* was playing at the Rex in Zurich in November, *The Wizard of Oz* at the Apollo. Although department stores had installed a new section for air defense, offering customers "shovels, picks, pails, hand pumps, and, to put out fires, paper bags of sand by the kilo," none of these implements of survival sold very well.[37] Evidently, "matters of fact" did not drown out other sounds or other distractions. By the end of the fall, the crisis that had begun at the beginning of the summer had largely passed.

The failure of the Germans to invade Britain in the summer of 1940 and the demonstration that "London can take it!," as the title of Britain's resilient film rendition of the Blitz put it in 1940, ended the high summer of new time. Stock in the "new European realities" was no longer such a

sure bet. "Terrible and wonderful," the great air battles between Germany
and Britain in the summer and fall of 1940 marked a new, unresolved
phase of the war, so that "there was still hope," as schoolteacher Jean
Guéhenno noted. By the end of 1940, the British had succeeded in winning time, which was Guisan's strategy as well. The effect was tremendous.
Already in October 1940, Willi Bretscher reminded readers of the *Neue
Zürcher Zeitung* that "the war is still ongoing": "nobody can predict how
long it will last, what the outcome will be, and what permanent changes
it will bring to the map of Europe and of the world." As a result, "It
makes no sense to demand fundamental changes or a radical revision of
the Swiss state."[38] Even if it was not until November 1942 that Churchill
detected the glimmer of victory, declaring that El Alamein, the British
victory in North Africa, was not the "beginning of the end" but was,
"perhaps, the end of the beginning," by November 1940 Hitler could no
longer be sure about beginnings and endings himself. With the Battle of
Britain, ambiguity contaminated the concept of "new time."

"New time" also failed to take hold fully in Switzerland because "old
time" retained sufficient legitimacy. Despite the trauma of the country's
general strike in 1918, the political divisions between Left and Right had
healed considerably over the course of the 1930s. In this regard, political
developments in Switzerland more resembled the direction they had taken
in Scandinavia than in France or Germany. And whatever their differences
in assessing the state of Switzerland in the summer of 1940, French and
German speakers were not divided by the western front as they had been
in the years 1914–1918. As a small but independent nation, Switzerland
tilted decisively in favor of the countries the Germans had overrun.

And finally, ingrained notions of Swiss exceptionalism resisted the
universal claims of "new time" and "new order." The historical legacy
of federalism undercut arguments in favor of uniformity, standardiza-
tion, and coordination—as it was, middle European time itself had been
quite difficult to impose on the cantons in 1894. Moreover, the daily lived
experience of linguistic diversity contradicted the tenets of race and virtues of hegemony that National Socialism preached. Switzerland represented a "counterworld to totalitarianism," concludes one historian. The
"spiritual national defense" the army promoted in countless gatherings of

troop units throughout the war strengthened the "disposition to return, to go back home," that had already been apparent in the 1930s. History was popular, and historians spoke with authority. Guisan's Rütli address had made use of Switzerland's past and its intertwined traditions of self-defense and self-governance all the way back to 1291. Indeed, Switzerland was deliberately created as an exception to "what was taken to be valid all around it," as Ernst Schürch, an influential newspaperman, reminded. The exceptionality of Switzerland was a burden; citizens should remain faithful to "the principles handed down to us," while understanding that they were surrounded by neighbors who "avow other methods and ideals." In other words, the argument for the viability of the constitution of the Swiss nation went hand in hand with the acknowledgment that a new order might well pertain for the rest of Europe. Swiss history was the exit from world history. "Swiss stay Swiss," argued Willi Bretscher. For the Swiss, "a revolution does *not* speak to us."[39]

Nothing had cultivated Swiss tradition in recent years as much as the National Exhibition in 1939. More than 10 million visitors swarmed to the enormously popular "Landi" in Zurich between May 6 and October 29. Historians agree that the "Landi spirit," with its emphasis on "unity in diversity," created a genuine feeling of collective belonging that was strong enough for the Swiss to navigate the crisis of the summer of 1940. Precisely what the "unforgettable" Landi confirmed was Switzerland's capacity for political and moral renewal that could be nourished only by the "resources of the federal union." In his response to Pilet-Golaz's 1940 radio address, Albert Oeri, the feisty editor of the *Basler Nachrichten*, invoked the 1939 exhibition; at that time, he mockingly noted, members of the Federal Council never hinted that "the Swiss folk" needed to improve themselves. The exhibition was widely hailed as a demonstration of achievement. "Really," insisted Oeri, "the 'old person,'" whom Pilet-Golaz hoped to discard, was "not as bad as the Federal Council now suggests," a realization that would come when the council itself "recovers the very composure it presently demands so categorically from the people."[40]

The Landi was an attempt to reformulate the contradictions tearing Switzerland apart in the 1920s as differences that would strengthen the country. The most popular exhibit was *Wehrwille*, or *A Strong Defense*, along the Landi's main concourse, the Höhenstrasse. It underscored the military character of Swiss self-reliance. The placards read: "Switzerland wants to defend itself," "Switzerland can defend itself," "Switzerland must defend itself."

After mobilization at the end of August 1939, whole regiments toured the grounds, making "field gray" the color of the Landi in the fall. Other pavilions celebrated the exhibit *Rural Life* as well as modern manufacturing, in the exhibit *Spirit of Progress, Quality of Work, and Capacity to Labor*. Nonetheless, the "homely nationalism" of the Landi was strongly influenced by "tradition and conservatism."[41] The acerbic novelist Max Frisch later wrote that the Landi had the "subtle odor" of the "blood and soil" ideology that had taken root across the Rhine. The "traditional Freyerzer livery," the "traditional Langnauer costumes," the "Emmentaler Chüejer dress," and the "garlanded Düdinger daughters" represented a "triumphant parade of the homeland" and an affirmation that Swiss character and Swiss virtue resided in the "countryside, not in the city."[42] But the signposts in French, Italian, and German also resisted racial thinking. In the end, the Landi anticipated the idea of the national Réduit, Switzerland as an "alpine fortress."[43]

The Landi offered a usable Swiss past in which conceptions of the present-day compulsion of "new time" could be countered with the depth of "old federal history." There was something very anti-Promethean about the professed self-sufficiency of the homeland. "Cute," wrote Frisch derisively. "A pristine Switzerland, as healthy as its cows." Yet precisely that cuteness ultimately made the country much less open to recalibration. The Nazi press itself wrote derisively about its "cute" neighbor, providing a slightly different way of thinking about Frisch's stern antifascist critique. Swiss expatriate Otto Philipp Häfner, a convinced National Socialist who would volunteer for and die on Germany's eastern front, prepared for *Das Reich*, the influential weekly published by Nazi propaganda minister Joseph Goebbels, a table of contrasts that differentiated "Greater Germany" from "Switzerland." As was often the case, the Nazi description of national characteristics is not inaccurate. It could even have been written by an anti-Nazi. Wildly off the mark, however, was its assumption that the German characteristics were self-evidently noble, while the Swiss ones were base:

Greater Germany	Switzerland
Power	The Safety of Property
Honor	Domestic Happiness
Glamour	Peaceful Afternoons at Home
Flags	A Quiet Walk Around the Lake
Eagle	A Quiet Evening by the Fireplace
Victory Clarions	Études on the Piano

For Häfner, the Swiss wanted nothing more than to steer "the wheel of history" away from their homes, which gets it about right.[44]

However, with its "porcupine mentality," "Helvetian nationalism" also spawned the rejection of "non-Swiss" elements. The "alpine fortress" protected its inmates, but it could reproduce a Maginot mentality that made citizens suspicious of the very existence of unpleasant outside events. When news of the Katyn massacre, in which the Soviet secret police slaughtered thousands of Polish officers held as prisoners in April and May 1940, emerged three years later, Switzerland's ambassador in Berlin, Hans Fröhlicher, noted in his diary that he hoped Switzerland would not join Germany in condemning the Soviets for murdering Poles, "because then we would have to take similar public interest in the fate of the Jews." To get involved was to get off Swiss time. Swiss newspapers showed little interest in reporting on the civilian victims of World War II, including persecuted Jews. Similarly, the Swiss federal policy toward refugees was characterized by a deep unease concerning the presence of non-Swiss elements in Switzerland. Switzerland's "spiritual national defense" was premised on creating an attitude of "between ourselves" that was antitotalitarian, but humanitarian in only a limited way. The Réduit idea itself reproduced parochial suspicions of foreigners, socialists, and city dwellers who tended to live in the "flatlands," the territory to be abandoned in the event of a German invasion. In any case, the Réduit strategy required only partial mobilization and thus left most Swiss men in their workplaces, where many ended up aiding the German war effort by manufacturing export goods destined for the Reich. As the standard joke put it, "Six days a week, the Swiss work for Hitler, on the seventh they pray for the victory of the Allies."[45]

In many ways, "Resistance" and "Adaptation" reinforced each other; the Swiss ultimately resisted setting their watches to German time, but Swiss time nevertheless facilitated withdrawal from events taking place in the war, encouraged suspicion of refugees, and ultimately justified economic cooperation with Germany. Pétainism and *attentisme*, or waiting it out, operated in a similar way in France: Pétain enjoyed wide legitimacy as France's savior in 1940, but, in the minds of most French people, Vichy remained a provisional solution.[46] In Switzerland as elsewhere, "between ourselves" deflected the geopolitical thrust of Germany's sword but not the ideological challenges of its antihumanism. As such, Swiss solidarity was inherently self-limiting. For all its unique aspects, the case of Switzerland reveals the ways in which Europeans outside Germany adopted a wait-and-see attitude to the prospect of a new German-dominated continent and sought to refurbish historical traditions to protect their national sovereignty, even as they never quite rejected the ideology underlying the "new time."

THE SWISS DID NOT HAVE TO ENDURE THE GERMANS UNDERFOOT; the French, the Dutch, the Poles, and others in German-occupied Europe did. In those places, people not only grappled with the compulsion of new time but were forced to react to German soldiers and respond to German regulations. Like the Swiss, they slowly and with difficulty created their own time in opposition to the German time the occupiers hoped to impose. They struggled with the self-evident nature of German rule. In the end, some did so physically, with bodies, guns, and bombs, but first they did so intellectually, with words.

4

Living with the Germans

EVERYONE IN GERMAN-OCCUPIED EUROPE HAD TO MAKE SENSE OF the "Bekanntmachung," the black-lettered notice German authorities posted on cheap colored paper, puzzling out the words and implications of the threatening lettering that spelled out the curfew regime, market regulations, and restrictions on Jewish life. Everyone had to size up the German soldiers they encountered on the street, decide how menacing were the daggers and pistols they carried, and learn the differences between the Wehrmacht and the SS, or Schutzstaffel, the Nazi paramilitary force. Everyone had to fit memories of the Great War into experiences of the new war. Everyone had to make judgments about why neighbors were arrested or killed. Where were the lines that separated what could be explained or rationalized away from what was clearly malevolent or arbitrary?

Over time, most people came to see few differences between the individual soldiers they encountered and the ideology of the German government. But initially, many thought that ordinary Germans were not so different from other Europeans, and this idea, which had been the lesson of Remarque's *All Quiet on the Western Front*, did not disappear all at once. Occupiers and occupied made deals; they found common ground; they fell in love. Lessons about the sinister politics of the German occupier were learned more quickly in the East, in Warsaw, where Germany's racial regime was infinitely more crass—Hitler wanted the place leveled—than in the West, in cities like Paris, which was supposed to survive in the new European order as a sort of old-fashioned, plushly upholstered resort for German tourists.

. . . in Paris

"WHAT IS THE DEFINITION OF COLLABORATION?" WENT THE JOKE that made the rounds in France in early 1941. The punch line: "Give me your watch, and I'll tell you the time."[1] After a harsh winter during which Parisians endured forty-eight days in which temperatures did not rise above freezing and suffered chronic shortages of coal and basic food-stuffs such as butter, pasta, and bread, the joke suggested just how much the French had been forced to give up under the German occupation. It made clear that the Germans were firmly in control, keeping the time, setting the curfew, and requisitioning French goods. Collaboration was not a two-way street, as Vichy leader Maréchal Pétain had suggested, but an exploitative relationship in which more and more French felt like suckers. The image of a French man handing his watch over to a German soldier also indicated how it was civilians who bore the burden of war and occupation in their everyday lives.

The French had to deal with German boots, not German bombs. The war turned out to be very different from the total destruction imagined and feared before 1939. Paris was not destroyed. Germany's rapid vic-tory over France also spared the country a repetition of the long war of attrition between opposing armies that had been waged in 1914–1918. Nonetheless, the new war required civilians, at least in the occupied zone, to live among military overlords. It was noncombatants who would have to deal with the occupation in ways they had not before considered.

Forced to flee the towns and cities the government could no longer defend, many French in June 1940 felt completely abandoned by the Third Republic, which quickly slipped into an almost irretrievable past as the "ancien régime." They lived in temporary housing scattered across France, and when they returned home, it seemed they had moved to another era altogether. Automobiles—Citroëns and Renaults—disappeared from the streets. One day on the Place de la Bourse, almost no vehicles could be seen: a grand total of three automobiles, one motor-bike, and a horse-drawn cab passed by in one ten-minute period around noontime. Meanwhile, dust gathered on big faded letters attached to the facades of buildings; neon lighting had been turned off. "As one walked along one could read in the shop-windows advertisements which seemed to be engraved on tomb-stones," recalled Jean-Paul Sartre: "*Choucroute always on sale, Viennese pastries, Week-ends at Le Touquet, All you need for your motor-car.*" The old signs and advertisements mocked city people who, by the fall of 1940, were spending a large amount of their time simply lining up for the basic necessities of life. "Before" was not so long ago—"I am talking about 1938," Colette clarified—but everything had changed.[2]

Amid these morbid scenes, Philippe Pétain appeared as a genuine savior, the guarantor of order even at the price of diminished sovereignty. But with Wehrmacht soldiers stationed across most of France, it was difficult to work toward a new French future. Most people waited. They waited for the British to win, or they waited for a decisive turn in fighting, or they simply waited for an end to the war. This *attentisme* initially helped the Vichy regime, because it was regarded as a necessary caretaker, but in the end Pétain's government was left without political purpose or energy. There were few people in France who wanted German soldiers underfoot, and French hostility toward the occupiers grew. However, this hostility was always qualified by prudence and fear, by everyday struggles to find food, by a desire for security after the exodus, and by resentment at being abandoned and displaced in the first place. For the families of prisoners of war, concern for hundreds of thousands of French men "over there" outranked worries about tens of thousands of German soldiers "over here." Mistrust of Germans also mingled with more general mistrust of foreigners and communists. Anti-German feelings therefore did not take any particular political form or have an immediate unifying effect. They certainly did not lead straightaway to resistance. Even so, disdain for the *bottes* of the *Boche* was something most French in the occupied zone shared. In unoccupied southern France, the equation was a little different: it was easier to speak up, but the calamity of the exodus had also been far less widespread and the absence of German soldiers made occupation a less urgent issue. Peace seemed closer at hand and war farther away.

Especially in the first years, people wavered between positions. Even a fiercely loyal republican such as schoolteacher Jean Guéhenno felt the insincerity of an absolutist approach. "What to do, what to do?" he asked himself repeatedly. "Despite everything," he felt it necessary to support Pétain, and "despite everything," he abhorred what Pétain was "*obliged* to do." Genuine collaborators quarreled among themselves; fascists in Paris such as Robert Brasillach looked up to the Nazis precisely because Vichy was too bound by tradition. When it emerged in 1943, the organized resistance was itself divided between communist and noncommunists. As we will see, feisty adolescent Micheline Bood not only recorded patriotic graffiti in her diary, but herself chalked slogans on the wall. She volunteered to recite "England, My Beloved England" in school. Yet she flirted again and again with German soldiers—right up to the *débarquement* in June 1944.[3]

Historians have worked hard to reveal the extent of collaboration and the variety of collaborationist positions and to resist the black-and-white judgments on patriotism, loyalty, and treason that were made so easily immediately after France's liberation in 1944. People did make choices, but they did not always think they were making free choices, since they were conscious of the risks of reprisal or denunciation. A careful analysis of French public opinion reveals a general wait-and-see attitude, but over time the center of gravity shifted unmistakably to a pro-British, anti-German position with doubts about the Vichy government and even about Pétain, the hero of Verdun, beginning to grow long before the Germans began to lose the war. That not all French were *attentistes* became clear in the winter of 1940–1941, and this realization steadily whittled down the wait-and-see majority.[4]

When it came to the offerings of the media and the cultural rhythms of daily life, however, the center of gravity was more on the side of collaboration and "live and let live." Whatever a particular individual's choices and hesitations, the background music to the occupation was provided by Radio-Paris, which was under German control. Photographer André Zucca, who had access to color film because he worked for the Nazi propaganda magazine *Signal*, spent his free time taking hundreds of photographs that showed a "casual, even carefree" city: Parisians bicycling under swastika-emblazoned flags, sitting in cafés among German soldiers, and showing off the latest white-rimmed sunglasses. These unsettling photographs are a reminder that life under German occupation was not just a matter of standing in food lines or rushing home to beat the curfew. Liliane Schroeder, a Parisian schoolgirl, began her diary on June 21, 1940, with the fall of France, and she knew where she stood: her American father, a soldier during the Great War, made her "French by birth, American by law, and half-way Anglo-Saxon at heart." She quoted "Monsieur Winston Churchill" to her diary; on May 11, 1941, she followed the patriotic call, broadcast on French radio in London, to re-occupy the streets between three and four o'clock in the afternoon; but she also enjoyed a Coca-Cola at a café on the Champs-Elysées and, one Saturday evening, attended a big show at the Vel' d'Hiv, a venue available to anyone who wanted to use it, including the Paris police in their round-ups of Jews. The occasion was the establishment of the Association of the Parisian Press and featured its president, the "délicieux" Jean Luchaire (who would be executed after the Liberation), clowns Pipo and Ruhm, Emile Prud'homme and his ensemble of accordionists, and, finally, singer Maurice Chevalier; "the trip was worth the effort," Schroeder mused.[5]

The collaborationist big-city press was part of life's routines; every-body still read *Paris-soir* (circulation 970,000 at the end of 1940) or *Le Petit Parisien* (680,000) with its snappy feuilletonist style. The latter reported the deadly serious "triple *execution capitale*," the replacement of three stat-ues of Marianne by busts of Pétain in the rooms of Versailles's Palace of Justice through the banter of municipal workers: "She sure is heavy," said one, taking the head of the republican icon in his hands; "she doesn't have to live under austerities," added another. The glossy illustrated mag-azine *Signal* offered a French-language mix in "Mozart and *Volkssturm*," "harmony and heroism," and sold more than 400,000 copies in Paris every two weeks, 800,000 in France as a whole.[6] The French-language programs of the BBC eventually attracted the most listeners (much of France stopped to listen to the 9:30 news from London), but Radio Paris retained popularity. Its hosts promoted the "New Europe" and warned against Jewish criminals at large in the city, but interviews with *gars* (or regulars on the streets), soap operas, and the ballads of Maurice Chevalier, Tino Rossi, and Charles Trenet made the overall tone youthful, energetic, and upbeat.[7] All three pop stars had to defend themselves against charges of collaboration after the Liberation in 1944. The insouciance of popular

culture manufactured a casual, even carefree city in which Parisian fans
and German officers mingled together. Of course, the line between the
carefree city and the occupied city was tenuous: concertgoers went to the
same Vel' d'Hiv near the Eiffel Tower to which arrested Jews had and
would be taken. While the underground in Warsaw urged a boycott of
cinemas, in Paris and elsewhere in France half again as many people went
to the movies in 1943 as in 1938, enjoying what one scholar has called
"soft-core" Vichy propaganda.[8]

As soon as the Wehrmacht entered the capital, Parisians had to figure
out how to comport themselves alongside the Germans with whom they
now shared the same urban spaces. By their presence, the Germans raised
difficult questions for the French, who had to come to some sort of conclusion as to what kind of Germans they were mingling with.

After midnight on June 14, 1940, the streets of Paris were deserted,
the windows shuttered. At 3:40 in the morning, according to the "live"
transcript prepared by Roger Langeron, the prefect of police, "a German
motorcyclist is crossing the Place Voltaire."

> 5:20—Three truckloads of German soldiers arrive in front of the
>   barracks in Saint-Denis.
> 7:55—Several German officers arrive at the Hotel Crillon.
> 8:15—A German column is passing Saint-Ouen in the direction of
>   the Porte Maillot.
> 8:50—The raised flags on the buildings at the corner of Place de
>   l'Étoile and Avenue des Champs-Elysées are taken down.
> 9:10—German soldiers are passing along the Avenue de Versailles.
>   The main post office, Rue des Archives, is occupied by the
>   Germans.
> 9:27—The German flag has been raised at the Air Ministry.
> 9:45—The Germans raise the Nazi flag at the Arc de Triomphe.

Suddenly, the Germans were everywhere; the fall of Paris was not
going to usher in a worldwide struggle on behalf of France to resist its
foe. Three days later, to his surprise ("Hélas!"), Langeron heard Pétain's
order to lay down arms. A week later he recorded the fact that five cinemas on the Champs-Elysées had reopened their doors: the Portiques, the
Triomphe, the Colisée, the Petit Journal, and *Paris-soir*.[9] The newsreels
that opened the shows were now German productions.

Requisitioning buildings and moving about the boulevards on motor-cycles or in trucks and automobiles, the Germans took over Paris as if they were playing on a "sinister Monopoly board," in one historian's words. Black-bordered traffic signs sprouted on the main intersections to guide the vehicles of the occupation forces to the "Hauptverkehrsdi-rektion Paris," "Feldzuglager (N) 2," "H.K.P. 656," or "NSKK Gruppe Todt." Parisians made do with bicycles, which numbered almost 2 million by the end of the occupation. German officers moved into the best hotels, beginning with the Crillon on the Place de la Concorde, as Lan-geron noted. Military headquarters was set up at the Kommandantur on the Place de l'Opéra. The Grand Rex cinema on the Avenue de Poisson-nière served as a German-only soldiers' cinema. Paris's largest English bookstore, W. H. Smith on the Rue de Rivoli since 1903, became a Weh-rmacht bookstore. Corner kiosks carried Germans newspapers such as the *Völkischer Beobachter* and *Das Reich* alongside French-language offer-ings, including *Elle*, *La Semaine*, and the ubiquitous *Signal*. No one could overlook the large swastika-emblazoned flags outside the new German properties, "horrible and hideous symbols of German domination" that "hung in the direct line of vision, suspended like huge carpets waiting to be beaten," as one American observer put it.[10]

Green-uniformed German soldiers were "everywhere," one resi-dent wrote, "in the streets, in the buildings they have requisitioned, in the hotels, in the shops where they meet their daily needs, in the stores where they raid everything the proprietors agree to sell them, in theaters, cinemas, restaurants, cafes, tea-rooms." Parisians leered at their black boots, which became a metaphor for the occupation, and the belt buckles inscribed with "God with us," which said something about the occupiers' arrogance, but also their seeming unassailability. Throughout 1940, thou-sands of German soldiers on leave augmented the occupation forces; they came as tourists to enjoy the benefits of victory. (After the German invasion of the Soviet Union, soldiers on the eastern front were consoled with the unkept promise "At least once in Paris.") German soldiers with guidebooks of the city tucked under their arms could be seen clustered around the base of the Eiffel Tower, strolling among the artists' easels on Montmartre, and browsing the *bouqiniste* stalls along the Seine. A few days'

leave in Paris were long enough to fill the seats in dozens of new caba-
rets that opened on the Champs-Elysées and in Montmartre and Pigalle,
offering mostly German audiences evening entertainment provided by
mostly French performers. As tourists the soldiers were "hustled along
and tossed together" with the rest of the Parisians in "the stream and
swirl of urban existence." "We were squeezed against them in the Underground," recalled Sartre, "and we bumped into them in the dark streets."[11]

In one of the first pamphlets of the resistance, "33 Conseils à l'occupé", written in the late summer of 1940, Jean Texcier expressed his
disgust at the sight of Parisians offering the new visitors their services.
"They are not tourists," he declared. "They are conquerors." If they address you in German, he urged, forget what you have learned and go
on your way. If they try to speak French, do not feel obliged to show
them the way; "they are not your walking companions." Texcier warned
against listening to the military band concerts, suggesting readers take
a walk in the countryside and listen to the birds instead. He advised his
fellow countrymen to buy suspenders somewhere else if the shop they
frequented advertised "German Spoken Here." He also appealed to the
French to think for themselves, since French-language newspapers and
radio no longer did so. The only thing permitted was to offer a soldier
a light if he asked, Texcier added; you don't refuse your worst enemy a
light. Texcier urged the French to watch out, to take care not to mistake
Germans for tourists or to mislead French observers about one's own
behavior: "watch yourself."[12]

After the war it seemed as though most Parisians had taken Texcier's
thirty-three pieces of advice to heart. The Germans were "everywhere,"
wrote Edmund Dubois, and Paris responded with silence. The saying
went: "Paris is a city of downcast eyes."[13] But the reality was more complicated. It was not just a matter of victors and vanquished, since the
question of "good Germans" lingered. After all, thousands of anti-Nazi
German refugees had come to Paris before the war. Widespread agreement that the Germans had acted "correctly" in their role as occupiers
also seemed to allow some degree of flexibility in interacting with them.
Moreover, as Langeron noted in his diary, Pétain's appeal to the French
to lay down arms, to examine their conscience as French patriots, and

eventually to work with the Germans in a new European order introduced a third element to Franco-German relations: collaboration. Even in Paris, Vichy was always present in the ways the French related to themselves as well as to the Germans. And as Texcier's unease indicated, Parisians did not act simply as conquered people; they went to movies, listened to the radio, read newspapers. Such behavior was difficult to interpret. Parisians responded with silence or disregard, but only sometimes, and they worried about the times they responded differently in a more lighthearted or even cooperative way. Silence not only revealed the disdain of a stoic, vanquished people, but also expressed suspicions the French had about themselves.

What to do when an old friend from Germany arrived for a short stay in Paris? Maurice Toesca, an official with the Paris police, considered himself a writer at heart, and one day in January 1943 he received a warning from his publisher Gaston Gallimard that a German sergeant wanted to contact him. When he heard the name, Toesca reassured Gallimard that Walter Heist was an old friend with whom he shared literary interests and with whose family he had stayed in Mainz on a student trip back in the 1920s. Even so, Toesca was not sure what to do. On the one hand, Heist had been a genuine comrade, a scholar of leading republican authors such as Romain Rolland and Henri Barbusse. On the other hand, Heist might have changed; once a Social Democrat, he might have become a Nazi.[14]

On account of the old friendship, Toesca refused to play the coward: he would meet Heist. To meet in a bistro, however, was to risk "character assassination," because the patrons would witness his friendly relations with a German officer. Yet to invite him home on the Avenue Niel, where he was known as a police official, came with its own problems. Neighbors would gossip about how the police were taking up with "Fritzes." It would be impossible to explain the innocent nature of his relations with the Wehrmacht sergeant and the fortuitous nature of the meeting. In the end, he telephoned the hotel near the Gare du Nord and explained to Heist that he was busy with work but could spend a "few moments together" at home after ten at night, a time when Toesca figured that most Parisians were no longer "roving the streets." But what about the concierge? He confided in her, since he had to explain why he was waiting downstairs. And his wife? She retired to the bedroom, and Toesca told Heist that she was in the country with relatives. The two friends stayed up until four in the morning talking about the persecutions the old Social Democrat had suffered under the Nazis and the war that Heist believed Germany would lose. The fact that Heist, who was very nearsighted, was off to deploy with the Afrika Korps was a sign of how desperate the Germans really were; he did not believe he would come back home alive. As it was, he survived, and Toesca and Heist resumed their literary collaborations after the war.

The incident played out completely outside Texcier's prescriptions, and Toesca worried deeply not about what sort of signals he would send Heist, but about how he would be seen by others, anonymously among restaurant patrons, as a police official among neighbors, and even as a husband in the eyes of his wife. After safely driving Heist back to his hotel, Toesca considered his "imprudence"; had he been recognized, he would have been branded a "collaborator, a traitor, a Nazi." It was French suspicions that vexed Toesca and forced him to hide his friend; in the background lurked the fact of collaboration and the continuous judgment of the French by the French. But Toesca's behavior also reveals the powerful French desire to recognize the good German, to see beyond the uniform, and to avoid reproducing wartime caricatures, all impulses that had been part of the effort of rapprochement with the Germans before the war.

The idea that ordinary people had more in common than not, the premise of Remarque's *All Quiet on the Western Front*, still flickered in the troubled relations between German soldiers and French civilians. When sixteen-year-old Flora Groult first saw Germans enter Concarneau, in Brittany, on June 21, 1940, she admitted they were "handsome," but despised the other girls for "getting up onto the running boards" and "giving the Germans oranges": "the sluts," she wrote, "ignoble bitches in heat." When her older sister, Benoîte, who also regarded men from the vantage point of "a woman," realized that the "three plump-faced Germans" she came across a week later were "eating vanilla ices under the cowlike eyes of five or six Breton women," she imagined how amazed the women must be to realize that Germans "ate in the same way as

Frenchmen, and that in the last analysis conquerors and conquered are very much the same." One sister emphasized the violence of the German "enemy," the other the violence of tiresome national stereotypes.[15]

The French willingness to contemplate the existence of the "good German," the ordinary German, like Remarque's Paul Bäumer, reveals the French anxiety that correct relations with the occupier were imaginable; the suspicion alone set France apart from Poland, where there was no such thing as the problem of the "good German." But honestly reckoning with the "good German" during the occupation meant discarding the all-encompassing category of the "bad German," which threatened to undermine the idea of innocent French and thus sharpened feelings of shame about the defeat of France, its political divisions before the war, its collaborationist tendencies, and even its anti-Semitism—the whole complex summed up by the Vichy regime. For many, the only solution to this problem was a determined effort to keep the categories "German" and "French" clearly distinct and to smear the Germans by creating the German type, *sauterelles vertes* (green locusts), as Texcier suggested on account of the green Wehrmacht uniforms that swarmed into France, "darkening the sky and covering the ground," or *haricots verts* (green beans), or simply "them" (*ils*).[16] France grappled continually with the problems of living with the occupier and with the challenge of drawing lines between German and French, from their behavior on streets and subways to their literature of home invasions and the graffiti wars on city walls.

For Sartre, it was precisely the "harmless sight of the German soldiers strolling through the streets" and "sitting in the metro" that troubled the French. The uniforms constituted a "pale, dull-green unobtrusive stain" among "the dark clothes of the civilians." Depending on where Parisians were in the city, the stain became more or less conspicuous, but it was always there, a daily reminder of illegitimate usurpation. Many Parisians cultivated the fantasy that they could, through the sum of averted glances, completely ignore the Germans and envelop them in silence: "silence in the trains, in the metro, in the street." While each passerby "keeps his thoughts," concluded economist Charles Rist, together the French sensed the collective hostility that "we" had declared against "them." In the metro Parisians had to "squeeze together to make room for you," Jean

Guéhenno wrote, addressing the German in his mind's eye directly. But "I lower my head a bit so you won't see where my eyes are going, to deprive you of the joy of an exchange of glances. There you are in the midst of us, like an object, in a circle of cold silence." It was therefore not surprising that German writer Felix Hartlaub, stationed in Paris, described the atmosphere surrounding him as he went about town as "arctic." When the soldiers did break the silence to ask for directions, Parisians mumbled "I don't know" or "*nix compris*" and left Germans to fend for themselves. A few dared to retort, "You wanted to come here, figure it out for yourself," before running out of the metro car. Another German could not figure out the location of the Bréguet-Sabin station. "What the hell are you doing here?" muttered an old worker in exasperation; obviously, "it's too complicated for you."[17] The Germans' own metro stories mostly told about how to navigate the system by one's own wits, and not one featured an actual encounter with French commuters. But all the metro stories, whether recounted by the French or the Germans, imagined the possibility of contact. The stories suggested that German soldiers were out of place, but not sinister. Sartre himself recognized this. He felt dissatisfied either way, whether he refused to give directions or whether he pointed the way to "the second turning on the Left." "What was the right thing to do?" he wondered. The question stayed with him because "the idea of who is one's enemy is only clear and definite when that enemy is on the other side of the fighting line."[18]

Was there a collective silence, a silence of refusal and resistance, a silence in which Parisians recognized each other in their individual gestures and averted glances? Or was the silence one of suspicion, based on the fear of being judged and misunderstood? If most commuters on the metro were silent, we know that they could also see each other reading the collaborationist press, *Paris-soir* or *Le Petit Parisien*, which certainly qualified the notion of the unbroken spirit of the vanquished. Ultimately, the France of the Resistance existed in only very incomplete form. Silence also resulted from uncertainty about where people stood on the question of collaboration and resistance. Sometimes the atmosphere on the streets seemed to be pregnant with conspiracy, yet observers also described the silence of despair and solitude. Guéhenno was quite sure about himself when in his diary he addressed the fictional German on the metro. But he was not always sure about others around him. One evening in December 1943, he was walking along the Boulevard Saint-Michel when he heard French prisoners singing the *Marseillaise* from inside a locked paddy wagon; only a "few people barely stopped to watch." He hoped others were "at least clenching their fists in their pockets."[19] But in this case, silence made Guéhenno suspicious about passersby. It divided rather than unified.

In Vercors's famous novel *The Silence of the Sea*, published clandestinely in 1942, silence constituted the central element of an ethics of self-determination. The German invasion of France becomes an invasion of the home when the novel's unnamed narrator and his niece must provide a room for a German officer, Werner von Ebrennac. They resolve to remain completely silent in the presence of Ebrennac, who recognizes in their behavior the love they have for France. Vercors, the pseudonym for artist and writer Jean Bruller, portrays the hard work involved in keeping silent and the oppressive, heavy atmosphere that results from the occupation of the narrator's house. Silence is an achievement that contrasts with the "cowardice" of those who had purportedly welcomed the Germans. This "stern expression" restores Ebrennac's faith in France, and he fills the room with soliloquies about his love for French culture, his opposition to the Nazis, and his dream of a Franco-German marriage in a new Europe. Sitting at the harmonium, he plays Bach's preludes. Paradoxically, French silence serves to introduce the "good German," who in turn tests the resolve of the silent householders not to recognize distinctions among the occupiers. In the end, Ebrennac comes to learn, after a trip to Paris, what the narrator and niece already know: there is no benevolence in Germany's presence in France. His dreams crushed, he volunteers for the eastern front. "Off to Hell," he announces. The niece's first and final word, "Adieu," confirms the mutual knowledge of the very different collective fates of the French and the Germans, who cannot reconcile in the war.[20]

Vercors ultimately dismisses the idea of the "good German," but the plot introduces him; French silence makes Ebrennac loquacious and thoughtful. Furthermore, the trespasser in the novel is not just the

German officer in the French home but also the residue of doubt, accommodation, and mutual recognition among the French. There is something terribly austere about the silence; the suffering is made more intense because the narrator and his niece do not speak to each other. Even after Ebrennac departs for the last time, the two remain silent. "My niece . . . got my breakfast ready . . . in silence, and in silence we drank," Vercors writes. Moreover, the mutual suffering is not necessarily accompanied by mutual understanding. The two French householders are constantly watching each other. The niece admonishes with a look, arches her eyebrows, although the narrator admits not being able to "decipher" her "messages." He notices the "faint fluttering" of her fingers when Ebrennac talks.[21] An atmosphere of suspicion undermines the freely chosen resolve to remain silent. *The Silence of the Sea* is not just about the problem of the German presence in France; it is also about the problem of speaking and understanding in the context of occupation and collaboration. The silence is as much a silence of appearances as it is a silence of conviction.

Wartime texts revealed considerable anxiety as "good Germans" enter French houses. Irène Némirovsky portrays small-town France under the occupation at cross-purposes. In *Suite Française*, written in 1941 and 1942, the character Lucile feels confined by her mother-in-law's house and the expectation that she will assume the proper role of wife to a French prisoner of war whom she no longer loves; Bruno von Falk, the billeted German officer, enters her life as a music lover who plays Bach and Mozart. Rather than being a trespasser, he provides Lucile an "island in a hostile house." Despite the happiness she feels, Lucile breaks off the relationship when she hides a French fugitive. Némirovsky thus returns her character to the patriotic community, but does so on Lucile's terms, not her mother-in-law's. Divisive issues of marriage, class, and politics complicate relationships with German soldiers; for Némirovsky, Vercors's silent niece would not be true to life. Other wartime novels are more simplistic, but they similarly play with fears about the ability of German soldiers to encroach upon the intimate spaces of French women who have been left alone after the imprisonment of French soldiers. These highly gendered projections of the loss of male French authority in time of war are just that, but they also stand in for more general concerns about the integrity of the French nation.[22]

In fiction, and in life, music posed the question of whether there existed a realm of the spirit beyond the war, a realm in which the French and the Germans might meet. For Némirovsky, music did not conform to national borders but crossed them like religion or ideology. She thus placed the music lovers (and potential lovers) Lucile and Bruno on their own "island." The Nazis themselves recognized the ability of the classical music tradition to reconcile the vanquished with the victors. No aspect of the Nazis' cultural mission in France had more success than the attempt to create "collaboration through music." German-sponsored concerts of Bach, Mozart, and Wagner provided blocks to build a "temple of pure music" that would establish common ground between Germany and France. "Wagner's brass," in effect, was supposed to drown out "the cries of the tortured and the rounds of gunfire," writes one historian.[23] This is precisely why Vercors described music as a seductive, dark, otherworldly force, delegitimizing the differentiations that music might permit between "good" and "bad" Germans by rooting it in demonic power. Music thus persistently raised the question of accommodation: Should one listen to German programming? Was music German or universal?

Even before townspeople could see the German soldiers coming up the street, they heard the loud songs of military units. What astonished listeners was the military comportment, the collective exaltation, and the sheer lung power of the group. Maurice Toesca disparaged the discipline of the German collective and took comfort in the disharmony of French individuality.[24] Classical music, however, recalled an idealist, romantic Germany that had not completely disappeared from view. Liliane Schroeder listened carefully to the notes drifting from the concert on the Place Colbert in Marennes; a "very good interpretation," she judged, but precisely because it was good, she made it a point of honor not to cross the square and decided to contemplate something less interesting instead—just as Jean Texcier had recommended. It was quite easy "to turn one's back to the 'Prinz Eitel Friedrich March,' the 'Reiterlust-March,' or the waltz '*In lauschiger Nacht*,'" but, according to Anne Somerhausen, an American resident in Brussels, it was "more difficult to resist" performances by "the famous boys' choir of the Regensburg cathedral" or "a Beethoven concert of the excellent Cologne symphony orchestra." Of course, uniformed Wehrmacht personnel attended such events in large numbers as well, so it was a question of not just listening to German performances but sitting alongside German occupiers. "Secret Annex Rules" in Anne Frank's Amsterdam hideout included a prohibition on listening to German radio stations except "in special cases, such as classical music and the like." In the Lodz Ghetto, Oskar Rosenfeld reported on "German classical composers in demand. Handel: *Largo*; Bach: *Air*; Haydn: Serenade."[25] Vercors was right to identify music as a point of contact between occupation forces and occupied civilians.

In reality, most German officers were not billeted in French homes, and those who were undoubtedly endured awkward conversations about weather rather than a regime of total silence. But the panic about the home invasion in *The Silence of the Sea* and other wartime literature suggests something more than how unbearable was the German presence. It expresses anxiety about the extent to which the French in fact responded positively to German appeals to common ground in music or sex or regarding transnational ideas such as Christianity, a new Europe, anti-Bolshevism, or simply the shared experience of World War I that had been so important in shaping public attitudes in 1938. The trespass was not simply the stamp of German boots in French homes but the suspicion that the French were divided on the issue of what the Germans had to say. Silence was a demonstration of resistance in the face of the victor; it was also a reaction to uncertainty about collaboration among the vanquished.

Throughout the winter of 1940–1941, fourteen-year-old diarist Micheline Bood continued "her struggle against the Germans." Micheline was exactly a year older than Anne Frank, but because she wasn't Jewish she never had to contemplate going into hiding and could choose how to respond to German occupiers. She decided "*never*" to cross the street on the designated crosswalks because to do so was to follow a German directive, nor did she *ever* put a leash on her dog, Darak. On the first of January, she indulged in the "pleasure" of writing "Vive de Gaulle!" in the snow on the Rue de Marigny. She reported her success in chalking two "*V*s" and one "The English will triumph" on the walls. She scratched out German posters, even though friends of friends had been arrested for doing so. She loved the English and hated the Germans. No other airplane had ever given her the impression of such "security, suppleness, and nimbleness" as the Spitfire she watched flying over Paris. With its slender frame and perfect lines, it was "the most beautiful airplane in the world." Micheline also watched, this time with disgust, as German soldiers drove along the boulevards in chauffeured cars, buying candies and other "delicious things." "They're swiping everything" was what Parisians remarked about the Wehrmacht's shopping spree, which was subsidized by a drastically devalued French franc.[26]

Micheline's "struggle" was part of a grand drama that played itself out over the skies of Europe as Britain repelled the German air assault in the Battle of Britain. "Planes have been rumbling in the sky all day long," noted Jean Guéhenno on September 7, 1940. For the next weeks, he anticipated, "we'll follow this battle, crucial to our destiny, hour by hour, as if we were at a play by Aeschylus." On the streets below, in a small-scale version of the battle between the Luftwaffe and the Royal Air Force, Germans plastered propaganda posters on walls of French cities and towns, and French high school students ripped them up. Most of the anti-English propaganda posters that the Germans had put up had been defaced or crossed out with red and blue crayons, reported Henri Drouot, a local historian. In Lyons alone, it was "at least 7000 posters (an average of 20 x 360 rues = 7200)." "The power (and impotence) of ambitious propaganda campaigns!" he remarked.[27] Although students divided themselves into Anglophiles and Germanophiles, the friends of France's old ally were very much in the majority.

The resilience of the British also legitimized the defiance of Charles de Gaulle, one of the few military and, for that matter, political leaders to flee France in the summer of 1940 to organize resistance to the Germans. More and more people listened to French radio programming on the BBC, an outpost of France on undefeated British soil, which facilitated the choreography of French resistance against German occupation. French radio, or "London," as it was called, organized a stay-at-home action for January 1, 1941. Between two and three o'clock in the nonoccupied zone and between three and four o'clock in the occupied zone, de Gaulle's people urged the French to stay off the streets and to shutter their windows. "To-morrow I will demonstrate," enthused Jeanne Oudot, a schoolgirl in the small village of Mancenans. The next day she reported: "Not a soul in the streets. Everybody understood and stayed at home." On the occasion of the Feast Day of Joan of Arc, Sunday, May 11, 1940, London urged the French people to stroll the streets together. It was a manifestation of recognition: as de Gaulle pointed out, "When you look yourselves directly into the eyes, you will recognize yourselves." According to Liliane Schroe-der, Parisians packed the streets; smiles had replaced suspicions.[28]

And in the most successful action, on March 22, 1941, London called on the French to write the first letter of the word *Victory* on walls and pavements. The idea was to give the French the "feeling that they were part of the show." The campaign was later extended across Europe. Within days, "Vs have blossomed everywhere." The BBC received a let-ter from a clandestine listener in the Marne Department who reported, "Nothing but Vs and still more Vs everywhere on the walls, on the roads, telegraph posts, etc." Pedestrians also crossed two pins in their button-holes to shape a *V*; "we were able to count 75 in five minutes, Yvette and me," reported Micheline. It was a victory in a cat-and-mouse game, as the German response confirmed. In some places, in reaction to the graffiti, the local German commander prohibited adolescents from leaving their homes on successive Sundays in March and April. Shopkeepers bore the responsibility of cleaning the *V* by the start of business. And school-teachers were required to make sure that children did not leave school with chalk in their pockets. Micheline herself had been caught writing slogans in school, but despite her promise to stop, she continued to trace *V*s on German military vehicles.[29]

These demonstrations were impressive. It is necessary, however, to remember that there were other graffiti and other texts. As Jean Texcier noted, shopkeepers advertised "German Spoken Here." Framed portraits of Pétain adorned shop windows. Graffiti was a weapon in a war that the French waged among themselves. Every day, Liliane Schroeder noted the different factions who announced themselves: "All power to Thorez—Long Live the King—Long Live the PSF—Long Live Pétain—Jews Out—Down with Laval—Long Live the PPF." But it is likely that the slogan she read just "this morning" was most representative: "Patience, de Gaulle will come."[30] The Franco-French conflict also staged itself in the life of Micheline Bood, who dared to chalk Vs, yet, at the height of the campaign, also began to meet German soldiers at public swimming pools, places where the half-naked men, out of uniform, did not stick out so much.

Once Micheline met Walter and started frolicking with him in the pool, she had to justify her relationship with a German soldier, the enemy. She saw the Germans in terms of the English, and in her diary she repeatedly expressed her unwavering loyalty to England. But she liked Walter a great deal: "(He's blond, twenty-five years old, he is very big and thinks that Paris is the most beautiful city in the world.)" First there was the question of sex, and Micheline was "shocked" by the "crudeness and violence" of the conclusions to which people jumped. "Why can't I speak to a young man without people immediately thinking that I am flirting or that he's my lover?" she asked herself. For the French to think otherwise was an expression of a "disgusting attitude." Then there was the problem that Walter was a German and that she was consorting with the enemy. Micheline was aware of public approbation, and she promised her mother that she "would not say anything to anyone about Walter," to which her mother replied that Micheline "should not say anything to Walter." She went back and forth on the issue in her diary. She found the German soldiers to be more polite than French boys, who always wanted to hit on her; she felt she could approach Germans as "comrades" and just talk. And even though she continued to hate Germans as the "Boches" who had invaded France, "the Germans, taken individually, are very nice, on the whole, well-mannered and correct." In any case, she asked, "How can one hate someone one doesn't know?" The priest to whom she confessed told her it was not a sin to meet with Walter.

Micheline then began to think about Walter and the other German soldiers in terms of the French. "There are plenty of cowards, traitors, and mean creatures" among the Germans, she began to explain to herself, "but they cannot be more cowardly than the French who betrayed their country." She justified relationships with Germans by pointing to the collaboration of the French. She was appalled: "To consider nowadays all the people who have become collaborators, who lick the boots of the Germans out of fear or cowardice, even in my own family! This dirty country just disgusts me." Intimacy with Germans raised questions about French behavior. The Germans, by contrast, had previously assumed the role of vanquished more honorably. According to Micheline, "In 1918, when the Germans were beaten, they conducted themselves much better than the French; they did not accept collaboration, and they neither humiliated themselves nor groveled."[31] Germany remained the enemy, and although Micheline held hands with Walter, she did not kiss him, but the genuine betrayal had been French.

After Walter, Micheline met Peter, an airman, and Rolf, and then there was the mysterious "Bébé," with "his clear blue eyes." Because Micheline sometimes went on double dates, she met girls who had even fewer scruples about going out with Germans than she did. Her friends Monique and Jacqueline had serious relationships with more than one German, and Micheline condemned them for their vulgarity, although she remained friends. And she continued to think of herself as "Anglophile": she had running arguments with her soldier friends, teasing them about drowning in the English Channel ("glouglou, glouglou!"); telling them of her firm belief in Britain's victory, which was rooted in her conviction of the rightness of Britain's cause; and criticizing the Germans for bombing women and children. She scrawled "Vive de Gaulle" in Walter's cabin at the pool. After an argument about Jews, Micheline and Rolf "separated on rather bad terms." This banter showed that Micheline had not changed sides. Indeed, making the case for Britain was very much part of the relationships she cultivated with Germans. Micheline was a bit like the character in Joseph Kessel's wartime novel *Army of Shadows*, whose "favorite pastime, when she traveled in the *métro*, was to put anti-German tracts in the pockets of German officers and soldiers."[32] Even so, Micheline could regard Germans in ordinary terms, as individuals. She regarded the German soldiers she met not as particularly sinister or even as Nazis, although they would never match up to the British. Given these sorts of social interactions, it was possible to see their redeployment to the eastern front in 1941 in a tragic light, as Vercors did with Ebrennac and Némirovsky with Bruno in their stories.

In daily life the French generally regarded the Germans as a group apart, but neither the German "they" nor the French "us" was nearly as unanimous as postwar memory suggested. Actual wartime realities contradicted self-righteous postwar accounts at numerous points. Conversations between the two groups were plentiful. The French did not conflate all Germans with sinister Nazis, as was the case among the Poles. It was Jews in France who saw the Germans as "them" and as sinister Nazis and who would never have imagined themselves saying "Adieu" to Ebrennac or sharing an "island" with Bruno. The Jews' necessarily uncompromising view of Germans set off the more ambivalent relationships the French pursued during the occupation.

. . . in Warsaw

THE HISTORY OF THE GERMAN ASSAULT ON WARSAW AND ON POLAND was almost immediately written by reference to a series of black and bloody days, a litany that invoked the tradition of the martyrdom of the Polish nation, often encapsulated in the phrase "the Christ of nations." This calendar of dark days also reflected the extreme violence the Germans deployed against Poland from the very outset of the war. Sunday, September 10, 1939, when the Germans launched seventeen air raids on Warsaw, was labeled "Bloody Sunday." Two weeks later, a fearsome sky full of bombers returned to the city. In some twelve hundred sorties, the Luftwaffe dropped five hundred tons of bombs. As a result, on "Black Monday," September 25, 1939, hundreds of fires raged uncontrolled, as Warsaw's water mains had been badly damaged. The smoke rose to a height of ten thousand feet and could be seen seventy miles away. Never before had such a destructive air raid been launched on a city, and the assault would remain one of the most fearsome in the entire war, comparable to the German raid on Coventry on November 14, 1940, or the British raid on Lübeck on March 28, 1942. The total number of civilian deaths due to air raids and artillery shelling as the Germans approached the Polish capital was fifty or sixty thousand, many times more than Coventry's dead and more than the number killed by Allied raids on Hamburg in July 1943 or Dresden in February 1945. More than half of Warsaw had been destroyed or damaged. Poles had assumed that both France and Britain would enter the war in early September 1939 not simply as self-declared belligerents but with active fighting forces who would relieve Poland's defenses in a matter of weeks. Such support never came, but there was still considerable confidence in an eventual Allied victory when the two nations' armies rallied the following spring. The news of the French armistice on June 17, 1940, thus came as a stunning, dispiriting blow—a second "Black Monday."

Less than four weeks after the German invasion of Poland began and almost precisely one year after the Czechoslovakian crisis when Londoners and Parisians anticipated the doom of their own cities, the destruction of Warsaw seemed to confirm the extraordinary capacity of airpower. Civilians were the primary victims of the assaults on the first "Black Monday," and the ruined city and the casualties among its inhabitants prompted the military commanders overseeing the defense of the capital to initiate talks to surrender Warsaw. That surrender occurred on September 28, 1939; German troops entered the city two days later.

Hitler himself hoped that the *Schrecklichkeit*, or frightfulness, that the Luftwaffe had meted out to Warsaw would serve as a warning to Poland's allies Britain and France. The invincibility of German airpower and the vulnerability of civilians were supposed to be the lesson of the propaganda film *Feuertaufe* (Baptism by Fire), released the following year. The first propaganda posters in Warsaw drove the same points home like a picture book: surveying dead civilians lying across the streetcar tracks, a wounded Polish soldier angrily confronts Chamberlain, who, arms crossed, turns away with a look of calculated disregard. The caption was simply: "England, This Is Your Doing!" Audiences who viewed *Feuertaufe* in Berlin in April and May 1940 sat in "dead silence"; according to security reports, scenes of the destruction of Warsaw made a "deep and lasting impression," a cross between "genuine admiration" for the Luftwaffe, pity for the Poles, and fear for Germany as the new offensive in the West got under way. As the new face of war, the Luftwaffe's air assault frightened civilians across Europe in a way that the much more popular film about the Wehrmacht ground invasion *Feldzug in Polen* (The Campaign in Poland) had not.

However, for all the brutality it depicted, *Feuertaufe* misrepresented the basic nature of the Nazi assault on Polish civilians. It was German boots, not bombs, that ultimately wrought the worst havoc. "Warsaw was the capital of that war," recalled writer Kazimierz Brandys about the German effort to systematically turn the city of 3 million Poles, including 400,000 Jews, into a permanent field of battle on which a new racial order would emerge.[33]

Warsaw in early October 1939 resembled a city of the dead. It was described as a "coffin" or a "corpse." Wrecked cars, overturned streetcars, broken lights, and glass shards littered the streets, which constant rains and early snow turned to sludge. What caught the eye of passersby were the smashed interiors of private life torn open by the collapsed facades of shelled and bombed buildings: "beds made up from the night, paintings on the walls, curtains and flowers in the windows, books on the shelves, and dishes, furniture, and clothes broken or torn." Every day in September, neighbors who had perished were buried in little cemeteries dug out of public parks, along streets, and even in courtyards of tenements. Hundreds of notices fluttered from walls and fences: black-bordered obituaries, inquiries into the whereabouts of residents who had fled or been bombed out, and advertisements for the sale of goods and services. This flimsy patchwork of private tragedies gradually covered up the vigilant appeals to Warsaw's people to resist ("To Arms—United, we will defeat the enemy") that the city had printed only a few weeks earlier. Everywhere people formed "ragged lines," standing in queues before dawn to purchase potatoes or bread. Because cash withdrawals were limited to fifty zlotys, residents who needed to buy food had to line up in front of banks first. Everyone noticed refugees, the homeless, and newly unemployed professionals joining ranks of street vendors. On Warsaw's Koszykowa Street and in the Square of the Iron Gate, they offered for sale a few candies, an onion, maybe some bread, or else their own personal belongings, a pair of worn leather shoes, kitchen utensils, books. "Doctors, lawyers, artists, scientists—men who only a few months ago had never been inside their own kitchens"—sold potatoes, weighed horse meat, and wrapped soup bones, "as if to the manner born."[34]

The Germans quickly prohibited Poles from posting advertisements and obituaries and quickly substituted their own notices. Beginning in the first weeks of October, posters appeared on the streets of Warsaw with the "Announcement" in German (*Bekanntmachung*) and Polish (*Obwieszczenie*) of executions by order of the German police commander. The names of the victims and the crimes with which they had been charged followed: Józef Sadowski, Stanislaw Lasocki, Samson Luksenburg. Most had been executed for the possession of firearms or hand grenades, but by December Poles were also shot for "complicity in acts of sabotage," a nebulous charge that included minor offenses such as ripping up German posters or insulting German authorities. The victims came from all walks of life—Catholics and Jews, men and women, workers, professionals, and Boy Scouts.[35]

Even more frightening were arbitrary roundups and executions in reprisal for the killing of German soldiers or their Polish agents. In the case of such reprisals, German authorities did not publish the names of the dead, but rumors quickly spread throughout Warsaw. On November 20, a week after the murder of a policeman, a crime in which the shooter was apprehended, the Germans summarily executed 53 male Jews from the same building at 9 Nalewki Street. (In a year, Nalewki Street would be in the heart of the Warsaw Ghetto: Emanuel Ringelblum's documentation of the ghetto included *The History of the House-Committee of Nalewki Nr. 23*, and the street was also the scene of fierce fighting in the Warsaw Ghetto Uprising in May 1943.) After the Nalewki Street executions, wrote Rulka Langer, a researcher for the Bank of Poland, "the ghost of a dead German began to haunt Warsaw."[36] The massacre of 107 men in the Warsaw suburb of Wawer on December 27, 1939, after 2 German soldiers had been wounded in a tavern caused an even "greater stir" throughout occupied Poland. "Within a few hours," remembered Wladyslaw Szpilman, a prominent pianist on Polskie Radio, "a wall of hate separated Germans and Poles." A year later, on the anniversary of the shootings, "Wawer, Wawer, Wawer" became a siren of Poland's underground. The keynote to the German occupation was the phrase repeated on legal notices: "will be punished by death." Nowhere else did the Germans make use of the death penalty as promiscuously as in Poland.[37]

The executions on Nalewki Street and in Wawer paled beside the ferocious wave of terror that swept through western Poland, which

Germany intended to annex. During the German invasion in September, an estimated 16,000 Polish civilians were killed, mostly for suspicion of being irregular "franc-tireurs." The Wehrmacht conjured up "an invisible enemy" led by priests (*Pfaffen*, as they were disparagingly called) and nationalists who allegedly fought in the rear and in the shadows. By the end of the year, as many as 50,000 Poles had lost their lives, many in reprisals for the murder of German civilians, as had occurred in Bromberg (Bydgoszcz) on September 3, 1939. In the hands of Nazi propagandists, the number of German victims killed in Bromberg increased by many thousands; Hitler himself set the total number of German victims in Poland at 60,000, although the Wehrmacht initially put the figure (high) at 5,000. In response to the German deaths in Bromberg, units of mobile SS killing squads and ethnic German "self-defense forces" murdered 1,200 people, including the district's leading citizens and its entire Jewish population in ten days. Indeed, in 1939 Jews were victims of gratuitous, brutal violence, as numerous "Blitz pogroms" across Poland indicated. But they were not yet primary targets.[38] Reprisals, executions, and massacres of Jews and non-Jews alike continued throughout western Poland long after Polish armed forces had surrendered.

The first refugees began to arrive in Warsaw, Lublin, and outlying towns in the winter and spring of 1940. Since the end of the war, there had been very little news from western Poland, which had been annexed by Germany. Even the early underground resistance groups that had sprung up among remnants of the Polish army around Warsaw and Kraków had no contacts in Posen. However, once Nazi authorities started to push Poles across the border, out of the annexed region, and into the German occupation zone, as part of an ethnic cleansing campaign, horror stories proliferated. At the end of May 1940, in Szczebrzeszyn, a small town in the Lublin district with a few thousand inhabitants, Zygmunt Klukowski, the local doctor, reported that "yesterday just before midnight, a transport of 1,070 evacuees from Kutno, Wloclawek, and Lodz arrived," "mostly women, children, and older men." "They had been removed from their homes with only fifteen minutes given to pack their necessities," he continued. They were then "loaded into freight wagons and moved east." Once in Szczebrzeszyn, Klukowski could see that they were in "terrible condition, resigned to their fate, completely broken."[39] In December 1939, the Germans deported some 87,000 Poles and Jews from the Posen region. Thousands more were also deported from the Wartheland, the other annexed territory.

Deported Poles confirmed rumors of mass executions. When the Latinek family finally made it to Warsaw, utterly dispossessed and living in a "small, almost bare room," they related how on December 8, 1939, they had been forced out of their apartment in Posen at a moment's notice, held for eight days in an abandoned factory on the edge of town, then loaded onto sealed freight cars and dumped days later into snow-filled ditches somewhere around Lublin. Friends asked the Latineks about mutual acquaintances: "How are the Manowskis, the Hoppes, the Hedingers?" "Killed. All killed," victims of the "unbelievable murder and terror that had descended on the western provinces of Poland." New deportees were pouring into Warsaw every day, wrote Hania Warfield, from "Poznan, Katowice, Bydgoszcz, Grudziadz." In this way, Rulka Langer, another resident, heard the "first news" about "the bloody terror in the district of Posen." She learned that "prominent people, people we knew and liked, men with whom we had played bridge and danced were now daily facing the firing squad."[40]

In the minds of many Germans, the early anti-German violence in Bromberg provided emotional rationale to wage war on civilians. According to one junior officer, it could "justify *any and all* measures on our part."[41] German occupation authorities repeatedly described Poland's crime in the most lurid terms, a reason to commit their own on a much grander scale. However, Bromberg was effect, not cause. Germany's imposition of harsh martial law in Warsaw, its effort to murder "prominent people" in Posen, and its campaign to deport Poles en masse from the western territories were not parts of a reprisal policy in response to Polish resistance. They were the aim of the invasion. The victorious Nazis sought to destroy the Polish nation by tearing out the traces of Polish life in the annexed districts and by subjugating Poles through harsh colonial-style rule in the occupied territories. The events of 1939 did not at all resemble the German occupation of Polish territory in 1915–1918; in the minds of many contemporaries, 1939 was the prelude to cultural, economic, and political slavery. The Allies themselves accused Germans of carrying out a "systematic plan of extermination."[42]

In the run-up to the invasion of Poland, Hitler was very clear that his public declarations concerning the rights of ethnic Germans were mere cover for a more ambitious racial reordering that his leadership would oversee in eastern Europe. He reminded Wehrmacht commanders that "Danzig is not the objective that we are concerned about." The aim of the military operations in Poland was "to eliminate active forces, not secure a particular frontier." That meant "first and foremost" the "destruction of Poland" and the expansion of "German living space." Greater Germany was to last for one thousand years. That achievement depended on a "brutal course of action," spearheaded by "my Totenkopfverbände," or Death's Head Units, as Hitler affectionately described the mobile SS killing squads, who had been mobilized "under the order to send every man, woman, and child of Polish origin to their deaths without remorse or mercy. Only in this way can we attain the living space that we need." The injunction "to harden the heart against pity" was the necessary and oft-repeated companion to every step in the expansion of racial war against the Slavs and, later on, the Jews. It might "seem hard, but it is simply a law of nature," Hitler reiterated on October 2, 1939, after the conventional military campaign had concluded, but as the political or "administrative" struggle was just beginning: "There is only one master for the Poles, and that is the German"; "therefore all representatives of the Polish elite are to be murdered." And on October 17, Hitler once again unambiguously laid out the emergency conditions in which the racial struggle would be waged: "Uncompromising racial struggle cannot admit any legal strictures."[43]

The existential ethnic nature of Germany's war aims represented a fundamental break in modern European warfare. The idea of German life and death taught the SS, Hitler's black-shirted paramilitary elite, to think in terms of the "big picture" in the acquisition of territory, in the subordination of occupied peoples, and in the radical and extralegal methods available to meet those ends. In this regard, the war in Poland prepared the way for and anticipated the invasion of the Soviet Union in 1941 and the implementation of the "final solution" against the Jews in 1942. As for Poles, it became very clear that defeat and occupation in 1939 were the beginning and not the end of a relentless German assault on the entire nation.[44] In Europe's East, the war never ended; there was to be no peace, no armistice, no collaboration, no Pétain or Vichy, only the terrifying and not quite imaginable prospect of complete German victory.

Short of the total biological destruction of the Polish people, a goal that was contemplated by some Nazis, "uncompromising racial struggle" was pursued along a variety of tracks. In terms of administration, Germany annexed western Poland into the old Reich, establishing two new German districts, with appropriate mail and telephone area codes, administered by Nazi Party Gauleiter Reichsgau Wartheland (Arthur Greiser) and Reichsgau Danzig–West Preussen (Albert Foster). Simultaneously, the Soviet Union, in accordance with secret protocols of the Soviet-Nazi Non-Aggression Pact of August 1939, annexed eastern Poland into Soviet Belarussia and Ukraine. What was left of Poland, around a shrunken triangle formed by Warsaw, Kraków, and Lublin, became German colonial territory that superseded old Poland, an entity that ceased to exist, as the generic designation "General Government," ruled directly by Nazi "Governor-General" Hans Frank, indicated. The racial war the Germans pursued also aimed at the liquidation of the Polish elite so that Poland would never again emerge as a "political factor." Mass arrests and executions of professionals, civil servants, teachers, merchants, and priests took place throughout the annexed and occupied territories in 1939 and 1940 in a project of "land clearance," which euphemistically adapted an agricultural term for political purposes; a March 1940 *New York Times* report titled "2000 Intellectuals Disappear in Warsaw" was basically correct. Finally, the Gauleiter of the newly annexed districts sought to fortify the German racial element by reclaiming "Polonized" ethnic Germans, even snatching suitable children for foster care in the Reich; resettling Germans from the Baltic countries, Romania, and the Soviet Union into the Wartheland and West Prussia; and deporting as many Jews and Poles as possible into the General Government, which would serve Germany as a "big Polish labor camp."[45] The Germans intended eventually to ship millions of Poles back into Germany, but only as forced laborers on temporary assignment as designated by the *P* stitched to their clothes. To implement the goal of a "Jew-free" Greater Germany, the Nazi overlords surveyed land for a reservation around Lublin in which Polish, as well as German and Austrian Jews, would be corralled. This plan came to nothing but indicated the basic direction of German thinking.

By the end of 1939, eastern Europe resembled a gigantic marshaling yard in which human freight was shunted back and forth according to differentiated bills of lading. German racial administrators grouped and regrouped the population in order to achieve the new racial order, an extraordinary plan limited only by the carrying capacity of the railroads and the exigencies of new wars in western Europe and then the Soviet Union. Administrators, entrepreneurs, and volunteers from the Reich poured into the annexed territories and the General Government to take up new colonial posts. Ethnic Germans rushed to acquire new political and economic opportunities in Posen and Danzig.

"We are thinking imperially here, on the grandest scale of all times," Governor-General Hans Frank reiterated again and again. Success would be measured by the degree to which the Germans eliminated "the prospects that Poland would ever again reestablish itself." As the first "colonial territory" of the German nation, the General Government would be treated as nothing more than "booty," its resources to be picked clean and its people to be exploited as a "labor reserve" under the "absolute leadership" of Germany.[46] "The mistakes of the German, Russian, and Austro-Hungarian empires" before 1941 that, the *Warschauer Zeitung* explained, had left "Polish hopes alive for more than a century and finally led to the resurrection of the Polish state are not to be repeated." As it was, Germany's newly established 1939 protectorate in Bohemia and Moravia left the Czechs with too much "independence."[47]

Nothing was to be left standing between the German "master race" and the labor reservoir of the "subjugated." The Germans banned almost all voluntary associations in Poland except for volunteer fire companies and social welfare organizations, which had obviously utilitarian purposes. Grammar schools remained open, in order to teach Poles basic skills, but otherwise education was dismantled. The Nazis also purged the Polish civil administration down to the county level. One of the reasons that

German administrators prohibited Poles from owning radios (effective October 20, 1939, just a month after a similar prohibition was applied to German Jews) was to destroy any pretension they might have to participate independently in European cultural and political affairs. The model for what Poles needed to know was loudspeakers, known as "barking trumpets," installed in public spaces; the "subjugated" would hear only what the "master race" wanted them to hear.[48]

The most audacious effort to destroy Polish society, however, was the physical elimination of the Polish elite. This was the first genocide in the war, one aimed at wiping out the Polish nation, although it would pale in comparison to the second genocide, Germany's all-out war against the Jews. To his underlings, Frank quoted Hitler: "What we have now determined to be the leadership in Poland is to be liquidated, what grows back" should "be removed." With the invasion of France in May 1940, he continued, the Germans had become "completely indifferent" to their opponents' (accurate) "atrocity propaganda," since there was no reason any longer to mollify European public opinion. Victory in western Europe opened the way to launch the so-called Extraordinary Pacification Operation. "This will cost the lives of some thousands of Poles," mainly "members of the Polish intelligentsia," Frank explained at a police conference on May 30, 1940. "Gentlemen," he went on to say, "we are not murderers," yet Frank also did not want to "saddle the Reich concentration camps with our problems"; "suspected people are to be liquidated immediately," "on the spot." To conduct executions was "a terrible burden," Frank admitted, but "every police and SS Führer . . . has to be one-hundred percent certain that he is carrying out the judgment of the German nation."[49]

Raids and executions continued throughout the summer and fall of 1940. "One of the blackest days" of the action was August 12, 1940. "The net was spread over the whole city," wrote Ludwik Landau, a chronicler of the occupation of Warsaw. "German patrols stopped and searched pedestrians in the streets; they flagged down trams, turned out the passengers, examined their papers and detained those they were after. Riding in a tram down Marszałkowska Street, I was twice subjected to such a check." The "main element was surprise," so the number of victims caught was high; "everywhere one heard of someone having been caught" by the end of the day. Prisoners were interrogated at Gestapo headquarters on Szucha Street or the SS barracks on Podchorażych Street and sent to Warsaw's refurbished nineteenth-century prison, Pawiak, or to the newly opened concentration camp at Auschwitz, where the prisoners received the numbers 1,513 to 3,179 (sown onto the sleeves of their uniforms). Others were simply executed at the woods at Palmiry outside the city.[50] Throughout the occupation, German authorities and the Polish Blue (uniformed) Police conducted similar raids on streets, streetcars, and movie theaters to round up young men and women for forced labor in Germany.

The Germans were not everywhere, but the raids filled the atmosphere of Warsaw and other cities with a trembling sense of foreboding. "Every inhabitant," wrote one resident, "woke up fully alerted to it; he could sense it throughout the day in the streets, in workplaces, in cafes, even in churches; he went to sleep, continuously conscious of its existence, and bolted out of his bed, instantly awake, at the slightest sound in the street, in the house entrance, or in the stairway." "At any moment he could be caught in a street roundup."[51]

Frank prided himself on his brutal imperial "style." In 1943 he joked that he had "the honor to be Number 1" on "Mister Roosevelt's list of war criminals." Methods that "apply in the Reich," he insisted again and again, "by no means need to apply in the General Government." What were needed in the colony were "men who have the courage to carry out new assignments in a bold, new fashion." On one of the Advent Sundays before Christmas 1939, the newly installed German officials in Lublin whom Frank had recruited resolved among themselves to behave "like bastards" toward the Poles, "exactly the other way round than at home." In occupied Poland and especially in the annexed territories, Germans acted as absolute lords and masters, treating their subjects like "Polish pigs." "My pride," remembered Melita Maschmann, a young Berliner who worked as a young civilian volunteer in the East, "would not permit me to betray any human weakness vis-à-vis the Poles." She wore a "rigid mask," "cold armor."[52] There was a constant push to destroy any social relations between Poles and ethnic Germans, many of whom had been longtime neighbors.

In the annexed territories, the party even established official workshops to educate Germans as to their responsibilities as representatives of the master race.

The brutality of Germany's occupation policy ensured that the space for fraternization remained extremely limited as compared to France. Although the wall separating Germans and Poles was most impenetrable in the annexed territories, even in the General Government, German oc-cupiers expected a high degree of deference from Poles. Streetcars, or, as the *New York Times* put it, "Jim Crow" cars, were strictly segregated, with German and Polish sections. (Anatoly Kuznetzov, at the time a teenager in Kiev, remembered that "when I had read about the Negroes in books like *Uncle Tom's Cabin* and "Mister Twister" I never imagined I would one day have to ride in a tramcar in the same way.") On Królewska Street, one day in February 1940, when Hania Warfield attempted to enter the front of the car because the back was crowded, a German soldier grabbed her, called her "you Polish pig," and slapped her in the face. On another evening, Warfield was standing in the back of a streetcar going along Nowy Świat Street as more and more passengers got on. She saw an "old gentleman" pressed against the bar separating the Polish from the empty German section. He "glanced towards it several times, then hesitantly, lifted the bar and, with a look at the conductor, timidly seated himself in the forbidden part." Later, two "brown shirts" entered; "stretching their stocky legs, in their shiny black boots, they sprawled insolently," and when they caught sight of the gentleman, they asked "*Deutsch?*" and, when they realized he was not, "hit him in the face with such strength that the old man fell to the floor." These were the "metro stories" in Warsaw.[53] The exhibitionism of German victory involved not military bands and group song, as in France, but insolence, swagger, and contempt.

The dividing bar on the streetcar extended to all realms of daily life. Poles largely withdrew to modest cafés, *cukiernias*, the "only meeting places for friends and business associates," where one could get "a steam-ing cup of substitute tea or coffee and an almost genuine piece of pastry." As for the Germans, who were not allowed in Polish cafés, they settled in newly acquired spaces in the city center, from which Poles were barred. Wehrmacht soldiers were under orders: "Do not share a table with Poles!"

At one point, Klukowski returned to Szczebrzeszyn from Bilgoraj so disgusted that he had "a severe headache": "Everywhere there are new signs in German. Buildings have been taken over for German offices, stores, and clubs. New buildings have been built for German use. The streets are crowded with Germans and you hear only the German language." In Zamosc, "the beautiful Citizen's Club building is now the German officers' casino; the city movie theater is now a *Soldatenheim*; the brandnew building on the marketplace is the new *Deutschehaus*; the big Czerski building next to the cathedral is gestapo headquarters." "On both sides of Lwowska Street," Klukowski added, "the Jews are digging trenches and installing air-raid shelters."[54]

The "well-equipped and healthy," "smooth-shaven" Germans in "their trim, grey-green uniforms" with "shiny boots" at first took Poles talking in the *cukiernias* by surprise because, before the war, they had been told a great deal about the impoverished conditions in the Third Reich. But the Germans soon took on ominous roles in the Polish imagination. Although Poles did draw some distinctions among the Germans, finding younger ones to be more brutal than older ones, distinguishing "an eagle on the chest," the "good" army, from "the eagle on the armband," the "bad" SS, and considering any act of kindness "Austrian" rather than "Prussian"—on the whole, they came to regard German soldiers and occupation authorities simply as "they," or *Szwab* or *Panie tymczasowy* (temporary masters). In the spring of 1942, the Polish Home Army undertook an undercover survey of the eleven hundred Germans who came and went in the region around Mielau (Mława), north of Warsaw. Only nine Germans, including a pastor, a warehouse supervisor, two artisans, and three policemen, treated Polish residents decently. A much larger group of Germans acted like "Huns" and referred to Poles as pigs, while most others simply took advantage of their status as "occupiers and victors." The prisons at Pawiak and Auschwitz, the death notices, and the executions at Palmiry convinced more and more Polish observers that the Germans considered the Poles to be "the most dangerous historical enemies," not only to be treated without kindness but also to be wiped off the "face of the earth." From the vantage point of the "German houses," meanwhile, the Poles appeared to be silently insolent or overly obsequious.

"Hate and enmity" "sat in the eyes" and "resonated with each word," recalled a German teacher serving in the Wartheland.[55] Eventually, these suspicions gave way to trepidation, as the posted regulations against any social contact with Poles were extended to warnings about assaults and going out at night.

The only way to cross the line that separated Poles from Germans was to become a German, as surprising numbers of so-called racially redeemable Poles did in 1939 and 1940. The Germans were in fact anxious to reclaim hidden German bloodlines for the Reich that they determined on the basis of cultural or political bearing or physical physiognomy. Those Poles willing to reclassify themselves as Germans in racial selections secured for themselves the benefits of German citizenship, German rations, and employment, and in the annexed territories they could hold on to their farms, but all at the cost of renouncing contact with former friends and neighbors. Germany's need for soldiers on the eastern front and settlers to fill the new "living space" eventually made these conversions increasingly coerced affairs. By 1943, with the onset of partisan warfare, the advantages of being German had become rather dubious, and circumstances would compel many of the "new Germans" to share the fate of the old Germans in the evacuations that followed the steady westward retreat of the Wehrmacht in 1944 and 1945.

Eventually, Frank grew impatient with those "valiant warriors who were absolutely determined to destroy the Poles," the very Germans he had initially encouraged, a development that indicates just how gratuitous German violence in the General Government had become. Simply on practical grounds, Frank took issue with Nazi officials who thought that Germany's task should take the form of a vast "machine-gunning extermination campaign." "After all we can't murder 14,000,000 Poles" he argued. "We don't have the men to carry out such a mission." Economic stability and internal security became more and more important to Frank once the German invasion of the Soviet Union in June 1941 allowed him to upgrade his dominion from "borderland" to heartland. With the eastward expansion of the borders of the German empire, the General Government no longer occupied the frontier but had moved closer, in Frank's words, to becoming "the very heart of greater German power."[56]

The recentering of the territory coincided with Frank's intentions to Germanize the General Government and make it an integral and productive part of the Reich. He dreamed of the day when the Vistula would be as German as the Rhine. At least as long as the war continued, he opposed policies that would undermine the goods and services his territories provided the Reich. If the choice was to be "extermination" instead of labor, he wanted to know who would staff the East Railway and move trains to the eastern front or deliver the annual 450,000 tons of grain and 500,000 liters of vodka to Germany. "Politics is more than violence," he asserted. For Frank's pretensions to statesmanship, SS officials derided him as the "King of Poland." They laughed at his "Frankreich." An official from the Reich Chancellery in Berlin reminded him that "rulers" in places like Kraków had to impose a consistent policy and could not have "clean hands."[57] It says a great deal about the Nazis that they thought Hans Frank had gone soft.

The occupation of Poland was the continuation of war, but this time a war against Polish civilians, Polish elites, and Polish Jews. The state of siege eventually laid the foundations for the most dense resistance network in Europe and the reconstitution of a "secret state" and a "secret society." But if the German occupiers drastically limited the parameters of collaboration and accommodation with their unceasing brutality, they also shaped the resistance that, for the first years, struggled with the difficulties of organizing a demoralized and frightened population. The bitter cold winters, the loss of social amenities, the scramble for food, and the fear of arrest created an increasingly atomized population. "Life takes place in silence," wrote novelist Zofia Nałkowska at the end of 1939. Six months later, Ludwik Landau made the same observation: "Nothing interrupts the silence." The early resistance fighter Jan Karski believed his landlady, "Mrs. Nowak," to be typical of Poles in the terrible years 1939 and 1940. "She had sold nearly every article of value to pay for goods" for herself and her son, Zygmus. Her days were spent "hunting for a bargain in bread or a pinch of margarine." After "many toilsome hours," "she once told me, 'I fall asleep as though I had been drugged.'" Observing his small town, Zygmunt Klukowski agreed: "People live completely occupied by their own personal problems and the struggle for food." The food itself was of poor quality: "The little loaf of bread that one buys with ration tickets smells moldy, the crust is soft, the dough is spongy, damp, and gluey. It tastes bitter and acidic, like one part soaked newspaper and one part old dustrag." Again and again, observers described men and women trudging through city streets and train stations; the bags of food they clutched appeared as burdens that kept them from understanding the wider situation or joining the resistance. People appeared trapped by day-to-day necessities.[58]

Fear of the Germans was also paralyzing. "The only things that can disturb me are nightmares," recounted Mrs. Nowak, "loud voices in the street, a bell ringing, or heavy steps on the stairs. Often one of these wakes me and I jump to my feet—my blood running cold and my heart beating wildly. . . . I stand next to my bed, rooted to the spot, listening, waiting for the Gestapo to come and separate me from my boy." For others, the "constant news about arrests, executions, death in concentration camps, and torture in prison" made it impossible to concentrate. "We are exhausted. Life is nerve shattering. We are living in uncertainty about what will happen to us, not in a month or a week, but in one hour," concluded Klukowski.[59]

In these circumstances, crime and alcoholism and general antisocial behavior soared. "Under the occupation," lamented one patriot, "the Polish people drank more liquor than before the war. . . . The desire to escape the grim reality, uncertainty about the future, and the feeling that death might come any day produced an atmosphere of hopelessness which was overcome by heavy drinking." There were "shady characters everywhere," offering their homemade "bimber": "vodka, vodka, vodka." By 1942 there were more than five hundred bars and cafés in Warsaw, many times more than in 1940. "From the 'Fregata' it was only a stone's throw to the 'Nectar' in St. Cross Street," and along the way "one passed a bar called 'Behind the Curtain.'" "A few steps from the 'Nectar' brought one to 'The Shilling,' in Marshall Street."[60] The underground press warned ceaselessly against the dangers of alcohol and the dispiriting impulse to drown one's sorrows, which was a little bit like signing a private armistice with fate instead of struggling against misfortune by collectively resisting the Germans.

In these debilitating circumstances, Polish patriots warned against the collaboration of Poles with Germans. Zygmunt Klukowski noted that in the first weeks of the occupation, "some of the girls" in Szczebrzeszyn were "having very intimate relations with the Germans." Several months later, a leaflet identified one of them, Leokadia Hascowna, a grammar school teacher. In Warsaw underground newspapers issued warnings, for example, to "the lady" who "drank wine with a German in the 'Paradise' yesterday"; "next time we will publish her name." The underground press eventually published "ten commandments for the civil struggle" that called for "an absolute boycott of cultural, social, and business relations." In any event, the collaborationist "reptile press" such as the *New Warsaw Courier* enjoyed growing circulation, and people continued to flock to movie theaters, despite a targeted campaign against "swine" who go to the "cinema" (the words rhyme in Polish).[61] It is unlikely that Polish shame was gendered, but Klukowski believed that women were more likely to inform on Poles for possessing weapons or hiding Polish officers. The Germans certainly believed Poles could easily be bribed with money or alcohol.[62] Later on, after 1942, when German policy against the Jews turned murderous, the most frequent victims of denunciation and blackmail threatened by so-called *Schmaltovniks* were not Poles working for the underground or peasants involved in the black market but Polish Jews.

In Poland, as elsewhere, Germans relied on local administrative forces: county-level civil servants as well as mayors and village heads in the General Government were largely Polish (except for Galicia, where Ukrainians predominated); fewer than one in five towns had German mayors (and even less in Galicia). The number of Poles who worked in Warsaw's city government increased from twenty to thirty thousand, many of them in the social welfare apparatus. These individuals needed to establish some sort of relations with the German occupiers. In addition, the Germans required the cooperation of the police, about twelve thousand men and later sixteen thousand, who, reconstituted as the Polish Blue Police, were expected, as Frank put it, "to unconditionally send their fellow countrymen to their doom." They generally met German expectations, especially when it came to anti-Jewish actions in 1942 and 1943. Less reliable were the fifty thousand or so Poles who worked for the East

Railway. Some joined the resistance; many more used their positions to steal from the Germans and sell tools, coal, and other goods on the black market.[63]

Zygmunt Klukowski was surprised when Jan Franczak, Szczebrz-eszyn's acting mayor, who had been so "very loyal" that he had invited German officers to a party celebrating the birth of his first grandson in January 1940, was arrested along with the principal of the high school in June, undoubtedly as part of the "Extraordinary Pacification Operation." Franczak was released six months later after a forced march through German prisons in Zamosc, Lublin, Oranienburg, and Dachau, which left him a "complete wreck, both physically and mentally"; he "looks terrible, and his feet are so badly swollen that he cannot wear shoes." What Klukowski regarded as a "surprising" turn of events became standard operating procedure.[64]

Peasants benefited from the yawning gap between the supply of food and the demand for it, and many were predisposed to accommodate themselves to German rule, but whenever German officials arrived in the villages to enforce food quotas, peasants found themselves insulted as "Polish pigs" (the second word seemed to self-evidently follow the first) or beaten, even killed; food-quota committees were often arrested en masse and sent to concentration camps. In addition to the food quotas, higher taxes, rising criminality, and later partisan activity threatened "the timeworn patterns of life" in the village on which peasant acquiescence to German rule was predicated.[65] Everything in the occupation regime, from its ostentatious brutality to the labor corvées, pushed Poles into the resistance.

Fear, demoralization, and the constant struggle to acquire food, as well as the destruction of the structures of civil society such as clubs, schools, and courts, all weakened the bonds of solidarity and cooperation. It took some time before the underground resistance movement overcame these corrosive circumstances. The increasing fierceness of the Nazis also induced more Poles to live as outlaws in the underground. The sheer violence of the occupation regime created an extremely sinister perception of the Germans, but it also accelerated the dynamic of self-containment in the underground. It fortified suspicions of foreigners, outsiders, and strangers. Much of the time, Polish resistance operations resembled a "secret self-help society." Underground groups, which described themselves as a "circle," "square," "triangle," or "rectangle," protected their own members first and undertook operations only close to home.[66]

However fragmented, the underground resistance revived Catholic conceptions of Polish suffering and martyrdom and of a besieged, pure Polish nation. It benefited from a history of Polish conspiracies going back to 1863. Many activists, including Klukowski, had rebelled against the Russians in 1905 and revived underground traditions by building clandestine civic structures. As soon as the war was lost in 1939, Klukowski began to read patriotic literature: first Stefan Zeromski's *The Ashes*, since he could not immediately put his hands on Henryk Sienkiewicz's trilogy, consisting of *With Fire and Sword*, about the Cossack Chmielnicki Uprising; *The Deluge*, set against Sweden's invasion of Poland; and *Fire in the Steppe*, which followed Poland's war with the Ottoman Empire. Each part of Sienkiewicz's trilogy lingered over seventeenth-century threats to the Polish nation from the North, the East, and the South, just as twentieth-century Poland had been invaded by both Germany and the Soviet Union in September 1939. Ethnic existence amounted to survival in an ongoing war of all against all. Sienkiewicz and his readers stressed the continuity of Poland's martyrdom and Germany's depredations, "from the Teutonic Knights to Hitler."[67] War in 1939 confirmed rather than "made" history, and despite the suffering Klukowski and a great many other Poles firmly believed that Germany's victories were merely "provisional," while Poland's resurrection, "our final victory," was certain.

There was a ready-made topography of martyrdom. Palmiry, where about 2,000 residents of Warsaw were executed through the summer of 1941; Pawiak, in which more than 100,000 were imprisoned over the course of the war; and Auschwitz, to which a total of more than 150,000 non-Jewish Poles were sent, became widely known sites of national suffering. These locations fitted easily into established traditions of Polish suffering at the hands of foreign occupation. Polish resistance heroes had been imprisoned in Pawiak in 1863 and again in 1905 (the subject of Ryszard Ordynski's patriotic 1931 film, *The Ten from the Pawiak Prison*). And

Auschwitz was the new Siberia. While Nazi terror in 1940 decimated the ranks of the underground, it also upholstered Polish patriotic traditions; it was sadly recognizable as Polish history.[68] Concepts like the "ancien régime," "old time" and "new time," or a dawning "authoritarian age," which dominated thinking in France and Switzerland, made no impact on Polish conceptions of history. The resistance knew exactly what time it was; it was the age-old time of Poland's marytrdom, an interlude of the dark followed by the light.

The image of Klukowski devouring one Sienkiewicz novel after another in the fall of 1939 suggests the living quality of Polish history. This history was highly defensive; it described a permanent state of siege in which Poland was beset by foreigners, the Cossacks, the Ukrainians, the Swedes, the Russians, and now the Germans. In this sense, it produced a Polish resistance that was self-strengthening but also more self-containing and more suspicious, unlike the more heterogeneous, republican character of the French Resistance. The prevailing account of Polish history did not intersect with the history of other citizens of Poland such as the Jews—for all his popularity, Sienkiewicz was not widely read by Polish Jews. The distinctive Catholic imagery of Polish nationalists, who drew a parallel between the sufferings of Christ and the sufferings of Poland, was of little use to Jewish participants in the Polish struggle. Indeed, the uniform oath that bound together the various parts of the Union for Armed Struggle in fall 1940 read as follows: "Before God the Almighty, before the Virgin Mary, crowned Queen of Poland, I lay my hand on this holy cross, the symbol of martyrdom and redemption, and swear that I will defend the honor of Poland with all my might so that Poland will be released from slavery."[69]

Because the violence of the German occupation precluded collaboration, the anti-German front was extremely broad politically and included extreme Polish nationalists and anti-Semites. It was as if de Gaulle's movement in France had included characters like fascist Robert Brasillach. Alexander Smolar described the paradox of the Polish situation: the behavior of "the invader served to unite organizations and parties that before the war had nothing at all in common." Whereas elsewhere in Europe resistance was, "as a rule, anti-fascist, democratic, and

anti-antisemitic," in Poland anti-Semitism was "compatible with patriotism (a correlation considerably strengthened under the Soviet occupation
in 1939–1941) and also with democracy." Because it was "not tainted by
any trace of collaboration with the Germans, it could prosper—not only
in the street, but also in the underground press, in political parties, and
in the armed forces." In Auschwitz the imprisoned Poles were the only
national group whose ranks included fascists because everywhere else
anti-Semites tended to work cooperatively with the Nazis and thus were
not imprisoned for anti-Nazi activities.[70]

The graffiti on the walls of Warsaw's buildings, *Polska Zyje* (Poland
lives), *Polska Zwyciezy* (Poland will win), and *Polska Walczaca* (Fighting Poland) denoted a Poland that was much more socially inclusive and socially
responsible than the prewar governments in the 1930s. The underground
celebrated the "masses" and the "people" and relied less exclusively on
the aristocracy or the intellectuals, whom the Germans had targeted for
liquidation in any case, but it remained ethnically exclusive.[71] As a result,
the underground saw past Polish Jews. The Jews, the great majority of
whom were slaughtered by the Germans, were not part of the overall
story of Poland's martyrdom, as the resistance would tell it.

THE EXTENSIVE RUINS OF THE CITY OF WARSAW IN THE FALL OF 1939
provided the backdrop to the occupation that lasted four long years. The
Germans thoroughly destroyed civil society and liquidated the Polish
leaders who had guided it. This collapse created dispiriting conditions
in which the black market, shadowy clubs, and crime prospered. People
just wanted to survive, and they generally looked out for themselves. Yet
the extreme violence of the occupation also steadily produced resistance
fighters who filled the ranks of a broad-based people's movement. Because they operated in local precincts, however, they also remained widely
scattered on the ground, fragmented in many pieces with diverse political aims, and were suspicious of outsiders and particularly Jews, the
very group who became the target for absolute elimination. The resistance placed itself in the heroic history of Polish martyrs who had risen
up against outside invaders over the course of hundreds of years, but

on closer examination it hardly reflected the noble record it sought to
emulate.

By contrast, the German occupation in France was a more multi-
faceted, less oppressive affair and produced a more complex mixture of
accommodation, collaboration, and resistance. At least at the beginning,
there was little confidence in the fundamentals of French history, which
gave more legitimacy to the idea of a new authoritarian age in Paris than
in Warsaw. The history that France shared with Germany, particularly the
harrowing experience of World War I, made it possible to distinguish
"good Germans" from bad, creating French suspicions about French
motivations that never entirely disappeared. Nonetheless, there was little
love for the German soldiers on French soil, and this fact placed limits on
what Vichy could achieve and eventually created more and more goodwill
for the republican resistance that slowly established itself.

Although German occupations could look quite different, and civilian
responses varied, there was always an element of compromise or concession, of self-doubt and self-reproach, as people realized that tough
repression hardly built good character. Wherever the Nazis passed, they
called up feelings of contempt and disdain, but also feelings of envy, a
sense of powerlessness, and temptations of treacherousness. Wherever
the Nazis passed, the weak became weaker and suffered more. Wherever
the Nazis passed, Jews would find themselves endangered on all sides,
trapped by the evil intentions of the victors and the shortcomings and
preoccupations of the vanquished.

5

Journey to Russia

IT IS REMARKABLE HOW OFTEN FRENCH ACCOUNTS CAST THE DEPAR-
ture of German soldiers for the eastern front, after the German invasion
of the Soviet Union in June 1941, as tragedy. In Vercors's *The Silence of the
Sea*, it was the German officer Ebrennac's disillusionment with the German mission in France combined with his decision to sacrifice himself
in the "hell" of Russia that finally broke the silence of the two French
patriots and elicited the niece's "Adieu." In Jean-Louis Bory's novel *Mon
village à l'heure allemande*, the fact that the former occupiers of "my village"
undoubtedly met their deaths in the faraway offensives strikes a note more
sorrowful than spiteful. In *The Forests of the Night*, Jean-Louis Curtis sent
Friedrich Rustiger, a German officer with a Jewish grandmother, to Russia.
The fate is not deserved, since Curtis deliberately made the character to be
as much a Jewish victim as a German aggressor. In the very last lines of
her novel *Suite Française*, Irène Némirovsky described the departure of soldiers from France in a folksy manner that deliberately evoked Leo Tolstoy,
writing of "the Red Cross vans, with no passengers—for now." These
were followed by "the field kitchen, bumping along at the end of the procession like a saucepan tied to a dog's tail. The men began singing, a grave,
slow song that drifted way into the night. Soon the road was empty. All
that remained of the German regiment was a little cloud of dust."[1] The
mood of untimely, unnecessary death lingers. The scene is tragic.

Némirovsky hoped to make Tolstoy her model. She made notes to
herself to "reread Tolstoy," the master nineteenth-century novelist whose
1869 novel, *War and Peace*, brought a full range of characters onto the

historical stage to depict the impact of the French invasion of Russia in 1812. Némirovsky took pains to humanize her characters by bringing them into association with everyday objects like the saucepan. The "little cloud of dust" evokes the blustery, opaque wartime circumstances that have thrown together different sorts of individuals, the rich and the poor, German and French, Bruno and Lucile, in ways that create new sorts of contact, much like the battlefield encounters at Borodino in *War and Peace*. Once sent to Russia in 1941, German soldiers became, in Némirovsky's eyes, more like the French civilians they had vanquished in 1940 and more like characters in Tolstoy. In fact, in notes for new installments to her unfinished epic cycle, Némirovsky wrote that "parallel to" the death of the virtuous French soldier Jean-Marie Michaud, she "must show the death of the German in Russia, the two full of sorrowful nobility." "Must." Like Tolstoy, the novels Némirovsky envisioned were deliberately reconciliatory, moving from "storm" to "peace" and putting individuals into comparable situations marked by the inability to determine the course of events or anticipate responses. Like Tolstoy, Némirovsky located virtue in simplicity and humility.[2]

As she pieced together the meaning of the German war against the Soviet Union, Némirovsky was hardly the only one thinking about Tolstoy. Jean Guéhenno began rereading *War and Peace* in January 1941. Charles Rist found reading the novel in November 1942 "ever more satisfying in light of events." World history caught up with writer Mihail Sebastian in July 1941: "I have been reading in *War and Peace* the episode of the fall of Smolensk in August 1812—and just as I read, the same battle takes place in front of the same Smolensk, 129 years later." Both cities were on fire— the Smolensk of 1812 and the Smolensk of 1941. After September 14, however, the date Napoleon entered Moscow, Sebastian noted that "from now on, Hitler is lagging behind the 1812 schedule."[3] Sebastian was one of the first observers to introduce the theme that Hitler was not simply following Napoleon into the Russian winter, but was not even keeping up with him. Hitler told his confederates that the inescapable comparisons about the crossing of the Niemen did not apply; he was not Napoleon. "History does not repeat itself," insisted the slick propaganda magazine *Signal*. With the invasion of Russia, however, it was difficult not to make comparisons between 1941 and 1812. It was almost impossible to find *War and Peace* in a London bookstore. For a time, the novel was allegedly the most read book in Germany. No other book was checked out from Vilna's ghetto library in 1942 as often as *War and Peace*—"despite the long waiting list for the multi-volume edition." Demand for Tolstoy there increased by more than 600 percent after the German invasion.[4] In July 1942, Alexandra Epstein wrote to a friend from the assembly camp for Jews at Drancy, listing the things she was taking with her on her involuntary journey to the East: "warm gloves, grey pullover, red triangle, small mirror, toothbrush (hard), shoelaces, knickers, petticoats, bra, books especially, I packed 4 volumes of Tolstoy, woolen socks, winter overcoat."[5]

Readers usually picked up Tolstoy because they were haunted by the parallels between Napoleon's and Hitler's invasions and wanted to find clues to the outcome of the present-day engagement; a Wehrmacht general in Russia asked his first lieutenant, who was planning to visit a bookstore in Smolensk, for "the thickest book about Napoleon's campaign in Russia!" Some readers found the outsize role of fate and surprise on the battlefield in *War and Peace* fascinating; Tolstoy provided both an explanation for and relief from an overwhelming sense of powerlessness. Others took comfort in "the powerful resistance of the Russian people." Fighting an increasingly defensive war on the eastern front in 1943, German soldier Kurt Erichson appreciated Tolstoy's arguments regarding the "unavoidable falseness of representation." According to Emanuel Ringelblum, who reported on what was being read in the Warsaw Ghetto, Jews "love to read about Napoleon because his story proves that the star of the dictator, the so-called 'invincible' man, fades inevitably, and much faster than anyone could ever imagine."[6]

Not all readers, and certainly not Jewish readers, mistook Hitler (the "Cursed One," in Ringelblum's words) for Napoleon, but the search for parallels between 1812 and 1941 as well as the parallel reading programs among very different kinds of readers from London to Smolensk indicated the legitimacy of Tolstoy's basic premise about the fog of war. As Tolstoy would have it, all participants in war were shaped by similar experiences of madness, helplessness, and demoralization; as they faltered, they could be portrayed without sentimentality, but also with sympathy for the ordinary. With the invasion of Russia, World War II entered a new phase—what Churchill referred to as the "deep, slow-moving tides" of a long engagement—that appeared to make Germans and others increasingly alike. In a matter of months after the German offensive began, Soviet counterattacks put an end to the blitzkrieg campaigns. The balance of power shifted, as Germany's invincibility gave way to more complex and messy calculations. It was not so much that the Allies had gained what Germany had suddenly lost; rather, Germany's unique power to dictate the terms of the war dissolved into a confused repertoire of mixed motivation, unintended consequence, and accident. The various combatants now "engaged" with each other as if they were in a great storm or heavy fog. They faltered, producing the kinds of situations that Tolstoy had probed carefully to ascertain the nature of war. Tolstoy's *War and Peace* seemed to be a very appropriate guide to what one scholar referred to as the new "inexhaustible openness of events." Tolstoy gave readers a better sense of Germany's gamble, and across Europe readers came to find that the events of 1941 gave renewed credibility to Tolstoy's account of the incidents of 1812.[7]

Tolstoy popularized the literary convention of following the common threads of humanity in all its repugnant and noble forms across the battlefield. In one example of how contemporaries embraced Tolstoy's style, one Swiss journalist walked off the "via dolorosa" in the aftermath of an engagement. "The brief army communique reported two to three divisions destroyed." But "as we hesitantly venture along the forest path," "the battlefield still lives as a bloody heap, where only a few hours ago the dead succumbed to their wounds." "For seven kilometers an uninterrupted tangle of mutilated corpses, dead dogs, shot-up and undamaged vehicles, tractors, weaponry, uniforms, medical equipment, and paper, a great deal of paper—the notebooks and letters of soldiers, here and there a poem. A tambourine and a harmonica lie underneath a smashed wagon; these soldiers had once sang and laughed on bright summer evenings."[8] Here war is depicted as the accumulation of the untimely deaths of ordinary men.

The young Polish writer Czeslaw Milosz read Tolstoy in a slightly different way. Wandering among the "ruins and ashes" of Warsaw, writing his impressions in notebooks, Milosz was struck not by the misfortune of dying but the ferocious embrace of killing. For Milosz, war was a state of alien being. In considering *War and Peace*, he focused on Tolstoy's unlikely and ungainly hero, Pierre Bezukhov, the illegitimate son of a nobleman, who in the summer of 1812 threw himself into the melee with an "excitement bordering on madness." Dressed as a peasant, Bezukhov hoped to save Russia by assassinating Napoleon. According to Milosz, such "madness" prevailed in the summer of 1939 as well. With the "frenzied movements" of refugees on the road, the abandonment of homes, and the slaughter of civilians, "everything collapsed," and, in Tolstoy's words, "became a heap of meaningless rubbish." Pierre's "faith in the purposeful design of the work, in humanity, in his own soul, and in God, had suddenly died," summarizes Milosz. For him, "everything" in the present day was not restricted to just Poland but included Germany too, and indeed all of Europe: "the cruelty of human beings that is identical in its results with the cruelty of nature; the ease with which in one second a sentient, thinking creature turns into a dead object; the treatment of individuals . . . as toys to be destroyed, thrown from place to place."

As Milosz examined the situation in 1812 (and 1939), without the framework of civilization Pierre, just like many of Milosz's contemporaries, "falls into a stupor, a completely vegetative state." "More active and crafty" individuals succumbed to "completely cynical activity," "since nothing enduring exists." They became "indifferent to murder." Also dangerous were those who found a comfortable existence "in the ruins of the ethical world, in the ruins of faith." Many turned to worship their "own tribe against the enemy tribe" in "place of the overthrown gods." However, in one scene pointed out by Milosz, the general loss of faith, the extensive collapse of structure, was relieved by Tolstoy's introduction of the "simple peasant Platon Karataev," who shared Pierre's pallet in a French prisoner-of-war camp. Platon revealed to Pierre the possibility of loving "one's neighbor." "A touch of a hand," Milosz wrote about his own times, "the word of a prison cell mate, will break down difference and enmity." It will again "raise man aloft."

Milosz insisted on keeping the "altar of suffering" of all "mankind" in view, seeking to "renew" the entire "tradition of Western Christianity."

He emphasized not only the parallels between 1812 and 1939 but also those between Germans and Poles. To have introduced telling national distinctions in his analysis would have short-circuited the movement from Pierre to Platon, from hallucination to touch. To dwell only on bad Germans and good Poles would have endlessly reproduced Pierre's "excitement bordering on madness." There was no specific geography to the "intellectual disarmament" or the "captive mind" that Czeslaw Milosz diagnosed. Yet reading Milosz after many decades, one cannot but feel Germany's heavy hand in the crimes. The examples Milosz summoned up in "The Experience of War" lined up in a way that simulated the dire situation in Warsaw where the young Catholic writer lived: the false gods were mostly German, the cell mates Polish.[9] Milosz's parallels to indict and to redeem all of humanity are somewhat misleading because the evidence of the actual war simply does not permit the dissolution of the German and the Polish into a single exemplary case.

Tolstoy's *War and Peace* was much read during World War II because it refused to be a simple patriotic text for any one nation, creating recognizable situations for readers as disparate as Polish patriot Czeslaw Milosz and German soldier Kurt Erichson. It disavowed the rudeness of national character. It declined history's imperious periodization of new time. This refusal was the novel's strength, particularly after Germany's blitzkrieg campaigns in Russia came to a full stop at the end of 1941. Readers could imagine new possibilities and new combinations. At the same time, the novel's even-handedness had a major drawback. Nothing in the events of 1812 could compare to Germany's single-minded violence against Russian prisoners of war or its implementation of the "final solution" against the Jews. Pierre and Platon, Poles and Germans, and Christians and Jews could not, in fact, easily stand in for one another as actors portraying universal themes before "altars," amid "tides," and in scenes of five-act theater. As observers took up *War and Peace* in 1941, Tolstoy was both helpful and unhelpful: it suggested precedents for the hesitant "Adieu" in Vercors's family room outside Paris or Bruno and Lucile's cooled leave taking in Irène Némirovsky's "Bussy," but not for Zygmunt Klukowski's account in his diary of the forced labor of his Jewish neighbors at German airfields outside Szczebrzeszyn. In the end, the parallels that gave structure to Tolstoy's "4 volumes" fell apart in Smolensk, the very place where he had first drawn them. Smolensk in 1941 was not Smolensk in 1812.

Smolensk 1941

IT WAS IN SMOLENSK IN OCTOBER 1941 THAT THE NURSES AND DOCtors of the Swiss Medical Mission caught up with the German forces in their push east into Russia. The medical mission, under the auspices of the Swiss Red Cross, was initially organized as a kind of Swiss peace offering to the Germans, who had become increasingly impatient with the studiousness of Swiss neutrality and the generally critical stance of most Swiss newspapers. In their journey to Russia, the Swiss nurses and doctors did not see the tragic, deadly embrace of two flawed but human opponents on the battlefield. They increasingly defined themselves in contrast to the Germans' celebration of hard, even merciless, violence. They expressed shock at the actions of the Germans, whose language and culture they in large part shared.

At first, the Swiss team had a basically chummy relationship with the German soldiers they encountered, as they sang, joked, and flirted together. But over time, these Swiss and German cousins felt out of sorts with one another; the Swiss increasingly found the Third Reich too totalitarian, while the Germans believed themselves to be misunderstood. This combination of intimacy and growing distance made the Germans loquacious. They were eager to talk and to explain themselves, and the Swiss were sufficiently surprised by what they heard to keep careful records, which survive in the writings of at least eight diarists. Although the Swiss were strictly forbidden to have "discussions of a political nature," as Wehrmacht and SS personnel became increasingly plainspoken about their willingness to accept extreme violence and about the place of the Jews in the "new Europe," the Swiss grew more argumentative, a forth-and-back that generated an extraordinary record of Nazi self-justification.[10]

The organizer of the voluntary commission, surgeon Eugen Bircher moved in pro-German circles around Hans Fröhlicher, the Swiss ambassador in Berlin ("The Swiss would be more happy if Happier [Fröhlicher in German] was more Swiss" went the joke), and he hoped to win greater Swiss understanding and support for Germany's anticommunist struggle in the East. But most of the doctors and nurses who signed up did so for humanitarian and educational reasons, "in the spirit of Henri Dunant" (one of the founders of the International Red Cross) or simply for the adventure. The cover of Simone von Wurstenberger's scrapbook of her trip featured exciting words arranged in modernist collage—"Warszawa, Warsaw, Res.-Base Hospital VII, Warsaw, Battle, Soviet, Major Offensive, Germany, Rollbahn! U.S.S.R., Deloused! Free of Bugs and Communicable Diseases, Stuka, Shellfire, The Front"—and paired a Prussian eagle holding a swastika with the red star and hammer and sickle of the Soviet Union.[11] The scrapbook represented the mission as a pell-mell of exciting war experiences, not as a contribution to the German cause.

At first the trip went well. Arriving in Berlin on October 17, 1941, the company set out to "conquer" the capital: "Funny, how so many of the male members of the mission eventually met up again in 'Haus Vaterland,' the big entertainment emporium" on Potsdamer Platz. The hospital train that left the next day for Smolensk was comfortable: "We were two to a compartment in upholstered seats." The hours were passed with games and lectures. The doctors sought "new friendships" and went over to get to know the nurses better. "Overall we are astonished," wrote Elsi Eichenberger, a twenty-nine-year-old nurse, "soup, asparagus, meat, and rice for lunch," and also a glass of wine, and in the evening "fish, meat spreads, bread and butter, and tea," delicacies that were difficult to get in wartime. In fact, the goods were nicknamed "French inheritance," because many had been plundered from occupied France. The good cheer lasted into the night: "We mostly stayed together until the radio played the song 'Lili Marleen,'" a favorite of the Germans, "to which we quietly sang along." But the Swiss responded to the German greeting "Heil Hitler" with "Grüss Gott"—"Good day." "Oh, how that sounds, 'Grüss Gott,'" remarked one of the German doctors, "a ring from the old days. Totally charming, my little girl."[12]

There was even a touch of Tolstoy. On October 23, shortly after midnight, the train crossed the Beresina River, where thousands of Swiss mercenaries had defended Napoleon's rear during the chaotic retreat in late November 1812. Most never returned—it was Switzerland's greatest military disaster in modern times. Awakened, the doctors and nurses pressed their faces against the windows from which they saw the "river as big as the Rhine in the moonlight," and together they sang the "*Beresina Lied*," which Swiss countrymen all knew well:

> Our life resembles a journey
> Of a wanderer through the night;
> Everybody carries something
> That causes him to grieve.[13]

Very quickly, however, a much more gruesome view of history unfolded before the Swiss volunteers who passed all the train stations of the cross in the terrible year 1941. As the doctors and nurses traveled from Warsaw to Minsk and on to Orsha and Smolensk, the train slowed down: "We travel for 1 or 2 hours and then stop for 3 to 4 hours." The signs of war accumulated. "We see supply trains of every kind passing by in both directions." Along the road that paralleled the tracks, motorcycles and trucks picked their way through piles of rubble: "a fully burnt-out train on the tracks . . . rusted locomotives, cars, trucks, tanks, telephone poles and wires." Barefoot children ran along the slow-moving train, begging for bread and cigarettes. Cemeteries for fallen German soldiers dotted the way. Elsi Eichenberger noted the "hospital trains" that "speed past us." At one point, the Swiss were able to hand cigarettes to soldiers, who told them they were "crazy" to come to Russia, "this pig-sty of a country."[14]

Still in the rear, the journey was interrupted by a long train "loaded with garbage. Old men and half-grown boys, who all wear a yellow-brown Jewish star on the right side, busy themselves with shovels." The Swiss diarists expressed shock at the sight of trains filled with Russian prisoners of war. Between Orsha and Smolensk, four or five such trains passed every day, each one with "20–50 freight cars, some open, some closed." "The sight is nightmarish," commented Ernst Gerber, a doctor. "It was as if they had been loaded from the field of battle like cattle. Unkempt beards and dirt disfigure their faces. Mongols, Ruthenians, Ukrainians— everything that we think of as Russian is represented." The Swiss were startled by the corpses lying along the tracks. "Those are Russians," explained the train commander, "who died while being transported in the cattle and coal cars and were thrown out when the transport slowed down." "Basta! An easy funeral, free-of-charge," he added. The Swiss started to count the bodies, which numbered in the hundreds. Even before they had reached Minsk, the Swiss doctors and nurses heard shots fired at night and then saw what the Germans identified as dead partisans lying along the tracks the next morning. Hundreds of trains traveled the route from Warsaw to Smolensk, but it was the Swiss cousins who noticed the scale of death in the German war.[15]

The depressing sights prompted some of the volunteers on the mission to sit out the evening song. The commander, Eugen Bircher, scolded the women, pointing out that singing and soldiering belonged together. "Haven't you understood the life of a soldier yet?" he asked. "You have to be jolly for as long as you can. Being a soldier means raising your spirits, laughing, making yourself helpful, lending a hand." Then the commander came to the point. "Whether you believe it or not, you have to be hard," and that was "something we don't understand at home." In Bircher's view, the singing should get louder as the sights along the route from Minsk to Smolensk became more gruesome. A German nurse "jubilantly" pointed out another passing train with Russian prisoners of war, "penned in like chickens in a cage," but her Swiss colleague asked her not to bring "all that misery" to her attention: "Otherwise how else could I sing on command?"[16] The ironic tone measured the growing distance between the Swiss and the Germans, as the latter embraced the discipline of hardness.

The Germans made a point of displaying the hardness they had learned and their willingness to use and even exult in violence all along the mission's journey to Smolensk. In response, the Swiss diarists recorded unsettling revelations about the central role of killing in German conduct in the occupied territories of the Soviet Union. The talk between cousins was much more open than the more guarded and infrequent references to the deaths of Jews, partisans, and other civilians in soldiers' letters or in the secretly taped discussions among Germans held prisoner by the Allies. The showmanship of death began in Minsk and never let up, ending only on the return journey after several Swiss nurses and doctors had toured the Warsaw Ghetto and boarded the train back to Berlin and home. Albert Oeri, the editor of the *Basler Nachrichten*, was not wrong to refer to the Swiss venture as a "swastika mission."[17]

As the train sat in Minsk, one Wehrmacht soldier was brutally frank about the murder of Jews. "The Jews," Elsi was told, "they are fast disappearing. We already bumped off 1,600. There are just thirty left, mostly shoemakers and handymen. For now they have to work for us, then it will be their turn. They are rounded up, have to dig deep ditches, and then 'piff-paff.' And all of them, the elderly and children." The German soldier explained that "we have had more than enough of that lot." The violence was both self-evident ("piff-paff") and spectacular ("bumped off 1,600").[18]

Out for a walk after they had finally arrived in Smolensk, two Swiss doctors, Bucher and Weber, came across a detail of six Jews, some wearing high heels and fur coats, hacking at the frozen ground with "scarred hands." The Swiss "allowed themselves" to engage the "annoyed" guard in conversation. Looking around cautiously, the German confided to the doctors: "You know, these poor devils—the whole thing disgusts me. As far as I am concerned, they can live, but I don't call the shots around here." But when confronted with the doctor's plea to "throw the musket away!" the guard replied: "You can lick my . . . I'd get shot myself." In this case, the equation came down to "you" or "me."[19] A few days later, Bucher passed by the spot again and saw disturbed earth covering what he believed were shallow graves.

In Smolensk corpses lay openly on the street. As she went out to go shopping, Elsi suddenly nudged the Swiss doctor who was talking shop with his German colleague and slowed her step. In front of her was a "blood-covered Ruskie, starring at her with dead eyes." Two more bodies were lying next to him. "What was that?" she asked. "Rebels, reprisals," the German doctor dryly replied. Elsi thought that this sort of "deterrence" was actually "incentive." "Where will all this slaughter lead?" she wondered to herself. Dead bodies were a daily sight in Smolensk, as elsewhere in German-occupied Russia; men, women, and children were shot simply for violating harsh curfew regimes. "Every night at least four or five people are shot around here," the chief nurse, a German, had warned her Swiss charges on arrival.[20]

Throughout October and November, the Germans marched huge columns of prisoners through Smolensk. The long, slow-moving lines of starving, unwashed soldiers sometimes took an hour to pass. Left behind on the streets were the dead who had collapsed and been shot. Ernst Gerber guessed that half the prisoners he saw would not survive the march to the railhead in Orsha. He was not far off in his estimation; 2 of every 3 Soviet soldiers taken prisoner would not survive the end of the year, 2 million men in all. In Roslawl, where he was later stationed, Gerber was able to save 20 "European looking types," whom he selected from among the prisoners to work as helpers in the field hospitals.[21]

As a female nurse, Elsi Eichenberger fell into long conversations with convalescing German soldiers, and her diary contains the longest transcriptions of wartime talk. Both violence and faith were central to the way the patients represented themselves to Elsi. One evening a captain named Erich Funke stepped into the hall: "Sister, do you know what the SS is?" He explained to Elsi that "our Führer's elite" had already done so much for Germany. A history lesson followed. Before Hitler, "the life of every German had been at risk," and Erich retailed (true) stories about communist revolutionaries shooting hostages in Munich in April 1919. He even knew the names of the victims ("the Countess Westarp and the Prince of Thurn and Taxis") and the place (Munich's Luitpold High School). Erich was attentive to the details when it came to German life and death. And he was prepared to die for his Führer and the new Germany: "Death is the father of life," he declared.

As for the war, Erich knew that answer, too. "The Jews started this war," he explained to Elsi; they "suck the last drop of blood." But Germany had woken up in time and was prepared to fulfill its mission. "Germany has to fight and bleed on behalf of the whole world on account of this plague," as he told her. "Poor Germany, but you will triumph, you have to triumph!" Erich promised Elsi that the German exterminators would "eradicate" Switzerland's Jews as well. With that his "torrent of political propaganda" dried up, and he took his leave, but not before giving Elsi a copy of Hitler's *Mein Kampf*.[22]

Elsi was curious, but she knew she had a big mouth and she did not want to offend the Germans. "I am prepared to answer all your questions openly and honestly," the SS captain reassured her. She asked about the SS. Known for bravery and sacrifice, it represented "the core of the new Germany," he told her. "We consider fear to be our biggest enemy." The captain went on to tell Elsi about his two daughters, who "did not know fear." "They should grow up to be whole, free, and go-getting people, who are armed against anything," although he regretted that his wife was so frightened that she would not go down to the "dark cellar alone."

Then Elsi allowed herself to ask about the "horror stories" bouncing back and forth around Switzerland. "He fell into an unbelievable rage," when she got to Lebensborn, or "fountain of life," the program that took care of and even encouraged the birth of illegitimate "Aryan" children. "No other people reveres women as the Germans do," he insisted. It was all lies, "Jewish propaganda." Thankfully, he added, "the Jews were now being driven away." The figure of the Jew was persistently on the tip of the German tongue. The captain tried to explain more fully. He assured Elsi that "the German cannot hate," even if he is not always a "diplomat." Here the language showed a trace of shame. He was mulling over the subject, an example of how German encounters with the Swiss drew out explanation. The captain tried again: the Jews were bent only on revenge—"'an eye for an eye, a tooth for a tooth,' say the Jews."

And what about the gassing of crippled soldiers in hospital trains as they passed through tunnels, which the Soviet news agency, TASS, had recently reported? "That's also a big huge lie," retorted the SS man, although he conceded that "we've cleared out the mental asylums, in a humane way, obviously. . . . [W]e release mental cripples from their useless and agonizing existence, but war cripples are holy."[23]

For their part, the Germans were also curious about their Swiss "cousins." As Elsi sat at the edge of his bed, a wounded soldier from the Rhineland asked her what "Swiss gals" were like. "Hmm, how should I answer that," Elsi pondered: "peevish, sanguine, melancholy, dispassionate, harmonious . . . a little bit of everything, as it goes." "And what does Switzerland say about us?" Elsi fielded the question frankly, acknowledging the bravery of Germany's soldiers but admitting the "unbelievable risk" Germany had taken in invading Russia and wondering by what "right" it dared to do so. "As if stung by a wasp," the soldier and his comrades provided a chorus of heated objections to the idea that the Germans were wild, barbaric aggressors: "They would have attacked us," "plans were found," "How was Germany even to survive after Versailles?" The boy from Heilbronn even took out a book with appropriate quotations from Hitler to support the case of German victimhood. But once the soldiers mentioned "the cannons" that had been directed at Switzerland the previous fall, Elsi kicked apart the line of argument: "Did the German Supreme Command also find Switzerland's invasion plans?" She had lost her patience. These "men who year after year had been hammered with propaganda" could not conceive of how "wrong" and "inhumane" their ideas were. A little chastened, the soldiers moved on to admire Elsi's pullover and shoes, but they rallied again when they showed her photographs of "Russians who were dangling from trees." "Deterrence," they said—the photographs were taken to publicize the fury of the Germans. "We cannot let ourselves go soft," explained the Rhinelander, who hoped to return to the front soon. "Convalescence makes you soft, sister."[24]

The Swiss volunteers repeatedly encountered Germans' sense of duty and their efforts to cultivate the hardness it required. Elsi's colleague Dr. Bucher had no luck comforting a soldier whose hands and feet had been amputated due to frostbite the day before. "I am in tears," the seventeen-year-old SS recruit explained, "because I promised my mother I would fly with the Führer to England." "It is really unbelievable," Dr. Bucher shook his head in dismay. "Ice creeps into the limbs, but the poison deceiving their hearts sits even deeper!"[25]

A few members of the missions were outright Nazi sympathizers, giving the Hitler salute, speaking ostentatiously in "formal German" (so-called *Schriftdeutsch*), and deriding "Jewish emigrants around the world" and the "yellow press" they controlled. Others recalled Switzerland's own "battle against the Bolschewki" in 1918 and admired Germany's "defiant fighting will." One of the nurses, named Babettli, was completely overwhelmed by German military might and admitted that it made no sense for Swiss soldiers to even try to defend the country against a German attack if it came. To "count on a military victory would be pointless"; "we can only lose," she declared. "And what would we lose? Men." Questions about Swiss honor did not interest her either: "'*Paperlapapp!*' answered

Babettli. "History, History! I don't give a damn. The innocent shouldn't lay down their lives just because of history," she argued. However, most of the nurses and doctors grew more estranged from the Germans as the mission went on, more indignant about Swiss volunteers on the eastern front, and more loyal to Swiss traditions of democracy and human rights. When one of the patients, "Lieutenant Schmidt," wanted a kiss from Elsi before he returned to the front, she refused, which he interpreted as the result of the dividing chasm of "nationality." She quickly corrected him: "Aside from the fact that I imagine my future husband somewhat differently, two people who really love each other will certainly not let the question of nationality . . . " But she left her reply unfinished.[26]

While the Swiss were quick to bring up democracy and humanitarianism, the Germans spoke up—at least in the Swiss transcripts—with stock phrases and Führer quotations. The Germans' words astonished the Swiss, who found intolerable what they regarded as the Germans' "totalitarian" mind-set, which shuttled between the profane and the sacred, between "mental cripples" and "war cripples," between extreme violence and complete faith. "Everything else," that is, anything that did not have to do with Germany, "had no reason to exist, was just nonsense."[27] By contrast, the Germans found the violence they meted out acceptable, even appropriate, even as they ably detailed the suffering they had endured after World War I. The Germans whom the Swiss encountered were completely absorbed in their own national drama. Indeed, the narcissism they displayed was instrumental to their use of extreme force.

Although the Germans clearly wanted to profess their "hardness" to the Swiss, bringing "my little girl" into confidence also revealed some of the brittleness of Nazi convictions. The SS man, for instance, was aware that winning Elsi's favor required more than bluster, a slight consideration to the possibility that others might see the Germans in a light different from the one in which they generally saw themselves. The news that Germany had declared war on the United States on December 11, 1941, opened the door to more practical conversations regarding matériel and schedules. One doctor looked Elsi sharply in the eye: "Well, you believe that Germany will still win, don't you?" Elsi reminded him that neither the United States nor the Soviet Union had really begun to mobilize yet.

In any case, "Nazi Germany has created so many enemies for itself, all of whom are waiting feverishly for the moment to rise up." The doctor was silent for a while and then acknowledged that Germany's actions made it necessary for Germany to win: "Germany must triumph, otherwise, woe to our people." This common formulation, with the words *must* and *woe*, implicitly acknowledged the unprecedented criminal nature of German occupation policies. He then confided to Elsi that he had requested a transfer closer to the front. He was willing to take this risk in order to apply his "method" in controlling gangrene so as to avoid so many amputations. The doctor had been warned that with his blood transfusions, he endangered the lives of patients. "Nonetheless, I am completely outraged when the lads are dismembered so quickly"; surgeons at the front were too quick to give the order: "Cut the leg off!" He, for one, did not see the situation as requiring such radical triage.[28]

When Elsi Eichenberger was back in Berlin a few weeks later, she was struck by two things. First were "Jews swarming the streets with the Jew star on their breasts." Everywhere she could read the notice "Jews not welcome!" At the beginning of 1942, the first wave of deportations to the East that the Nazis had forced on some fifty thousand readily identifiable German Jews had just concluded. And second, she noticed the "war cripples, whom I am especially aware of. Whenever I see them, I think about the stories about them being gassed and I breathe a sigh of relief." In this case, Elsi identified more with the wounded Germans than the endangered Jews, who, later, would in fact be gassed.[29]

But before returning to Berlin, the doctors and nurses had been treated to one more stop on their tour of the German empire: Warsaw. Swiss truck driver Franz Blättler was struck by the odd contrasts, "ragged . . . hungered-out faces" and "photographs of classy, half-naked women" outside a nightclub. He wandered into a German club. Perhaps because he was a man, and a truck driver at that, he was offered a fistful of war stories about how German soldiers had treated prisoners of war—"Yup, comrade, you have to come up to the front and then you'll see the fine methods with which we deal with this shit people. Recently, I captured a rear guard with my tank: just don't take any prisoners, that is our watchword." Another German, a young man from Berlin, topped the story with his account of clearing bunkers with a flamethrower and then shooting the Russians as they fled. War stories from France were recollected as well: in a prisoner-of-war camp, German soldiers had accompanied French African troops for an evening walk and simply shot them in the back. "Do you think there is place for that colored riff-raff in the new Europe? . . . You will be amazed how we will clear out what doesn't suit us." The truck driver muttered something about the Geneva Convention. "Man, you mean that League of Nations crap—all nonsense. What is right is what helps us, that is our motto, and we hold on to it with a grip of iron." In the company of the Swiss trucker, the German soldiers said what otherwise went without saying.[30]

Time was short in Warsaw the next morning: "We set out in cars to at least see the ghetto." Apparently, the ghetto was the "highlight" of any trip to Warsaw. Hubert de Reynier made notes: "In the city center . . . a quarter is reserved for Jews. There are as many as 600,000. The quarter is surrounded by a wall or otherwise barbed wire. The whole thing is guarded by the military. Every Jew who tries to flee is bumped off." Swiss doctors toured the ghetto, inquired about living conditions, and discussed among themselves the four to six hundred Jews who died of hunger every day. De Reynier summed up: "Saw the most unusual Jewish types. Overall, powerful impression."[31]

This sort of ghetto tourism was by no means unusual. On subsequent missions, Swiss doctors, accompanied by SS officers, again visited the ghetto. One even spoke "for a long time" to the ghetto's "mayor" and gained insight into "the huge difficulties that the problems in the East pose for the German state and how they are approached and tackled." Ghetto diarists in fact mentioned visits by Swiss doctors. According to a May 1942 report by the Polish Government-in-Exile, big tour buses organized by the Nazi leisure organization "Strength Through Joy" drove soldiers through the ghetto almost every day. It was "like going to the zoo." But it was the Jewish cemetery, with its cartloads of dead stacked in the outbuildings, that was the most popular stop on the tours. What German visitors sought out was not human exotica, something that intrigued the Swiss, but the "triumph of death," which served perhaps as a visual charm to protect non-Jews in the *danse macabre* of Germany's ghetto.[32]

On her sold-out concert tour of Wehrmacht installations in the spring of 1942, Lale Anderson, whose big hit was "Lili Marleen," *the* song of the Wehrmacht and a merry one for the Swiss volunteers as well, refused to join the "Tourneetruppe" on its visit to the Warsaw Ghetto. As a result, she was put under house arrest and later prohibited from singing "Lili Marleen."[33] The Nazis were quite keen on getting Germans from all walks of life into the ghetto, and most visitors to Warsaw very much wanted to go. The tours were organized to strengthen anti-Semitic clichés and thus ultimately served as an incitement to violence. They also created among Germans a kind of complicity that extended far beyond the SS and the Gestapo. Ghetto tours were a performance of violence in which perpetrators justified murder, lest they become victims. For German visitors, the tours were part of the everyday socialization of violence; for the Swiss, however, they were evidence of the violence that set Germans in the Third Reich apart.

When Elsi Eichenberger and her colleagues crossed the border to Switzerland at Schaffhausen at the end of January 1942, they were met by reporters and photographers. Asked about her impressions of the eastern front, Elsi replied, "I don't want to say that I would not have gone to Smolensk," but she stressed her conviction that "the soul makes a nation, not propaganda and rabble-rousing, not cannons and airplanes, not troops and war." She wasn't sure she should have opened her mouth at all. In fact, the members of the Swiss Medical Mission had agreed not to talk publicly about their experiences. However, one doctor, Rudolf Bucher, refused to keep this commitment. He lectured to Swiss military units, social welfare groups, and political gatherings. He carefully outlined the challenges of modern military medicine and the hostility of Germans toward Switzerland, but also clearly informed his audiences about conditions in the ghettos. In the context of the generally circumspect commentaries in the Swiss press, Bucher's revelations became the "talk of the town"; they were loud and clear enough for Bucher to run afoul of federal authorities, who were anxious not to unduly provoke the Germans.[34]

The Swiss diarists left behind astonishing evidence of the centrality of violence to the Germans' self-representation. It was not simply that the Germans whom the Swiss encountered were enduring extremely difficult

conditions on the eastern front. Rather, these Germans felt themselves
to be protagonists in a racial struggle that justified merciless behavior toward the unarmed and weak and murderous action against Jews and other
civilians. They openly discussed "the destruction of whole nations and
the extermination of peoples and races." Other sources such as records
of conversations among German prisoners of war in Britain and the
United States do not reveal the primacy of ideology in the Germans' acts
of violence. Scholars who have studied these records conclude that the
time has come "to put an end to the overestimation of the ideological."
This conclusion seems premature. It may well be that among themselves,
as members of a group, soldiers did not have to explain themselves. However, in the early stages of what they imagined to be a victorious campaign against the Soviet Union, when Germans introduced themselves *as
Germans* to their Swiss "cousins," notions of a "Jewish world conspiracy,"
"Bolshevik subhumanity," and the "National Socialist People's Community" were very much on their minds.[35]

It is impossible to know just how representative this racial bluster
was, but Swiss as varied as a doctor and a truck driver took note of it.
Their German interlocutors were themselves diverse and included doctors, nurses, and Wehrmacht soldiers. Because the Swiss volunteered for
the medical mission, it is unlikely that they were predisposed to find fault
with the Germans. Yet almost every conversation circled around the question of race and violence. What also struck the Swiss was the collective
nature of the Germans' faith, evident when soldiers raised their voices to
sing Nazi hymns or fell silent to hear Hitler's speeches—on subsequent
missions, doctors would find individual Germans more introspective
and conversations with them more satisfying. Moreover, the Swiss diarists appear to have been genuinely shocked by the German barrage of
self-justification. They shared some of the Germans' racial prejudices,
particularly when picking out in their descriptions the "Mongols" among
the Russian prisoners of war. But the Swiss repeatedly disputed the basic
fundamentals of racial science, not only in the name of humanitarianism
but also because it was offensive to Switzerland's multilingual identity. Elsi
Eichenberger, who at first tried to "make allowances," ended up in so
many arguments with Schmidt, Funke, and others that she reproached

herself for her impertinence. Other doctors considered quitting the mission entirely after they were barred from treating ailing Russian prisoners of war. This particular divergence from the humanitarian aim of the mission is what prompted Bucher to break his oath and talk publicly about the events in Smolensk.[36]

The Machinery of Destruction

WHEN THE SWISS DOCTORS AND NURSES GOT OFF THE TRAIN AT Smolensk in October 1941, they walked into a machinery of destruction that was accelerating with unprecedented speed. The casual killing of French African soldiers in the Oise Valley near Paris in early June 1940 and the deliberate murder of Polish intellectuals in the "Extraordinary Pacification Operation" the same summer had, by the 1941 invasion of the Soviet Union, developed into a much more massive killing process in which Wehrmacht soldiers and SS officers spoke a shared language as they sought out their designated targets: prisoners of war, partisans, and Jewish civilians. Hundreds of victims became thousands and then millions of men, women, and children. The Germans killed one of every five hundred people on the planet over the course of the summer and fall of 1941. By the spring of 1942, Germany's murderous assault on the Jews had spread to every place its troops occupied in Europe. You didn't need to go to Smolensk to see what was going on; you could stay at home. Even when (or precisely because) the armies of the Reich began to falter and fall after the Battle of Stalingrad in 1942–1943, the SS and the political police intensified their efforts to murder all the Jews, to hunt down the growing number of partisans and underground conspirators, and to avenge German losses by massacring civilians. Violence was both justified and enabled by the conviction that if the Germans did not act decisively as perpetrators, they would become victims themselves. In this way, violence was truly a way of life and the way to life.

Helmuth James von Moltke, the great-grandnephew of the famed Moltke of the Franco-Prussian War in 1870, and later a lonely prisoner of conscience whom the Nazis would execute in 1945, thought the world was coming to an end. Working in counterintelligence for the Supreme Command of the Armed Forces, he knew a great deal. "The day is so full of gruesome news that I can hardly write," he confided to his diary on October 21, 1941. "In Serbia, two villages have been burned to the ground. 1700 men and 240 women have been executed. That is the 'penalty' imposed for an attack on three German soldiers. . . . As I write, a large number of shootings are taking place in France." But "those are just the first ominous signs of the coming storm." Each and every day, he noted, "thousands of German men are becoming accustomed to murder." The result was sure to be the "eventual introduction into the Reich of measures 'tested out' in the occupied territories"; for example, "since Saturday, the Berlin Jews are being rounded up." "What do I say," he wondered, "if someone asks: and what did you do during these times?" How can "I sit at the table in my heated apartment and drink tea? Don't I make myself complicit by doing so?" A few weeks later, the "machinery of destruction" continued to supply a steady stream of victims: "Russian prisoners, evacuated Jews, evacuated Jews, Russian prisoners, executed hostages."[37]

Given Germany's treatment of Russian prisoners of war, which was publicly witnessed by thousands of Russian and Ukrainian civilians, and the overall brutality of the occupation regime in Smolensk, Minsk, and Kiev, the Germans quickly found themselves confronted with a hostile population. Although not yet a crucial factor in 1941 or even 1942, partisan warfare began almost at once, particularly since many Soviet soldiers found themselves stranded behind German lines. Already in November 1941, one German general remarked on "the steadfastness of the partisans." It would be a never-ending theme until the Germans quit the Soviet Union altogether. Moreover, "The Russians continuously throw new forces into battle." At every step, the notion "you or me" seemed to gain credibility. It was one of those watchwords that soldiers on the line, killers in the rear, and leaders in Berlin shared and expressed repeatedly. By the end of the war, the idea would be expressed as *"Friss, oder du wirst gefressen!"* (Devour them, or you will be devoured!).[38]

National Socialism aimed to exterminate Jews, to decimate or enslave Poles and Russians, and to destroy civil society in eastern Europe, and so

Germany's war in the East was not simply about advancing and retreating armies. The Germans proposed to occupy and dramatically rearrange space, which completely changed the relationship between forward and rear lines. "The criterion was not soldiers per kilometer on the front but soldiers per square kilometer," concludes one historian. The intertwining of war and occupation, with occupation serving as the continuation of war against civilians, meant that the "density of the layers of danger" was much greater in the East than in the West. The density increased manifold when the German advance finally stalled in the suburbs of Moscow in December 1941. Wehrmacht units were surrounded, outflanked, overrun, and crushed to pieces. One general on the front admitted privately on January 1, 1942, "War's lost!"[39]

The invasion of the Soviet Union altered the dynamics of the German military offensive in eastern Europe, and it altered those of the German occupation regime in western Europe. There were conservative elements who supported the German crusade against communism. More common, however, was satisfaction that the two tyrannies would destroy each other. Observers rubbed their hands together: "Better the graves of Boches and Bolsheviks than the graves of honest men!" as one diarist cited prevailing opinion. Charles Rist thought that this position was typically petit bourgeois because it refrained from taking sides.[40] But the real problem was that Germany's war in the East did not end Germany's occupation in the West. Whatever one thought of the "red peril" in Moscow, the "brown peril" was still in Paris. More and more people in France and even in Poland watched the confrontation between Germany and the Soviet Union with the realization that whatever hurt the Germans helped them. One of the effects of reading Tolstoy in 1941 was to make Russians out of Bolsheviks. For most Europeans, the eastern front became a war between Nazis, who had invaded in the name of imperial and racial goals, and Russians, who fought to save their country, not their regime.

The failure of the Germans to defeat the Soviet Union quickly released the energies of communist resisters—they had been nearly paralyzed by the German-Soviet Non-Aggression Pact in August 1939—and emboldened anti-German conspirators more generally. What at first were quite scattered acts of sabotage against German military personnel ended up proliferating once the Germans began to execute hostages in reprisals and thereby deepened hostility to the occupation. Terror and counterterror fueled resistance across Europe. The strains of the war also increased Germany's determination to acquire forced labor from all the occupied countries, a policy that provided more cover for the resistance.

The machinery of destruction that the Germans set in motion accelerated at every juncture in 1941: the invasion of the Soviet Union, the neglect and death of Soviet prisoners of war, the murder of Soviet Jews, the staggering blows of the Soviet counteroffensive in December, the ignition of partisan warfare in the East and armed resistance in the West, the hostage taking, and the labor corvées. According to one Polish historian, the brutality of the occupation regime that had once been confined to Poland was carried westward in a process of "Warsawization." For instance, the executions that had first been publicly advertised in Warsaw on October 13, 1939, came to Prague on November 17, 1939; to Paris on December 23, 1940; to Amsterdam on March 6, 1941; to Brussels on August 10, 1941; and at last to Copenhagen on April 8, 1943.[41] The confiscation of radios and implementation of the star decree for Jews followed a similar pattern. But there also remained fundamental differences between East and West. Western Europeans rarely saw bodies of civilians lying in the street. For both soldiers and civilians, Germans and non-Germans, the danger increased exponentially as one moved from West to East. The machinery of destruction speeded up dramatically, but not everywhere at the same rate.

When the members of the Swiss Medical Mission arrived in Smolensk at the end of October 1941, a German victory still seemed within reach, but when they departed in January 1942, they had become witnesses to the Soviet counteroffensive in the Winter War. Some of the doctors had taken part in the hasty, drunken evacuation of Roslawl and Juchnow. By the end of the mission, the field hospitals were overflowing with hundreds of wounded soldiers, many of them seriously frostbitten. As Franz Blättler, the truck driver, noted when he was back in Warsaw, the Russians were "neither cowardly subhumans nor an undisciplined herd, but tough, relentless fighters." Given the unexpected resistance the Wehrmacht faced, Blättler remarked to one of the German doctors that "the man who returns from the front is not the same one as he was before." The observation certainly applied to the Swiss doctors and nurses who had come face-to-face with unimagined violence. "My dear friend," the German objected, "you underestimate us."

"When our soldiers leave the field hospitals alive, you can be sure that they are spiritually back in shape," he explained. Then he went on to say that "there will never again be a second 1918." The reference was to the demoralization that had allegedly spread from the battlefront to the home front and back again during World War I, a weakness that made Germany vulnerable to a host of external and internal enemies. The aim of National Socialism was to armor the nation so that Germany would never be vulnerable again. Given what he had seen, Blättler conceded the point: "In the hospitals, the patients are worked over by the press and radio, by the doctors and the nurses, such that any potential doubts regarding the final victory are quickly overcome."[42]

The conviction that Germany had almost been wiped off the map after its defeat in 1918 and that the Nazi victory in 1933 forever barred another 1918 was widespread. Hitler announced war with Poland to the Reichstag on September 1, 1939, with the words that there "will never again be another November 1918 in German history." It was the specter of defeat, revolution, and Versailles that underlay the military and moral ethos of the Third Reich and its willingness to preemptively strike at and murder its designated enemies. Insofar as Germans accepted the notion that Germany had almost been destroyed in 1918, they accepted the basic premise of National Socialist aggression at home and abroad. It was a fantastically powerful myth, one that most Germans in the Third Reich— whether they were Nazis or not—came to share.

In fact, the determination to avert another 1918 left Germany increasingly isolated in a world of enemies. "Many hounds soon catch the hare" was the folksy expression most often used to describe Germany's overreach and brittle occupation policy. Just when this realization sank in differed from person to person, but it was wrapped up in the drama of Germany's war with the Soviet Union. In the ghettos, as the Russians held out for three weeks, for five weeks, then for twelve weeks, "hope began to gleam that perhaps this time the Germans had slipped up." "We watch as military ambulances and trains go west, loaded with wounded and frost-bitten soldiers," Zygmunt Klukowski reported at the end of 1941. But most Europeans, including many Germans, only seriously contemplated Nazi Germany's defeat during the Battle of Stalingrad in late 1942 and early 1943. Observers were riveted. "Tens of thousands are perishing in the gigantic battles at Stalingrad," wrote Yitskhok Rudashevski from the Vilna Ghetto in the middle of September 1942. For the first time, he continued, it was possible to expect "something tangible," the "final defeat of Germany," "when the weary world will straighten its back." "In town," noted Léon Werth, writing from the French provinces, "the only topic is Stalingrad." "Stalingrad is the center of the war," providing "the first signs of German disintegration." Numerous diary entries, such as those written by French economist Charles Rist, began with a reference to Stalingrad:

12 September: Astonishing resistance of the Russians at Stalingrad.

21 September: Stalingrad still holding out.

25 September: In Stalingrad, astonishing resistance, which surprises the entire world.

28 September: Stalingrad still holding out. You can say that the entire world is waiting for news about the siege.

11 October: Stalingrad still holding out, despite Hitler's prophecy.

14 October: Stalingrad has not been taken.[43]

Rist began reading Tolstoy's *War and Peace* in fall 1942.

Just after the Soviets surrounded the German Sixth Army at Stalingrad in November 1942, the call went out, probably from French-speaking programming at the BBC, to write the graffiti *1918*. If the *V* in spring 1941 gave people in German-occupied Europe courage to hope for an eventual British victory, *1918* or *1918 = 1943* made the much more specific prediction that Germany's capitulation at Stalingrad in the winter of 1942–1943 marked the beginning of Germany's complete defeat. "The inscriptions *1918* are everywhere," reported Henri Drouot from Dijon at the end of November 1942. In Vilna graffiti on the walls at the beginning of January 1943 asked *"Deutschland Wohin gehstu?"* and exclaimed: *"9. November—1918—Wiwat!"* In Warsaw the slogan was "Deutschland

Kaputt, 1918–1943." "The French have come up with a new dirty trick," recounted the Wehrmacht soldier Heinrich Böll. "When I saw it for the first time," it "hit me like a ton of bricks! Really the effect is amazing, they simply write 1918 on the walls, just this combination of numbers without commentary, just an oppressive little number." Böll contemplated defeat—it made him physically ill—and did so inside the National Socialist understanding of history in which 1918 and Versailles had swallowed everything up. "It would be terrible if everything once again is for nothing," he wrote during the Battle of Stalingrad—*once again* is the key phrase echoing the idea that in 1918 Germany itself had almost been annihilated. "We have already had at least 20 bitter poor and unhappy years since Versailles."[44] Germany's soldiers would fight on.

Germany's defeat at Stalingrad was disastrous. The Soviets advanced by "leaps and bounds" after February 1943. "The average rate of progress was 5.3 km a day. At that rate, with 592 km to go," the Russian armies would "enter Berlin on 11 December."[45] But the anticipated victory over Germany in 1943 did not come. The terror intensified, and soldiers like Böll would continue to board trains to the front for many more months before the Germans were finally defeated.

BETWEEN THE YEARS 1941 AND 1943, THE GERMANS EXPANDED THEIR ambitions, almost limitlessly. They advanced their war on Jews and other civilians, and even after they encountered setbacks in the Soviet Union and the tide began slowly to turn against them, the deeply held myth of Germany's stab in the back and near liquidation in 1918 stoked Germans' determination to defend a huge racial empire on foreign territory and to carry out murderous assaults on the innocent. The year 1942, in particular, made unmistakably clear that the regime of remorseless terror against Jews had transformed into an exterminatory "final solution," beginning in Poland in the spring and extending across all of German-occupied Europe by the summer. Most of the Jews who would be murdered by the Germans were dead before the German surrender at Stalingrad in January 1943.

With the German invasion of the Soviet Union, the war entered a new phase of unprecedented violence in which the Germans marched as virtual masters on the battlefield. It was at this point, in October 1941, that the Swiss Medical Mission encountered their uniformed German cousins. But the Winter War in front of the suburbs of Moscow in the winter of 1941–1942 and the Battle of Stalingrad the following year added dramatically new elements to the conflict so that the Germans no longer appeared invincible, even as they applied new degrees of violence against their military opponents and against civilians, particularly Jews. The new, unexpected revelations of the war in this phase bore out many of Tolstoy's propositions about the fog of war, the incapabilities of military leadership, and twists of fate. Stalingrad was indeed an epic drama that observers across Europe quickly recognized to be the pivotal point in the war. But the war in Russia also indicated just how little Napoleon's campaign resembled Hitler's, which was driven by the unprecedented violence that Hitler's soldiers openly acknowledged and justified. By the time the doctors and nurses returned home to Switzerland a few months later, it was clear that Smolensk in 1812 was not Smolensk in 1941, and it was clear also that Tolstoy's *War and Peace* and the parallels and generalizations that he drew from the human conflict could not provide a model to adequately render the brutality of World War II. Civilians and particularly Jews found themselves abandoned on a shifting terrain marked by merciless violence.

6

The Fate of the Jews

THE SUMMER OF 1942 MADE PLAIN WHAT SORT OF WAR THE GERMANS were fighting. It was a war waged by Germans against the demographic status quo of modern Europe and particularly against its Jewish communities. The deportation trains that left train stations across the Continent for a newly built archipelago of assembly camps, concentration camps, and death camps were vivid evidence of this war. The trains could be seen by anyone who cared to look. But looking was not always seeing, and explaining was not always understanding. When contemplating the fate of the Jews in the terrible year 1942, European observers more often than not themselves ghettoized Jews, imagining them as part of a separate, unthinkable current of events, distinct from the ones that affected them. The fate of the Jews, in this view, was not directly related to their own. Most Europeans had allowed themselves to be subtly transformed, from Jews' neighbors and fellow citizens into "Aryans," or at least into non-Jews. Nazi categories mattered.

Perpetrators

NINETY MINUTES INTO HIS TWO-HOUR SPEECH TO THE REICHSTAG ON January 30, 1939, marking the sixth anniversary of the Nazi seizure of power, Hitler made his notorious prophecy that, as he put it, "may be memorable for others as well as for us Germans." "If the international Jewish financiers in and outside Europe should succeed in plunging the nations once more into a world war," Hitler declared, "then the result will not be the bolshevization of the earth, and thus the victory of Jewry, but the annihilation of the Jewish race in Europe!" It is unlikely that Hitler actually conceived of the physical extermination of the Jews of Europe at this point. Germans did not yet exult in the extraordinary feeling of mastery that came only with the blitzkrieg victories against France in 1940, and they did not yet sense the existential conflict of "us" versus "them" that accompanied the invasion of the Soviet Union in 1941. But Hitler's prophecy regarding the "Jewish problem" pointed to the ethnic nature of the Nazi conception of war and the connection the Nazis saw between the fate of "others" and that of "us Germans." In the end, German life was premised on Jewish death.

For all the talk of "stolen colonies" in the Reichstag speech, the Nazis aimed not at the recovery of territory in Africa or the adjustment of borders with Poland but the reconstitution of "spaces and races," as one historian puts it, out of historically existing "lands and peoples."[1] The prophecy amounted to a declaration of war on Jews across the spaces Germany might occupy in a future war. Hitler publicly reiterated his intention "to reach a solution and settlement of the Jewish problem" in addition to "the disposition of the entire living space" of eastern Europe in his Reichstag speech on October 6, 1939, after the fall of Warsaw. The invasion of Poland inaugurated not so much a war between states but an assault on people: on Poles, Russians, Gypsies, and especially Jews. This fact was simply missed by most observers in Paris, London, and New York.

The Allies' misrepresentation of Hitler's intentions was evident in the way they reported on his January 1939 prophecy. As the *New York Times* noted in its front-page coverage, the words were heard "amid the evening's wildest acclaim." The London *Times* added (on page 13) that there was no "more sinister flourish than the suggestion that another war would mean the destruction of the Jewish race in Europe." But the balance of the commentary on the speech reflected the fact that "no new ground was broken," with little in Hitler's language that was "new or unfamiliar." With "nothing unexpected," in contrast to the perilous events of September 1938, Europeans were more apt to breathe a sigh of relief at Hitler's insistence that Germany was a "peace-loving nation" than to feel consternation at his direct attack on "the Jewish race." The "Jewish question," the Jewish Telegraphic Agency concluded, was "largely relegated to the background in today's press, whose voluminous quotations from foreign newspapers did not indicate that the warning of possible annihilation of the Jews had aroused any interest." This summary characterized understandings of Hitler's declaration of war on the Jews. He was not at all coy. His words met with great applause from Reichstag deputies, but they were also not really heard clearly by others.[2]

With the invasion of the Soviet Union in June 1941, as Goebbels put it, the "anti-Bolshevik waltz," an old record, could be put back on and the campaign against Jews and communists could once again be synchronized. At this point, Hitler returned to his prophetic words. Throughout the fall of 1941, in speaking to party leaders, he referred explicitly to the extermination of the Jews. He publicly repeated his prophecy to party members on January 24, 1942, and on the occasion of the opening of Germany's "Winter Relief" charity drive on September 30, 1942. Hitler's prophecy appeared as "The Word of the Week," a propaganda sheet that was displayed in "market squares, metro stations, bus stops, payroll offices, hospital waiting rooms, factory cafeterias, hotels, restaurants, post offices, train stations, schools, and street kiosks," as one historian has documented. The army newspaper *Der Kampf* discussed "the destruction of the Jewish race," quoting Goebbels's speech at Berlin's Friedrich-Wilhelm University on December 1, 1941, with emphasis: "*We are now seeing the implementation of this prophecy.*"[3] Even before June 1941, the threat to annihilate the Jews had already been featured in the final frames of the anti-Semitic propaganda film *Der ewige Jude* that Goebbels's Ministry of Propaganda released in 1940. Hitler's prophecy dominated the audiovisual space of the Third Reich.

Forced to work in a factory, Elisabeth Freund, a young Berlin Jew, reported on the debris that "a horrible wave of anti-Semitic propaganda" had left behind. "Along the whole Kurfürstendamm signs hang in almost every shop," Freund noted: "'No Entry for Jews' or 'Jews Not Served.' If you walk along the street you see 'Jew,' 'Jew,' 'Jew' on every house, on every window pane, in every store. It is difficult to explain why the Nazis, these devourers of Jews, want to paste this word all over their city." Nazi words spread into buildings and mailboxes: as Freund noted, "Early in the morning leaflets lying in the stairwell call openly for a pogrom. The notices that report that a soldier has fallen in action blame the Jews for his death!" According to Howard K. Smith, the CBS correspondent in Berlin, "The leaflet was jet-black, with a bright yellow star on the cover and under it the words: 'Racial Comrades! When you see this emblem, you see your Death enemy!'" Germany's frankness about its domestic enemies was startling. In Albert Camus's veiled novel about the war, *The Plague*, it took a long time before city officials dared to use the word *plague*, notices were put up where no one would see them, and newspapers only slowly reported on the death of victims; by contrast, there was no such hesitancy about what the Nazis considered to be the Jewish plague, although the loud public propaganda provided few details about the deportation of German Jews, which began in October 1941. However, the pronouncements were sufficiently clear for Karl Dürkefälden to come to the conclusion in the spring of 1942 that "the Jews are being exterminated." At the end of March 1943, Switzerland's Social Democratic paper, *La Sentinelle*, featured a front-page article, "La 'liquidation' des Juifs par le Troisieme Reich," that was based solely on official German communiqués.[4]

At a time when the death notices of soldiers who had fallen on the eastern front filled newspapers—"The men are falling like flies," noted one diarist already in July 1941—the idea that Jews constituted Germany's lethal enemy began to take root. "There is no difference between Jews and Jews"; no distinctions could be made among individuals of the "race," reminded Goebbels in a ferocious article in *Das Reich* in November: "The Jews Are Guilty." Jews would pay for the death of every German soldier, he promised, and the number of German casualties had soared in 1941 in comparison to the campaigns in Poland in 1939 and France in 1940. Goebbels's article did not mention deportations, but the party's declarations did not hide the regime's intention to attack Jews as the collective enemy of the German people. Nazi racial administrators even sought to reassure soldiers in the army newspaper *Die Front* that the home front was not falling behind but was instead doing its part in solving the "Jewish question." The newspaper published "Excerpts from the War Against Jewry":

Since 1 September a police ordinance has required those Jews still living
in the territory of the Reich to wear a yellow Jewish star. Jews are not
allowed to use public transportation or to leave their areas of residence.
The only exception is for the considerable number of Jews who have
been mobilized to work insofar as the distance to work exceeds 7 km.
The shopping hours for Jews have been set from 4 to 6 o'clock. . . .
Furthermore, Jews are not allowed to keep pets, to attend German
cultural activities or to avail themselves of German hairdressers. New
regulations will require Jews to turn over electrical appliances, record
players, typewriters, bicycles, and optical instruments.[5]

The detail is revealing: it suggested that the authorities could rely on
Germans' understanding that the Jews were getting *exactly* what they
deserved.

Most Germans recognized a "Jewish problem," but at the same time
it was hard to ignore the plight of impoverished neighbors. Local party
leaders acknowledged this difficulty when they reminded party members
of their duties as racial comrades and offered suggestions on how to sub-
due the feelings of pity. "An effective means to curb false pity and false
feelings of humanity is my habit of long standing not even to see the Jew,
to see right through him as if he were made of glass, or rather as if he
were thin air," wrote one obliging party member to his Stuttgart newspaper.[6] Even so, Germans were witnesses to the deportations wherever
Jews still lived. They exchanged news about the Jews as part of everyday
gossip—"one says," "one hears."

Isa Kuchenbuch, who worked for the German Red Cross, wrote long,
chatty letters to her fiancé, Fritz, a soldier, about her thoroughly Nazified
routines in Bremerhaven. She shared her joy that German armies were
marching from "victory to victory" in Yugoslavia and Greece. Going to
the movies, Kuchenbuch sympathized with the "very proud" Boers in
Ohm Krüger, a film that fortified her hatred for England and prompted
her to declare, "You want to pay back the British double!!" "We will *never*
lose courage," she promised Fritz on the day of the invasion of the Soviet Union, June 22, 1941. "Today we never left our places around the
radio," she added, although that did not stop her from going out to dance

in the evening. (Sitting at "our table" at Pschorr's in Dresden that night, Victor Klemperer also commented on the "general cheerfulness of the populace.")

The expanding drama of the war allowed Kuchenbuch to indulge herself in "world history"; "we will hardly allow foreign races and peoples to stay in German lands," she guessed. "Russians + Poles still have lots of room in Siberia," she added. "And where will the Jews go? There is no place left for them, maybe Canada?" Even so, the impressions of the newsreels depicting Soviet atrocities in Lemberg (or Lwów, in Polish), local Jews, and Russian prisoners of war were hard to shake: "How horrible must these Jews be? You probably imagine yourself in the ghetto." "Sometimes I wonder," she went on to say, undoubtedly passing on local gossip, "why we take prisoners at all?—those people are not worth eating the same bread as our soldiers. Or are these," and nothing was completely cut-and-dried for Germans contemplating war, "simply poor oppressed people, who suffer under the heavy hand of their leaders?" All in all, however, "we really do have the right to take pride in the Germanic race"; Kuchenbach finally reached her conclusion: "So it wasn't that easy to exterminate us." She completely accepted the premise that only the German invasion had prevented the Bolsheviks from massacring German civilians. Otherwise, she wrote, "We would not be alive, Fritz, that I know."

In the meantime, now that the threat had been checked, it was time to go shopping. Isa Kuchenbuch wanted "a pair of genuine Russian shoes" ("shoe size 38"), "stockings have to be 9½–10," and "Aunt Dede wants a silk 'Jewish dress,' but it has to be pretty big!" since she was supersize.[7] Isa's letters to Fritz shuffled together extreme fantasies of conquest and of vulnerability, hesitated between feelings of ruthlessness and of sympathy, and celebrated the German race as a whole while also revealing her own sense of entitlement—as it was, "shoe size 38" did not fit; Fritz needed to find something larger. With the invasion of the Soviet Union, Kuchenbuch became increasingly adept at seeing the world as the Nazis did, in terms of ethnic struggles for survival. She imagined her own demise as well as the demise of those who would have slaughtered her. She accepted deportation and mass murder as completely normal and acceptable aspects of the war in which Germany was now engaged.

The same summer, Isa and her companion Alma visited an auction featuring "goods from Jewish denaturalizations"; she had her eye on a "genuine Tabriz carpet." She did not get it, but she consoled herself: "I am actually happy and relieved that a keepsake from some Family Kohn has not passed into our household." In preparation for her marriage to Fritz, Isa also prepared papers documenting her Aryan identity. Watching the newsreels, listening to "Lili Marleen" on the radio in order to properly share the "atmosphere of army life," becoming a superior Aryan by ordering a "Jewish dress," assembling an Aryan household, and fantasizing about mass murder were all of one piece.[8]

In late November, Kuchenbuch passed on remarkably precise news regarding the deportation of her Jewish neighbors: "They are being sent to Poland, to Lodz. The ones from in our neighborhood have had to assemble themselves in Bremen, in 2 big schools, right near Heinz and Alma. There they reside with kit and caboodle and they look just terrible. They are allowed 100 M travel money. The railway journey costs 90 M, so 10 M has to cover necessities for an 8-day period. They leave the Reich as the poorest of the poor." The rich Jews—the real Jews, she noted—had evaded the deportations entirely, but Kuchenbuch's emphasis was on the divide separating Germans and Jews who would never again be able to ruin "good, old German families." Jews found this "bitter hard," she added, but "some were okay": "They all have to take responsibility for their kind. Now I have given enough 'honor' to the Jews, having sacrificed half a page of writing paper on their account. So let's change the subject." At first the details of the report revealed a flicker of sympathy—"the poorest of the poor," "they look just terrible." But in the end, the alleged sins of the collective justified the acknowledged suffering of individual Jews. Kuchenbuch had successfully rearmored herself. (On November 18, 1941, 440 Jews from the Bremen region were ordered to assemble at the Schule am Barkhof from where they were deported to Minsk to work as slave laborers until they were murdered at the end of July 1942; only 6 survived the war.)[9]

Others were more unsettled by the deportations. People did speak up for "old Jews" who "wouldn't hurt a fly." According to a security report from Detmold, "Even comrades who had proven their National

Socialist convictions . . . stood up for the Jews." Local Nazis themselves may have felt besieged, since the party probably received thousands of appeals on behalf of individual Jews in the fall of 1941. The concrete result of these appeals was the establishment of Theresienstadt, which allowed "friends" of the Jews to imagine their former neighbors incarcerated in an "old age ghetto," or *Endlager*, not a death camp. Himmler was still smarting from the overall lack of resolve among Germans that first fall when, in his October 1943 Posen speech, he bitterly denounced even Nazi Party members who had made a case to spare their "A-1 Jews."[10] As it was, Theresienstadt functioned primarily as a transit camp to Auschwitz.

As German armies advanced into the Soviet Union in the summer of 1941, rumors about the slaughter of Jewish civilians spread across the country like wildfire. Three common aspects of the rumors revealed a genuine sense of horror. First, there was the information that the victims included women and children, as advertised to Elsi Eichenberger by the soldier in Minsk; second, the fact that victims undressed and went to their deaths naked or partly naked; and third, the revelation that SS shooters sometimes went mad. To take just one example of the open talk along the home front: the city employee who came to read Anna Haag's water meter in a Stuttgart suburb at the end of November 1941 "told about a relative, an SS man, who reported that he had had to shoot down 500 Jews, including women and children, in Poland, that many were not dead, but others were just thrown on top, and that he could not take it anymore."[11] That the rumors foregrounded "women and children" meant that justifications regarding the general brutality of war or specific threats posed by partisans did not predominate. Many people understood the killings as something terrible. The rumors also clarified the identity of the shooters: the SS. Already in the fall of 1941, a division of labor was in place to allocate blame, with the SS acting in a way that set it apart from the "clean" Wehrmacht. This shift in blame was blatantly exculpatory after the war, since it allowed the majority of Germans to distance themselves from the crimes, but before 1945 the focus on the SS had a critical edge, indicting the regime for unacceptable conduct. The shape of the rumors revealed how shocked the Germans who relayed them were.

Loyal National Socialists such as Isa Kuchenbuch tended to embrace the racial doctrines of the regime, including "special treatment" for the Jews, who "have to take responsibility for their kind," with more and more fervor as time went on. The course of events, as persecution gave way to outright murder, pulled them deeper into the Third Reich. Perceptions of dangerous Jews and endangered Germans were central to the worldview of the Nazi loyalists who made up a large proportion of the population, stiffening their sense of victimhood and their feelings of righteousness as they considered the battles ahead. As they became "Aryans," preparing ancestral papers and racial passports, identifying with the Boers, and vilifying communists, they turned the Jews into an ominous collective danger. As can be seen in Isa Kuchenbuch's commentaries, the war was a culmination, a great simplifier, and an opportunity to become a new German being—entitled, superior, shoe stealing. By contrast, those who did not follow the anti-Jewish line, and it is not clear whether such Germans constituted a large minority or a small majority, responded with dismay to the murder of innocent civilians. But they also tended to push the crimes onto the SS, to see those crimes as isolated atrocities rather than as part of a comprehensive policy, and thus to locate them on the periphery of national events. They thereby preserved the soundness of the stories Germans told about themselves and their nation and allowed the Third Reich to remain a part of those stories. The first group, Nazis in one form or another, worked to excise empathy altogether, while the second group, doubters of all kinds, tended to manage it by putting the source of anxiety aside.

Witnesses

GERMANY'S "FINAL SOLUTION" WAS HARDLY A SERIES OF "NIGHT AND fog" operations; many of the most brutal roundups occurred in public and in broad daylight. That being the case, it is startling how little commentary the persecution of the Jews elicited in the underground press or in personal diaries and letters, particularly in western Europe. The war had the effect of creating new boundaries that separated friends from strangers. For instance, to most Poles, the Poland that was besieged by the Germans was a "true," Catholic, and ethnically homogenous Poland. In this view, Poland's victims were not all equal, not all members in the same community of suffering. The same was true in other nations under German occupation. Jews, national minorities, and refugees were often excluded from circles of empathy. People everywhere drew these boundaries because they were absorbed by their own problems: rationing, calories, air raids, men gone missing or stranded in prisoner-of-war camps. They also calculated that if an identifiable group such as the Jews was condemned to death, they themselves would survive because they were not Jews; distinctions between fellow citizens sharpened. Previously existing anti-Semitism compounded the indifference. By contrast, for Jews, Germany's unrelenting war was a central and terrifying fact of life, but even for them it was not always entirely fathomable in its ferocity or comprehensiveness. The sudden onset of deportations in the spring and summer of 1942, the departure of trains loaded with Jewish captives, revealed Europeans' wide range of perceptions and judgments. Jews did not belong in everyone's stories.

"In the beginning there was no Holocaust." With this provocative statement, Raul Hilberg, an eminent scholar of "the destruction of the European Jews" and himself a refugee whose family fled Austria in 1939, drew attention to the incomplete understanding that existed long after 1945 regarding the centrality of anti-Semitism in the Third Reich, the extent of the annihilation, the dynamic of the planning process, and the moral failures the operations against the Jews exposed across Europe. Some fifteen years after the liberation of the camps, key books on the "human condition" and on modern European history made no reference to the Holocaust. The Library of Congress introduced the subject heading "Holocaust—Jewish, 1939–1945" only in 1968, a year before *The American Heritage Dictionary* provided a definition for *Auschwitz*.[12] Only in the last three or four decades has the Holocaust become central to our historical accounts of the war and the way scholars understand this period.

Yet the assault on the Jews was witnessed and interpreted as it occurred. It was the most dramatic manifestation of what made World War II different: the willful persecution of people based not on what they had done but on who they were. It is sometimes easy to forget that the "Great Action," in which three hundred thousand Jews were deported from the Warsaw Ghetto and murdered in Treblinka in the summer of 1942, constituted "the greatest slaughter perpetrated within a single city in human history," a cost of lives greater than Hiroshima and Nagasaki combined. Across Europe anti-Jewish actions were very visible. The deportation of German Jews often began with a procession down the main street of town. Amsterdam's Jews waited on street corners for the streetcar that took them to the train station. In Paris in July 1942, thousands of Jews were arrested and transported on the city's green-and-beige municipal buses to the assembly point at the Vélodrome d'Hiver, near the Eiffel Tower. They were then interned at Drancy, a dilapidated housing complex outside of Paris, from where they were sent on transports to "an unknown destination"—the phrase was often repeated and hid more precise information about Auschwitz. Deportations continued on and off for two years. Horrific scenes of mayhem also occurred in Polish towns when German policemen and their auxiliaries drove Jews into market squares to await deportation or execution. For hours, Jews trembled and Poles watched. Most witnesses there knew the final destination as Treblinka or Belzec. All this occurred in a context full of anti-Semitic pronouncements and regulations. Yet even Jews, the victims of these calamities, did not fully understand Germans' actions or intentions. The war revealed the boundaries of empathy, but also historical, ethical, and philosophical limits to comprehension. The Holocaust took place at what one survivor described as "the limits of the mind."[13]

It must be true that "few Parisians remained unaware" of the events of "Black Thursday," July 16, 1942, the day of the first and largest raid on Jews in Paris. Forty-five hundred French policemen, beginning before dawn and working in teams of two or three, arrested more than fourteen thousand Jews in *La Grande Rafle* (The Great Roundup). "One is ashamed to be . . . present at such ignominious sights," commented novelist Claude Mauriac. The noise in the stairwell or on the street was unmistakable. Edith Thomas looked out the window and saw the car parked alongside the curb. A couple was hustled into the backseat, followed by the cries of two little children left behind. Although the raids concentrated on the northeastern parts of Paris, where most Jews lived, they took place across the city. Nonetheless, the diaries kept by French men and women make little or no mention of the deportations that and the following day. On July 16, Liliane Schroeder noted that Jews had been banned from many public places and prohibited from using public telephones (every time you entered a phone booth you saw the sign, big as a hand, "Accès interdit aux Juifs") and recounted rumors about entire Jewish families murdered in Poland and Czechoslovakia in retaliation for the assassination of German soldiers—probably a misleading reference to the destruction of the village of Lidice, northwest of Prague, on June 10, 1942, and the massacre of its (non-Jewish) male inhabitants. But she did not comment on the deportations taking place in the twenty arrondissements of Paris itself. Although economist Charles Rist took note of the "terror and horror" churned up by the arrests, his diary focused on military developments.[14]

When diarists did mention the assaults on the Jews, they tended to do so by stringing them together with other German depredations, including the forced labor corvées and the execution of hostages at Fort Mont Valerien in retaliation for the assassination of German military personnel. Detail accumulated around incidents of German terror, but not German terror against the Jews. "As I was approaching Boulevard Saint-Germain from the direction of Boulevard Raspail," Vercors recalled on Christmas Eve 1940, "I caught sight of a notice" posted across the street. "All I could make out at a distance was a name and a word. The word in huge capitals was SHOT, and above it, in slightly smaller capitals, the name: JACQUES BONSERGENT. A young engineer, having struck a member of the German Army, had been sentenced to death two weeks ago. HE WAS SHOT THIS MORNING, proclaimed the last line of the sinister notice. I could not take my eyes off it. Around me people stopped, read, wordlessly exchanged glances." Vercors continued down the street, and "every hundred yards or so the same poster was up" and "the same motionless, silent crowd before it." The next morning, "I found the posters surrounded by flowers, like so many tombs. Little flowers, of every kind"— "real flowers and artificial ones, paper pansies, celluloid roses, small French and British flags."[15] There were no such memorials after "Black Thursday" in July 1942.

In 1943 clumps of Parisians could be seen reading yellow posters the Germans had put up threatening the families of "saboteurs": "All male relatives . . . will be shot; the women will be sentenced to hard labor; children under eighteen will be sent to reform school." In the corridors of the République Metro station, "people said nothing, but horror was written on every face." However, there are no references to "wordlessly exchanged glances" or "horror . . . written on every face" when it came to the deportation of Parisian Jews.[16] Most of the diarists emphasized their shock and indignation at the German occupation, and when they did mention the deportation of Jews they tended to assimilate the events into a larger pattern of German repression, diminishing their extraordinary anti-Jewish nature.[17] By including mention of Jews, the commentaries corroborated German barbarism, but their spare details suggested that, while diarists could imagine themselves in the shoes of "male relatives" or "children under eighteen," they could not so easily put themselves in the place of Jewish neighbors. Jews were not self-evidently part of the French "us." In some ways, the very vulnerability of Jews reassured non-Jews that they were safe; German violence against Jews kept broader German violence in check, the thinking went. "It is an appalling thing to say," admitted twenty-one-year-old Benoîte Groult after a curfew had been lifted and a group of hostages executed, "but it is thanks to these hundred shot Jews, that I was able to go to a concert on Sunday—Berlioz, Ravel, Wagner."[18]

Communist Edith Thomas was one of the few writers to express her shock when she "saw a train go by," "cattle cars sealed with lead": "Thin arms of children clutched onto the bars. A hand outside fluttered like a leaf in the storm. When the train slowed down, voices cried out: 'Maman!'" But "the only reply was the grinding of axles." To break the silence, which she felt was suffocating, it was necessary to "cry out the truth."[19] Thomas's emphasis, however, remains on defenseless children, not defenseless fellow citizens.

The major novels dealing with the occupation, including Vercors's *The Silence of the Sea*, were usually set in the countryside, the precincts of the "real" France. They contain almost no references to Jews or Jewish experiences. Edmund Dubois, in his 1946 account, "Paris sans lumière," mentions the deportation of the city's Jews but does not make them part of the overall story of French resilience during the German occupation.[20] These oversights indicate how the Jews slipped out of sight because they were not considered equivalents of or stand-ins for the French and their suffering.

The stories of the occupation both during and after the war provide rich detail on arrests, escapes, and betrayals, but they involve men and women who chose to actively resist. The scenes are often dangerous and dramatic, but they are quite unlike the terror experienced by Jews as they encountered the German assault on innocent families. Every day, for instance, Hélène Berr, a student of English literature at the Sorbonne, returned home to parse out the rumors with her parents, who fielded phone calls informing them of friends and acquaintances who had been arrested: "Papa says we have to think about when we should leave," but "I've still never left home." "If they ring the bell, what do we do?" she considered. "If we don't open the door, they'll knock it down," so she wondered whether they should maybe "make a run for it." For Jews, the German presence was not an incentive to rebuild a clandestine but honorable civil society by taking a stand, or chalking graffiti, or entombing the metro in silence. It represented a constant advancing, murderous threat. Their experiences as innocent victims who were rounded up indiscriminately had the effect of undoing the deliberate, purposeful heroic work accomplished by the French Resistance. The fact that non-Jewish French individuals were at least passively complicit in the persecution of Jews made the heroism of resistance even less tenable. As a result, Jews did not have a welcome place in France's virtuous underground republic.[21]

The Polish resistance and the underground state it constructed also neglected the terrible fate of the Jews. This was so because non-Jewish Poles had the opportunity and occasion to fight the Germans, whereas the collective German assault on all Polish Jews left Jews almost completely powerless. Writing in the Warsaw Ghetto, Wladyslaw Szlengel drew the distinction in "Two Deaths":

> *Your death is a death by bullets*
> *For something . . . for a country;*

Our death is a stupid death . . . Our death is like a dog's
In a corner of a street.
Your death comes with decorations
And communiqués.[22]

Because the Polish nation was often defined in an ethnic and religious way, Jews also tended to be written out of stories of its suffering. The German intention to destroy the very existence of Polish culture and nationhood reinforced the idea of a crucified Poland whose resurrection depended on Poles returning to social, religious, and ethnic roots in which Jews had no place. Before the war, Polish Jews and Polish Catholics had generally lived in two communities. Especially in the countryside, they were separated by patterns of sociability, language and accent, and historical traditions. Lines between Poles and Jews were not set in stone, and many Jews strove to integrate themselves into Polish life and culture, but the divisions were more rigid in Poland than in France or elsewhere in western Europe.

Nonetheless, in comparison to France, the Polish underground press reported on the destruction of Jewish communities far more extensively and thus with potentially more compassion. The largest underground newspaper, *Biuletyn Informacyjny*, which was associated with the Home Army and the Government-in-Exile in London, is the outstanding example. By contrast, smaller nationalist and conservative papers were often explicitly anti-Semitic and even took a measure of satisfaction in the disappearance of Poland's Jewish minority. In any case, until the Warsaw Uprising in late summer 1944, when the Home Army launched a failed assault on the German occupiers, the Polish underground was a major conduit through which information about Germany's war on the Jews reached London. Moreover, given the ferocity, extent, and proximity of Germany's roundups, there was no way Polish observers could be shielded from witnessing the extraordinary brutality directed toward Jewish civilians. During the deportations, the corpses of Jewish victims could be seen along the streets and in the squares of Polish towns. Jews made up a large percentage of the population—10 percent in Warsaw and often more in towns and villages. They were not invisible. When the first armed resistance to the German occupiers broke out in the Warsaw Ghetto in

April 1943, shelling could be heard and black smoke seen throughout the city. Poles were very well aware that the Germans had turned their country into a vast cemetery, and many wondered if they were next in line.

Again and again, Poles were witnesses to the roundup and brutalization of Jewish neighbors in small-town settings in ways the French or Dutch were not. Zygmunt Klukowski, the genial doctor and amateur historian in Szczebrzeszyn, a small town about halfway between Lwów and Lublin, reported on the proximity of terror. He was extremely well placed. From the windows of the hospital, he could see over the low-timbered one- and two-story buildings around the marketplace, and, standing on the wall surrounding the building, he could catch sight of the railway station and the approaches into town. The hospital itself was a place where people came and went. As a doctor, Klukowski felt responsible for and maintained good relations with both Poles and Jews. He also had access to an automobile, which made possible trips to the countryside. And as a Polish patriot, who, as a student, had been imprisoned for taking part in the 1905 revolution, Klukowski took the effort to keep a careful diary of events during the German occupation. He recorded the beatings and roundups in the marketplace that he witnessed and the gunfire he heard around town. During the deportations in the summer and fall of 1942, he noted, "People walking on the street are so used to seeing corpses on the sidewalks that they pass by without any emotion." But neighbors did talk. "Now when people meet on the streets," he reported, the normal way of greeting is, "Who was arrested? How many Jews were killed last night? Who was robbed?" Klukowski also made it his business to get information from his Jewish neighbors, learning about the deportation of Czech, German, and Belgian Jews to death camps in Poland in March 1942 and about massacres of Jews in the countryside, including the killing of fifteen hundred people, "mostly women and children," in Jozefow, about twenty miles south, in mid-July 1942. "I am sure that this is true," he wrote, "because Jewish information is most reliable."[23]

Klukowski's diary is also notable for its detail—on the persecution of Jews, the German efforts to extract forced labor, the collaboration of the municipal administration, the destruction of schools, the resettlement of peasants around Zamosc in 1943, and the spike in partisan and criminal activity. He named names; interestingly, there are references to Poles who helped Szczebrzeszyn's Jews (the "rope-maker" Dym in town, also a villager from outlying Gruszka Zaporska who, when caught, was executed with his family), even if there are more to those who tormented and killed ("Particularly active was Matysiak," and "Skorzak, a city janitor," who roamed the Jewish district armed with an ax, as well as the "'blue police' Muranowski, Tatulinski, Hadjuczak, and Jan Gal"). In the diary, both Poles and Jews were victimized, but in the way Klukowski deployed collective nouns it is clear that both groups are included in the "we" of his Szczebrzeszyn chronicle. As someone who knew his neighbors well, he also made a sorrowful observation at the end of 1942: "It is hard to believe but the attitude toward Jews is changing. There are many people who see the Jews not as human beings but as animals that must be destroyed."[24] Evidently, sympathies in the town had drained dry.

The Germans entered Szczebrzeszyn for the second time in mid-October 1939, when the Soviets evacuated the town after final border negotiations—"I have to admit, I like them better than Germans," commented Klukowski regarding the Soviets. From the very beginning, Germans put Jews to work as forced labor to "sweep the streets, clean all the public latrines, and fill all the street trenches." Regulations and notices were "plastered everywhere," though, Klukowski carefully pointed out, "most of the orders are aimed at the Jews." Violence against Szczebrzeszyn's Jews escalated quickly. By the fifth day of occupation, Germans "cut their beards; sometimes they pull the hair out." A week into the occupation of the small town, "the Germans are beating the Jews without any reason, just for fun." The Germans began plundering Jewish homes and shops at the end of the second week, parking furniture trucks along the curb while holding Jewish men hostage in the town square. They completely expropriated Jewish businesses a year later, at the end of August 1940. In the winter and spring of 1941, new military installations and an airfield that the Germans were building in preparation for the invasion of the Soviet Union required larger and larger contingents of forced Jewish labor. The airmen stationed nearby came into town only once in a while, Klukowski remarked, but when they did, "they begin drinking, making lots of noise, and beating Jews." Beatings turned into shootings in January 1942, when the Germans caught Jews violating regulations; "their crimes: leaving town without a permit, transporting a cow without a permit, hiding a fur coat, and walking without wearing the Star of David on the sleeve."[25]

Intimate knowledge about the shooting of individual Jews in town gave way to ominous news about mass deportations in the area. At the end of March 1942, "Entire railroad trains loaded with Jews" from western Europe "passed through, possibly to Belzec," along with Treblinka, Sobibor, and Auschwitz-Birkenau, a special death camp. Around the same time, other trains transported Jews deported from Izbica to their deaths in Belzec. The information that Klukowski received from local Jews was extremely accurate. Presumably, many other Poles had heard as well. By early April 1942, Klukowski provided some details about the death camps: "All Jews are forced behind the barbed-wire enclosure. Some are killed with electricity, some with poison gases, and the bodies are burned."

On the morning of August 8, 1942, "shouting in German, Polish, and Yiddish" announced that deportations from Szczebrzeszyn itself had begun. Jews were herded to the marketplace at the main crossroads of town, while "patrols of Gestapo, gendarmes, *Sonderdienst*, 'blue police,' along with members of the *Judenrat* and the so-called Jewish militia" searched for hidden Jews. Many Jewish residents were killed in the operation, and it was not until eight o'clock in the evening that hundreds were taken to the railway station. "No one believes that the Jews will be moved to the Ukraine. They will all be killed," Klukowski reported. This was news passed on by gendarmes and railroad men, but since Jews tried desperately to find hiding places and even fought back, it is likely that the victims themselves also understood that deportations led to death. A few days later, Klukowski learned that "the train carrying the Jews went to Belzec."[26]

For Klukowski, the day was "so terrifying" that he did "not have the strength to describe it." A little more than two months later, at six o'clock in the morning on October 21, 1942, the Germans launched a second and final operation to deport Jews, "in reality a liquidation of the entire Jewish population in Szczebrzeszyn." By three o'clock in the afternoon, nine hundred Jews had been assembled on the marketplace and then taken to the outskirts of the town. Klukowski tried to report on the "terrifying day": "I cannot describe everything that took place. You cannot even imagine the barbarism of the Germans. I am completely broken and cannot seem to find myself." What Klukowski witnessed was completely bewildering. Shots rang out throughout the city, as German and Polish police, armed with guns and axes, pursued Jews in hiding. Grenades were thrown into cellars and men, women, and children killed indiscriminately. Total war against the Jews had come home. To Klukowski's horror, Polish civilians also joined the "Jew hunts." In both operations, in August and October, municipal workers cooperated with the Germans by "removing the belongings" of the Jews, loading them onto wagons, and taking the stuff to warehouses around city hall or else stockpiling furniture, bedding, and other items in the marketplace, where "some townspeople . . . stole the best pieces." Over the next several days, German police and the Polish Blue Police continued to search for Jews in hiding; "on all sidewalks there are numerous blood stains."[27] The familiar world of custom and obligation among neighbors, who had lived however uneasily in the same place, had completely broken down.

In July 1943, many months after the last of Szczebrzeszyn's Jews had been hunted down and murdered and after they no longer appeared in the diary's entries, Klukowski compared the Germans' roundup of young Poles who were drafted to work in Germany with the roundup of Jews a year earlier. "Everything looked the same," he commented, "except for one thing; the big difference was attitude. The Jews marched in complete resignation, guarded only by a few gendarmes. Here these marching men showed hatred toward Germans and were being guarded by hundreds of soldiers carrying machine guns." Yet Klukowski's description of the deportations in August and October 1942 in fact indicated utter mayhem as Jews sought to escape or find hiding places. The operations took many hours, stretching into the night, and required the police and their auxiliaries not just to stand guard but to actively search "barns, cellars, attics, and other hiding places." At the end of the day, streets in Szczebrzeszyn were stained with blood and littered with bodies of Jews, who obviously did not obey orders "in complete resignation."[28] The popular narrative of Jewish passivity came later or was constructed on the basis of hearsay from elsewhere. It could not have derived from the events that Klukowski himself had witnessed. Klukowski knew a great deal, and there were many others like him, but looking back in retrospect Klukowski succumbed to Poles' tendency to make fundamental distinctions between themselves and Jews. In July 1943, he rewrote the horror he had felt in October 1942 into contempt; he was now among those whose "attitude toward Jews is changing." Without the Jews, the Poles could be seen in a better light, no longer as partial collaborators, as ax wielders, but as robustly patriotic young people who "showed hatred toward the Germans." The Jews became passive, the Poles heroic.

What had occurred in Szczebrzeszyn, and in hundreds of towns and villages across Poland in 1942, in full view of local residents, quickly made its way into the underground press. Newspapers associated with the Home Army and the Government-in-Exile enjoyed the largest circulation, had the most reliable information, and showed the greatest sympathy with the plight of Jews. The Home Army's *Biuletyn Informacyjny*, a weekly with a circulation of forty-five thousand, began to report on the murder and liquidation of entire Jewish communities by "gas" or "poison gas" in the death camps of Belzec and Treblinka in the spring of 1942. After the deportation of Warsaw's Jews in the "Great Action" in July, August, and September 1942, the full scale of "German barbarism" became clear. It amounted to "mass murder without precedent in world history." Like Zygmunt Klukowski, who lacked "the strength to describe" or the ability to "describe everything" or "imagine the barbarism," commentators felt the inadequacy and loss of words: "I am convinced that the civilized world does not and cannot believe what is happening in Poland. We ourselves, who see and know, can scarcely believe it." Witnesses tried to string together a portrait of the tragedy from different angles: "Day after day, week after week, month after month people are being murdered. Whole families, whole groups. Women separately, men separately, children separately. It goes on in Warsaw, Lwów, Cracow, Lublin, Przemysl, Prezeworsk. In hundreds of small towns. In hundreds of villages. . . . Every day thousands of people are being deported from Warsaw. Their destination is Belzec, Sobibor, Treblinka and Pelkiny. Every day masses of people are being poisoned by gas."

On September 17, 1942, in an often-quoted editorial, the *Biuletyn Informacyjny* tried to tally the dimensions of the murder: "Infants, children, youth, adults, the elderly, the infirm, the sick, the healthy, male, female, the converted and unconverted alike are ruthlessly murdered, poisoned by gas, buried alive, or pushed from windows to the pavement." But although a few papers insisted on seeing "the murder of human beings," not simply "the liquidation of the Jewish element," most papers still kept Jews separate from Poles. Even the *Biuletyn Informacyjny*'s strong statement placed the Jewish tragedy "alongside of" the "tragedy" engulfing Polish society and referred to Jews in the third person as being "systematically slain in our country," thereby creating a grammar of witnessing characterized by an "us," who inhabited "our" country, versus "them," who just happened to be in it.

To make distinctions between Poles and Jews did not necessarily foreclose empathy. Many Polish commentaries regarded Germany as an "unbridled beast" that would, after the annihilation of the Jews, prospect for new victims. In this view, Jews and Poles were both victims of Nazism; Poles could see themselves when they regarded the fate of Jews. The socialist newspaper *WRN* (its initials stood for Freedom, Equality, and Independence) concluded that Poland had become "a testing ground" for "the eradication of entire people": "In the event of Hitler's victory, the Polish people and surely most of the Slavic people can expect the present-day fate of the Jewish population in Poland." But this conclusion once again relied on making a distinction between "the Polish people" and "the Jewish population in Poland." "There have already been roundups of old beggars in south-central Poland," warned the Peasant Union of Women in September 1942, and people passed on rumors that the Germans were preparing "to kill the elderly right in their homes."[29] Given the "Extraordinary Pacification Operation" of 1940, which had aimed at decapitating the Polish nation by massacring its elite, these were not incredible fears. Occurring just after the deportation and murder of the Jews, the SS initiative to deport and resettle Polish peasants in the Zamosc region in the spring of 1943 made even more plausible the suspicion that the Poles were next in line. Hans Frank, the Governor-General, worried about growing numbers of partisans in light of the unrest that the Zamosc "resettlement" had created, since "from the child to the most aged woman had been witnesses to the Jewish deportations."[30]

In contrast to the uneven and somewhat detached commentary on the mass murder of Jews, the entire Polish press reported on the Zamosc deportations in great detail. "The whole of Warsaw," wrote Ludwik Landau on January 7, 1943, "has only one thing on its mind: these children from Zamosc." To Vladka Meed, a young Jew hiding outside the ghetto walls, the difference was obvious: Poles "welcomed with open arms the first trainloads of Polish children evacuated from the eastern section of the Zamscz region," but those "same Poles remained utterly indifferent to the fate of the children of the Jews, their ghetto neighbors." In the end, the conviction that "yesterday they poisoned the Jews—today we are next in line" ended up only embellishing the long history of suffering that the Polish nation had endured, as opposed to producing real sympathy for Poland's Jews. Polish patriots did not so much avert their glances at the sight of the ghetto as constantly refocus onto themselves. Germany's war against the Polish nation overshadowed its war on the Jews. Indeed, for decades after 1945, the site of Auschwitz stood as a poignant symbol of Polish, not Jewish, suffering.[31]

Polish observers believed the Germans intended to target the Poles after murdering the Jews, but they also insisted on a crucial difference between themselves and Jews, precisely the differences that Zygmunt Klukowski had identified in his 1943 diary entry: "attitude." Again and again, the Polish underground elaborated the theme of the passivity of the Jews and the complicity of the Jewish "police" during the deportations. According to *Wiadomsci Polskie*, a paper close to the Home Army, the Jews "went unquestioningly to their certain deaths: with a pfiff of a whistle they left their homes and accepted the separation of their families. . . . Everything functioned smoothly and punctually under the clubs of their own people—the [Jewish] police." As a result, the Jews had lost their "human dignity." The Jews provided the Poles with a cautionary tale, as when editorialists warned at the beginning of November 1942, invoking a very religious rhetoric, "We have to countermand these sins with the feeling of national unity, individual courage, and collective action."[32]

Jews in the ghettos themselves debated the issue of passivity and questioned whether they were going like "sheep to slaughter." Such ideas were not simply an invention of the Poles. But the Polish emphasis on Jewish passivity served to mark the difference between Poles and Jews; sheep-like behavior was elevated into an ethnic characteristic. Indeed, the assault on the Jews was often regarded by Poles in strictly ethnic terms. German barbarism, Jewish passivity, and Ukrainian and Lithuanian collaboration were all collective attributes that set these other groups apart from Poles. Thus, outrage at German depredations did not necessarily prompt sympathy for the Jews. Instead, the attribution of such group characteristics within the dynamics of mass murder strengthened nationalist and anti-Semitic arguments that postwar Poland had to be ethnically homogenous, cleansed of its unvirtuous prewar Jewish, Ukrainian, and German minorities, as well as geopolitically secure from its enemies to the east and west. The view that passivity not only distinguished Jews from Poles but also made the Jews complicit in their own deaths had the final effect of covering up the participation of Poles, particularly the Polish Blue Police, in Germany's anti-Jewish actions. Repeated references to Jews as sheep helped burnish the self-image of the Poles as noble eagles. Polish participation in the persecution of the Jews could be purged from memory only by indicting Jews for their own suffering.

If the idea that the Poles were next in line created some sympathy for Jews, allegations of Jewish passivity in the face of extreme violence worked in the opposite direction, creating indifference to the plight of the Jews. A number of observers worried about "the moral depravity of Polish society," which had become one of "the inevitable consequences of Germany's crimes." Klukowski himself had noted that acts of violence had become "so common that, really, no one seems to care."[33] "Once murdered all the Jews publicly, in broad daylight," commented Lwów's *Biuletyn Informacyjny Ziemi Czerwienskiej* in July 1944. "We were witnesses to all this, we and our children, who could not understand it. We saw how people were shot on the streets." What the Germans had accomplished, wrote Zofia Kossak, a conservative Catholic writer, in her famous August 1942 proclamation, "Protest," was "the forcible participation of the

Polish people in the bloody spectacle taking place on Polish soil." Shock and horror could lead to their opposites: emotional "numbing" and indifference and "the dangerous conviction that it is permissible to murder your neighbor with impunity." This evacuation of empathy was at the core of Kossak's protest: "Anyone remaining silent in the face of this murder becomes an accomplice to the murder." Yet Kossak deployed a completely nationalized discourse in which she addressed a "we" defined simply as "Catholics, Poles." She conceded that Jews remained "political, economic, and ideological enemies of Poland." Even as she maintained that "awareness of this fact," which "remains a mystery of the Jewish soul," "does not release us from the duty of damnation of murder," she provided evidence for the way perceptions of national difference tended to produce indifference.

Kossak's "Protest" relied on the very categories—"Catholics, Poles," and "the Jewish soul"—it sought to overcome. Even in protest, it reproduced the ghetto, the two worlds separated by a wall. In the summer of 1942, an amusement park was installed in Warsaw's Krasinski Square, a park tucked into a crook made by the zigzagging walls of the Warsaw Ghetto and named in honor of a prominent Polish family that included nineteenth-century romantic poet Zygmunt Krasiński. The square was originally supposed to be incorporated into the ghetto, but when the final borders were drawn, it lay outside the Jewish district: "We have been robbed of every tree and every flower," fumed one ghetto resident. Poet Wladyslaw Szlengel could "look on the pretty Krasinski Park / With its wet autumn leaves . . . Aryan trees peering into my Jewish window." From the other side, Vladka Meed strolled into the square, "crowded with youngsters and adults engaged in sports, dancing and amusements. It was a joyous scene and a noisy one. The small cafes were bursting with young men feeling their oats." At one point, two men, blackmailers, identified someone they took for a Jew: "Jew! Dirty Jew!" Vladka carefully watched the responses of passersby. They "were not particularly proud of what they had just witnessed. Some shook their heads, others smiled wryly," but they "all resumed their Sunday stroll." The amusement park remained open during the Warsaw Ghetto Uprising, which began after the Germans attacked the precincts on the eve of Passover, April 19, 1943. Easter fell on the following Sunday, April 25. Poet Czeslaw Milosz recounted the Warsaw scene where "the bright melody . . . drowned / The salvos from the ghetto wall":

> *At times wind from the burning*
> *Would drift dark kites along . . . That same hot wind*
> *Blew open the skirts of the girls*
> *And the crowds were laughing*
> *On that beautiful Warsaw Sunday.*

The carnival carousel spinning alongside the ghetto walls became "the symbol of Jewish isolation."[34]

It was hardly unusual for the two worlds, the Jewish and the Polish one, to inhabit the same space. Theater director Edmund Wierciński, who often took the local train from Warsaw to the nearby resort town of Otwock, happened to see the town's Jews rounded up. With Wierciński's diary at hand, a postwar novelist imagined the scene he had witnessed, "the Jews squatting in rows and the Germans drinking beer at the mahogany table." The local train then crossed a small river. "Groups of slender, pleasantly suntanned boys and girls" came into view; passengers could see them standing "around the ice-cream kiosks and the kvass stands." The passengers "slowly began to look more cheerful."[35]

As German violence against the Jews grew more extreme, Zygmunt Klukowski noted that "some Poles" behaved in a manner that was "completely out of line." "During the massacre some even laughed," he wrote. Others "went sneaking into Jewish houses from the back, searching for what could be stolen." There were certainly elements in Polish society who welcomed the "German mass murders," because "they will reduce the scale of the [Jewish] problem," even if "they cannot eliminate it entirely." The nationalist press offered plenty of examples of satisfaction that "the victory" over the Jews "has been won."[36] One of the things that worried Zofia Kossak was that the silence of the Poles or, even worse, their cooperation with the occupiers would enable blame for the murder of the Jews to be shifted from the Germans to the Poles themselves. Anti-Jewish actions by the Poles were also a function of the worsening conditions of the Jews, who had been expropriated, ghettoized, and completely isolated from their neighbors. Their helplessness made them "fair game." As Jacob Gerstenfeld put it with bitter sarcasm, "Aryans in their Christian abnegation wanted to free the Jews of the trouble of this world's goods." "I myself lost my coat in this manner on 4 January 1942 at 5 o'clock on [Lemberg's] Krakowski square." More important was the fact that Germans deliberately lured Poles into complicity by offering them the opportunity to repossess the belongings and homes of deported Jews. During the deportation of Jews in Otwock in August 1942, Calel Perechodnik could see that "a part of the ghetto was already inhabited by Poles. Women were straightening out the apartments, where the not-quite-cold bodies of the owners were lying about. Others were peeling potatoes in front of the houses." One day he even saw a girl pushing a baby in a carriage; "my legs buckled under me. I recognized my daughter's stroller."[37]

Gerstenfeld's coat and Perechodnik's daughter's stroller were small examples of a massive redistribution of property from Jews to Poles during the German occupation. As one of the advisers to the Polish Government-in-Exile put it, "In this respect a cardinal and irrevocable change occurred." He went on to warn that "if the mass of the Jews ever return, our population will not recognize their restitution claims, but will treat them instead as invaders, resisting them by violent means if need be." Jan Karski, a Polish diplomat and courier for the underground, hardly disguised his contempt for "the Polish peasant, laborer, and half-educated, stupid, demoralized wretch" who welcomed the fact that the Germans were "finally" teaching the Jews "a lesson." But unfortunately, he was accurate in describing the abiding economic interest in the transfer of property. Commitments made in London in November 1940 to grant equal rights to Jews in postwar Poland were therefore not widely accepted at home. In German-occupied Poland, the confiscation of Jewish property by the Germans and its partial redistribution to the Poles deepened the demoralization of Polish society. It fortified both the silence of the Poles and the dehumanizing stereotypes of Jewish passivity that circulated so widely. If Kossak's protest lamented the Poles' silence, it also upheld the legitimacy of Poland's economic struggle against the Jews. Ultimately, Kossak's proclamation expressed the complicated political crosswinds that rejected

Auschwitz but not the ghetto. Economist Kazimierz Wyka, writing in 1945, accurately described the moral consequences of this state of affairs:

> Shielded by the sword of the German executioner, who was carrying out a crime never before seen in history, the Polish shopkeeper took possession of the keys to the till of his Jewish competitor and believed that he was acting in the most moral manner. To the Germans are left the guilt and the crime, to us the keys and the till. The shopkeeper forgot that the "legal" destruction of a whole nation was not staged by history so that the sign could be changed on someone's shop. The manner in which the Germans liquidated the Jews falls on their conscience. The reaction to the liquidation, however, falls on our conscience.[38]

In Poland, the thorough knowledge of Germany's crimes against the Jews did not break down but more often reinforced structures of ethnic prejudice.

The Polish underground and the Home Army informed the Government-in-Exile of Germany's murder of Polish Jews in specific detail, but the first comprehensive report on the systematic nature of Germany's annihilation program was prepared by Emanuel Ringelblum in the Warsaw Ghetto and the socialist Jewish Bund. The so-called Feiner Rapport provided an overview of the slaughter that had taken place since the German invasion of the Soviet Union. It provided details about the destruction of Jewish communities in Lithuania, Belarussia, and Ukraine; about the use of gas vans at Chelmno, where at least 40,000 Jews perished; and the onset of deportations in Poland in the spring of 1942. It estimated that the total number of victims exceeded 700,000—the actual number was much higher. The report concluded that "the criminal German government has begun to carry out Hitler's prophecy that five minutes before the end of the war, whatever its outcome, he will have murdered all the Jews of Europe." A Swedish businessman with connections to the Polish underground delivered the document to Stockholm; it reached London at the end of May and provided the basis for the BBC broadcast publicizing the murder of 700,000 Jews on June 2, 1942. By the end of June, further BBC broadcasts confirmed to Ringelblum—he was one of the rare people in Poland able to hear them—that the news about Poland's Jews had reached London. "It has alarmed the world to our fate, and," Ringelblum allowed himself to hope, "perhaps saved hundreds of thousands of Polish Jews from extermination." In its public pronouncements, the Government-in-Exile tended to play down the estimates provided by the Bund, said little about Warsaw's Jews during the "Great Action," and generally overlooked the gravity of the peril in which Jews found themselves. But it did publish a widely circulated book, *The Mass Extermination of Jews in German Occupied Poland*, based on a communiqué dated December 10, 1942. Prepared by the Ministry of Foreign Affairs, it represented the government's first official acknowledgment and condemnation of the German effort to exterminate the Jews.[39]

The BBC broadcasts on June 2, 1942, and again on June 26 provided one of the most reliable confirmations of the terrible rumors that had begun to gather. In Amsterdam Etty Hillesum recorded in her diary on June 29 that "the English radio has reported that 700,000 Jews perished last year alone, in Germany and the occupied territories." Confronting this stark news made more urgent the challenge of comprehending what exactly awaited Jews sent to the East. "Even if we stay alive we shall carry the wounds with us throughout our lives," Hillesum noted. She imagined herself in Poland, "on the battlefields, if that's what one can call them. I often see visions of poisonous green smoke; I am with the hungry, with the ill-treated and the dying, every day." She found that her "mind has come to terms with it all," but her body had "disintegrated into a thousand pieces and each piece has a different pain." "The English radio speaks of their being gassed," wrote Anne Frank on October 9, 1942, about the Jewish deportees. "Nice people, the Germans! To think that I was once one of them too!"[40]

Victims

WHAT EXACTLY DID THE BBC REPORTS ABOUT THE GASSING OF HUN-dreds of thousands of Jews in Poland mean to those Jews, mostly in western Europe, who were able to hear them? Using the BBC's own estimations, one historian maintains that as many as 15 million Germans listened to illegal radio broadcasts by 1944. These broadcasts carried frequent references to gas chambers: "Fifteen million German listeners were left in no doubt as to what was going on." This is a remarkable statement not so much because it accepts the rather high estimate of 15 million, which, in any case, would have applied to 1944 but not to 1942 or 1943, nor because it overlooks the fact that German listeners, as we might guess, were more interested in unvarnished news about the military situation than anything else, but because it assumes that facts broadcast by the BBC were taken or could be taken at face value. Even for Jews, who were most interested in news about events in Poland, the news about gas chambers, about Auschwitz, did not register as clear and unambiguous information about which there could be "no doubt."[41]

In November 1943, eighteen months after the first BBC broadcasts, Hélène Berr recorded in her diary that "British radio has apparently rebroadcast frightful details about life in the camps in Poland." She did not hear the reports directly, but it is unlikely that this was the first time that she heard the calamitous news. The reference to "life in the camps" suggests the elision or suppression of the true nature of the death camps. Berr remained trapped inside the world of Nazi euphemism: deportation, resettlement, labor colony, and so on. Berr, like many Jews faced with knowledge about Auschwitz, tended to parse the news about the gas chambers in ways that broke the information apart into smaller, more manageable parts that no longer necessarily added up to the systematic mass murder that the Germans were in fact carrying out. A week later, Berr tried to make sense of the deportation of "whole families" from Drancy: "What do they think they will achieve? Set up a Jewish slave state in Poland? Do they believe for one minute that these unfortunate families who have long been settled here, in some cases for five hundred years, will ever think about anything except coming back."[42] Berr was remarkably well informed, since she worked for the Union of French Jews, and she had even sorted through the rings, watches, and other personal belongings that had been confiscated in Drancy after Jews had been deported to Auschwitz, but she continued to think in terms of new settlements that made German directives appear simply impractical or irrational.

The resolve to work the whole thing out remained strong. Although metaphors of shipwreck struck an ominous note, they also left room for a few survivors. Berr was haunted by "the line from the Book of Job at the end of *Moby-Dick*: 'And I alone am escaped to tell thee'" (Job 1:19). The stormy scene lifted suddenly with the receipt of a postcard from Auschwitz-Birkenau at the beginning of December 1943. "A mooring for a blindly drifting mind," she wrote with relief. Berr also unwittingly rearranged chronology to suit the logical sequences she had such a hard time abandoning. She heard about "twenty-thousand Jews" "massacred" in Kiev only at the end of 1943; that was news about the murder of more than thirty-three thousand victims at Babi Yar more than two years earlier. This delay in transmission allowed her to place massacres after rather than before Germany's military setbacks in the East, which made them more understandable. "What will they do with the camps when events turn against them?" she wondered. Berr's diary entries practically argued with the "German soldiers I pass on the street"—"opening a door for me one day and perhaps deporting me the next day"—because Berr thought she could argue her way out of, and possibly escape, the fate that she feared so much.

However, Berr got much closer to the truth when she commented on eleven children who had been deported in February 1944. "What use are the children?" she wondered. "They don't send wives and children with the non-Jewish workers who go to Germany. The monstrous incomprehensibility and illogical horror of the whole thing boggle the mind. But there's probably nothing to work out, because the Germans aren't even trying to give a reason or a purpose. They have one aim, which is extermination." The word *extermination* had now entered Berr's vocabulary, and so had the term *asphyxiating gas*. Berr thereupon contemplated her arrest, after which "I'll be in Upper Silesia, maybe dead, and my whole life, with the infinity I sense within me, will be snuffed out abruptly."[43]

Hélène Berr was acutely aware of how others diminished or even denied the catastrophe that was unfolding even if she could not always see how she did the same herself. She knew much more than the "woman of the lower classes" she had run into, who had concealed the truth from herself because it was too hard to acknowledge, but Berr was not so different. Berr's acquaintance "reckoned there were a lot of Jews in Paris, obviously, you notice them with that label stuck on them, and then she said: 'But they don't bother French people, do they, and anyway they only arrest people who have done something.'" Later on, another acquaintance, Madame Agache, who was not Jewish, was astonished: "You mean to say they are deporting children?" "It's impossible to express the pain," Berr wrote about such encounters. But she herself had difficulty with the problem of "not knowing, not understanding even when you do know." That "you have a closed door inside you," and that it opens and shuts again, was, Berr concluded, "the enormous drama of our age." The drama was the challenge of understanding something that had not been imagined before, the need to question precedent, and the obligation to imagine irrationality and incoherence in ways that had not been necessary before the great assault on the Jews began to gather force in 1942. "In the face of absolute evil," poet Léa Goldberg surmised, "the imagination of the assassins exceeds the imagination of the victims," the opposite of the case during the war scare in 1938 when the lords of the air assumed fantastic forms in the minds of the designated victims of air war. It would have taken the most strenuous effort on Berr's part to think like a Nazi and to have "no doubt" about the BBC broadcasts. Berr knew about not knowing, but she herself still did not know. "I can't hold it against the woman."[44]

The Jews in the ghettos in Poland acquired much more precise information about the mass murder under way, and did so more quickly, but even so, their comprehension of the overall German design was uneven and disrupted by hope, what one author refers to as the "magical thinking of the Jews." In retrospect, historians write about the noose tightening around the ghettos in 1941 and 1942, but at the time the danger was not always clearly seen. Understanding German actions was refracted through commonsense assumptions about Germany's need for labor or was mitigated by the local nature of atrocities. For a long time, deportations were "evaluated as single episodes," explains historian Raul Hilberg, "rather than as a patterned destruction process." "If surrounding ghettos were wiped out," he continues, "the remaining one might be spared. Never was the past the inevitable future."[45] Jews also drew on the long experience of persecution in Europe to make sense of the events of 1942, which the Jerusalem-based Jewish Telegraphic Agency continued to describe as "pogroms," terrible, but local, incidents.

News about the massacres of entire Jewish communities behind the advancing German front reached the Warsaw Ghetto in September and October 1941. Underground newspapers reported "Bloody Days in Vilna," and the execution site in Ponary quickly became a "synonym for death." In the midst of the murderous operations of the SS death squads in the Polish territories annexed by the Soviet Union in 1939, a few refugees made their way westward, providing further information on the death toll, including 9,000 Jews murdered in Slonim, about one hundred miles south of Vilna, on November 14, 1941. Such information likely took time to circulate and become widely believed. The scrupulous diary kept by Chaim Kaplan, the sixty-two-year-old principal of a Hebrew elementary school in the ghetto, mentions neither Vilna nor Slonim until May 16, 1942. Reports on the murder of Jews in gas vans in Chelmno beginning in January 1942 reached the Warsaw Ghetto at the end of that winter and formed the basis of a detailed report prepared by its historical section, Oyneg Shabes. However, ghetto residents could interpret the German assault on "Grabow, Kutno, Krosniewice, Gostynin and Gabin" in different ways. Were they local disasters much like the pogroms endured by their grandparents, or were they the first step toward the realization of Hitler's prophecy to exterminate all the Jews of Europe in the event of a world war? Surely, with the entry of Japan and United States into the conflict in December 1941, a world war was under way.

For Kaplan, writing for days without any "real" food, it was the destruction of the Jewish ghetto in Lublin in March and April 1942 that shocked him into contemplating the unprecedented scale of Germany's genocidal ambitions. The murder of more than 30,000 Jews was especially ominous, because it was around Lublin, as Kaplan knew from the BBC, that the Germans had initially planned to create a "Jewish reservation" in 1939; outright liquidation thus marked a new strategy. Kaplan now strung together the sites of Germany's war: "Vilna, Kovno, Lublin, Slonim, and Novogrudok." Since Lublin, "not a day passes without some Jewish settlement being completely wiped off the face of the earth," he wrote. This was something more than pogroms. For the first time, residents in the Warsaw Ghetto began earnestly debating their own fate, whether it would come "during this summer or next summer. As usual, there are those who rush the end and those who put it off." But the sheer size of the ghetto, with more than 350,000 people, the largest Jewish settlement in Europe, also made it difficult to imagine a final operation, one that would have to be ten times larger than what had taken place in Lublin. Perhaps, Kaplan wondered, taking a different tack, Lublin's Jews were treated "so much more cruelly" because of the community's "spiritual" or deeply religious history. If true, it did not necessarily follow that Warsaw would be next. A few days later, however, Kaplan concluded that there was nothing special about the massacre except chance: "Lublin was the first to drink the cup of sorrow to the dregs, but not the last."[46]

Kaplan contended, "There is no doubt that they are no longer alive," although, he admitted, "no one knows their burial place." Others continued to ask, "Where did deportees settle?" Kaplan's friend Hirsch—his alter ego, perhaps even an imaginary figure—considered those who continued to pose such questions "optimistic fools." "No one knows their whereabouts," he asserted, "simply because they were killed along the way and never reached a new destination." Lublin was the beginning of the end, the start of a more comprehensive "final solution," in Kaplan's words. "The Nazis created ghettos in order to annihilate us but their plan did not succeed"; indeed, Kaplan had regarded the endurance and self-organization of the ghetto Jews in 1940 and 1941 as an extraordinary accomplishment. However, in the spring of 1942, the Germans "decided upon . . . annihilation through murder." Again "Hirsch is screaming": "Are you better than the people of Lublin? The people of Cracow? The people of Lodz?" "If not today," he concluded, "then tomorrow or the next day you will be taken out like lambs to slaughter." It is worth noting that Kaplan basically agreed with Hirsch, but could not, at least in the diary, say so directly. He was aware that his own hesitancy on this matter was "no more than self-deception." Yet he allowed "my wise friend" Hirsch to articulate his own worst and well-substantiated fears. At the end of June 1942, Kaplan began to write in the past tense and to consider "our strength" in the past perfect, after it had given way.[47]

After so many months of rumors about the deportation, resettlement, and murder of Jews in Poland, the talk in Warsaw on July 22, 1942, was about the imminent destruction of the ghetto. This made the period from dawn to late afternoon "the most tense hours of our lives," when "the spark of hope flared up and then died," Kaplan wrote. The notice was posted at four o'clock. Vladka Meed was also in the ghetto that day: people "streamed from every doorway." They "elbowed forward, determined to see and read the notice for himself, unwilling to take another's word—not even the word of one who had just read it. Each person had to interpret the announcement in his own way," stoking renewed doubts and counterarguments. "I devoured the printed words," Meed remembered. "Again and again I read them, until the letters seemed to leap and dance before my eyes, as though to elude understanding: 'By order of the German authorities, all the Jews of Warsaw, regardless of age or sex, are to be deported.'"

There were exceptions: Jews employed in the German workshops, the Judenrat (or Jewish Council) itself, and the Jewish police. The Jewish ghetto was assaulted piece by piece, beginning with "the removal of the prisoners from the Jewish prison in Gesia Street," the consolidation of patients to the hospital on Leszno Street, the roundup of beggars. Meed and many others tried, sometimes successfully, to get work documents, although this division of the ghetto into productive and unproductive parts, Kaplan surmised, simply anticipated two kinds of death: "One half was for sword, pestilence, and destruction; the other half for famine and slavery." The exceptions the Germans made for workers were dubious, because in his view they were basically being told, "May you be recompensed by being the last one to be shot." The selections may have offered a slim reed of hope for those deemed useful, but only at the cost of acknowledging that the expendable had been sentenced to death; to be deported was to be murdered, not resettled. In any case, Chaim Kaplan did not have money for a bribe or a work document.[48]

The assault continued block by block: "After Nowolipie," which was just a block from Kaplan's residence at 20 Nowolipki Street, "came the turn of Leszno Street from the corner of Zelazna to Solna"; the police had moved in the opposite direction. But on August 3, doubling back but skipping over Nowolipki, "they slaughtered Zamenhof and Pawia Streets." "All day," on August 4, "my wife and I take turns standing watch, looking through the kitchen window which overlooks the courtyard, to see if the blockade has begun." At one point, dozens of Jewish police entered the courtyard, but then "the destroyers passed on to the Nalewki-Zamenhof block." By four o'clock in the afternoon, "the furies subsided"; "the numbers of passersby increased." The quota had been filled and thirteen thousand people seized. The entry is the last one in the diary. Kaplan's side of Nowolipki, including number 20, was eventually blockaded and formed one of the boundaries of the "wild" part of the evacuated ghetto. After Kaplan's deportation, news circulated that deported Jews were transported directly to a death camp at the end of a spur off the Warsaw-Bialystok railroad line: Tremblinka, Treblinki, Trebblinka—many variants of the name were offered before it became well known to Jews as Treblinka.[49]

Many Jews in the ghetto came to see the basic elements of the "machine of destruction." News about Ponary, about Slonim, Lublin, Warsaw, Kraków, and Vilna, made it to most ghettos. In September 1942, reports reached Vilna that "250,000 Jews were taken out of Warsaw"; near Malkinia, where the spur to Treblinka began, "they are poisoned with gas." Even residents in the well-sealed ghetto in Lodz heard about the "Great Action" in Warsaw in a matter of days (on July 27 Dawid Sierakowiak referred to the deportation of "10,000 persons a day").[50] Local Jews in Szczebrzeszyn not only knew the facts about massacres in Jozefow but also the nationality of the passengers whom trains from Germany or Belgium transported to nearby Belzec. The comprehensive, European-wide scale to the "final solution" was clear to many Jews in Poland. Again and again, witnesses made reference to Hitler's prophecy about the elimination of all the Jews in Europe. Diarists minced no words about the "destruction" or "liquidation" of Jewry that was taking place.

Kaplan, as Hirsch, screamed that the Jews of Warsaw were doomed and urged them, "Alarm the world!" But Kaplan as Kaplan ladled up hope when he doubted Germans' abilities or reconsidered their intentions. Seeing German designs clearly took time, and the farther away Jews were from the ghettos and the death camps, the easier it was for them to believe that deportation to an "unknown destination" meant resettlement in a labor colony. From the very beginning, the idea that the Jews were being sent away to work was a ruse, and the deportation of the very young and very old made that much clear. But it nevertheless deceived Jews, who themselves saw their Gentile neighbors recruited, often against their will, to toil in labor brigades in Germany. Most Jews, at least at the beginning, could not imagine why the Germans would deviate from the model of setting up work camps and penal colonies, especially since Jews in Poland, and also in Germany and elsewhere, were conscripted on a daily basis into little battalions of latrine cleaners, snow shovelers, and building contractors.

As Jews in western Europe faced the first wave of deportations in 1941 and 1942, they gave considerable thought to how they should pack their knapsacks. Local Jewish Councils encouraged them to do so, often repeating German assurances that Jews were to be resettled in labor colonies across Europe. "We assumed that we would have to perform heavy labor under difficult circumstances," recalled one survivor from Kassel in Germany, but we had no "evidence that the aim of our journey was to be our physical destruction."[51] Photographs depict Jews arriving at assembly camps with extra clothing, tightly packed knapsacks, and turned-over mattresses.

In Amsterdam Etty Hillesum repeatedly imagined the moment when the notice of deportation arrived in the mail. How would she prepare for life "in a labor camp under SS guards"? "I wouldn't tell a soul at first but retire to the quietest spot in the house, withdraw into myself and gather what strength I could from every cranny of my body and soul," she wrote in her diary on July 11, 1942. (The first notices had been sent on July 4; Margot Frank received hers on July 8, which impelled Anne Frank's family to go into hiding in the Secret Annex two days later.) "I would have my hair cut short and throw my lipstick away," Hillesum continued. "And I'd have a pair of trousers and a jacket made out of that heavy winter coat material I've got left over." It was important to get hold of a sturdy knapsack; the Jewish Council recommended against suitcases. This careful planning for life in a labor camp contrasted with the "lovely stories" Jews were telling themselves, most likely after continued BBC broadcasts, about the Germans "exterminating us with gas." "But what is the point of repeating such things even if they should be true?"[52]

In Prague, too, thousands of Jews could be seen "hunting for backpacks, hats, caps, suitcases, tableware, and nonperishable provisions." Then they "flung themselves into the turmoil of packing, of cleaning up, choosing objects, attempting to assume a casual attitude, putting on airs toward their surroundings as if everything happened according to the laws of the world order." "What do you bring?" considered one Jew in Hamburg. "Photographs of relatives? Later, you think, no, pull them out. Better to take a warm coat or a scarf."[53] Etty Hillesum also decided against photographs.

The Jewish Council in Amsterdam warned deportees not to "pack the rucksacks *too full*," but they urged on them a long list of practical items that were undoubtedly difficult to acquire in wartime, especially given the restrictions under which Jews could shop: "a favorite book," perhaps, but otherwise winter jackets; work overalls; a pair of strong shoes, "preferably with iron fittings"; blankets; a penknife; and so on. "The entire philosophy of compliance was packed up in the rucksacks," argues one historian, "the assumption that deportation was probably inevitable and could be mitigated by following instructions from above." And more, the well-provisioned, not "too full" knapsack suggested that the deportations to "an 'unknown destination'" ("That's what they call it," noted Hillesum) could be managed in an efficient, practical manner.[54] "Unknown destination" was a German euphemism, a lie, but it was also adopted by Jews who calculated the odds and hoped for the best.

Even in the East, the assumption that "a sewing machine can save your life" never completely lost its grip on ghetto populations. Jews assumed that the Nazis were motivated by need-based rationality and aimed to calibrate themselves accordingly. Such calibration proved to be illusory because the Nazis desired the destruction of the Jews more than they wanted their labor. In the Third Reich, the machinery of war did not enslave living Jews to help produce victorious German outcomes; rather, the machinery of destruction functioned to produce dead Jews. Moreover, even to the extent that "salvation through work" made sense, the strategy meant accepting a selection process that separated out

allegedly nonproductive Jews from productive ones. "Those who maintained that the best prospects lay in increased production, especially of
war supplies, tended to accept the fact that unproductive elements would
not be spared," concludes one historian. "The circle became smaller and
more select." In Lodz parents were "exhorted to sacrifice their children,
children their parents, and the healthy the sick," as the son of one survivor puts it. Moses Merin, a member of the Jewish Council in Sosnowiec,
outside Katowice, bluntly declared himself willing "to sacrifice 50,000
of our community in order to save the other." Unfortunately, while the
sacrifice was real, the safety achieved remained terribly uncertain, and deportations continued from Sosnowiec throughout 1942 and 1943. Merin
understood his helpless position vis-à-vis the Germans: "I stand in a cage
before a hungry and angry tiger. I stuff his mouth with meat, the flesh
of my brothers and sisters, to keep him in his cage lest he break loose
and tears us all to bits."[55] But he felt he had no choice, one of the many
choiceless choices imposed on Jews in the war. In the end, all the principal ghettos and almost all the outlying ones were liquidated before the
Germans finally retreated from the territories they occupied. Selections
for labor continued in Auschwitz even in the fall of 1944, but "salvation
through work" was no longer a viable strategy for survival once the ghettos had been destroyed.

In the workshops, the remaining Jews were haunted by deported Jews.
A considerable amount of the labor they undertook involved sorting
through personal belongings abandoned in the ghetto or the small items
returned from the death camps. In the Warsaw Ghetto, after the "Great
Action," more than 700 men and women worked for "the *Wertefassung*, to
clear out and collect up the booty in the ghetto"; Abraham Lewin's daughter found this work shameful. In Lodz some of the factory "ressorts"
were dedicated to sorting out packs and sacks of clothes and shoes that
came from surrounding ghettos. One survivor remembered heartrending
scenes when "mothers recognized the things of their deported children
and working Jews those of their parents." Some of the clothing came
back "torn and bloody" or contained letters and identification cards of
friends or relatives who had been alive weeks earlier.[56] The shoes and letters, the rumors and the memories, did not allow any peace in the ghetto.

Jews across Europe also debated the sheer scale of Hitler's prophecy. On the lists maintained by the SS, as they prepared to implement the
"final solution," the designated victims, from the Jews in Ireland to the
Jews in the Soviet Union, numbered 11 million in total, roughly as many
people as had been killed in World War I. The talk at Lwów's Café Wells
in April 1941 was the usual: "the theme of German atrocities against us,
the Jews." A longtime resident, Jacob Gerstenfeld did not doubt the murderous intentions of the Germans. His point was simply that they would
not be able to realize their plans. "In Poland there were 3.5 million Jews,"
he pointed out. "For the sake of argument," he began reasonably, "let us
assume that the Germans, with all their atrocities would murder 100,000,
maybe even 200,000 Jews, or, let us take the worst-case scenario—half
a million Jews, which of course was an impossibility, who could imagine
such a thing? This would mean that every seventh Jew would be murdered. Why should I be the seventh? I would do everything possible to
be among the six that would not be murdered."[57] The very arithmetic
seemed to hold out hope.

What strengthened the argument against total solutions was the
staggered nature of the deportations: nothing happened right away,
and then once it did, it happened only incompletely. Thousands of Jews
were grabbed, but the thousands who were left behind, accompanied at
times by new arrivals into the ghetto, found it more difficult to see German operations in a machinelike way, undeviating and systematic. In the
Lodz Ghetto, Oskar Rosenfeld reminded himself to "paint the zigzag of
in- and outsettlings!" among Polish and German Jews: "a) Into the
ghetto. . . . c) Germans in. d) Poles out. e) Germans out. f) Neighboring
Poles in. g) Some of the same out. h) Again, Poles out." Of course, in "this
confusion, thousands die."[58] But confusion also protected thousands.

After deportations, those who remained in the ghetto continually
attempted to create a new center of gravity. After friends and relatives
had disappeared to an almost certain death, chroniclers often referred to
survivors catching their breath, finding their footing, albeit in horribly
adverse conditions. "Under the overcoat of Ponar," one inhabitant of the
Vilna Ghetto looked about in March 1942, "a life creeps out that strives
for a better morning. . . . The literary evenings burst their seams, and

the local hall cannot hold the large number that comes there." Surveying circumstances in Lwów, Jacob Gerstenfeld remarked that "the mass slaughters called *Aktions* were interlaced with periods of relative calm." "Two weeks without an 'action' sufficed for people to delude themselves again that a remnant will be saved," noted one diarist in Peremyshliany, a small town in Galicia. The hardships of daily life, remembered one survivor, "were like water, which leaves no trace. After every new loss, after every blow, the calm surface resettled with terrifying indifference."[59]

Before the final evacuation of the Lodz Ghetto in early August 1944, it was possible to hear the boom of Russian artillery, to fantasize about "Apocalypse or Redemption," the title of the last entry in one of Rosenfeld's notebooks. For years, Jews had tried to dispute the ability of the Nazis to carry out the "final solution" by imagining that the war would end or that new allies would join the fight so that they would be saved before they were murdered. Soviet counterattacks on German positions and the entrance of the United States into the war in December 1941 appeared to interrupt the steady military advance of the Germans, although with the new year the Nazi assault on the Jews accelerated rather than slowed down. In 1942 it was hardly surprising that "when acquaintances met each other on the ghetto streets," they would ask for "the latest news" about the war against Germany and the war against the Jews: "Open your mouth and tell me what you know." "If there is the slightest hint of any Nazi defeat or political setback," Chaim Kaplan explained, "it serves as a cure for our bones." And "when the news doesn't tell us what we want to hear, we twist and turn it until it seems full of hints, clues, and secrets that support our views." This practice bothered Kaplan when he saw ghetto residents prepare for eminent liberation: "We even set dates and hours for the end of the war." But the twisting itself, Kaplan believed, had the salutary effect of strengthening the spirit. After all, he pointed out, "a nation which for thousands of years has said daily, 'And even if he tarries, I will await the coming of the Messiah every day,' will not weaken in its hope." The challenge was to wait, to endure; Polish Jews would be murdered, but Polish Jewry would survive. Jews in the ghettos remained steadfast in their belief that the democracies would eventually vanquish "the other side, the enemy of the Jews and the enemy of humanity."[60]

So long as this faith held, it served to ward off the threat of Treblinka or Auschwitz, replacing the Nazi future with the Allied future. But, of course, the Allies were in Britain and the Jews stuck with the Germans in Poland. There was great anxiety that time was not on the side of the Jews. Despite setbacks on other fronts, the German war against the Jews proceeded remorselessly. After the Allies invaded North Africa in November 1942, Dawid Sierakowiak, sitting in the ghetto in Lodz, commented bitterly, "They are doing everything except coming here, damn them!"[61]

The great reversals in 1943 that marked the beginning of the end of German power—Stalingrad, "Tunisgrad"—found fainter echoes among Jews because the Nazi "machine of destruction" had relentlessly destroyed most of the ghettos in 1942. Time had run out. "From morning to night," hiding in "Miss Hela's" Warsaw apartment, Calel Perechodnik could "hear shots from machine guns and the boom of dynamite." "The whole sky was red." Through the shutters, he could see Poles "standing for hours on the roofs of their houses, observing this unusual sight." "Against the background of the burning Warsaw ghetto," Perechodnik realized that he was witnessing "the twilight of Polish Jewry." "It occurred to me that sooner or later I too would be forced to share the fate of all the Jews," Perechodnik reflected. "I thought to myself that in such a case no one will be left to weep and to honor the memory of my wife, that no one would transmit to posterity her suffering, that maybe no one would demand vengeance for her innocent life, for the death of millions of Jews."[62]

Faced with oblivion, Perechodnik was tormented by the last thoughts of his wife, Anka, who had been herded onto Otwock's market square the year before, on August 19, 1942, and then deported, with their daughter, Aluśko, to Treblinka. "Anka, my wife, what were you thinking then? . . . [M]aybe you are looking at the Polish policeman who is guarding you with a rifle in hand. He came to the movies for so many years, always kissed your hand through the glass opening of the cashier's booth, paid you compliments, told you how beautiful you were with the lamp shining on you, in the flush of youth—and now he is ready to shoot you if you get up." It was the full realization of utter betrayal and abandonment. Perechodnik dared to imagine the train: "You have just passed by Swider,

Josefow . . . You are already in Falenica. The train stands at the station a
long time. . . . The train goes farther. It is already in Warsaw. The last time
you were in Warsaw was in January 1940. You traveled to the bank to pay
off the old debt on the movie house. . . . Aluśko, Aluśko, are you still alive?
Have you not yet suffocated? Anka, do you still have a little water?" Then,
"the train leaves Kosów and detours to the special railroad siding of death
that leads to Treblinka." Perechodnik goes even further, writing in 1943,
"The crowd of naked, silent women, mostly with children in hand, moves
forward to a huge building, where they are supposed to bathe. . . . The
sun sets in blood red color and with it, hope. . . . [T]he doors close auto-
matically, from the interior is heard an enormous cry—it is all over. The
door is opened; people's bodies are thrown out. The building is readied to
receive new people so that they may 'bathe.'"[63]

After the deportations, the streets and houses in smaller ghettos, such
as the one in Otwock, could be reoccupied by Poles. Perechodnik had
walked around the ghetto in Otwock, looking at "empty apartments,"
"broken windowpanes," and "open doors": "Feathers from bedding, old
ration cards, photographs, and identity cards" blew "in all directions"
along empty streets. After the "Great Action," the borders of the Warsaw
Ghetto were redrawn, restoring parts of the district to the Polish city. But
large parts of the ghettos were simply abandoned, "whole rows of flats,
facing each other," "stark empty." The opening lines of a November 1942
underground report on "the liquidation of Jewish Warsaw" contrasted
the "radiance of the incomparable golden Polish autumn" with the bright
sparkle of a new layer of snow:

> This snow is nothing but feathers and down from the bedding of the
> Jews, which along with all the belongings, from the wardrobes and
> suitcases full of linens and clothes to the pots, pans, plates, and other
> household goods, the 500,000 Jews evacuated to the 'East' left behind.
> These things, which do not belong to anyone anymore, the tablecloths,
> the coats, the down blankets, the pullovers, the books, the scales, the
> documents, the photographs lie in a jumble in apartments, in court-
> yards, in swept-up piles covered with the snow of the thousand-fold
> German murder of Warsaw's Jews, the slashed entrails of their beds.[64]

CALEL PERECHODNIK'S ANGRY INDICTMENT OF GERMAN MURDERERS and Polish neighbors doubled as his own self-indictment for being a Jewish policeman. Clarity about the final solution could be achieved among the victims, but Perechodnik's insight was soiled, since the policeman had been able to save himself while watching his wife and daughter and his fellow Jews go to the deportation trains. At the same time, there were many Jews who were not able or willing to comprehend the radical intentions behind the Germans' thoroughgoing racial designs. Given the history of tolerance among Jews and non-Jews over the past century, and given ordinary faith in civilized behavior, it was understandable that Jews had difficulty accepting the unprecedented nature of the Nazis' murderous aims. They made wrong assumptions about the rational basis of German behavior. Yet to resist understanding the Nazis was to hold out hope, and it helped victims survive under the most extreme circumstances.

Because many Jews, at least at the beginning, misled themselves, even when they knew a lot—Hélène Berr is a telling example—it is not surprising that non-Jews also misunderstood the nature of what awaited the Jews when they arrived at the "unknown destination" to which they had been deported. Involuntary labor service, not death camps, was the tragedy most people were acquainted with. But the historical record is clear: neighbors in France and in Poland surmised a great deal about what they were witnessing along the streets of the towns they shared with the Jews. They were far from ignorant of what was happening. But usually they subordinated this terrible knowledge to their own sufferings. Their reckoning confirmed how far most Europeans had come, in the circumstances of the German occupation, to see themselves as "Aryans," or least as non-Jews, whose fate was disconnected from that of Jews. As a result, among non-Jews, knowledge about the murder of the Jews generally did not translate into empathy commensurate with the concerted attack on the innocent, and among Jews faith in non-Jewish neighbors and common-sense assumptions about the Germans tended to blunt sharper insight into the unrelenting nature of the Nazis' pursuit of final solutions. Everything was corrupted in the conditions of extreme violence that prevailed in German-occupied Europe: insight into what was happening, empathy toward victims who were known to be special targets, and trust in the brakes that had traditionally checked complete moral depravity. These shortcomings raised questions about how this manifest corrosion in the ability of human beings to look out for themselves had come to pass in the twentieth century. And they raised the question, "Where was God?"

7

The Life and Death of God

IT WAS IN WORLD WAR I THAT THE SAYING "THERE ARE NO ATHEISTS in the trenches" was first popularized. World War II updated it to read "There are no atheists in foxholes." The premise was that the exposure of human beings to extreme danger, as in these conflicts of man-made mass death, would induce them to seek shelter in the grace and mercy of God. To tolerate terrible events, contemporaries needed to acknowledge the realm they could not control. Another wartime maxim pushed the other way, however, following the remark in Ernest Hemingway's *A Farewell to Arms* that "All thinking men are atheists." While the restored presence of God in the "trenches" or "foxholes" provided meaning in terrible times, and presumed the sufficiency of faith, to reject God was to register that somehow events were so terrible that they could not be reconciled with ideas of God and his ability to protect or offer solace to the believer. The two contradictory ideas share the assumption that, in the modern age, extreme events force individuals to fundamentally reassess their place in the world, either by refurbishing faith as a source of abiding strength or by abandoning it altogether on account of its flimsiness.

Thus, it is perhaps most surprising that twentieth-century Europeans continued to muddle along without moving in large numbers to one or the other position with regard to God. After World War I, most soldiers and citizens shared what one scholar calls a "diffusive Christianity." This "comprised a general belief in God, a conviction that this God was both just and benevolent although remote from everyday concerns, a certain confidence that 'good people' would be taken care of in the life to come, and a belief that the Bible was a uniquely worthwhile book."[1] They prayed in a rationalist and petitionary manner, assuming that God had the capacity to intervene and that events were subject to divine agency, but they also did not have clear answers as to why God chose to intervene when he did. As a result, Christian faith had a certain flexibility; people did not feel the need to avow God in their everyday lives but also did not question his presence or existence. This diffusive Christianity explains why, even in conditions of extreme violence, there were not large numbers of people who either reestablished intimate relations with God or rejected him altogether. If anything, parishioners became less deferential to the priests and preachers who had so effortlessly justified the declaration of war in 1914 and grew less convinced that God was somehow present in the bloody course of events that mocked such justifications in the years thereafter. After World War I, relationships to God became more personal and less a matter of public routine.

Christians continued to hold church funerals, but they were less committed to baptisms, confirmations, and religious weddings. World War II barely budged these secular trends. Yet the unquestioned, almost commonsense faith in God and in a Christian way of doing things, as embodied in the "Golden Rule," "Do unto others as you would have them do unto you," also made any concerted ejection of Christ or God from daily life extremely difficult, as the Nazis themselves would find. Perhaps because the experience of God was no longer so central to the lifeworld of modern Christians, the extreme violence of the occupation in World War II did not shake the premises of the "diffusive Christianity" that people in the end did hold on to. Neither the fate of the Jews nor the part Christians played in their torments disturbed theological assumptions or raised general questions about Christian responsibilities. Observers may have condemned this or that religious figure for not protesting specific un-Christian or antichurch policies the Germans carried out, but they did not reconsider in a fundamental way the relationships between God, faith, punishment, and suffering.

By any measure, church attendance increased modestly during World War II. There were those who believed that parishioners were rejecting the corruption of modern life that the outbreak of the war, the rise of

the Nazis, and the defeat of the republican regimes had allegedly confirmed. While church pronouncements in France in the first year after
the armistice with Germany did refer to God's punishment of a way-
ward, self-indulgent French republicanism, most parish priests sought to
rally parishioners behind ordinary Christian virtues of humility, patience,
charity, and love. They used the liturgical calendar to provide structure
to everyday lives disrupted by the difficulties and displacements of war.
They urged Christians to love their neighbors, without explicitly suggesting they should engage in radical or subversive acts of solidarity with
Jews, the most imperiled neighbors.[2] The focus on the parishioner and on
the neighborhood, as well as the ability of Catholic traditions, particularly
in France and Poland, to reaffirm national identity, meant that religious
experience tended to uphold social and theological conventions rather
than to question them. The violence of the occupation was evidently
never so great as to create "foxhole" conversions, nor so unsettling when
human suffering was contemplated as to force the issue of the existence
of God as such.

    This broad brush applies across much of Europe, but not to the Jew-
ish experience of the occupation. Here there was much more querulous
discussion, even if most Jews remained believers throughout the war.
Jews were in a much better position than Christians to see the hypocrisy
of Christian injunctions to show mercy and love, because they were on
the sharp receiving end of Christian anti-Semitism or indifference. Jews
also had developed a relationship to God in which the integrity of the
Jewish people, its history of suffering punishment and renewing faith, and
its particular covenant as God's chosen people all combined to encourage
more theological debate. And finally, the nearly boundless scale of the
calamity that nearly wiped out the Jewish communities of Europe threatened the very existence of Jewish God, who could not be imagined without the presence of Jewish believers. The Nazi war against the innocent
raised questions about divine justice and biblical authority. It raised the
question of precedent since the Jews had suffered not only in the annals
of modern history but in the ancient books of the Bible.

    Paradoxically, it was also the tormentors of the Jews, the Germans,
who, in small theological circles during World War II, began to reconsider
their relationship to God on account of the massive suffering that defined

Germany's enduring experience of the war. But their God was one who remained focused on Germans rather than on their victims. The presence of suffering on the part of the perpetrators, but the absence of Jews, who had been their victims, makes the German reckoning with God at the end of the war worth examining; it reveals the stubborn limits of new theological insights. In an odd way, both perpetrators and victims, Germans and Jews, began to formulate new ideas of a wounded, suffering God that resonated in the postwar era.

The God of the Jews

THE MOST EXTRAORDINARY TRANSCRIPT ABOUT THE GASSING IN Chelmno in January 1942 came from an escaped prisoner who has now authoritatively been identified as Szlamek Winer. A thirty-year-old native of Izbica, a village about two-thirds of the way up the road from Lwów to Lublin, and not so far from Zygmunt Klukowski's hometown of Szczebrzeszyn, Winer had been confined to the ghetto since 1941. In January 1942, Winer volunteered to work with about forty other men and found himself assigned as a "grave digger" in Chelmno, about twenty miles away. Under the guard of SS policemen, including one leader known as "the Whip," Winer and his fellow Jews emptied customized furniture vans filled with murdered Jews who had been asphyxiated with carbon monoxide—there were about seven or eight loads each day—and buried the bodies in ditches. They often saw friends and relatives among the dead. At night and in the morning, the men in the various cells of the dilapidated "mansion," where the workers were housed, prayed and talked about "politics, God, and our situation." After a week, Winer managed to escape and flee to the Warsaw Ghetto, where Oyneg Shabes archivists urged him to reconstruct a diary of the horrifying events he had witnessed. Written in Yiddish, the report was transcribed into Polish and eventually made its way to the Polish Government-in-Exile; *The Ghetto Speaks*, the newspaper of the New York City branch of the General Jewish Workers' Union, published a detailed summary of the "gas-executions" in a special edition dated August 5, 1942. It provided dates, locations, and the names of the grave diggers, their murdered relatives, and the SS men, including "the Whip." Ghetto leaders, believing that Winer was in danger in Warsaw on account of what he knew, arranged for him to flee to the ghetto in Zamosc, where he was rounded up and murdered in Belzec in late April 1942. The original Yiddish diary survived the war as part of Emanuel Ringelblum's Warsaw archive.

In his diary Winer detailed the operations of Chelmno and recounted the horrified conversations among the teams of Jewish grave diggers, who saw the "whole Jewish community being swept away."[3] At "about five in the morning everyone was awake because of the cold," he wrote, and the work began around seven. "We began talking," and the talk was about God. "Gecel Chrzastkowski, a member of the Bund, and Ajzensztab (Ajzensztab owned a fur shop in Wloclawek)—both from Klodawa—had lost their faith in God. The others, however, myself included, were strengthened in our belief." They repeated what a man named Mojzesz Asz from Izbica had said the previous evening: "It has fallen to us to be victims, because the time of the Messiah is approaching." Despite his faith, Winer also felt the great pain of abandonment. In the middle of the night, he had been awakened by nightmares or the cold: "O despair, if there is a God in heaven, how is it possible to permit the murder of innocent people! Couldn't He perform a miracle?" At the end of the day, new grave diggers arrived and brought (false) news that "the Russians had already retaken Smolensk and Kiev" and were "advancing toward us." Even so, some of the older people had "completely lost their faith in God. They said that those are fairy tales. There was no God. How could He see our suffering and do nothing?" Others "remained firm in their faith," even though "we are not able to understand God's actions."

Some in the group recited evening prayers and, the next morning, the Psalms, though "weeping bitterly"; "others lay still, completely indifferent." A few "even mocked us for our piety saying that there is certainly no God and that all attempts to console ourselves seemed childish," Winer recorded. "But we responded that our lives are in the hands of God and that, if this was His will, we would accept it with humility. All the more so, since the time of the Messiah was coming." "Even Ajzensztab," who earlier had lost faith in God, took part in the prayers.

The events recounted in the diary became widely known among leaders of the Warsaw Ghetto, and the diary undoubtedly prompted renewed
discussions about God and about questions regarding faith, the suffering
of innocents, and the coming of the Messiah posed by Winer and his
fellow Jews. Winer depicts the divisions among Polish Jews quite clearly;
perhaps more than half of the grave diggers remained firm in their belief in God. In face of the terrible course of events, a good number of
others, perhaps more secular Jews (such as those mentioned by Winer
who had been active in the anti-Zionist Bund or in more worldly business
dealings), had lost their belief. Believers professed not to know the will
of God, while nonbelievers could not comprehend a God who would
permit terrible suffering or would not intervene to help.

Holocaust survivors Primo Levi and Jean Améry argued that the
clearly defined groups of believers and nonbelievers in the camps approached the horrors unfolding around them in fundamentally different
ways. According to Levi, "believers lived better," because the frameworks
of the Bible kept their sorrows from overflowing into "despair." In his
view, "Their universe was vaster than ours, more extended in space and
time, above all more comprehensible." In an odd way, believers knew
where they were even if they did not know the will of God, while nonbelievers were genuinely cast adrift from all intellectual anchorages.
There was a self-sufficiency to believers because, as Améry put it, even
in Auschwitz "nothing unheard-of occurred." As a result, "The grip of
the horror reality was weaker." By contrast, assimilated Jews neither had
God nor, once they found themselves in the camps, could they put stock
in Enlightenment ideas about morality, which the catastrophe had completely debased. As a result, they had fewer resources to confront their
conditions, which they found more shocking and disorienting. They were
left speechless in the face of the "unheard-of," while believers could use
the precedents and lessons of Jewish history to make sense of events that
they did not consider to be "unheard-of."[4]

Levi and Améry both approached the believer, who whittled down
the "horror reality" with the sure knowledge of tradition, with a mixture
of envy, of those who lived better, and resentment, against those who
could diminish in some way the scale of the crimes against the Jews. But

the distinction between believers, who could assimilate what was happening, and nonbelievers, who could not, is too tidy. The distinction does not account for the enormous labor of comprehension, the challenge of doubt, and the effort to reconcile God with the accumulating evidence of the destruction of Jews, even for the most fervent believers. In their efforts to explain the horrible events, Jews drew on different aspects of biblical interpretations and Jewish history, giving different weight to precedent, to the ability of the faithful to understand the divine, and to the presence of God in the suffering of the innocent. Although many Jews lost faith, most did not. But even among believers, new conceptions of God as less powerful and more vulnerable and also more aligned with suffering victims took hold. If Germans during the Nazi period shared the question of how to become "Aryan," Jews shared the question of how to remain Jewish.

Many thousands of victims faced death singing "Ani Ma'amin," a hymn whose title translates as "I believe." "Ani Ma'amin" was widely sung in the Warsaw Ghetto.[5] To sing the lines, each of which begins with the phrase "I believe with perfect faith," gave powerful expression to the idea that the Jews had entrusted their lives into the hands of God. This perfect faith sometimes troubled Jews and other observers because it seemed to imply complete submission, a lack of engagement with the world, and an unwillingness to acknowledge the "horror reality." Indeed, German killers regarded the alleged passivity of the Jews as evidence of complicity in their own deaths that were ultimately willed by God. But Germans were also puzzled by the unbrokenness of the Jews' faith and trust in God. Perhaps they did not see that the Jews refused to be defined by their enemy. Instead of "going to one's death degraded and dejected," Jews confronted it "with an inner peace, nobility, upright stance, without lament and cringing to the enemy," a stance that dignified and sanctified God.[6] Indeed, the biblical phrase "sheep to slaughter," which was widely quoted at the time to describe Jews' alleged passivity, in fact has a different meaning in the well-known "Suffering Servant" lines in the Hebrew Bible's book of Isaiah. In those verses the metaphor connotes obedience rather than passivity—obedience to God, not to the tormentors of the Jews. The more "marred" the suffering servant's "appearance" was,

the greater the suffering of the Jews, "despised, shunned by men," as
the poet wrote in Isaiah, and the higher the value placed on the apart-
ness of "my people," the Jews, in relation to other evildoing "kings" and
"nations," and the higher the value placed on silence during the Jews'
"maltreatment" (Isa. 53). "Sheep to slaughter" was often, undoubtedly, a
phrase of bitter self-criticism in the ghettos. "Why did we allow ourselves
to be led like sheep to the slaughter? Why did everything come so easy
to the enemy?" asked Emanuel Ringelblum after the Germans had completed the "Great Action" in the Warsaw Ghetto at the end of the summer of 1942.[7] But the phrase also registered steadfast, even untroubled,
faithfulness, one that distinguished the "sheep" from "those who shear."
In similar fashion, the New Testament also refers to Jesus as the "lamb
of God."

"Ani Ma'amin" also contains words about the coming of the Messiah:
"And even though he may tarry, Nonetheless I will wait for him." The
word *tarry* summed up the painful experience of God's silence or his absence and even the possibility that he had abandoned the Jews. Although
ending with a declaration of constancy and faith that makes do without
definitive answers, the text nevertheless poses the question of how long
the suffering can be endured, how long its alleviation can be postponed.
Upon hearing about the murder of Vilna Jews at Ponary at the beginning of September 1941, Herman Kruk tried to write in his diary: "The
hand trembles, and the ink is bloody." "Hard to describe," the "dreadful
thing" demanded more of the witnesses of history. "Can the world not
scream?" And it demanded more of God: "If the heavens can open up,
when should that happen if not today?"[8] Szlamek Winer himself wondered, "Couldn't He perform a miracle?," one that would have prevented
"the murder of innocent people" in Chelmno? Why God tarried was a
question widely discussed among Jews as the Germans expanded their
murderous policy in 1941 and 1942. The ultimate promise, "Nonetheless
I will wait for him," did not erase fretfulness about the knowledge that
"he may tarry" and about the dire consequences of tarrying.

The notion of "nonetheless" or "despite everything" is an important
plank in Jewish theology. "Despite everything," *ken-lo* (yes-no), writes one
scholar, is "one of the permanent values of Jewish thought" in which

faith "causes a 'yes' to spring up out of the roots of 'no.'" The key text for this theological perspective is the book of Job in which Job, certain of his piety and aware of how he and those around him have suffered, experiences an unjust, indifferent God yet persists in believing in justice. Both Job himself and the angry, grieving poetry of the book of Job figure in what has been called "a theology 'in spite of' God for the sake of God."[9] But the years 1941 and 1942 strained that theology, as the "everything" behind the "despite" kept getting larger, the "no" louder, and the "nonetheless" more terribly contrived.

The "nonetheless" revealed the degree to which Jews understood the gap between expectation and experience, understanding and faith, and suffering and sin. It acknowledged that the universe was not legible, and therefore it moved past the foundational story of God's covenant with the Jews. In the book of Deuteronomy, the Jews are presented with a covenantal relationship in which the Jews as a people are enjoined to worship and obey, promised the favor and blessings of God, and, though warned against transgression, comforted by the possibility of repentance. The legalistic structure of the book creates a shared sense of expectation and understanding that is consistent with a covenantal relationship between the people of Israel and God. "Nonetheless" ponders the difficult things the Jews learn long after establishing the covenant with God in Deuteronomy: that the innocent may suffer for the sins of others or for no clear reason at all.

There were still numerous Deuteronomic interpretations of German actions against the Jews, which some Orthodox Jews interpreted in terms of the wrath of a God angry at the secular ways and "false religions" (Zionism, communism) of Jews, but they steadily lost their plausibility. For more and more Jews, the scale of the disaster had completely wrecked the balance between punishment and sin. In the space of the ambiguities created by "nonetheless," Jews, in increasing numbers and with sharper arguments, wondered not about their own mortal sin but about God's divine justice. What was at stake was the meaning and pertinence of interpretations about Jews' suffering in the Jewish religious tradition. Could the Jewish people, as they had done before, preserve faith in the face of biblical and historical ruptures? Or was the calamity of Europe in the 1940s of a different order, one that exceeded the Jewish suffering documented in the book of Lamentations and the book of Job? Jews looked to precedent in an attempt to hold on to the validity of the books of the Bible and God's covenant with the Jewish people and thus the credibility of the survival of both the Jewish people and the Jewish God. As it was, ancient Jewish texts themselves thematized the question of precedence: "Is there any agony like mine?" cries the despised city of Jerusalem in Lamentations 1:12.[10] Lamentations did not necessarily soothe the agonies in the present.

Following the tradition of Talmudic and Midrashic literature, the role of the rabbinical commentary was "to place the events in a comprehensible theological and ethical framework," but this labor of orientation became increasingly tormented over time. In Warsaw the Hasidic rabbi Kalonymus Kalman Shapira at first located the "wickedness" of Amalek, the recurring but ever-same enemy of the Jews in the Hebrew Bible, in terms of present-day Jews' admiration of "secular wisdom." Amalek's "murderous character" was easily aligned with the waywardness of the Jews. Shapira himself attributed the death of his son, daughter-in-law, and mother in Germany's bombing campaign against Warsaw in September 1939 to his own sins. As the crisis worsened, however, Shapira set aside the arithmetic of the book of Deuteronomy, in which God distributed punishments for sin. He took more seriously the questions of his congregation about the unmistakably "murderous character" of the Germans in Poland by widening the scope of contemplation: "We know and believe that whatever God does to us—even when God forbid, he smites us—it is all for the good." What "seems like a plague" was in truth a "good for Israel." Historical precedent also provided perspective. "Why should a person's faith be damaged now," he asked in a homily delivered on Hanukkah in 1941, "if it was not damaged when he read descriptions of Jewish suffering from antiquity to the present day in Scripture, the Talmud, or Midrash? Those who say that suffering such as this has never befallen the Jewish people are mistaken." In other words, it was time to let go of the idea that the Jews were being punished for their sins and should repent. The scale of the disaster exploded such a simple model of cause and effect. If such a model did not apply, it would take more intellectual work to make sense of the terrible events befalling the Jews. However, what Shapira wanted Jews to remember was that they had always suffered and done so in ways that did not immediately make sense. There was nothing about the scale of the disaster to lead Jews away from identifying with the already established resilience of their people and their faith. Precedence provided sufficient answers. Thinking about the stories of the destruction of the First Temple and the Babylonian exile in the Jewish Bible, philosopher Martin Buber went so far as to say that the experience of God's silence, the dreadful events that threatened faith, and the resulting incomprehensibility regarding divine actions were a central part of the history of Jewish faith; the Holocaust was not qualitatively different from other terrible events the Jews had endured. Therefore, the lessons of "nonetheless" still applied.[11]

Even if the catastrophes occurring in 1942 could be shown not to be without precedent, the perception that events in the present had exploded the frameworks of the past remained profoundly unsettling. Shapira himself had growing difficulty finding words of consolation. "The words are now stale," he wrote in the third winter of the war; "they will not have any effect" on the rabbi who might attempt to console or on his listeners. After the "Great Action" in the summer of 1942, Shapira returned to his earlier sermons and added postscripts, which offer extraordinary evidence of the increasingly difficult labor of orientation. To an August 1941 sermon in which he had admonished Jews to continue their "study of Torah and divine service" for the sake of the future, he added in September 1942 that such admonishments were no longer possible. "When our communities are almost completely destroyed," and when "even those few individuals who are spared are . . . crushed and suffused with the fear of death, there are no words with which to lament our sufferings; there is no one to admonish, there is no heart to rouse to religious activities." A few months later, in November 1942, he appended the following to a sermon delivered the year before: "Only until the end of the year 5702 [summer 1942] was it the case that such sufferings were experienced before. However, as for the monstrous torments, the terrible and freakish deaths which the malevolent, monstrous murderers invented against us, the House of Israel, from the end of 5702 and on—according to my knowledge of rabbinic literature and Jewish history in general—there has never been anything like them."[12]

Shapira's amended sermons indicate how the Holocaust had begun to make understanding God and his ways exceedingly difficult. Faith that, despite his tarrying, God would intervene to save the Jews crumbled. Shapira admonished Jews in Warsaw to remain faithful despite the lack of evidence that he would be able to save them. He spoke in sermons of God's withdrawal into "His inner chambers," where he had fled to weep and grieve in silence.[13] But while faith in a God who could not save the Jews revealed the pure and martyr-like qualities to faith, it also opened the door to suspicions that God could only weep as all the Jews disappeared, a complete burning or devouring that would completely short-circuit the thousand-years' history of the Jews and their faith.

Many similar scenes of theological torment unfolded in Jewish ghettos and hiding places across Europe in 1942 and 1943. To explain their experiences, Jews looked to their own sinfulness, reminded themselves that the innocent suffer disproportionately the sins of the guilty, and reassured themselves that ancient Jews, too, had suffered in mysterious, incomprehensible ways. Only such ancient precedents could offer hope of containing the scope of the present calamity by making it simply horrible but not comprehensive and final. Yet the calamity seemed more comprehensive and more final. Thus, the relationship between ancient narratives and present-day suffering was intensely debated.

Jews read and reread the book of Psalms, the book of Lamentations, and the book of Job. They studied the expulsions, the Crusades, and the pogroms. In the Brussels apartment where he lived on false papers with his parents, sixteen-year-old Moshe Flinker "realized once again that the troubles of the Middle Ages and our troubles today are identical." From the perspective of two thousand years, "all our troubles, from the first to this most terrible one, are multiple and endless, and from all of them rises one gigantic scream." The cry "is identical to the cries in other places or at other times." Yet if Moshe heard the echoes of the past, he was almost deafened by the cries of the present, the "one gigantic scream." The present witnessed such great suffering that the time of the Messiah was surely drawing nearer. Deliverance, he maintained, would not come from the

Russians, or the British, or the Americans, whose postwar world would be at least as anti-Semitic as the prewar world: "Salvation will only come when the whole world and particularly the Jews have given up the hope for an Allied victory. . . . Precisely when all expectations have come to an end, God will stand by us." Amid the suffering of the innocent in the present, Moshe hoped he recognized the "birth pangs of the Messiah." Many rabbis similarly assured that "the harsher the persecution of the Jew, the greater the ground for the rescue."[14] In this view, the agonies of the present beckoned the Jewish future by hastening the coming of the Messiah.

But Moshe's time management fell apart. He wondered why the chain of calamities was so long, and he imagined the possibility of time without end, without future or redemption: "Perhaps this is only one link in a long chain of anguish which will continue in the future."[15] In this case, empty, repetitious time without meaning would win out over the cumulative redemptive promise of Jewish history as described in the Bible; a litany of terrible events would be left unorganized and unreflected by the words of God and merely confirm his eternal absence. In Moshe's reading of Jewish history across five thousand years, the present could reaffirm the historical time of the Jews who maintained faith despite everything. This expressed the authority of precedence. The immense suffering of 1942 could also redeem Jewish history in an "eye blink" if the unprecedented disaster of the present hastened the coming of the Messiah. But Jewish history could also be invalidated altogether if the unendingness of suffering no longer fitted with precedents and simply had the effect of removing the idea of the end, the idea of resolution and redemption.

Moshe's reflections never quite found a harbor. They moved constantly between comprehension and incomprehension, and they took up consideration of the books of the Bible as well as news releases from the BBC. But untethered to a particular model as it was, the despair grew larger and more unmanageable; this is the "plot" of his diary, so to speak. "Before," he reflected, "that was three or four months ago, it did not cost me any effort to answer these questions. With every fiber of my being I felt linked to my people and to my brothers. But now," at the beginning of 1943, he wrote, "everything is different. Since the time that emptiness has caught me in its clutches, I feel that nothing concerns me anymore, as if I was already dead."[16] Commentary gave way to cries, prose to poetry and song. In some ways, the diary, typically a record of events, began to document the impossibility or futility of keeping such a record. In a poem titled "An Event," Moshe was still able to fit the events of 1943 into the Jewish calendar's 5703, though the tenses flicker between present, future, and conditional:

> *Now we are here*
> *here we are standing*
> *In this year of the twentieth century*
> *We stand here and wait*
> *Our God, will you stand by us*
> *Yes, our God, you will stand by us*
> *Yes, our Redeemer—you will redeem us*
> *You have forgotten—you will remember*
> *You have abandoned—you will return*
> *You have pity on us*
> *And have mercy on us*
> *You will plant us once more*
> *In the earth of our land*
> *You will bring us to stand once more*
> *In the place of our heritage.*

But in moments of despair, as in another poem, titled "Before Afternoon Prayers," 1943 threatened to push 5703 into the abyss of total catastrophe. Flinker anticipated the death of God, who would not exist in a world without the Jews. He therefore appealed to God's own self-interest, urging him to save the Jews "for Your sake." He wrote:

> *Over our head, catastrophe upon catastrophe has come and comes*
> *Not long, and then everything is destroyed*
> *Two thousand years we bore the yoke of exile*
> *Two thousand years we allowed children*
> *to be burned*

for catastrophe—for suffering . . .
If it is not for our sake
Do it for Your sake.
Quick, Eternal God—save us!

The juxtaposition of *Quick* and *Eternal* perfectly expressed the quandary of Moshe's consternation and his faith. Everything depended on "the speed of an eye blink."[17]

Why was it no longer possible to easily contain the disastrous events befalling the Jews in 1943 in the larger framework of historical Jewish time, in the calendar in which it was the year 5703? And how did Europe's persecuted Jews come to conceive of God as a result?

First of all, the manifestations of the calamity were increasingly general rather than specific or localized. This omnivorous quality qualified the pertinence of precedence in the past. The news of events in Chelmno or Treblinka indicated that the German assault on Jews was systematic. The death camps were no longer the work of a "roving execution squad or a localized pogrom," and they were not associated with offensive military operations in the Soviet Union or with a German withdrawal. Their operation seemed to be a directed, well-organized, and sustained war on civilians, like a new world order. Moshe himself came to believe that precedent did not apply because of the sheer extent of the catastrophe. "First of all," he reflected, "in former times the persecutions were always localized," giving the examples of the expulsion of Jews from Spain and pogroms in recent eastern European history. "In one place Jews were very badly treated, while in another they lived in peace and quiet." "The second difference," he continued, "is of the official character that the present-day persecutions take, and the organized manner in which one continuously increases our suffering." In Warsaw Rabbi Shapira agreed: "In all our previous troubles, there was always at least a refuge for us. In one land they considered us expendable and spilled our blood out like water, yet in another land we were free people and nobles. If we were to only flee the land of blood, we could bring ourselves into the hands of its foe and king, with praises. Such is not the case today, when it is as if the entire world has risen against us—this one raises the axe before our eyes, and this one prepares to stab us with the spear." We alone, he added, our "faces blackened and hearts confused, must wander about, with fear and suffering, insulted, degraded and pursued without refuge, every step a danger for us, every morning presenting new dangers for us."[18] In both Brussels and Warsaw, the disaster seemed unprecedented, although it was less so when Jewish commentators in Jerusalem or New York looked at it.

The second reason the calamity seemed to be outside the boundaries of Jewish history was the complete disassociation of the imprisoned Jews from the rest of humanity for whom they had always considered themselves torchbearers of truth and justice. Jews often identified with the fate of the Armenians who had been slaughtered by the Ottoman Turks in 1915, for instance, and Franz Werfel's account of the catastrophe, *The Forty Days of Musa Dagh*, was a popular book in the ghettos. But if Jewish writer Werfel had "bewailed" the Armenians, poet Yitzhak Katzenelson asked, "Who will write a Jewish *Mousa Dag*?" Captive Jews emphasized their terrible isolation and the total silence of the rest of the world. To be sure, Emanuel Ringelblum pointed out, "Demonstrations are held in democratic countries protesting the massacre of Jews in Europe. Various parliaments permit discussion of the persecution of the Jews."[19] In the end, however, no French steamer *Guichen* and no Captain Joseph Brisson arrived on the horizon in 1942 or 1943 to shell German positions, as Werfel had plotted the happier end to the suffering in Turkey. The Jewish people were murdered before the war ended; as Paul Celan noted, the one who kept his promise was Hitler.

The third reason for the unprecedented nature of the calamity was the murder of children. Certainly, there is plenty of infanticide in the Jewish Bible. Abraham was enjoined to sacrifice Isaac; the wind came, and Job lost his sons and daughters. But the death of children is not the primary point of these Bible stories, which address through radical means the motives of Abraham and Job, yet contemporaries in 1942 and 1943 remarked repeatedly on the murder of children as marking a new, unparalleled phase in the catastrophe. Rabbi Shapira wrote at the end of June 1942, when the inhabitants of the Warsaw Ghetto had heard of the wholesale slaughter of children: "Now innocent children, pure angels, as well as adults, the saintly of Israel, are killed and slaughtered just because they are Jews, who are greater than angels. They fill the entire space of the universe with these cries and the world does not turn back to water, but remains in place as if, God forbid, He remained untouched?!" In this turn of events, "the father is as orphaned as the world is cold."[20]

Jews in the Warsaw Ghetto contemplated the "theology of the child." In June 1942, Ringelblum referred to the fact that children "are the first to be exterminated." He continued: "Except for Pharaoh, who ordered the newborn Hebrew babes thrown into the river Nile, this is unprecedented in Jewish history" (in fact, Ringelblum's point about precedence is even sharper since only male infants were murdered by the Egyptians). "In the past," he wrote, "whatever was done with the grownups, the children were always permitted to live—so that they might be converted to the Christian faith. Even in the most barbaric times, a human spark glowed in the rudest heart, and children were spared. But the Hitlerian beast is quite different. It would devour the dearest of us, those who arouse the greatest compassion our innocent children." Yitzhak Katzenelson made a similar observation. He knew that Jews in the sixth century had been defeated in battle, that their soldiers had been massacred and their people exiled. But the Germans, he insisted, "do not kill us in battle." This was not like Babylonia, as described in the book of Lamentations, because "they destroy us while we are peacefully employed in their ser-vice. They transport us in trains; tens of wagon loads daily, to Treblinka and other like places."[21]

When Yitzhak Katzenelson sang "The Song of the Murdered Jewish People," the poem he wrote in the holding camp in Vittel, France, where the Germans had deported him after the Warsaw Ghetto Uprising, he removed the year 1942 from the traditional Jewish calendar. The calamity that had befallen the Jews was almost completely coextensive with the Jewish nation, which had almost ceased to exist. The song mourned a people unable to honor and cherish God or to wait for even a tarrying Messiah because it had been murdered. To be sure, Katzenelson him-self was a survivor and recorded the song, but "the Murdered People" registered the victory of Amalek, the enemy of the Jews, over the Messiah and thus the end of Jewish history. In all previous disasters, Jews had been able to reassemble and to mourn their dead according to the stories of faithfulness and devotion as told in books of the Bible. Living Jews had recomposed the living spirit of the Jewish nation, but Katzenelson wrote from a place where that living spirit was completely in tatters. This unparalleled situation demanded a new accounting. If God had been forced to abandon his people, had not that led them astray?

When Moshe Flinker urged God on with the imperative *Quick*, he placed himself in the Jewish tradition of arguing with God, just as Job had. The book of Job uses the horrible sufferings meted out to Job, the end of his prosperity, the death of his children, the wrenching of his body, to dispute the idea that there is meaning in human pain but also to give voice to the questions that the faithful nevertheless have about God's relationship to his people. As they witness Job's torments, his friends insist that he repent because, if Job had not been sinful, God's punishments would make no sense. His wife would simply curse God and see God as merely human. But Job does not go down either route, because to do so would mean betraying himself and his faith. The book of Job thus associates faith with suffering. God eventually speaks to Job without answering his questions, and Job must live with the unconsoling thought that God is both incomprehensible to and distant from his human creations. In fact, God reminds Job of the sheer awesomeness of his universe, which includes the beasts of Leviathan and Behemoth, terrible things that faith must accept. In this universe, intellectual justifications or understanding of human suffering is puny and insufficient. The book of Job can do nothing more than propose for Jews a vexed faith in a powerful, arbitrary, and, last, silent God—he withdraws completely from the Jewish Bible after the book of Job. With Auschwitz among the beasts of creation, however, Jews quarreled with greater obstinacy. They did not let it go, as Job had, when he heard about Leviathan and Behemoth, and God's unknowable nature, and they disputed Job's notion that suffering was a simple expression of faith. The comfort Job took in his own "dust and ashes" was not satisfactory as long as the terrors of God's universe manifested themselves exclusively in Jewish "dust and ashes."

In some ways, Jews in the 1940s began to read the book of Job from the perspective of Job's children, who were swept out of the Bible by God's capriciousness, and not from the perspective of Job's friends, who continued to believe that punishment came from sin and therefore could not be malevolent, nor from the perspective of Job, who remained steadfast in his faith despite the afflictions he suffered. What possible lesson was there to learn when the children of Jews were being murdered and when the Germans always took the children first and wanted more? (The resurrection of Job's children is a Christian, not a Jewish, idea.)

Job's successors, as they undoubtedly thought of themselves in the Polish ghettos of the 1940s, did not just press God with questions but prepared briefs of indictment. The anger and impatience of the faithful revealed how Jewish relationships with God had begun to change and no longer accommodated Job's conclusions about God's awesome or distant nature. He came to be closer at hand, and more dirtied up. In his poem "Slaughter Town," poet Simcha Bunem Shayevitch, who was deported from Lodz and murdered in Auschwitz in 1944, sounded out: "Poet of wrath and vengeance . . . Mother Rachel . . . And Rabbi Levi Yitzhok . . . go, all three, to God. You will thunder and demand." You "will weep and plead." One day in Warsaw, after the "Great Action," Wladyslaw Szlengel finally took "out a large book," and "a Waterman pen," and "opened an account" with God, the "gentle elderly Man / with whom I drank at the same table." "I prayed," Szlengel began, weighing his part of the bargain, "I fasted," "I have said: God will help," "I have had faith: God is with me." God had not done his part. "Look!" Szlengel concluded the argument, "The page of Your deeds / In relation to me—is clean." Like Job, Szlengel in Warsaw demanded an answer. "For all my deeds," what did Szlengel's Jews get? Only "the tin tablets" identifying the remaining laborers in the workshops, only "the Umschlagplatz," "Treblinkas," and "Prussian gas." In fact, Jews in Lodz staged a trial of God in the fall of 1942, after the deportations of thousands of old, ill, and very young residents. Elie Wiesel imagined a similar court in Auschwitz, writing in his autobiographical novel *Night*, "I did not deny God's existence, but I doubted His absolute justice," in which case, "I was the accuser, God the accused." For poet Itzik Manger, writing in London, the judgment was harsh:[22]

Creator of the worlds, You are mighty and terrible beyond all doubt.
But from the circle of true lovers of Israel, we Galicians,
for ever shut You out!

For a number of Jews, God had betrayed the Jews rather than the Jews having disobeyed God, but this did not induce them to give up the faith of their fathers, which provided the resources for the judgment against God. If God had abandoned his people, the Jews would not. In this regard, Jews were anticipating the postwar idea that the Torah was more important to cherish and to love than God.

Wladyslaw Szlengel's poem "It's About Time" is the most dramatic account of imaginary trial at which God is not only brought to account for his guilty actions but also punished and killed. It is hard to imagine the tremors of doubt, anger, and fear as Szlengel refused the reconciliation of *ken-lo* in the last months of the Warsaw Ghetto. "We will pay back!" shouted his Jews in "It's About Time." "For the agony of the Ghetto," "For the death in Treblinka." The people promised that the punishment would be terrible. Once God has been transported by the Jews to the "slaying place," Szlengel imagines the events that follow: the hangman, who is presumably the German, the same hangman who had murdered the Jews, will push God "into the steam chamber / And hermetically closed the hatch behind you." After the "torture of dying," "they" take over from the Jews who had overseen the trial and the transport of God. "They will drag your body along and throw it into a monstrous pit." "They will pull your stars out—the gold teeth out of your jaw." In the end, "they will burn you," as they had burned the Jews, and "you will become but ashes," intermingled with the ashes of the Jews that God had abandoned.[23] The future-perfect construction suggests that the punishment has not yet taken place. Szlengel's anger, and his contemplation of God's execution, remain fantastical. But more Jews contemplated how God had become wounded or incapacitated or even culpable.

When Moshe in Brussels appealed to God to save him for God's own sake, if he was not going to save the God-fearing Jews for theirs, then in effect he was warning God that in a world without Jews, there would be no God, either. Moshe's lament was a final expression of faith, an attempt to save God. But this God was a God who had to be cajoled to act, a God who was possibly crippled or wounded, a God who tarried because he could not do otherwise. Contemplating God's vulnerability, Moshe began to see God in terms of his people's sufferings, to see God, that is, as a Jew in 1943. If, in his "Song of the Murdered Jewish People," Katzenelson composed the "last song by the last Jew," after which there would be no more Jews to "fight or sacrifice" or to "soothe someone's pain," a bitter scene in which God stands by as a third party, alone amid murdered Jews and victorious Germans, in his diary he imagined God as the dead Jews themselves. "They are God!" Katzenelson exclaimed. "A great and vast nation of Jesuses," "not only Jesuses of thirty years of age, but old and venerable Jesuses," "infant and child Jesuses," all of them "murdered Gods." Katzenelson's God is not Job's, awesome and distant; he is no more than the Jewish people and no less than their suffering.[24] Perhaps Katzenelson finally has his murdered people provide a sanctuary to the grieving, weeping, hidden God who was no longer able to save his people but would remain with them. Instead of being given a trial and perhaps executed, God is returned to the community of Jews, if only as "ashes and dust."

In her Amsterdam apartment, where she had learned to pray, Etty Hillesum sought to protect and console God just as her fellow Jews began to be deported. "Paradoxically," writes one scholar, "in a world in which God is powerless his existence is predicated on the faith of those whom he cannot save." Etty came to recognize herself as "the girl who could not kneel but learned to do so on the rough coconut matting in an untidy bathroom." On July 12, 1942, she wrote, "One thing is becoming increasingly clear to me: that You cannot help us, that we must help You to help ourselves. And that is all we can manage these days and also all that really matters: that we safeguard that little piece of You, God, in ourselves. And perhaps in others as well." "The jasmine" behind her house, she wrote, had been "completely ruined by the rains and storms of the last few days"; "white blossoms are floating about in muddy black pools on the low garage roof. But somewhere inside me the jasmine continues to blossom undisturbed, just as profusely and delicately as ever it did. And it spreads its scent round the House in which You dwell, oh God. You can see, I look after You. I bring You not only my tears and forebodings on this stormy, gray Sunday morning, I even bring you scented jasmine. . . . I shall try to make You at home always."[25]

The catastrophe of 1942 and 1943 did not deny the God of Deuteronomy because many victims believed that God had indeed chastised his people for their sins, even as the faithful innocent were afflicted more than the assimilated guilty. The calamity did not deny the God in Job because many Jews believed that faith always required a leap of faith, a *ken-lo*, a despite everything, even if that meant the death of children who made orphans out of parents, a condition of childlessness that imperiled the very existence of Jewry. But the events of 1942 and 1943 did make more pertinent the idea of a crippled God who stood in for his horribly wounded people, of God weeping in the hidden inner chamber that Shapira imagined, of God who was the Jew in the train cars and in the gas vans, of God as "seven million" Jesuses. Kneeling on her rough coconut matting, Etty Hillesum neither overturned nor validated anyone's theology. But the rough matting in her untidy Amsterdam bathroom on which she knelt provided a foundation for postwar theological reassessments that saw God as present exactly in the wounds of his people. In the Nazi attempt to kill God, God's people deliberated, they argued and raged, they shared the anguish of Katzenelson and Szlengel as they contemplated the end of Jewish history. For some Jews, God was indeed dead, or else did not exist; it is estimated that about one-third of Holocaust survivors, most of them Orthodox, lost faith in God, and almost no nonbelievers became believers in the same period. Yet for most believers, and that is for most Jews, God remained present in the catastrophe, first and foremost as the God of the Jewish Bible to whom they expressed faith when they sang the words "I believe with complete faith," but also as an "old-new God" who would share suffering but could not annul affliction.[26]

The God of the Germans

THE NAZIS' MOBILIZATION OF VIOLENCE AGAINST INNOCENT CIVILians was so unrelenting that it is hard to think of the perpetrators as anything but godless men. In some ways, this state of fearlessness and godlessness is what the Nazis wanted to achieve in their racial revolution. In their view, Germany would prosper only if its citizens accepted their responsibilities as racial comrades who were willing to sacrifice the weak and crippled among their own families and to exterminate the dangerous and alien among the inhabitants of Europe they conquered. To destroy biologically unworthy elements in modern life meant rejecting the Judeo-Christian God of mercy and love and the humanistic ethic that had developed as a common part of European civilization. According to the Nazis, morality had to be oriented around Germany, not "Man."

The Nazis had considerable success in producing genuine conversions to National Socialism, especially among the young people on whom Hitler had set his sights. Across the Third Reich, individuals debated for themselves the whole question of *becoming*, becoming a National Socialist, becoming a comrade, becoming a race-minded German. They grappled with questions about the importance of fitting in, the convenience of going along, and the responsibilities the individual owed to the collective. Their answers were never absolute, but, almost until the end, Nazism remained a highly relevant moral and ethical current, and an alternative to Christianity, in Germany. The Nazis certainly accelerated secular trends: 50 percent more Germans left the church during the Third Reich than had done so during the Weimar Republic. Although exits slowed dramatically after the beginning of the war, because there were very few returns, the churches, especially the Protestant churches, continued to lose parishioners.[27]

Yet on such matters as the divinity of each individual, the consolation of the afterlife, euthanasia, and even the deportation of Jewish neighbors, the Nazis found they could go only so far before encountering arguments. The Ten Commandments and the Golden Rule were not so quickly erased from conscience. To be sure, most Christians succeeded in reconciling their diffuse Christianity with fervent National Socialism, and they hoped that the Nazis would not impede such a reconciliation by moving in a concerted way against the churches. But the Nazi project to undermine universal humanitarian impulses, to argue that instead of "Man" there were only men or races, to contravene international law, required *effort*. It gained traction but not without friction. Christians were deeply complicit in the policies of the Third Reich inasmuch as they made deliberate efforts to reconcile Nazism with Christian principles, but they continued to distinguish themselves from those they considered to be fanatic National Socialists. As a result, they experienced life in the Third Reich as a series of acceptable compromises and as a sequence of tense standoffs.

The Third Reich was a predominately secular place, and so soldiers who were religious found themselves isolated and even ostracized, mocked as "praying soldiers" or "brothers" who never fully fitted into the military cultures of the fighting unit, which was based on comradeship. In World War II (as in World War I), the virtues of (military and ethnic) comradeship were prized over (sectarian or universal) Christian brotherhood and were routinely enforced by soldiers themselves through collective hazing rituals, ranging from visits to brothels to the execution of prisoners of war and even the murder of Jewish civilians. For most soldiers, the conventional Christian view of war as punishment for sin and as a test of faith did not make sense; *Volk*, nation, and especially comradeship cut deeper. Whereas Christian soldiers saw the war as an opportunity to bring theologically inclined young people into contact with comrades in order to spread the word of God and strengthen religious experience in the postwar world, most soldiers simply wanted to return to the prewar world.

Most Wehrmacht soldiers accepted the National Socialist premise that Germany was fighting for its very existence, and their faith in this idea made it less likely for combatants to question whether the war against civilians was right in God's eyes. What they did begin to wonder about was why God was subjecting them to unrelenting war and violence, which meant that a universal humanitarianism did begin to slip back into the discourse. It was a humanitarianism that tended to erase differences between Germans and their enemies by merging the fate of the two groups. Some soldiers on the eastern front came to refer to the killing simply as murder, with both Germans and Russians as victims. These sorts of equivalencies across the military front suggest the growing difficulty soldiers had in continuing to explain the war in the National Socialist terms of "us" and "them," but it did not produce real insight into the nature of National Socialist violence against civilians. It certainly did not lead to equivalencies between Germans and Jews. In the end, German soldiers experienced violence as mobile military forces free to advance and retreat. They could not see themselves as the Jews did, as a people or nation overtaken by death and abandoned by God. The insights they gained about how suffering did not confer meaning, the lesson of Job, they gained as soldiers who, on the battlefield, suffered and faced death, but not as active agents in a machinery of destruction. They forgot that it had been the Germans who had acted in God's name by wreaking such terrible judgments on the world in the first place.

Mimeographed newsletters produced by two close-knit Protestant groups contain extensive excerpts from letters written by their members who were fighting in the field. These letters indicate how conceptions of God in Germany's war changed over time. The *Sternbriefe* were newsletters that Hans Graf von Kanitz, the commander of the Chemical Warfare School in Celle, sent to about four hundred Christian Wehrmacht officers who had participated in Kanitz's Bible-reading groups in the 1930s. They recorded more conservative theological views and a robust patriotism. The *Rundbriefe* were produced by soldiers who, before the war, had studied with Marburg archaeologist Erich Dinkler and theologian Hans von Soden, both of whom were members of the quasi-dissident Confessing Church and were strongly influenced by a colleague of Soden, liberal theologian Hermann Bultmann. These newsletters provided more open-ended and inquisitive views. In contrast to the officers' *Sternbriefe*, the students' *Rundbriefe* were much less tied to the state and National Socialism. Both are singular sources for understanding the religious thinking of Christian Wehrmacht personnel. Although they are not representative—they do not include Catholic voices, and the soldiers who contributed were much more self-consciously Christian than most Wehrmacht members—they document writers who deliberately searched for religious meaning, just as Moshe Flinker and Etty Hillesum had. The collections reveal both changes in German religious experience over the course of the war and German soldiers' limited reckoning with the nature of Nazi violence.[28]

The *Sternbriefe* quoted patriotic writers such as Gorch Fock, Walther Flex, and especially Otto von Bismarck. The officers repeatedly cited Bismarck's words—"I am *God's soldier* and I must go where he sends me, and I believe that he sends me and *fashions* my life as he needs it,"— almost as much as they did the Old and New Testaments. The career officers made little distinction between soldiering for God and soldiering for Germany. "This double duty does not imply a division," wrote Kanitz. "On the contrary, we do not want to be surpassed by anyone differently minded in loyalty, dutifulness, and readiness for action." They adopted the militant language of National Socialism—*Führer, Final Victory, Terror Attacks*—with ease. There is only one reference to tensions between a Christian and a Nazi worldview that discussions about "the war and the Fifth Commandment" (Thou shall not kill) and "the universality of Christianity and the ethnically specific nature of belief demanded in the present day" were intended to reconcile.[29] In contrast to the *Rundbriefe*, the *Sternbriefe* did not promote a vision of a new, respiritualized Germany after the war. For Kanitz's group, being Christian represented a better way to serve Germany, a country that had found God's favor. The *Sternbriefe* took note of officers' promotions as they made their way up the Wehrmacht chain of command, as well as the deaths of those who had been called to God's side.

Again and again, the letter writers described their isolation as Christians in the army; fellow officers stationed in France showed little interest in discussions about the Bible or in Sunday worship, preferring movies and cafés, "femaleness" and "food." When things became tougher in Russia, the Christian officers felt terribly estranged from the casual code of conduct expressed in the words of singer Lale Anderson's big hit "Es geht alles vorüber, es geht alles vorbei" (This too will pass when all is said and done), which comrades quoted repeatedly in letters home. In one field hospital in Stalino, "all the wounded" sang it, "slowly, wistfully," whenever it played on the radio.[30] To the Christian officers, such an attitude indicated a lack of faith in God as well as in Germany. Kanitz's officers believed that Christians, with their sense of duty and discipline, and seriousness of purpose, made better soldiers than the itinerants who sang along with Anderson. The reverse was also true: the ordeal of soldiering offered the opportunity to combat personal weakness, to wrestle with "the bastard in us," "our good old boy aspect," and thus to become better Christians.[31]

"God with us," the phrase stamped imperiously on the belt buckle of every Wehrmacht soldier, embossed around the Prussian eagle and swastika, well describes how Kanitz's Christians thought about God's relationship to Germany. Major Boesenberg, writing from France at the end of June 1940, reflected on the "incredible" and "inconceivable" turn of events that had resulted in Germany's victory, but at the same time he knew what "God has done to us and for us." "Christians have the obligation," agreed Oberleutnant Fligge, "to thank God that he so obviously blessed our weapons." After the invasion of the Soviet Union, the Christian officers believed not only that God remained on Germany's side but also that he had chosen Germany as his tool in the "holy crusade" against Communism. "If in Poland God's purpose was not recognizable," commented First Lieutenant Loetsch in August 1941, "then the devil is literally here," in Russia, "without a mask."[32]

The Nazi condemnation of Judeo-Bolshevism meshed seamlessly with biblical descriptions of the struggle between light and darkness. "Isaiah 1, 3–4; Genesis 28, 15; Matthew 27, 25, and probably also Psalm 109, 16–18" could be cited to confirm "God's judgment against the still-cursed Jews," one letter writer declared. The fact that the war became more brutal and German casualties mounted made the struggle against the "devil" more recognizable and righteous. "So we can see," wrote First Lieutenant von Dietlein in November 1941, "that this war, in which everything is heightened in excess, is a judgment on the nations, and particularly violent states such as Russia and England."[33]

Theoretically, the horrors of the battlefield could intensify unremittingly and only further confirm that an apocalyptic struggle with the forces of evil was under way. Even after Stalingrad, von Dietlein confidently read "all the events of the last years" into "the prophecies in the Bible." The "what" was clear—Germany's victory; what was not clear was the "when," which only God knew. But by 1942, the bitter course of the war made it more and more difficult to see the viciousness of the fighting as evidence of the righteousness of the cause. The spectacular violence of the war, which had brought no quick or clear resolution, began to disperse Germany's unified crusade against Bolshevism into countless individual struggles of endurance in battle. This dispersion was manifest in the "brooding" or "chatter" that the Christian soldiers repeatedly enjoined themselves to resist. Kanitz himself remained convinced in December 1941 that "the Wehrmacht had proven itself to be the best in the world," but he also admitted that "we have also had to learn how little man can do, how dependent he ultimately is" on God, "the Lord of history."[34] Whereas in France God was acknowledged as "the Lord of history" because he had ordained Germany's victory, in Russia he was "the Lord of history" because he withheld it.

The sense of desperation grew worse over time. "The people are being tossed about by the endless hardships" of the war, observed First Lieutenant Schröter in November 1942. "There is no quiet, no peace in sight, no way out of this misery." It was from this terrible place that God would finally lead the faithful. "We have to first find ourselves at a dead end, where no amount of doing and thinking will get us over the wall, only God who will then be able to tell us: my ways are perfect!" References to suffering and anguish drenched the *Sternbriefe*, which sought consolation in the unfathomable nature of God or in the mercy that he extended to those who suffered in adversity. Officers reported a widespread feeling among the troops they led that God had fallen silent. But, objected First Lieutenant Sturm, "God is never silent! He speaks to us, but in his fashion." Images of "dead ends" and high "walls" indicated the sheer difficulty of the circumstances, but left open the possibility of a breakthrough, although it was no longer clear whether this opening coincided with Germany's victory. In considering Germany's fate after Stalingrad, Lieutenant-Colonel Bösenberg recalled the ancient Jews. "God doesn't need our people, as little as he needed the chosen people in the Old Testament!" he warned: "Whether the German people continue to be the decisive instrument of God in the reorganization of the world of nations and remain the blessed vessel of the divine mission, or will be cast aside, will depend on whether Germany allows itself to be called to its God and to be prepared for his tasks. Otherwise, God could also abandon our people and let them perish in the Bolshevist collapse."[35] Kanitz's

Christian officers began to conceive of God as wrathful, judgmental, and even capricious. As the war turned against the Germans, they were humbled, but generally remained true to their conception of themselves as "God's soldiers."

Unlike Kanitz's *Sternbriefe*, Dinkler's *Rundbriefe*, circulated for members of Marburg's "evangelical student community," were written without calibrating the religious texts to Germany's national history. Letters made few references to Germany's triumph over France or to a Christian, anti-Bolshevik crusade in Russia. The soldiers did not express devotion to the Führer, hope for a "final victory," or indignation at "terror attacks" on German cities. On the contrary, the letters documented a growing sense of alienation from the Third Reich and from the ordinary soldiers who had been raised under the "influence of propaganda and in the hustle and bustle of life."[36] If Christian soldiers at first regarded the war as an opportunity for self-examination through suffering, a period of probation from which better Christians would emerge, the offensive in Russia undermined the pedagogical model of the "punishment rod" by producing unrelenting violence and suffering. In the end, soldiers emphasized not the comrades who had yet to become better Christians, but the Christians who had been called to suffer and fight alongside their comrades. The Christians came to identify with the very comrades they had disparaged at the beginning of the war. In contrast to the *Sternbriefe*, the *Rundbriefe* reveal much less anguish about the judgment of God because the students did not interpret the war in terms of Germany's certain victory. If anything, although the letters did not explicitly say so, the students regarded war as punishment for the Third Reich.

Before Christmas 1940, Erich Dinkler described the war as "a great time of waiting, a great time of advent, when we listen with particular attention to the word: open the 'gates, that the King of glory may come in!'" (Psalm 24). It was first and foremost a "battle against ourselves." The students also expressed the hope that the simple struggle to open hearts and minds to the word of God would have an ecumenical effect, bridging the differences between the "parties" within German Protestantism, that is, between the Confessing Church and the pro-Nazi German Christians, and between the confessions, between Protestants and Catholics. Both theological dogma and institutional interests had betrayed the hopes and hardships that ordinary Christians shared in common. The students' ecumenical spirit had taken shape in face of the hostility of the Third Reich to the churches. Simply to pose the question "Will there emerge a Christendom in Germany which in unmistakable attachment to God and Christ is compatible with being a 'genuine citizen' of the 3. Reich?" indicated the perceived gulf between the religious and the party-political spheres. Long conversations with an "old SS leader" about church-state tensions, and the dangerous Jewish influence of the Old Testament, did not leave Erich Dinkler much hope that he would return home to "a world of peace" in which his "probation on the front" had earned him the right to "practice Christian religion and seek a Christian calling"; rather, he suspected that his fight with the Nazis would continue, "but with unequal weapons."[37]

The key to creating Christianity in Germany was to approach comrades in arms as Christians. The war presented this opportunity. "Never again will theologians have such intensive contacts with German men" as they have on the battlefield, observed Heinrich Giesen in May 1940. The young theologians tried to approach their comrades, but discussions never went beyond the "quotidian." Given the "spirit of the age," explained Günther Dehn, most soldiers had lapsed into "lazy" National Socialist thinking. They were far too "transfixed" by "big historical perspectives," that is, by Germany's victories, to accept the war as punishment. For Kanitz's officers, most soldiers were bad Christians and thus bad National Socialists, whereas for Dinkler's students, soldiers were bad Christians because they were good National Socialists. As a result, members of the "student community" constituted a "community of loneliness" in the fighting units.[38] Kanitz's officers were lonely because they read the Bible; Dinkler's were lonely because they rejected the historical grandeur of the war.

If German victories kept comrades from accepting Dinkler's interpretation of war as punishment, the stalled offensive on the eastern front made Dinkler's brothers ready to abandon the whole idea of punishment altogether. This revised understanding of suffering made it possible for the Christian brothers to come closer to their comrades. Just a week before he was killed in Crimea in December 1941, Gerhard Wackerbarth wrote about his war experiences: "All horrors and miseries are served up here, it is the deepest darkness that can be imagined. The eternal light with its bright glow is supposed to light the way." Wackerbarth's confidence that only great darkness can bring light seemed about to give way to despair that any light would emerge from such darkness. Fighting near Moscow, Dinkler himself wrote to Hans von Soden that "the individual is literally being devoured in the battle with nature and men. The manifestations are more ghastly than ever." The war in Russia prompted the students to reassess their comrades. "Here in the trenches I have learned," acknowledged Gerhard Arning, exactly "what our German soldier can achieve and what is demanded of him." "To be a soldier" was the state of being in which "war, death grief, and suffering belong together." Soldiers were called to act, and as actors they were also condemned to "impotent suffering." To "actually be a soldier" "in the firezone" facilitated a relationship to God, which is why Dinkler felt that he belonged "with the comrades right on the front lines."[39] In their suffering, he saw soldiers as almost Christlike figures. God affirmed his presence amid the misery the soldiers endured, but this meant that he could not or would not alleviate the afflictions of the faithful, a motif Jewish quarrelers with the Lord outlined as well. A handful of German and Jewish commentators alike anticipated postwar theologies that scaled God to twentieth-century calamity by reducing his power but discovering his presence in suffering.

Hermann Bousset's reasons for transferring to the front lines were more specific. "From the very beginning," he had seen things in the rear that "were not easy to cope with—they were about the Jews." In his view, "German soldiers distinguished themselves fundamentally from the administrators of the master race," that is, the SS.[40] However, his was a minority voice even in the *Rundbriefe*. The silence is conspicuous; the calamity of war was usually understood as something German soldiers shared with other belligerents, but it is not imagined in scenes of the mass murder of the Jewish people.

In the end, many of the theology students fighting on the eastern front had nothing more to say. Writing early in 1945, Gerd Wicke reflected on how hard it had become "to open one's mouth to speak."

The *Rundbriefe* quoted German novelist Gertrud von Le Fort: "Today we fall silent quite easily, simply out of helplessness in the face of the size and terribleness of events, which words can no longer master. We have the feeling that we have to fall silent! All we can do is endure in silence to God."[41] If Kanitz's *Sternbriefe* focused on interpreting the outcome of the war in terms of God's judgment, Dinkler's *Rundbriefe* discovered the spirit of Christ in the ordinary soldier whose sufferings the students came to share. Both sets of letters reveal how the violence of the war gradually overwhelmed theological knowledge. The result was more speechlessness.

What is missing in either the *Sternbriefe* or the *Rundbriefe* is any compassion for or reference to the civilian population, Russian prisoners of war, or Jews. Only German soldiers embodied suffering in these pages. The example of Konrad Jarausch, a reserve officer who had studied theology before the war, shows that it was possible for soldiers to see the extraordinary suffering of Russian prisoners of war—Jarausch considered them Christlike figures—but the vast majority of soldiers saw only people like themselves. Moreover, there was little sense of the extreme violence that German soldiers in particular deployed, although the student letters drew distinctions between the ordinary *Landser* on the front and more sinister SS officers in the rear. Erich Dinkler noted the growing moral degradation among the troops, but interpreted cold-bloodedness in terms of human weakness and frailty. Especially in the extreme conditions of the eastern front, "God talk" tended to emphasize the helplessness of soldiers, not their agency; it thus overlooked the terrible imbalance between the force projected by the Germans and the vulnerability of unarmed civilians. For most Wehrmacht soldiers, like most Germans, God at the end of the war was not the God of Deuteronomy, who meted out punishment according to sin; he had withdrawn and remained unfathomable, but in ways that permitted Germans to behold their own sufferings without seeing the suffering of others. They consoled themselves without raising further questions about their parts in the war. Perhaps the advancing speechlessness at the end of the war indicated how inadequate theological discourse was when it addressed only German victims; perhaps it revealed the moral desert in which more and more Germans found themselves. In

November 1943, a young twenty-five-year-old Catholic who was serving as a medic wrote home to Passau: "Serious and most serious matters . . . What am I supposed to recount? The shot-up limbs, the stomach and lung wounds, the dying . . . What should I write to you . . . Once in a while I have time to write, but I almost never do. What ever. What for?"[42]

8

The Destruction of Humanity

AT A CONFERENCE AT WAYNE STATE UNIVERSITY IN 1970, A YOUNG rabbi angrily asked, "How is it possible to believe in God?" He directed the question to Elie Wiesel, Holocaust survivor and author of the auto-biographical novel *Night*, who replied, "That is not the question. After Auschwitz, the question is how can one believe in man?" Wiesel's re-sponse suggested that the focus of any consideration of the Holocaust must be the collective moral compass of Europeans in the 1940s. Could human beings be trusted, and their compassion relied upon, when the powerless were persecuted? Wiesel insinuated that the crimes of the Ger-mans in occupied Europe could not be understood in terms of Germans or Nazis alone. Both Germans' actions and the responses of civilians across Europe, both Jewish and Christian, to those actions challenged ba-sic assumptions about what it meant to be human. It was not difficult to demonize German perpetrators and dwell on the "yawning gap" that sep-arated "a Gestapo man from myself," as French critic Léon Werth admit-ted in 1942. But such an easy exercise displayed "the sin of pride." Werth contemplated that "the distance was perhaps no greater than the greatest differences imaginable between any two men." The fact that the positions might be reversed "is what is frightening." Werth's line of inquiry into the reversal of positions became pertinent fifteen years later when France's counterinsurgency campaign in Algeria transformed former "victims into executioners."[1]

During what many French quickly termed the "dark years" of Ger-man occupation, contemporaries wondered about how anchored people really were to such precepts of Judeo-Christian morality as compassion and empathy. Over and over again, they anticipated Wiesel's question. Werth himself, considering the struggle to find compelling proofs for the existence of God, declared, "Let us be modest and find the proofs for the existence of Man." In the terrible year 1942, writer Czeslaw Milosz despaired as well. "Locked in this great laboratory of time between 1939 and 1942," he observed, men and women had shown themselves to be no less cruel than nature itself. Milosz emphasized that in this "spectacle," "we all are also actors." Living in Poland and witnessing the treatment of human beings "as toys to be destroyed, thrown from place to place," hearing the arguments denying the existence of Man, "with a capital *M*," apart from individual tribes, classes, or races, Milosz was astonished by "the plasticity of human nature." As a result of trends stretching back to the Renaissance and the Reformation, Milosz argued, and now embodied by Nazism and communism, morality had become something to be ratio-nalized. In an age characterized by historicism—the idea that we are who we have become—morality seemed autonomous from general and bind-ing rules. Only such developments, Milosz continued, could explain such phenomena as "young men in perfectly clean uniforms [who] can shoot people while gnawing on a ham sandwich." In these conditions, "the beast that slumbers in every man" could go on "a rampage with impunity," still "leaving him clean hands that can stroke a child's head or light the candles on the tree on Christmas eve." Put another way, the real catastrophe was that men could take part in the catastrophe of the war and then remain onstage to take part again. According to philosopher Maurice Blanchot, writing after the war, "There is no limit to the destruction of man," who appeared and reappeared in new, viable, and terrifying life forms. Rather, "There is disaster only because, ceaselessly, it falls short of disaster."[2]

For contemporaries, the background readings supporting this pes-simistic thesis were often the gloomy explorations of the human soul of Fyodor Dostoyevsky, the nineteenth-century Russian writer. In the ghettos witnesses recalled his first novel, *Poor Folk*, and his classic *Crime and Punishment* as they tried to make sense of the conditions of extreme squalor that imprisoned Jews endured. In Lodz getting an apartment was no easy thing after thousands of German Jews were resettled into the

ghetto beginning in October 1941. "In the dark room with only one, finally cleaned, window, a distraught-looking woman, torn dress, unkempt,
haircut . . . lice-ridden"—in this setting, Oskar Rosenfeld, a Czech Jew
who, once he was deported to Lodz, became one of the chroniclers of
the ghetto, felt "the nearness of Old Russia: Dostoevsky." And when the
last remnant of Jews were "settled out of the ghetto" in 1944, Rosenfeld
saw before him utterly destitute "figures as those described by Dostoevsky": "a woman: loose gray strands of hair draping her shoulders . . .
her legs are swollen and they hardly fit into the flat loafers; in her hands
smaller and larger bundles, on the left shoulder a rucksack patched together from various materials; in front, dangling over her thighs, a soup
bowl and a *menashka*," the ubiquitous soup ladle. Rosenfeld's description
of the woman recalled Dostóyevsky's declaration, strikingly similar to
Blanchot's, in his short story "An Honest Thief." "Man is a creature that
can become accustomed to anything."[3]

Ultimately, however, Rosenfeld believed that Dostoyevsky was not
adequate. The Russian writer "recounts conditions." But in Lodz, "the
freedom to make decisions," which was key to Dostóyevsky's spiritual
dramas, was "absent." The ghetto "therefore defies presentation through
the means of the epic in the conventional way." Jews were constrained,
lacking the dramatic radius of Dostoyevsky's characters. When German writer Ernst Jünger learned through a friend that Lodz's Judenrat
felt compelled to participate in the deportations of Jews "under ten"
and "over 65," as demanded by German overlords, he felt that not even
Dostoyevsky could have "foreseen" the moral and ethical circumstances
in which the victims operated.[4]

Still, Dostoyevsky resonated. Many looked to the Grand Inquisitor
who, in the famous scene in *The Brothers Karamazov*, argued with Christ
and, by extension, with Christians that the "burden of free will" was too
heavy for God's creatures. They could not be relied upon to make ethical
choices. Hélène Berr bitterly denounced the absence of mercy among
Christians who, as they did nothing as Jews were being deported, "crucify
Christ every day." "I reread the chapter about the Grand Inquistor in *The
Brothers Karamazov*," she wrote in October 1943. She came to the conclusion that "Christ would no longer be wanted, because he would give men

back their freedom of conscience, and that is too hard for them to bear. 'Tomorrow, I will have you burned,'" Berr quoted the Grand Inquisitor telling Christ.[5] Dostoyevsky anticipated the way many Christians abandoned Christ during Germany's war on Jews and other civilians.

Dividing into Categories

IN MANY WAYS, THE GERMANS DID TRY TO BURN OR ABANDON CHRIST because they expended so much effort in denying universal obligations and shared humanity. They wanted to replace a global conscience with a Nazi conscience. The influential "Aryan" administrator Walter Gross, head of Germany's Office of Racial Policy, declared that "Man as such does not exist"; "there are only men belonging to this or that race."[6] For the Nazis, it was not the species as a whole that was biologically valid, but the distinct "races." The notion of species, or humanity, was dropped in favor of race. It followed that universal principles did not apply.

If National Socialist biology promised Germans their destiny, National Socialist history indicated their jeopardy. With Germany's defeat in World War I, the German "race" had been threatened with extinction. Arrayed against it were a whole series of military, political, and biological dangers, France and Poland but also communism, as well as domestic strife and racial degeneration. The great success of the Nazis was to get more and more Germans to adhere to the fundamental premises of the Nazi account of history: the conviction that Germany had faced extraordinary suppression after 1918, the belief that the Third Reich attained a measure of real "freedom" in the years since the Nazi seizure of power in 1933, and the fear that this freedom was imperiled by the new war, a war that demanded and justified harsh methods to ensure German victory. Ordinary Germans, from skeptics to true believers, echoed back National Socialist history when they insisted, as the German doctor did to the Swiss truck driver in Warsaw in January 1942, "there will not be a second 1918" and regarded the war as a struggle between peoples in which the stakes were "existence" or "nonexistence," us or them. This doctrine justified preemptive war against Poland, France, and the Soviet

Union, and it rationalized the murder of Jews. The year 1918 was the historical, sentimental vestment that could clothe the application of pitiless, but absolute, laws of racial biology.

Germany's historical and racial struggle depended on purging humanitarian impulses that, unchecked, would only give advantage to the enemy. *Humanitätsduselei*—drivel about universal imperatives rooted in notions of a collective humanity—impeded the paramount task of ensuring Germany's future, building the Greater German Reich, and reshaping world history. At a party meeting held in the newly installed German movie theater in Lublin at the end of January 1941, Hans Frank, the Governor-General of occupied Poland, addressed the topic of the "remnants" of non-Germanic people in the occupied territories. He complained that among his administrators, "there were still some humanitarian dreamers about and those, who out of genuine German *Gemütlichkeit* [or coziness], tend to oversleep world history. . . . Here, I appeal to your resolve." This was rhetoric characteristic of German entitlement and empowerment. There was a constant push at every level to create perpetrators, to move from "coziness" to "resolve" in order to make "world history." "Auschwitz, not 1933, was the real 'German Revolution'—the real 'overthrow' of the existing social formation," writes one scholar. "In the process, the Nazis 'liberated' themselves from humanity."[7]

The Nazis disputed the existence of "Man" most perniciously through the proliferation of categories. Humanity was dismantled by drawing boundaries. Categories both lumped and divided. As one observer notes, "the Jews," a lethal threat completely separated from "Aryans" and all other "races," gathered up "the lively, quarrelsome, sometimes loving, sometimes nasty collection of loosely affiliated neighbors" into a "single anonymity."[8] Not even "Aryan" had the unambiguous quality of the category "Jew," since the Nazis distinguished between their own worthy and unworthy lives on the basis of physical and mental health and disabilities. As they trawled for "Aryan" blood wherever they could find it, the Nazis distinguished between four kinds of ethnic Germans, emphasizing, first, the strength of one's intention to return to one's racial origins and, second, in the case of probationary Germans, racial attributes. The flexibility

of the German *Volksliste* itself varied from place to place, as racial administrators applied different interpretations; it was much easier for a Pole to
become a German in Katowice than in Posen.

In the Nazi view, Poles were, of course, racially inferior to the Germans, so much so that they did not merit proper classification. For many
years, before he tried to change course and grudgingly enlist the Poles in
Germany's anti-Bolshevik struggle, Hans Frank took to simply calling his
subjects in the General Government "foreign elements," people without
a nation or a state. In Himmler's view, eastern Europe was just "ethnic
mush," while other racial administrators sorted Poles into the categories
"Little Poles and Masurians" and "Masurians," in turn, into subgroups
from Kurpie, Łowicz, and Podlasie. Whether by lumping or splitting, they
denied the anthropological integrity of the Poles.[9]

The business of dividing people into categories took place across
wartime Europe. The distinction between "Aryan" and "Jew," introduced by the Nazis, crept into everyday speech with astonishing speed.
While Jews were forced to identify themselves with yellow stars, non-Jews
posted signs assuring passersby that their establishment was "Christian"
or "Aryan." Everyone knew that there was an "Aryan" side to the war
and a "Jewish" side, and many sought to ensure they were on the right
one. Even more pernicious was the widespread association of Jews with
communists. This strand of anti-Semitism became more radical over
the course of the war, especially in Poland, where the Soviet Union had
annexed the eastern territories in September 1939. If, before 1939, many
observers regarded all communists as Jews, during the war all Jews suddenly became communists.

Across Europe the enemy was ethnicized. Beginning in October 1938,
when the Czechs forced anti-Nazi ethnic Germans from the Sudetenland
back across the newly drawn German border, they set in motion a process
in which the citizenries of states dissolved into their ethnic constituent
parts. Czechs did not recognize former German-speaking Czechoslovak
citizens as Czech, just as Poles did not recognize as Poles those Polish citizens who were German, Ukrainian, or Jewish. Likewise in France, in 1939,
foreigners were vetted and classified according to the strength of their
attachments to France. Over time, foreigners became more menacing,

and foreignness was defined in ever more exacting ways. Refugees from Belgium and northern France, and later from Alsace and Lorraine, where the Germans expelled politically unreliable elements after annexing the provinces in 1940, soon found that their welcome wore out, sometimes because of their "excessive patriotism," sometimes because they did not seem French enough. Even in Switzerland, Catholic, Protestant, and Jewish organizations were held responsible for "their" refugees; refugees no longer enjoyed the country's long-standing tradition of providing Swiss hospitality to all asylum seekers.[10] The fanciful idea that German armies relied on a "fifth column" of sympathizers also exacerbated fears among neighbors. As citizens became increasingly suspicious of strangers, the consequences for Jews were disastrous.

Across Europe people watched each other more closely. Accents and physical features mattered more in daily interactions. Even Jews began to scrutinize themselves, keenly aware of their "good looks" or their too Jewish looks. As he was waiting in line at the prefecture in Paris to register as a Jew in October 1941, Jacques Bielinky found it "curious" that among the crowds, "strongly Jewish types are rare," with most people having "the physical appearance of the usual Parisian types." Degrees of separation multiplied, while bonds of fellowship and coresidency disintegrated.[11]

The ghettos into which the Germans shoved Polish Jews were the most radical consequence of the policy of classification and isolation. But even in the ghettos, categories proliferated. Wherever they were confined, Jews divided up according to whether they spoke Yiddish; whether they could be counted as "eastern" or "western" Jews; whether they were French or Dutch nationals, Polish emigrants, or German refugees; whether they were able-bodied or unfit for work; whether they were veterans of the Great War; and whether they had access to supposedly "safe" positions in the Jewish administrations and thus the coveted *shaynen*, or certificates. Confronted with the prospect of "renewed outsettlement" from the Lodz Ghetto in March 1943, Oskar Rosenfeld wanted to know "Which categories?". "Here's a brother, and here's a brother," at least at first glance, observed another inmate about how quickly bonds of solidarity frayed in Lodz, but on closer examination "the older one," the

Polish Jew, "is the real one," while "the new one," the German Jew, "is really only a stepbrother."[12]

Whatever the imagined principles behind the selections, which ultimately enveloped the entire Jewish community in ghetto after ghetto, each deportation order separated those who left from those who remained behind. In the assembly camp in Westerbork in the Netherlands, Etty Hillesum noticed how the arrival of the twice-weekly train "symbolically divided the camp into two parts." After its departure, she wrote, there was a palpable "Hurrah We Are Alive" feeling. In the Warsaw Ghetto, children played the game "German and Jew" in which the one beat up the other. In other words, Jews divided themselves up between "German" survivors and "Jewish" condemned. The selections were so horrifying, in part, because they often worked against the construction of solidarity, precisely because they were based on what many Jews took to be notions of expendability. With terms like *Musselmänner,* or "walking corpses," prisoners spoke with authority about those who had lost the will or ability to live and had become dispensable. In Auschwitz Primo Levi made distinctions: he shared water with Alberto but not with Daniele.[13]

Thinking in terms of categories, dividing up people required paying attention to differences that had previously not been thoroughly scrutinized. If the idea of "Man" was grievously injured in German-occupied Europe, it was not because passersby refused to acknowledge the stranger, but the reverse. Passersby quite self-consciously acknowledged their difference from strangers and, based on the degree of that difference, made decisions about whom to see and for whom to care. Making such distinctions became a zero-sum game. The Poles, the Czechs, the French created a "between ourselves," a shared solidarity that despised the Germans, indeed one that could resist the Germans, but one that also excluded anything foreign. "Between ourselves" was a nationalism that was "small Czech," or "small Polish" or "small French." It was anti-German, but also parochial, Manichaean, and distrustful of outsiders.[14] Paradoxically, the anti-German attributes of solidarity "between ourselves" were entirely compatible with anti-Semitism. Even when directed against the Germans, it bore the imprint of Nazi ideas about the value of purity, inclusion, and exclusion.

But thinking in terms of categories also broke down the solidarities of "between ourselves." Once set in motion, the process of division
and subdivision could go on for a long time, until only lonely individuals remained to fend for themselves. In the harsh conditions of wartime,
people improvised, lived day to day, and sought personal advantage, and,
since most lacked power themselves, they closely examined the (imagined) advantages of others. Most folks stood in the line, but, as they did,
they imagined vast numbers of their neighbors embracing the black market instead or outfitted them with other sinister powers. In nations that
were divided by suspicions about talkative and prying neighbors, by political loyalties, and by economic resentments, people felt like they had
woken up in a world turned mad. There are all sorts of indexes of the
breakdown of solidarity in wartime Europe. The combination of economic scarcity, nighttime curfews, and general mistrust meant that people spent more time scavenging for food and stayed indoors for longer
periods of time. Young people drank more, and they cheated; the line
between hoodlums and resistors was vague in the streets of Marseille and
in the forests around Szczebrzeszyn. Without reliable itineraries into the
future, they slipped the authority of school, home, and parents. Parisians
recognized themselves as Gaullists when they strolled together on the
streets on the occasion of the Feast Day of Joan of Arc, but they also
looked out for themselves. People employed what they called *le system D*,
derived from the French verb *se débrouiller*, that is, "to get by," "to wangle,"
"to weasel out of"; in German-speaking contexts, people acquired "Vita-
min B," that is, *Beziehungen*, or "contacts."[15] Public spaces were shabbier
and more dangerous, and people moved about them with more suspicion
and mistrust.

The Well of "Miracles"

IN HIS NOVEL *LE PUITS DES MIRACLES* (THE WELL OF MIRACLES),
written in 1942–1943, André Chamson explores this world gone mad, the
lack of solidarity among townspeople who are no longer recognizable,
and the attempts to stitch the place back together. Chamson's novel offers

a ghastly fairy tale set in the shadow of the powerful "land of barracks and barbed wire" into which the imprisoned fathers of local boys have disappeared. The unnamed narrator listens in on the sounds in his tenement building's corridors and stairwells and, from behind "heavy, worn damask drapes," observes the goings-on in the tenement courtyard, the shaft or "abyss" that becomes his "well of miracles."[16] From his post at the window, the narrator is an eyewitness, distant, uninvolved, but industrious in his observations. Not all the action takes place in the courtyard, but the "well of miracles" serves as a handy image for the fantastical shapes and occurrences accompanying the degradation of wartime life. A brick wall separates the courtyard from an alley, once a lovers' lane, but the couples who hurry past no longer walk arm in arm. The world is out of joint. It is also strange because it appears anachronistic. In the novel, for example, a plague of rats is followed by an epidemic of diphtheria; townspeople are reduced to searching for special potions and lucky charms. Medieval demons seem to be at work.

A general sense of sickness and squalor prevails. As he watches passersby, Chamson's narrator takes note of the leather handles of "half-empty hand bags" that have been mended with thread. From her window, Colette too noticed "new, distressing signs": "the right elbow of a man's jacket is a shade lighter than the left. Almost all the handles of shopping bags are threadbare and held together with string." Chamson overhears the conversations of a group of boys playing in the courtyard. It turns out that children have started to wet their beds because, as one doctor explains, a meatless diet of turnips and rutabagas retains much more water: "Oh, I'd like to control myself," one boy confessed, "but I can't tie it up with a string." For their part, the elderly are losing their teeth or can no longer fit dentures into their shrunken mouths.[17]

In fact, the number of calories the French consumed dropped by one-quarter to one-half between 1940 and 1942. "Nothing more than some frozen meat and, for vegetables, a few carrots and otherwise turnips, kohlrabi, and rutabagas," wrote Denise Domenach about her meals in Lyon in January 1941. Micheline Bood, who cavorted with German soldiers at Paris swimming pools, enjoyed even less variety at the dinner table. "Lunch on Saturday consisted of beans, two slices of sausage for each person and some cheese, while dinner was soup, chestnuts and more cheese. Sunday brought bean salad, boiled beef, and a dessert made of chestnuts for lunch, then soup, beans, and jam for dinner. Monday's lunch was an egg for each person with vermicelli, followed by jam, and Monday's dinner was beans, bean soup and jam again." According to one historian, people in Romania, Hungary, and Bohemia-Moravia ate better than the French, who quickly shared a common vocabulary of scarcity: "The epithet *national*, bracketed with coffee, tobacco, footwear or sausages could be translated as trash." These were all substitutes or *ersatz*—"a word, like *blitz* and *diktat*, which the Reich gave to the languages of Europe." According to Liliane Schroeder, the "kids in rags dragging their feet in huge ill-fitting shoes or old-fashioned velvet slippers" made "our catastrophe" terribly visible, and in Chamson's fairy tale Tinou, the "red-haired" boy, wears bathroom slippers that are several sizes too big and held fast with string. Unmistakable also was the loud clatter of improvised wooden soles on the street, which inspired Maurice Chevalier to compose the song "The Symphony of Wooden Soles."[18]

German expropriations and hoarding by French peasants prompted rationing that in turn created long lines outside the grocer, the butcher, and the baker. Chamson's narrator describes inching forward for hours, gripped all the time by the fear that when he finally makes it to the entrance of the store, the sign that has "already been laid out" will be hung: "No More Vegetables Today" or "Come Back Tomorrow." The proprietor, Delpoux, keeps order in the line to make sure that people do not crowd the entrance. At one point, he knocks to the ground a man who is not paying attention to his directions; no one in the line says a word. Standing in line himself, Chamson's narrator shamefully admits that shoppers have become so afraid that Delpoux reigns as the undisputed leader of his street corner.

In France's lines, the resolute silence of Vercors's characters had given way to the silence of despair. One observer looked around at the "incredible dirt and sadness in Paris." "People run around in half shoes with mostly wooden soles" and stood in line "in the snow in front of food shops," but "everything in silence." Pedestrians in the streets of Rouen "go their own way." They were "strangers to each other whom the bonds of sympathy do not bring together in any way. All they have in common are their separate preoccupations: bread, sugar, butter, meat." Of course, people gossiped in line. "We all spoke our opinion without restraint," wrote Janet Teissier du Cros about herself and the "other grumbling women."[19] But the grumbling gave way to backbiting and denunciation when neighbors exaggerated the power of big shots like Delpoux, freely assigned Jews and communists to positions of power in the black market, and scrutinized the advantages others had. In this atmosphere of mutual suspicion, the boundaries between "us" and "them" constantly shifted. The malevolent forces were not restricted to the Germans, or Vichy authorities, or the upper "two hundred," as in Chamson's story, but included all sorts of ordinary folks whom one simply did not like or did not know.

The long hours spent in lines turned people into censors and suspects and fed the wave of denunciations that inundated police stations and Wehrmacht offices in France and other places in German-occupied Europe. Neighbors suspected each other of offenses small and large, and the denunciations quickly became a routine, if disagreeable, aspect of wartime social relations. "One half of France spies on the other," remarked Léon Werth, "but most astonishing to me is not that one half of France spies on the other, but that the groups spied-upon seem neither distressed nor angry nor disgusted nor indignant at the groups doing the spying."[20] There was even a film made about denunciations. Henri-Georges Clouzot's *Le Corbeau* (The Raven [1943]), set in a fictional small town, Saint-Robin, was condemned by both the Resistance and Vichy because it disputed the idea of a virtuous France that both sides upheld, but it received good reviews, from among others the Germans, who were the primary beneficiaries of French bad-mouthing. Most letters of denunciation addressed blackmarket activities of one sort or another; they were rooted in envy rather than political conviction. One historian estimates that 3 to 4 million such letters were written over the course of the occupation of France.[21] Each one chipped away at the solidarity of shared suffering.

The widespread grumbling, censoring, and denouncing turned once familiar precincts into sinister landscapes. In the opening scenes of *The Well of Miracles*, Chamson introduces the menacing figure of the dog catcher who enters the courtyard every two or three nights. He locks the dogs in a windowless shed and later, beyond the narrator's field of vision, kills them. Stray dogs were among the many living creatures left stranded by the calamity of the war: "Perhaps only the small birds in the garden or the fish in the streams were still able to believe in the almighty benevolence of their creator," remarks Chamson. As early as the exodus in the spring of 1940, French dogs were abandoned to the dog catcher or left to fend for themselves; according to one estimate, the canine population of the Alpes-Maritimes dropped by half as pet owners saved on food expenses. In Chamson's tale, the dog catcher can be seen everywhere in town, along narrow alleyways, near bushes in the gardens, but the whimpering and howling of the dogs in the shed seem to go unnoticed; only the man at the window takes note. The "transports," as Chamson calls them, are both furtive and public, part of the horrible "universe of killing dogs," an allegory that anticipated the deportation of France's Jews and David Rousset's conception of the Nazi *Univers concentrationnaire* a few years later.[22] Unsatisfied with his dirty and low-paid work, the dog catcher eventually joins in the criminal activities of the butcher Delpoux and the black marketer Tourinas. He ascends to a position in the black-uniformed "Milice," the aggressive paramilitary guard formed by a weakening Vichy regime, becoming one of the well-dressed bullyboys who wear boots rather than slippers. "Instead of hunting animals roaming about he took up hunting people who were being persecuted," Chamson writes.

The boots in Chamson's story belong to dubious characters who have stepped in to represent the new order in the most outlandish ways. One scene set in a barbershop features a figure every bit as monstrous as the dog catcher. The "hydrocéphale ventriloque," the neighborhood's own Pétain. A harmless-enough creature before the war, contenting himself with memorizing the schedules of the French railways, he now finds his vocation in learning by heart the new French radio programming—he listens fifteen hours a day—from the pause signal ("Frr frr frr frou") to political speeches. After cutting in line at the barbershop and settling in his chair, he barks out these addresses to the terrified customers waiting for their own haircuts: "Frrann-çais! I have the duty to ask you to have faith. . . . You are suffering, I know, and you will have to suffer more, but you only have to follow me and you can be certain of salvation."[23]

One of the first victims of the misshapen new regime to be hauled in, after Chamson's narrator hears "unsettling comings and goings" in the apartment overhead one morning, is "Monsieur de Vienne"—no one knows his actual name. When the coast is clear, the narrator ventures down the stairs of his building, only to encounter another tenant who acknowledges Vienne's graciousness, but quickly gets to the heart of the matter: "Who will now move in there in his place? In these times, any change means a turn for the worse." Once outside, the narrator observes how pedestrians in the street rush indoors to avoid the police moving through the neighborhood. People watch, but they are also watchful, removed from the scene of the crime by windows and doors and imprisoned by their fears. They are witnesses to their own complicity in the violence, which they seek to contain by doing nothing to bring it upon themselves. In this time of troubles, the townspeople occupy their neighborhood, but they do not properly inhabit it anymore. They are no longer free people.

However, in *The Well of Miracles*, Chamson also offers a story of the triumph of hope over fear. The narrator is largely passive, but he is obviously appalled at the transformation of his town. He accepts his responsibility as sentinel and gradually notices new miracles around him: the confidence that allowed the arrested man from Vienna to accept his misfortune as a temporary humiliation, the confidence that allowed the children in the courtyard to believe in a reunion with their imprisoned fathers, the confidence that allowed the two "goddesses of vengeance" down the street to prophesy the return of the stern rule of republican justice. This confidence unnerves the powerful creatures of the new regime, the dog catcher, the butcher, and the black marketer. Chamson whittles them down to size. From the third story of his house, the narrator can see into the ballroom where the big "personalities" of the town, the dog catchers and people catchers, have gathered to celebrate in the most hypocritical and sanctimonious way the fallen soldiers of the wars. He realizes that the "two hundred gathered around the raised dais of the minister, surrounded by guards in black uniforms with badges and revolvers . . . would have felt isolated amidst the great mass of all the other people. . . . They were satisfied with the present state of the world, but this satisfaction is what made them different from everyone else and this difference filled them with fear." Suddenly, "armed soldiers," the Germans, enter the story and multiply through the town "like inedible mushrooms in the mouldering soil of a secluded forest glade." When they do, the entire ideological proscenium erected by the two hundred opportunists comes crashing down. "We awoke from our nightmare and stepped back into history."[24]

This is how Chamson captures November 1942, when the Wehrmacht occupied Vichy France in response to the Allied invasion of North Africa. The moment of liberation has not yet come, but the townspeople have recognized themselves as free men and women, which is the precondition to their liberation. At the end of the novel, Chamson returns to the dark courtyard where the dog catcher had operated. In the shadows, the narrator bumps into a worker who takes him for the black marketer Tourinas, until he is vouched for by the worker's son, La Sisse, one of the little boys who played in the courtyard. The narrator is shown where a gun has been hidden in the brick wall, and thereafter he is no longer a witness but a participant in the coming struggle to reconquer the town. The novel ends on a satisfying, though thoroughly sentimental, note. Its arc and its ending are consistent with the changing forms that *attentisme* took in wartime France, where generally positive feelings toward the "national revolution" or at least toward Pétain gradually dissolved over the course of 1942.[25] What is not persuasive is Chamson's emphasis on the "two hundred," who serve to contain the more general fear and suspicion that prevail in the opening scenes of the novel. Ultimately, Chamson wants to limit the damage to his idea of France, but in focusing on this limited group of elites, he de-emphasized the uncanny and frightening qualities to his fairy tale and to France under German occupation. He seeks to alleviate the feelings of abandonment that had dispersed and divided the French since the exodus in the spring of 1940.

In his essay "Republic of Silence," written immediately after the war, Jean-Paul Sartre also tried to pick up the pieces of the exodus to make them available for new accounts of the Liberation. Sartre did not address "the elite among us who were active members of the Resistance Movement," but rather addressed "each of us," who confronted on a daily basis a moral decision on how to behave toward the German occupiers. If ordinary French men and women had decided to cooperate with the military authorities, the Resistance would have been wiped out. But they did not. The big "No" of the Resistance was fortified by the little "no" of the more passive majority. The "silence" that reconstituted the Republic without leaders or institutions was the refusal to give evidence when stopped or detained. It was a republic of small gestures, the V's chalked on the walls; the propaganda posters defaced; the necklaces that featured the Cross of Lorraine; the blue, white, and red ensembles worn on July 14, Bastille Day; the BBC programs monitored at nine thirty; and the silence enforced against German soldiers as they barged into the spaces of everyday French life. Sartre recognized in these modest individual acts a collective ensemble of French autonomy and unanimity. Like Chamson, with his two hundred, Sartre consigns collaboration to the margins.[26]

Chamson's novel begins in nighttime, with a France that is difficult to read; he skillfully explores the half-open spaces of confusion and suspicion. But the novel ends with signs and sides clarified. In this way, *The Well of Miracles*, for all its fantastical and disjointed features, lays the foundations for the Gaullist myth of France as a nation of liberators, "the only France," "the real France," "the eternal France," "the France that fights," as Charles de Gaulle declared at the Hotel de Ville on August 25, 1944. The Gaullist myth was by no means entirely false. As historian John Sweets argues, "If one were forced to choose a myth, the Gaullist version of a 'nation of resisters' would be far more accurate than the new myth of a 'nation of collaborators.'"[27] This myth also had the salutary function of restoring France as an active subject in history. Nonetheless, reconstituting the "we" required a number of excisions: the evidence of opportunism and collaboration, the fear of strangers and suspicions of neighbors, and indifference in the face of suffering.

Sartre's "Republic of Silence" also left out Jews. Not only does Sartre's essay have nothing to say about the fate of the Jews, thousands of whom disappeared from the precincts of the republic, but it also uses a vocabulary of collective inclusion and individual empowerment that excludes Jews by being so inappropriate to their difficult circumstances. Jews were targets, not suspects. Sartre referred to the resolve to say "no," to stay silent during torture, and to accept death if necessary, but these represented choices, ones that were constitutive of the "republic of silence." There were few choices for Jews, who also faced torture and death, and there were none once they left France. Without the ability to make existential choices, they could not be part of the "republic of silence."

In Chamson's fantastic, out-of-sorts world, the bewildered bed wetters, the frightened shoppers, and the intimidated customers at the barbershop return to their homes. The narrator's apartment provides him a safe and stable vantage point to observe the changes that have been taking place in the courtyard and in the street. The small-scale dramas imagined in Sartre's "Republic of Silence" also take place mostly out-doors. In both accounts, private spaces remain relatively inviolable— except for the case of "Monsieur de Vienne," who, like the great majority of Europe's Jews, was turned out of his home, which subsequently be-comes available to new tenants. The unwilling residents of the ghettos in the "land of barracks and barbed wire" witnessed the changing makeup of social relations, just as Chamson had, but in the most extreme con-ditions of dispossession, destitution, and physical jeopardy. They were turned out of their homes and found no sanctuary. How did they reflect on the idea of humanity when they were still alive and had pen and paper and resources to do so?

"Ghetto Wonders"

THE SCALE OF THE ACCUMULATING LOSSES AFTER 1939 WAS SO GREAT that many Jews during the war remembered the difficult prewar years, in which Jews were, in one historian's words, "wholly defenseless, largely friendless, and more and more hopeless," as a time of exemplary order and security.[28] The disaster dispossessed Jews of their property, their homes, their relatives, and their lives. Victims steadily lost the ability to make themselves at home in the world. In his poem "Things," Wladislaw

Szlengel itemizes the things left behind as the Jews of Warsaw were confined to smaller and smaller spaces. In the weeks before the Warsaw Ghetto was officially sealed on November 16, 1940, "legions of Jews" could be seen trekking to the designated quarter. "From Hoza Street and Marzałkowska," streets among Warsaw's best, ones now off-limits to Jews, "carts were moving, Jewish carts." They were loaded with "furniture, tables and chairs," with "suitcases, bundles and chests," with "boxes and bedding, suits and portraits," with "cherry brandy, big jars and little jars," and "with books, knickknacks and everything" to install in the new apartment on Śliska Street, at the southern edge of the ghetto. Before long, that apartment, too, had to be abandoned. (In October 1941, Sienna and Sosnowa Streets, relatively good addresses, were "carved out" of the ghetto and placed in "Aryan" hands, but not Śliska; sixty thousand Jews were uprooted as a result.) At the other, northern, end of the ghetto, on Niska Street, the new rooms were smaller: "Furniture, tables and chairs, suitcases and bundles, and pots—gents, that's it." There was no room for the carpet; the silverware had to be left behind: "No cherry brandy this time. No suits or boots or jars or portraits." When the next move took place, to "the apartment blocks," there was "no furniture or stools, no jugs or bundles." There was still "a suitcase, a coat, a bottle of tea and piece of candy," hauled "On foot, without any wagon." The "gloomy procession" had not yet come to an end; the next move to Ostrowska Street, a much more impoverished area near Miła, was made with just "one suitcase, a warm scarf and that's it," "no big bundles or little bundles." When deportation came, along the "Jewish road" to Treblinka, "A small suitcase and a knapsack" would have to do, but after the German shouted the order "hands free," there was "only water—with a strong pill," a capsule of poison, usually Veronal, known as "Jewish drops."[29]

The Germans frequently transported Jews without their luggage, even though the carefully prescribed weight limits accompanying deportation orders—twenty-seven and a half pounds, sometimes even less here or a bit more there—seemed to suggest that "things" would be checked through rather than confiscated. Jews on the lists to be deported from the ghettos quickly gathered the bare necessities: "a warm blanket, a suit, a pair of shoes, some linens. When it's curtain time, also a cooking pot and a drinking cup"—"the leftovers of one's possessions." As it was, in Lodz, during the deportations in May 1942, the Germans cut off the straps to the packs, which, as a result, had to be left behind. Police shouted "Hands up" as people boarded the trains, so that even the small bundles stitched together out of sheets and blankets and tied together with "cords and ropes" fell to the ground. With hands up, Jews were able to save a ladle or a *menashka*; "some even save a single potato," reported Oskar Rosenfeld. In the Lodz Ghetto, euphemisms for dying included "threw away the spoon" and "packed his little bag."[30] This was the ghetto version of the condemned man "kicking the bucket" at his hanging.

After Jews disappeared down "the Jewish road," poet Szlengel had a vision of "all the Jewish things" coming out "from chests and houses." "They will run out through the windows, walk down the streets until they meet on the roads," putting in reverse the movement of the deportations. "All the tables and chairs and suitcases," "the bundles / the suits and jars" will install themselves once again in the old apartments "all the way to Marzałkowska," where "new people," "Aryans," already waited in the once abandoned rooms. They will "close the open windows," "empty the coffee from the glass," and "finish the hand of bridge" lying unplayed on the table.

"Things" is an inventory of loss, but also an inventory of the obliteration of the associations that once attached to the "things," the "household fairies," the knickknacks, the photographs, the books that had had enchanted lives on Marzałkowska Street. Evacuation meant the destruction of the familiarity of life itself. Polish hands acquired so much property in the first months of the German occupation that early assessments of Polish-Jewish relations, such as Jan Karski's February 1940 report to Poland's Government-in-Exile, emphasized in umambiguous terms that there could be no turning back; Polish attitudes toward the Jews were "overwhelmingly severe, often without pity." Envied and disliked, the Jews had finally been forced to "pay and pay and pay."[31]

In the ghettos the contents of the knapsacks and the "big bundles" and the "little bundles" deteriorated quickly, particularly since there were few opportunities to wash clothes and bed linens. Oskar Rosenfeld saw how "the colors fade, the shirts gets frayed, the garments disintegrate."

It was particularly difficult to keep shoes in good repair when the ground was wet and muddy. In Lodz there was nothing new in the shops because the only items for sale were those that had been brought into the ghetto in the first place. Rosenfeld listed some of the items available in May 1942: "broken mirrors, old toothbrushes, broken combs, torn nightgowns, eaten, worn shoes," also "pulped paper by weight as toilet paper" and cast-off "ribbons, tooth powder, socks, gloves, hairpins." And this list dated from a time when inventories had been recently replenished following the "selling-off of the sold out," when unfortunate German Jews, deported to Chelmno, sold their remaining possessions after packing up their allotted twenty-seven and a half pounds.[32]

The body itself decomposed. The majority of ghetto residents quickly became completely malnourished. After the fall of 1941, Jews in the Lodz Ghetto received about nine hundred calories a day, about one-third of what was necessary for a healthy life; in Warsaw, where 80 percent of the food consumed had to be smuggled into the ghetto, the allotted ration was even smaller. This was "a prescription for a slow death," commented Rosenfeld. (The Germans quite bluntly called the ghettos by the purpose for which they were designed: *Todeskisten*, or death traps.) Jews in Lodz had lost 1 million kilograms of body weight over the course of the year ending in May 1942 when Rosenfeld described the "face of the ghetto": "Faces are shriveling, thin so bones are visible everywhere, death skull, a horrid sight. Collapsed temples, protruding ears, unshaven, stubble beards, like convicts released from prison." Two teenage girls caught the attention of one resident in Lodz, who noted "the hair, already inflected with gray, that tumbles onto their girlish necks, and the deep furrows that crease their young faces." Irene Hauser, originally from Vienna, lost twenty-two pounds between her "arrival" in Lodz on October 24, 1941, and her diary notation in mid-May 1942; in the same period, her husband, Leo, lost twice that amount. The last time the couple had sexual intercourse was on January 30, 1942. By the summer of 1942 Irene described ever-worsening conditions for her and her six-year-old son, Erich (or "Bubi"), in short diary entries: "Sold Bubi's shoes. Got 35 Marks. Bought peas" (June 26); "Wonderful Sunday weather," but "dragging myself around, knees give out" (July 12); "Sold the summer dress for a bit of fat" (July 26); "Nothing to eat . . . My loved ones . . . where have you all gone?" (August 19).[33]

The single daily serving of soup dominated Leyb Goldin's "Chronicle of a Single Day," written in the Warsaw Ghetto in August 1941. Time "stretches like rubber," because anticipation of the one o'clock meal built over the entire morning: "'only' seven hours to go." Goldin tried to busy himself with an Arthur Schnitzler novel, but he could not get past the first line: "Eva looked into the mirror." He was completely consumed by his stomach: "Your stomach and you," he mocked: "ninety-percent stomach and the small part—you yourself." Still "six more hours," so "sleep, sleep, as long as possible." A little later Goldin wondered, "What time is it?" "Ten past eight. Four more hours."[34]

"Always the same problem," wrote Oskar Rosenfeld: "Is something in the soup? Is it thick or empty soup?" Usually, the soup was thin, "carrots, water beets, red beets, a few kernels of barley swimming around in warm water—that was called soup." Given the paramount importance of soup, it is not surprising that "in the streets, the man with the soup ladle in his hand is the characteristic feature of ghetto life." For Josef Zelkowicz, who wrote extensively about conditions in Lodz, "the symbol of the ghetto is the pot."[35] When he considered how to paint the Lodz Ghetto, Rosenfeld devoted one scene to the "people of any age and sex carrying their soup vessels across the street. . . . Striking here are the manifold containers: *menashkas*, bowls, pots, plates, even little buckets." "Scurrying, rushing, starving, quick-stepping people" filled the streets of the ghetto in Rosenfeld's sketch from April 1942, and each one of them had "vessels for soup: plates or bowls or cups of tin, pewter, or china, tied to their body with a string." Without some sort of *menashka* close at hand, it was not possible to quickly take advantage of unexpected opportunities. And it was always just the *menashka*; knives and forks were unnecessary, "since there is nothing to cut (knife) and nothing to spear (like pasta, baked goods, firm foods—fork)." Indeed, in the Lodz Ghetto, "there are thousands of young people who have never handled a knife and fork." (So ubiquitous was the *menashka* in the bitter years of the war that children in the Soviet labor camp in Kolyma who had been given two guard-dog puppies to raise named one "Ladle," the other "Pail.")[36] If the loss of carefully packed "things" registered the utter unfamiliarity of the world of the ghetto, the one single thing, the *menashka*, told of the complete destitution of its hungry residents.

By the time of the deportations in 1942, one in four residents of the ghetto in Lodz and Warsaw had already succumbed to disease or starvation. "The grim reaper" began to gather his harvest soon after the ghetto was sealed. In Lodz, by the end of the summer of 1940, death "decapitated heads of households—fathers; broken hearts—mothers; and shattered spines—sole breadwinners"; "he claimed a tithe of everything that fell into his grasp." Of course, those without resources or connections suffered in disproportionate numbers. In the poorest districts of the Warsaw Ghetto, around Smosza Street, for example, whole families and then entire tenement buildings died as typhus spread with plague-like severity. "Death is on the march. Births fail to appear. The ghetto is liquidating itself" was Oskar Rosenfeld's summary of Lodz in July 1943.[37]

The painful losses of personal belongings, the difficult decision to sell something dear for very little in order to buy something practical for a great deal, the constant thoughts about thick or thin soup, and the daily sight of carts collecting the dead for burial forcefully posed the question of privilege in the ghetto. So too did the role of the Jewish councils in the selections for "outsettlement" on the "Jewish road" leading out of the ghetto. Almost every ghetto diary commented on the abrasions of social conflict. "There was no social peace in the ghetto," explained Isaiah Trunk, "because there was no equality among the inmates."[38] Wealthier Jews or longtime residents of Warsaw and Lodz could supplement insufficient rations and draw on connections in order to evade labor roundups. Poor Jews, and those who had been fleeced before they were settled in the ghetto, had far fewer resources. They bore the brunt of the tragedies in the ghetto in 1940 and 1941: hunger, disease, and labor deployments for the Germans. Cultural differences aggravated those of class; middle-class Polish-speaking Jews, who dominated positions in the ghetto administrations, had little in common with the Yiddish-speaking "masses."

Most Jews trapped in the ghettos quickly became destitute; even in Warsaw, very few lived on assets. As a result, the most relevant resource was connections to the Jewish Council. For the thirteen thousand Jews who worked for the Jewish administration in Lodz or Warsaw, a position offered protection, the coveted *shaynen*, as well as opportunities to extort money from more vulnerable residents or to embezzle food and other goods. Ghetto residents perceived the ability of some to call upon connections as the main source of social friction. Oskar Rosenfeld described "four kinds of human beings" in the ghetto. At the bottom was "the vast majority who die of hunger" for lack of resources. At the top were "those who have everything in excess, the best of the best," a small number but with the power to help a third group, "those who have connections." And finally, there were "those who don't want to bite the dust and are looking around for rations, and who, if there's no other way, will organize them for themselves," that is, will steal food even with the risk of running afoul of the ghetto police if they did.[39]

The Jewish police were especially detested for their abuse of authority. In Warsaw they set up small-time racketeering operations, taking bribes to allow Jews to evade the dreaded labor deployment outside the ghetto or extorting money from house committees desperate to avoid the chaotic trip to the delousing facilities. The "shiny boots" that had distinguished the violent German occupiers in October 1939 soon came to characterize as well the Jewish police, whose "beautiful knee boots" contrasted with the "old clogs" worn by those at the bottom of the social pyramid. Indeed, Emanuel Ringelblum took note of "the era of high boots" favored by "heavy-handed people," "ambitious people," and "policemen." Even women started to wear boots; they were "the wives, or mistresses, of gangsters emerging at the top." In Yitzhak Katzenelson's "The Song of the Murdered Jewish People," it was these "Apostates and near-apostates with shiny boots on their feet," wearing "Hats with the Star of David, like a swastika, on their heads," who "smashed doors" and "hunted us" to get their daily quota of "heads" during the "Great Action" in the Warsaw Ghetto in summer 1942.[40]

As "gangsters" and "apostates," the ghetto police were hardly regarded as representative of the ghetto population. Observers were shocked to see that Jews agreed to carry out German orders in the hope of saving themselves, but most saw those who did so as atypical. Others, however, commented on the general spirit of meanness and the commonness of thievery in the ghetto. "The author of these lines," admitted Oskar Singer, another chronicler in Lodz, "has repeatedly attempted to look for and discover the nobler side of the ghetto resident, but the results have unfortunately been very unsatisfactory." The fact was that hunger "breaks steel," even "the hardest steel" of the traditional Jewish obligation to help neighbors. In Lodz an "alarming lack of consideration" prevailed. "The law that dominated the ghetto was that of the jungle, the law of might-makes-right." In this view, the Jewish police were only the most successful of the ghetto's many predators.[41]

Dawid Sierakowiak railed against the "big shots" and "dignitaries" in the Lodz Ghetto, but it was his own father who stole a piece of Dawid's bread, creating "tremendous anxiety" in the family and jeopardizing the pact that "everybody at home will live 'fairly.'" For a time, a period of "relative calm" returned, and "Father divided his bread into equal daily portions." But a few weeks later, at the end of May 1942, he devoured a pound of bread belonging to "Mom" and Dawid's sister Nadia. "My unfortunate once-powerful father" died on March 6, 1943, before Dawid could "settle accounts" with him. Irene Hauser too watched in despair as her husband, Leo, bought coffee, honey, and cigarettes for himself: "The child cries in hunger, the father in cigarettes, the mother wants to die—family life in the ghetto." In fact, the ghetto was filled with smokers; up to seventy thousand cigarettes, mostly Croatian Draws and Begrawas, were consumed in Lodz every day. They were carefully rationed (eighteen a week in May 1942), and the extras that Leo presumably bought cost one valuable mark a piece.[42]

Irene divorced Leo, and she also stopped writing her terse diary entries in the middle of the September 1942 deportations that targeted those "under ten, over 65." It is difficult to assess how representative the bleak picture of the broken Hauser household really was. Judicial proceedings in Lodz do reveal bitter family feuds in which wives accused husbands of prowling the streets and stealing food, while husbands complained that wives neglected the household. Despair and exhaustion played a part in weakening family bonds. But what really mattered was not the absence of solidarity but the fact that the cloth of mutual aid could not be stretched far enough in these grievous circumstances of disease and hunger. The death or deportation of breadwinners had catastrophic consequences, and family members made great efforts to protect each other from the "hammer blows" of ghetto existence. Josef Zelkowicz recounted the story of one woman, Braindel, who sold her wedding ring after her husband, Isaac, suffered a heart attack ("How swiftly the ghetto obliterates twenty-six years of life"). The doctor who attended Isaac also noticed how anemic the couple's thirteen-year-old daughter, Golda, had become. Braindel was torn between using the few marks she had left over after paying the commission on the sale of the ring to buy medicine for Isaac or bread and soup for Golda.[43] Undoubtedly, there were many more people in the ghetto like Braindel than like Irene's husband, Leo.

In the Warsaw Ghetto, a remarkable network of more than two thousand house committees, which administered the collective spaces of the tenement buildings and their interior courtyards, formed the basis of mutual solidarity. Wealthier residents shared the obligation to look after or "adopt" poorer tenants. Especially in the years 1940 and 1941, the house committees were held up as bright examples of self-reliance among Jews from various social, religious, and political backgrounds. Most Jews in the ghetto had moved into their new residences over the course of October and November 1940, many never having lived in Warsaw before, and so most people had to refashion local connections. This process took shape in the house committees. "There is not a tenant who is not among the members of some committee or in charge of some courtyard duty," wrote Chaim Kaplan. "Social action is thus diffused through all levels of the broad public."[44]

In some ways, the experiment worked so well that the thick solidarity of the tenement and the courtyard made obligations to the outside world much thinner. Ghetto residents looked after their own buildings first, and this effort alone absorbed their resources. It was difficult to get the overtaxed house committees to support wider ghetto initiatives such as orphanages and soup kitchens. Emanuel Ringelblum feared that his vision of a "disciplined, nationally conscious community" was falling apart into "a collection of hundreds of separate micro-communities." But often, what impeded efforts to save the child or feed the hungry was not so much unwillingness to help as the scarcity of food; this became clear when ghetto community workers sought to extract from housewives a single potato or turnip, or simply a spoonful of flour or sugar in the so-called spoon action.[45] The thousands of Warsaw Jews who relied entirely on the daily bowl of soup benefited from the remarkable voluntary efforts of the Aleynhilf, a mutual assistance organization, but such efforts were not alone sufficient to sustain life. Self-help could not ensure collective survival, because the German overlords had expropriated and stolen the resources of the community.

Under conditions of extreme duress, solidarity persisted. But circles of mutual aid tightened and thus threatened to exclude strangers to the community and the community's most vulnerable members—orphans, the sick, and the old. Family members fought each other to acquire bread, ghetto residents struggled to acquire privileges including exemptions from the deportations, and, according to one witness who had escaped from the death camps, in response to a question that could barely be posed, victims trampled on smaller and weaker bodies in the gas chambers in order to reach the last remnants of the poisoned oxygen. Suspicions about the fragility of the bonds that held the Jewish community together could be confirmed whenever residents left their apartments and their buildings' courtyards and walked in the streets. Like soldiers in the trenches of World War I, ghetto residents became accustomed to stepping over corpses. But neither could this erase evidence of solidarity, particularly among friends, comrades, and relatives. As the ghetto broke up during the deportations, people created and clung to intimate circles of mutual help that provided food and hiding places. They also recognized the unbidden heroism of figures such as Janusz Korczak, director of the Don Sierot orphanage since 1911, who accompanied his children as they walked two by two, holding hands in a "long crocodile" all the way from Sienna Street across the length of the ghetto to the Umschlagplatz on August 6, 1942.[46] On the ghetto's streets, one could see both the corpses of abandoned children and the "crocodiles" of solidarity and charity.

Compounding the assault on Jewish humanity in the ghettos was the bitter feeling of having been abandoned by the rest of the world. At night, lying exhausted in bed, Irene Hauser could hear church bells toll in "Aryan" Litzmannstadt. Standing at the edge of the Lodz Ghetto,

Oskar Rosenfeld also heard "unaccustomed noises": "roosters crowing, hens cackling, gramophones, radio music," and a "clock chiming." These sounds of life created for him the "most incredible effect," which was "to be for *the first time* completely cut off from the world." In the Warsaw Ghetto, the bridge along Żelazna over Chłodna Street, which connected the "big" and the "little" ghetto beginning in January 1942, offered fine views of Warsaw traffic and the Vistula River. But rather than connecting separate geographic parts or overcoming a great divide, the bridge provided "spectacular evidence" of the impossibility of movement. It symbolized being caged in rather than pointing a way out. Jan Mawult, a policeman in the ghetto, referred to the bridge over Chłodna Street as the Ponte di Sospiri, after the Bridge of Sighs behind Saint Mark's Square in Venice. Windows out of the ghetto also offered a view onto windows into the ghetto. During the ghetto uprising in April and May 1943, Warsovians scrambled onto roofs to witness the German bombardment of the district, but many Jews had the sense that the Poles across the way could look but did not truly see. Adina Blady-Szwajger recalled in her memoirs a scene from the Great Deportation: "In a house on Żelazna Street, over there on the other side, a woman came out onto the balcony in a flowered dressing gown and watered the flowers in the boxes. And she must have seen the procession [to the Umschlagplatz], but she went on watering the flowers." Jews often saw Poles tending their gardens on the other side.[47]

The ghetto that Oskar Rosenfeld called, invoking Daniel Defoe's resourceful shipwrecked hero, Robinson Crusoe, "a Robinsonade on the continent" provided heartening evidence of Jews' "spontaneous inventive spirit," a remarkable event in "the history of mankind." At the same time, this twentieth-century island no longer belonged "to the *world*. We are all dead for the world. The world has given up on us." ("Crusoe of York" lived "eight and twenty years all alone.") Emanuel Ringelblum was cheered to hear the BBC broadcast, in June 1942, summaries of the report that he and his colleagues had written on the murder of hundreds of thousands of Polish Jews, heartened that the world was no longer "deaf and dumb to our unparalleled tragedy." But he grew more despondent about humanity, and even about Jews in Palestine and the United States, after the Great Deportation had destroyed the heart of Polish Jewry and with it the heart of Jewry as such. After a secret visit to the Warsaw Ghetto in October 1942, following that summer's deportations, Jan Karski, an envoy of the Polish resistance, believed the whispers of despair he heard to be "roaring": "I was hearing cracking, tearing sounds of the earth opening to swallow a portion of humanity."[48]

Jews in the ghettos were also cut off from the most ordinary moments in life's journey. With the past as well as the future taken away from them, Jews no longer lived en route; the ability to make a home, to rear a family, to pursue productive goals, to create a meaningful life had largely been stolen. The ghetto was life without substance or structure: "Dogs are barking, horses neighing, birds twittering, *slaves are toiling*, but we," wrote Oskar Rosenfeld, "we here in the ghetto are vegetating . . . our lives have lost all purpose." For his fellow Jews, the railway station waiting room of war was a place where people whose homes had been confiscated and communities destroyed had been pushed and shoved, a place where fears of the deportation trains and of death left people hanging at the very edge of life. It was a time "saturated with finality" but without the ability to move, to act, or to resist. Jews were completely trapped, not by decisions they had made but by those decreed by others. This was the cardinal difference between "Aryans" and Jews: Jews found themselves in ghettos and camps not because of any choices they made but because of who they were condemned to be in the eyes of their tormentors. Even Poles had more room to maneuver, both to escape the blows of the Germans and to fight back. Thus, for Poles, writes one scholar, the experience of the war could be recast as "a sacred, heroic, lofty time," in which martyrs sacrificed themselves for a restored postwar Poland, whereas for Jews, the war was simply "a cursed, shaming time." Dawid Sierakowiak wrote that in the ghetto, "time is passing to no avail."[49]

Even before their deaths, Jews felt discarded. Ghetto diarists and chroniclers were thunderstruck by "the world's cowardice and heartlessness." Yet they kept a meticulous record of what was happening in the ghettos.[50] Witnesses took extraordinary care to preserve their documentation. Even if most of the writers did not survive, a remarkable number of their texts did; in the most awful places in eastern Europe, surviving pages exceeded surviving people. They wrote with confidence that the words of the victims would overwrite the words of the murderers. They wrote up their chronicles in the not yet entirely misplaced hope that the world would hear and understand Jewish testimony and ultimately judge the Germans on the basis of that written record. In this regard, Jewish writers felt a tenuous connection to a future humanity. Writing was a fragile recognition of humanity forestalled, a humanity that one day would mourn the consequences of not having prevented the sacrifices endured in the present.

If André Chamson wrote *The Well of Miracles* from behind the protection of "heavy, worn damask drapes," peering out to report on the new depredations taking place in the apartment courtyard, ghetto chroniclers wrote from inside Chamson's windowless shed in which the captured dogs had been locked. There are occasional glimpses of life beyond the ghetto—the toll of church bells, or, in Warsaw, the Vistula, neighbors seen across Żelazna Street—but most of the writing is about the ghetto itself, the space and time occupied between the initial deportation from home, which becomes the impetus for keeping a record, and the final deportation to the death camps, for which there are no records. The journals and diaries are more or less completely congruous with ghetto space and ghetto time. The German, the dog catcher, is there, striking cruel blows during the periods of "in-settlement" and "out-settlement," but is not an outsize figure in the episodes, which concentrate on the Jews, the dogs in the shed. The "ghetto wonders," a term used by chroniclers in the Lodz Ghetto, like Chamson's "well of miracles," are the features of a fantastic, horrible reality emerging out of the ruins of the old world, but the wonders in the ghetto are incomparably more intense, more expansive, and more lethal than Chamson's miracles.

Writers strained to describe the evidence of life in a new time and place. As part of a two-person team investigating claims for ghetto-funded poor-relief support, Josef Zelkowicz inspected twenty-eight apartments and thus twenty-eight households and twenty-eight groups of impoverished, suffering Jews. The title of his reportage, "A Bruise and a Welt in Every Dwelling," referred to the buildings Zelkowicz surveyed but applied as much to the people who inhabited them. The precincts of the ghetto were toxic and horribly, monstrously alive. "Get your eyes used to understanding that in the ghetto it is not enough to look around soberly and realistically," Zelkowicz urged his assimilated Polish-speaking partner, Ryva Bramson. "Looking and seeing isn't enough!" Zelkowicz called Bramson "to read behind the lines, as they say," but he also urged her to document the forcefulness of the catastrophe in which people died not from hunger but from "an illness called 'ghetto.'" "To sharpen your gaze" was to see the details that had to be discerned slowly, to piece together the back stories of misery. "Breathe slowly," Zelkowicz advises Ryva. "Drink the bitter cup with me, sip by sip until it's empty."[51]

At the end of the staircase was "a hole in the wall," "covered with a rag," "open to every gust of wind," "the First Apartment." In the room stood a "small iron stove," but because it was "rusted out," the ordinary object had come to resemble a "pus-invested wound." "Crumpled red sheets" covered the bed but were ghoulishly reanimated in Zelkowicz's description: "They look like hunks of meat from the butchered horses that they bring into the ghetto for the inhabitants to eat." A closer look reveals the "dishevelled hair" that "surrounds the face on the pillow like a spider's web that has trapped a dead fly." Although "Zlata died in February, Feivel in March, Zeinval in March, Miriam in June, Mendel in August" 1941, the ordinary ruins of their lives have taken on a grotesque vitality. In "the Fifth Apartment," the photographs that Lodz residents were permitted to bring with them during the resettlement in April 1940 stare "burning holes into yearning hearts." Zelkowicz sees the children in "the Tenth Apartment" "writhing and convulsing like worms in the sun."[52]

This rebirth of the world in grotesque, deadly forms is perhaps what Oskar Rosenfeld was trying to get at when he wrote that "in the beginning God created the ghetto." It was a lethal genesis, in which people counted the dead who had already passed—Zlata, Feivel, Miriam—rather than the generations to come. For his part, though, Rosenfeld did not see the vivid horror that Zelkowicz did. For him, when he tried to describe "the face of the street," "everything is old, mummy-like, as in an herbarium, people, houses, trees, memories. Even fresh vegetables, as soon as they are brought into the ghetto, shrivel, the leaves shrink, the little tails of radishes and turnips wilt. . . . Everything looks as in a secondhand shop." It was as if "the cosmic plan" revived the entire world in a state of decomposition. "As fishes, in accordance with their constitution, swim in the water, so," Rosenfeld concluded, "the inhabitants of the ghetto go hungry."[53]

The genesis of the ghetto allowed life, however dreadful its living, however extreme its lot. In the ghetto, "every resident has to tell himself: I must live in the ghetto the way others live outside in their cities and spaces." For Rosenfeld, the question was whether people would be able to accept "such a thesis" and learn to survive. Those "who have been deported here from the West"—that is, the twenty thousand German, Austrian, and Czech Jews dumped into the ghetto in the fall of 1941— by and large would and could not. A Yiddish song even mocked the impractical Jews from the West. It was set to the tune of a Polish military march:[54]

> *A German Jew*
> *goes around with his briefcase,*
> *looking for butter or margarine,*
> *nowhere, nowhere,*
> *nothing to buy,*
> *he takes a visa*
> *to Marysin*

In a terrible way, the genesis of the ghetto was life giving because it allowed a class of "fish" and "spiders" and "worms" to eke by, even when their numbers were persistently diminished. Lodz's ghetto chroniclers spent considerable time analyzing the deportations of German Jews in May 1942 and the evacuation of those who were "under ten, over 65" in September. For Oskar Singer, the German Jews were insufficiently resilient; they lived apart in communal housing assigned to them on the basis of the transports on which they arrived from Berlin, Vienna, or Cologne. For whatever reason, whether age, language ability, or comportment, they could not swim in the ghetto like the other fish. In his investigation titled "On the Problem East and West," Singer did not linger on the faces or intentions of the Germans, although they are present. The core problem is one of Jewish ability. The emphasis is on how unfortunate people found themselves in the wrong categories, not on the quotas the Germans themselves established to deport and murder thousands of ghetto residents. Singer's conclusions are unsettling, yet by making "the borders of the ghetto" into "the borders of explanation," they leave room for the consideration of Jewish sovereignty, even in the face of powerful outside forces.[55]

What Rosenfeld termed "the cosmic plan" in which "inhabitants of the ghetto go hungry" was the premise for exploring the ecology of ghetto life just as one would investigate the way fish "swim in the water."[56] Zelkowicz's fearsome grotesqueries, in which the ghetto comes alive in pus and blood, sought to preserve life in a similar fashion. Even the "terrible days" when the very young and very old were deported were framed by Zelkowicz in terms of natural calamities, in which the "ghetto" kills. The argument of the ghetto elder Chaim Rumkowski, that individual Jews had to be sacrificed in order to protect the Jewish ghetto, could appear as an extreme aspect of the cosmic plan of the ghetto as represented by pitiless tickings of time. "The hands of the clocks advance very slowly, like the long, twisting limbs of green spiders," writes Zelkowicz. "With each passing moment, the ghetto's pulse weakens and ebbs. . . . 'Cling-clang—one in five to be torn away. Clank-clank—one Jew in five.'" This displacement of German murder into a "cosmic plan" was a declaration of sovereignty, not a concession of utter helplessness. A month after the deportations of those "under ten, over 65," the "daily question" remained: "What's new in the ghetto?"—"in contrast to what is going on outside."[57]

The inquiries of Zelkowicz, Singer, and Rosenfeld gave an ecological cast to ghetto life and death. They impounded "ghetto wonders" from the Germans. Adopting the approach of the feuilleton, they reported on the "vitality of ghetto people," on their accomplishments and creativity; Singer, for example, thoroughly investigated the workshops where most of Lodz's population worked manufacturing everything from war matériel to women's fashion. Ghetto journalists also got at backstories that explained how individual Jews in the apartments survived and suffered, grim details such as the fourteen-year-old boy who left his dead mother in the room so he could continue to collect her rations, or the trademan's song "Sacharina orginalc sechs a marek."[58]

With a breezy, cosmopolitan style honed in the big-city newspapers at the turn of the century, feuilletons presented portraits of urban life in which diverse characters came vividly to life. In the ghetto, feuilletons introduced the vividness of the dead and dying. In old Lodz, "textile wagons" "driven by peddlers who collected unfinished fabrics" "circulated among houses and courtyards"; in new Lodz, "the wagon circulated from home to home and from courtyard to courtyard just as it used to, and the peddlers load it as before," but this time they collected unfinished lives. Zelkowicz wanted to introduce the actual lives of his apartment dwellers in order to sweep aside the views of the Jewish masses held by more assimilated Polish-speaking colleagues such as Ryva Bramson. (In Warsaw the Oyneg Shabes archive tried to do the same in order to preserve the voice of the urban Yiddish majority, for which the Polish-speaking Judenrat had little feeling.) As Zelkowicz visited apartment after apartment, he told stories, gave names, and tried to alert readers to revealing details: "a window that lost its wooden sill one winter evening"; "the banister [that] disappeared one tough winter night"; "the marks of furniture on the walls but the furniture is gone."[59]

When it came to chronicling "those terrible days" in September 1942, Zelkowicz's mind's eye went from apartment to apartment and household to household as he himself had done when he went out on his inspection tours with Ryva Bramson the year before. Suddenly, "The house at 45 Limanowski Street exploded. The policemen 'dealt' with it just a moment ago." "In that building," Zelkowicz reported, "they took away old Krell," a pious Jew. He continued, "The house at No. 45 Limanowski Street is blowing up," and he thought about Rysiek Fajn, who was so much like "a pet kitten." "When he was hungry—when was he not?" Zelkowicz remembered, "he neither cried nor nagged people as other children did." "Rysiek was but a boy, a six-year-old boy. So they took him." The calamity went on and on, paragraph by paragraph: "The house at No. 47 exploded . . . 5 Urzednicza Street . . . Building No. 7 has exploded."[60]

The chroniclers resolved to document both the good and the bad about the ghetto, and in so doing they preserved the sovereignty of the inhabitants. Almost everything we know about the internal politics of the ghetto we know because of what Jews wrote during and after the German occupation. Polish witnesses understood the dubious role of the Jewish policemen, and German visitors to Lodz spoke with Jews about the sorts of decisions Rumkowski and the Jewish Council faced when forced to meet German deportation quotas. But details about the actions of the police and the councils, and about the decisions reached in circumstances that have been pointedly described as "choiceless choices," are available only from Jewish sources. Ghetto chronicles did not constitute a "republic of silence," nor did they portray a mass of victims. They attempted to explore in unblinking fashion the scale of heroism, suffering, shame, and humiliation in order to reveal the living body of the mortally threatened Jewish people. Chroniclers had few illusions about what went on inside the walls of the ghetto, but by investing Jews with choices and by recognizing their accomplishments and failures, they maintained the illusion that the ghetto would ultimately survive as part of the "cosmic plan," however horrific its details. Tellingly, in his Warsaw Ghetto diary, Abraham Lewin described the German actions during the Great Deportation in the summer of 1942 as a "pogrom," indeed one "with all the traits familiar from the Tsarist pogroms of the years 1905–06."[61] For Lewin, the German and Ukrainian police were dangerous outsiders who had violated and invaded the Jewish space of the ghetto. In this way, Lewin's description both upheld the sense of home and obscured the mechanisms that confined Jews to the ghetto and then led them out again to be murdered. In this sense, the genesis of the ghetto—"in the beginning God created the ghetto"—inhibited an understanding of the apocalypse.

In "The Song of the Murdered Jewish People," Yitzhak Katzenelson linked together a chain of bitter accusations on behalf of the suffering Jewish people who are constituted and sanctified in their song, their scream of lamentation. Composing his modern-day Bible in the transit camp in Vittel in France in 1943, before being murdered in Auschwitz a year later, Katzenelson is unsparing in his indictment: of the Germans, "far crueller" than Amalek; of the Polish bystanders and thieves; of the "overseas" Jews; of the "apostates and near-apostates" among the Jewish police; of "Adamie" Czerniakow and the Jewish Council; and of God himself, who "invented a Jewish people," but now looked upon a world in which the "houses of prayer" were empty and the "Psalm of the Day" went unrecited. From the *kesl*, or cauldron, on Miła Street to the freight cars to Treblinka, he reimagines the Jewish people, beginning with his own lost son and wife, Benzionke and Yomele, who stand in for all the murdered Jews; to the orphans and children, who were deported first; to the "Menachem Mendels, Tevye the dairymen, Nogids, Motke thieves." Deceived and betrayed, the murdered Jews constitute the living body of the Jewish people whose suffering "in these terrible days" displaces the prophets themselves. "Evoke not Ezekiel, evoke not Jeremiah/ . . . I don't need them!" Katzenelson speaks directly to Isaiah: "You were not as small, not as great," as the small Jewish boy, "not as good, not as true, not as faithful as he." Katzenelson's radical theology disposed of God because Katzenelson found him instead in the Jewish people whose faith in humanity was so strong that they could not imagine the slaughter of 6 million: "We did not believe it could happen because we are human beings."[62]

9

Broken Words

LITTLE MORE THAN SIX MONTHS AFTER THE END OF THE WAR, ON November 21, 1945, US Supreme Court justice Robert H. Jackson delivered the opening statement for the prosecution at the "Trial of the Major War Criminals before the International Military Tribunal" in Nuremberg. Speaking in the name of the "common sense of mankind," he expressed astonishment as he described the "catalog of crimes" carried out by the "broken men" sitting in the docket. Goring was there, but not Goebbels or Himmler and not Hitler, all of whom had committed suicide. "You will have difficulty," he declared, to "believe that in this twentieth century human beings could [inflict] such sufferings." Jackson spent the morning detailing the Nazis' "Lawless Road to Power," the "Consolidation of Nazi Power," the "Battle Against the Working Class," and the "Battle Against the Churches." After a two-hour recess at noon, he turned to the "Crimes Against the Jews." In this part, Jackson provided unusual detail about "the most savage and numerous crimes planned and committed by the Nazis." He reflected on the unfathomability of the "incredible events," conceding that "if I should recite these horrors in words of my own, you would think me intemperate and unreliable." However, Jackson used the words "the Germans themselves" had written down. He cited reports on mass killings prepared by Einsatzgruppe A in Lithuania and Latvia and "the picture of horror" they painted in the town of Sluzk on October 31, 1941. He went down the list, "town after town, where hundreds of Jews were murdered": Vitebsk, Shitomir, Cherson. Another report detailed problems Germans encountered when using gas vans to murder Jews. He concluded this section of the indictment with "one more sickening document," the "Stroop Report," an "almost incredible text," "beautifully bound in leather with the loving care bestowed on a proud work," outfitted with the title in Gothic script, "The Jewish Quarter of Warsaw Is No More," and with one particular photograph said to document the effort to pull "bandits" out of bunkers but actually showing "almost entirely women and little children." The photograph, now iconic, shows a little boy in a buttoned coat and a cap with his hands up as German soldiers drive Jews out onto the streets in the aftermath of the Warsaw Ghetto Uprising in April and May 1943.[1]

Jackson drew attention to the obvious contradiction between the photograph's caption, "Pulled from the bunkers by force," and its content, women and children surrounded by armed men. But the "polar opposites" that Jackson saw in that photo, and that we continue to see, the contrasts, in one scholar's words, of "perpetrators vs. victims, military vs. civilians, power vs. helplessness, threatening hands of weapons vs. empty hands raised in surrender, steel helmets vs. bare-headedness or soft caps, smugness vs fear, security vs. doom," were not opposites at all for the German photographer who snapped the picture. As far as the Nazis were concerned, all Jews were partisans and bandits, and their apartments were therefore bunkers. Because, as Himmler would explain to the Wehrmacht in May 1944, Jewish women gave birth to future "hate-filled avengers," who threatened "our children and grandchildren," all Jews, especially women and children, had to be killed.[2] The unassailable guilt of Jewish children guaranteed the unassailable innocence of German children. The very photograph that observers today regard as evidence of the gratuitous violence of the Holocaust's perpetrators, those perpetrators themselves regarded as evidence of their resolute racial virtue.

"A child at gunpoint" is hardly the only picture that served the dual purposes of both the Nazis and their enemies. Another photograph, commonly known as the "weeping Frenchman," appeared both in *Life* and in the Nazi illustrated *Signal*. Whether the man was weeping in Paris, Marseille, or (most likely) Toulon, and whether it was taken in 1940 or 1941, the photograph is widely regarded as a classic representation of the "patriotic grief" of the French after the Germans occupied France.

According to one website devoted to "iconic photos," it is "one of the most heart-rending pictures of the Second World War"; the man "cries across decades from his faded photograph. He cries not only for his generation, but for his century." For *Signal*, however, the photograph, which it acknowledged had been originally published in the United States, illustrated the theme "Freedom is not easy." *Signal* also republished the ubiquitous graffiti that had appeared across Europe after the German defeat at Stalingrad, "1918 = 1943." But it did so in January 1944, immediately after "the year 1943 has passed, and the magic appeal of the slogan has vanished: '43 was not '18." For those the Germans occupied, the graffiti announced Germany's extreme vulnerability, but as 1943 gave way to 1944, "1918 = 1943" was for the Germans themselves evidence that they would not and could not be defeated. Indeed, in October 1943, Himmler averred that if the Jews were still alive, "we would now probably have reached the 1916/17 stage when the Jews were still part of the body of the German people."[3]

As Jackson's opening statement suggested, for many observers at the time and since, "common sense" recoiled at the horror of the "incredible events" and at their duration and scale. The Holocaust was so unfathomable that its victims themselves suspected that "nobody will *want* to believe us, because our disaster is the disaster of the entire civilized world." But as they wrote the initial drafts of the history of the victorious Third Reich, the Germans displayed little of the incomprehension that afflicts students of the Holocaust today. Germans put "loving care" into the commemoration of the "proud work" of destroying the Warsaw Ghetto, for instance; one teletype message on May 24, 1943, reported, "Of the total 56,065 Jews apprehended, about 7,000 were destroyed directly in the course of the grand operation."[4] Although they faced difficulties integrating the violence into their overall accounts of German history, the perpetrators were quite straightforward about documenting the "final solution." Almost all the documentary evidence of the murders of Jews comes from the Germans themselves. The document known as the Stroop Report was just one piece in a much larger record of wartime activity.

After the war, imprisoned SS brigadier general Jürgen Stroop, who had changed his name in 1941 from the too Catholic Joseph (and the childlike moniker "Jo-Jo") to the more SS-friendly Jürgen, recalled a meeting with SS general Friedrich-Wilhelm Krueger, in which he was urged to take "photographs of the Grand Operation." (The term *grand operation* comes up again and again in the Nazi sources; the action was the opposite of unspeakable.) Photographs would "serve as invaluable tools for future historians of the Third Reich—for the Fuehrer, for Heinrich Himmler, for our nationalist poets and writers, as SS training materials, and, above all, as proof of the burdens and sacrifices endured by the Nordic races and Germany in their attempt to rid Europe and the world of the Jews."[5] Although Stroop initially prepared only three copies of his report, his superiors indicated that it would eventually be made available to the public for the benefit of the master race. Even at the time, however, there was nothing secret about the events in the ghetto in the spring of 1943. The black smoke hung across the sky over Warsaw. From Krasinski Square, an open space that offered good vantage points to observe what was going on behind the ghetto walls, one could see artillery pieces trained on the ghetto and even Jews falling out of burning buildings.

The Unfinished Epic

JUST AS THEY HAD DOCUMENTED FOR PUBLIC CONSUMPTION THE "TIME of struggle" before 1933 and the achievements of the Third Reich after 1933, the Nazis carefully recorded all aspects of the war, including the various fronts, and the "administrative" operations of the SS behind the lines. The army and the SS deployed journalists, photographers, filmmakers, and even novelists to document the unfolding history of Nazi Germany. In the letters and films they sent home, ordinary soldiers did their part to commemorate the events. "Has any real event in history been more 'theatricalized'?" asks one scholar. "The Nazis documented their actions self-consciously and at length. They photographed themselves as if they were actors in a movie, as if they needed a record of their 'heroic' actions."[6] As Justice Jackson pointed out at Nuremberg, the Nazis easily found words to describe their actions. Nazi accounts of history did not tremble or stutter or fall silent in the same way as did Jackson's "common sense of mankind." Indeed, Hans Frank, Governor-General of occupied Poland, appealed to newly written history in order to erase the inhibitions of old-fashioned sentimentalism. The task of fitting events into a narrative of Nazi history would grow more difficult with time, but the challenge of finding the right words did not prevent the first versions of Germany's new "world history" from being drafted.

As Germans expanded the killing of Jews in the Soviet Union in the summer of 1941, they correspondingly expanded their collection of archival evidence. On August 1 of that year, the Gestapo chief, Heinrich Müller, ordered mobile killing squads to send "particularly interesting visual material" to Berlin "as quickly as possible," including "photographs, placards, leaflets, and other documents." Two weeks later, "Hitler's cameraman," Walter Frentz, who had learned his craft with Leni Riefenstahl, Nazi Germany's most famous filmmaker, and photographer Franz Geyl, whom Himmler referred to as a "film reporter," accompanied the SS leader to Minsk. The entourage visited the Jewish ghetto, a Durchgangslager (transit camp), and an asylum; held court at the Leninhaus; and witnessed the execution of local Jews, before Himmler reported back to the Wolfschanze, where he dined with Hitler on August 16, 1941. The implementation of the "final solution" accelerated whenever Himmler inspected and Hitler approved. In all probability, Frentz filmed the massacre; photographs reveal that the visit to the Durchgangslager was both photographed and filmed, despite Frentz's postwar claim that he was in Minsk only out of curiosity. Further corroboration is provided by Himmler's calendar; the entry for November 19, 1941, referred to dinner followed by "Newsreel and film from Minsk."[7]

The films, photographs, and "other documents" produced an archive that "future historians of the Third Reich" and "nationalist poets and writers" would be able to mine. Himmler recruited well-known novelist Edwin Erich Dwinger to Erich von dem Bach-Zelewski's SS operations in July 1941, just when Bach-Zelewski commenced the large-scale murder of Jews in "Russia Center," his area of responsibility. Dwinger had become famous for his "German Passion," in which he recounted his experiences as a prisoner of war in Russia during World War I, the outbreak of the revolution there, the agonies of the civil war, and his return to

Germany. Each volume of the work, which appeared between 1929 and
1932, registered the growing hold of National Socialism on Germany.
He had also written a number of instant histories of the new "Greater
German Reich," describing the German victories in Poland and France
that seemed to herald "a new Gründerzeit," or "New Beginning." Now
he was grateful for the opportunity to march alongside the SS in order
to "experience the new order" from an "administrative" rather than military angle. Dwinger was hardly fainthearted. In *Tod in Polen* (1940), he
imagined many of the elements that would characterize the Holocaust in
the course of describing events following "Bloody Sunday" in Bromberg,
on September 3, 1939, a rendition that cast the Poles as perpetrators and
Germans as victims. But evidently, he was disgusted by what he had seen
or was expected to witness in Russia in 1941, and he secured a transfer
back to the Wehrmacht, whose operations he chronicled in *Wiedersehen
mit Sowjetrussland*. (Bach-Zelewski, Himmler's "favorite general," himself
suffered "intestinal ailments" connected to the murder of Jews, before
recovering from his breakdown to emerge as a more hardened killer.)
Dwinger's transfer was the first sign of trouble in the production of Germany's new "world history."[8]

Himmler also engaged his good friend novelist Hanns Johst, president of the Reich Literary Chamber. Johst expressed his gratitude that
his "Reichsführer, my Heini Himmler," had allowed him to participate
in what Himmler himself described as "our task" to produce updated
"sagas" that would leave behind a "true-to-life memorial to our times." At
the beginning of January 1940, Johst accompanied Himmler to Poland in
his special train "Heinrich," where he welcomed newly repatriated ethnic
Germans from the Soviet Union. Johst commemorated this homecoming
in his 1940 book, *Ruf des Reiches—Echo des Volkes!* Including a reference to
a "reservation" for the empire's Jews, Johst celebrated the "pioneers of
the new state who confirm the legitimate claims of our race in the new
provinces." Johst also took part in Himmler's conference of SS leaders in
Wewelsburg on June 12, 1941, a meeting on the eve of the invasion of the
Soviet Union at which the sphere of activity of the mobile killing squads
was outlined and the death of 20 to 30 million Slavs discussed. He traveled with Himmler to newly founded German settlements in Hegewald,

near Shitomir in Ukraine, for nearly three months in the fall of 1942, and he attended the notorious meeting of Nazi leaders in Posen in October 1943.[9]

Although Himmler regarded Johst as a "kind of bard of the SS," Johst never published further installments of his "sagas." Perhaps Germany's imminent victory fell out of sight too fast. Nevertheless, Johst described his commitment to preserve for posterity precisely the epoch-making nature of National Socialism's accomplishments. In a radio address in July 1942, he held forth: "Not long after combat operations have been concluded, poets, novelists, and reporters will be taken to the battlefields, and tested men from the front lines will make every effort to give them a true, close-hand intimate picture of the decisions that have been taken so that no false, faded, or overly sentimental historical or aesthetically convoluted perspectives can take over these holy, solemn sites." The references to "tested men," to a "true picture," and to "holy, solemn sites" suggested the epic terms in which Hitler, Himmler, and Goebbels all discussed the "final solution." Johst called for historical narratives sufficient to the historic task that Nazism had taken on. One postwar witness recalled even clearer words from Johst: he allegedly urged "German writers to take part in executions in the east in order to let such events make them more virile."[10]

Joseph Goebbels, the Reich minister of public enlightenment and propaganda, was also hard at work. In the spring of 1942, just as the final preparations for implementing the decision to exterminate the Jews in a European-war "final solution" were being completed, Goebbels was planning a major show trial of Herschel Grynszpan. On November 7, 1938, Grynszpan, a Polish Jewish refugee, had shot Ernst vom Rath, a junior diplomat stationed in Paris. The assassination had provided the regime with the pretext for the pogroms it unleashed across Germany three days later. Describing the trial as "less a legal than a political proceeding," Goebbels intended for the world media, by covering the trial, to broadcast Germany's justification for the deportation of Jews to the East. The trial would prove, in the words of Goebbels's lieutenant Wolfgang Diewerge, that "the French people were incited into a war by World Jewry against its own interests." "The extermination of Jewry," Diewerge commented in an October 1941 memorandum for Goebbels, "is a pre-condition for the coming New Order in Europe."[11] Plans moved forward in early 1942: Hitler himself was "very interested" in the trial, and Diewerge secured the agreement of the former French foreign minister Georges Bonnet to testify about the political pressure exerted by Jews on French foreign policy. He drew up plans for a radio broadcast of the weeklong trial, in which it was agreed beforehand that Grynszpan (and presumably, by extension, Europe's Jews) would be sentenced to death. In the end, however, Grynszpan's claim that he had had a homosexual affair with the German diplomat and concerns about the reliability of French officials prompted Goebbels to scuttle the entire project. The French had themselves put on trial leaders of the Third Republic, but the officials stood accused of losing the war, not, as Hitler hoped, of declaring war on Germany in the first place. Vichy's trial was anti-Semitic insofar as leading French Jews stood accused, but its focus on the inadequate preparations for war sent the wrong message; as Germany saw it, the problem was that the Jews were warmongers, not that they were insufficiently bellicose. This sideshow, taking place in the central French town of Riom, posed an additional problem to the construction of a persuasive German narrative on the "final solution."

At the same time, in May 1942, Goebbels's Propaganda Ministry sent filmmakers to the Warsaw Ghetto, where they produced eight reels for a film, most likely intended to update, once the deportations from the ghetto had begun, the anti-Semitic feature *Der Ewige Jude*. As Jewish witnesses could plainly see, German choreographers carefully staged scenes to confirm the most blatant anti-Semitic clichés about poverty and luxury in the ghetto, all in order to deny so-called Asia in Central Europe any humanity. Given the many takes the filmmakers took the trouble to shoot, it is highly likely that the film was designed for propagandistic rather than documentary or archival purposes.[12] In the event, the film was never released or even completely edited. Exactly why this was the case is not clear, but by the conclusion of the "Great Action," the massive deportation of Warsaw's Jews, at the end of the summer of 1942, all eyes were riveted on Stalingrad. There, the challenge was not to justify mass murder but to avoid a repeat of the Soviet offensive in the Winter War of

1941–1942. As the world watched military events on the Volga, the fall of 1942 dramatized for the first time the possibility of Germany's defeat. After Stalingrad the appetite for huge propaganda productions on the order of a show trial or *The Eternal Jew* diminished considerably. Hitler came to realize that he could not rely on a European-wide consensus on the "Jewish problem," that not all Europeans would be receptive to the public documentation and justification of Germany's extermination of the Jews. (He later came to believe that a world without Jews would cement European alliances with Germany against the Allies.)

While Germany's military advance unfolded, soldiers themselves constituted an army of amateur historians and archivists. After listening to Hitler's announcement to soldiers on October 2, 1941, in which the Führer pronounced the "beginning of the last great deciding battle of the war," a delicatessen owner from Münster began writing an explicitly documentary letter to his wife in which he sought "to provide a bit of insight into our experience." A few weeks later, Albert Neuhaus was able to send Agnes the first fruits of his reportage: "I am sending you 6 rolls of film to develop. I don't have to tell you how important these pictures are to me. Let me ask you to develop these pictures with *total care* in a 6 x 9 format. Preferably, silk smooth matte finish." He was satisfied with the results, subsequently requesting bigger 18 x 24 centimeter enlargements to provide "an ornament for our apartment."[13]

The first indications of how extensively ordinary German soldiers documented field operations, including the execution of partisans and the murder of civilians, came from the Soviets, who discovered photographs among the possessions of the thousands of soldiers who had been killed in the first months of the German invasion. Already in France in 1940, CBS radio correspondent William Shirer had noted, "It seems funny, but every German soldier carries a camera." Advertisements for Agfa film and Voigtländer cameras filled the pages of Nazi periodicals. That many of the photographs of executions showed soldiers gathered around holding cameras indicates the keen interest in documenting this part in the war. In the Vilna Ghetto, Herman Kruk described how photographers captured their subjects: everywhere the German "stands ready with his camera" to begin the "hunt with Leica cameras." One disturbing sequence of photographs from 1942 shows Wehrmacht soldiers marching Serbian Jews into a field, forcing them to dig their graves, and then shooting them. The last shots depict the soldiers viewing the photographs they had taken earlier.[14]

Once arranged in photo albums, the photographs directed the viewer "seamlessly from picture-postcard views, drinks parties and social occasions, to poverty-stricken indigenous peoples in destroyed towns and cities, deportations, hangings, murders, and executions," as one scholar observes. Most of the photographs of Soviet civilians conformed to blatantly racist stereotypes, an indication of just how deep or intuitive distinctions between "us" and "them" had become. The photo albums also make clear the degree to which violence had been absorbed into daily life on the front. Taking photographs, sending the films home to be developed according to careful instructions, trading snapshots, and pulling them out to show comrades or Swiss and German nurses, Wehrmacht soldiers expanded upon the traditional practice of fashioning a family photo album; photography at the front created "a much greater family ideal . . . the nation-state itself." Soldiers shared the feeling of participating in something "completely new" and "groundbreaking" (gewaltig, which is related to the German word for "violence"). Photography documented their historic collaboration in the National Socialist project.[15]

The epic mode of writing history, which depicted Nazi Germany building a new world, allowed soldiers and citizens to at once mobilize themselves for an epoch-making journey while disregarding the suffering they inflicted. It introduced a newly conceived German civilization that distinguished itself from the newly designated barbarians it conquered and killed. This distinction was continuously shored up by the rhetoric of "us" or "them," existence or nonexistence, which circulated widely in Hitler's speeches and in soldiers' letters after the invasion of the Soviet Union. The idea of making history on an epochal scale justified the war against civilians as much as it enabled it. One postwar philosopher notes that the racial politics of the Nazis perceived the world in "architectonic" terms: "It is not a question to accept conditions, but, rather, to build a construct, in which the radicalism of the very making implied an idealism of barbarism and a puritanism of evil."[16] A worldview in which the world in view consisted of enemies or expendable people sustained violence and generated more violence.

But this was also its undoing. As German counterinsurgency efforts expanded and the number of partisans increased, the war seemed to be endlessly creating more enemies. In September 1941, Konrad Jarausch, a reserve officer on the eastern front, feared "the prospect of a long war": "I'm terrified by the thought that all these people whom we had to hurt and humble deeply, might at some time band together for revenge." Unlike "my comrades," Jarausch did not believe that killing all the Jews would solve the problem of escalating violence. There were Russians, Ukrainians, and others—"We . . . are sucking them dry." He wondered whether his little boy would eventually have to take up the same fight. These fears were widespread enough for one army newspaper to publish an article confronting the nagging question in its title, "A War in Perpetuity?," in October 1941. It assured soldiers that the only "forever" of the war was the shape that world history would take at its conclusion; "what we are fighting for is the *fate of great historical epochs*."[17] However, as the war continued, references to the "Thousand-Year Reich" were discouraged because the term's insistence on permanence had become too ambiguous. The titanic kept conjuring up the *Titanic*.

The Germans held the advantage for "a long time," noted writer Albert Camus in his "Letters to a German Friend." This was so because "you kill more easily than we do." But in the end, the Germans scorned "faith in mankind" and, as a result, had created an expanding world of enemies. They had marked themselves as "the men, who by thousands, are going to die solitary," whereas "we have our certainties, our justifications, our justice," a solidarity that made Germany's defeat "inevitable." The French had paused in 1940, ashamed, guilty, introspective, but they finally embraced their weakness as a virtue, whereas the Germans' superhuman effort to remake the world ultimately destroyed precisely those who believed they had liberated themselves from humanity.[18] Camus revised Hans Frank's opposition of humanitarian impulses to history making, putting the emphasis on the Germans who died for themselves and for a history only they could read and understand. At a basic level, Germany's escalation of violence undermined its maintenance of historical meaning.

Historian Saul Friedländer takes up this conflict between violence and history when he argues that the Holocaust's perpetrators came to regard the extermination of the Jews as a "singular" series of events that could not be integrated into the broader narrative of German history. Himmler's October 1943 speech in Posen, in which he referred to the annihilation of the Jewish people as "an unwritten and never-to-be-written page of glory" "in our history," reveals an awareness, Friedländer argues, of "some total transgression which a future generation will not understand, even as a necessary means toward a 'justifiable' end." Complete knowledge about what the SS elite had accomplished could not be revealed to "the eighty million upright Germans," Goebbels declared. Describing the "punishment" inflicted upon the Jews as "barbaric," Goebbels was also very aware of the limits to what the German public would understand. "What will we do with half-Jews, what will we do with their relatives, their in-laws, their spouses?" he wondered, calling these "extraordinarily delicate questions." He worried as well that "later generations" would not have the "gumption" and "vigilance" that present-day National Socialists possessed; this meant it was important to proceed immediately to find a "final solution" to the "Jewish problem." Elsewhere, Goebbels feared that in twenty or thirty years, Germans living in a land without Jews would lack "intimate" experience with the enemy and that their inability to understand the circumstances that made action urgent in the present would prevent that action from being understood in the future. Nazi leaders acknowledged that the resolve and hardness they so cherished would slowly dribble away.[19]

Although Germans hardly shied from documenting the murder of Jews, as the extent of the killings grew officials developed numerous strategies to explain or contain evidence about the scale of annihilation. The most compelling argument for Germany's preemptive assaults on the Jews rested on the notion that Germany had very nearly been destroyed in 1918. The fact that most Germans, both Nazis and non-Nazis, accepted this false recovered memory of defeat and revolution constituted the Nazis' greatest propaganda success. Hitler's injunction "Never again" urged Germans to mobilize tirelessly in order to avoid the fate they endured after the first world war. This history of 1918 was a huge accelerator of violence in the Greater German Reich. But was fear of another 1918 sufficient to foster complete understanding of the Nazi ambition to destroy every last Jew and to fight the entire world? The year 1918 was a self-limiting justification. Its aim, the peace, security, and prosperity of Germany in a postwar world, was inconsistent with the transgressive, expansive, and ultimately self-destructive means by which it was to be achieved. Nazi leaders therefore worried more and more about whether future generations would see themselves as heirs to the drama of the present day. In this way, they acknowledged the problems even National Socialist history had in assimilating the murder of the Jews, which as a result retained an "unthinkable" aspect.

Germans themselves also began to rethink their place in Nazi accounts of German history. This rethinking is audible in the ways they approached victory over the course of the war. The belief in an *Endsieg*, or "final victory," took on more desperate forms, mutating from "we will win," "we are winning,"—the plain evidence of 1939, 1940, and 1941— to "we can still win," the feeling in 1942, after the difficult Winter War, to "we must win," the resolve of total war after Stalingrad, before falling apart altogether in 1945. At the outset of the war, most Germans insisted on their patriotic part in the war effort. By the very end, most no longer wished to hold themselves accountable, and they lamented the war as a catastrophe that had befallen them. At the end of September 1939, Heinrich Döll, an owner of a large bookstore in Bremen, fully supported the war against Poland and Germany's firm stance against the intervention of France and Britain. He was also careful to explain to his son, Heinz, a soldier, that these were points on which all Germans agreed, whether they were Nazis or not; "patriotism is not at all determined just by the National Socialists" he insisted. Heinrich did not want to be left out of the history the Nazis were making. Five years later, he was again writing to his son, but this time he put as much distance between himself and the Nazi leaders as possible. "In any case, we are not, and neither are you nor broad elements of the people, responsible for the war," he wrote, and this had been the case "from the beginning," he assured Heinz. The "fanaticism" and "rabble-rousing" of its leaders, that is to say, Hitler, Goebbels, and the other high-ranked Nazis, were responsible for driving

Germany into war. The responsibility he had proudly accepted on behalf of the German people in 1939, Döll had abruptly withdrawn by 1944.[20] This shirking of responsibility was quite typical of Germans who, in the spring of 1945, blamed an ever smaller number of fanatic Nazis for losing the war and destroying the country. The shift was admirable in that individuals no longer identified with the Nazis or their crimes. But it was also entirely tendentious, because it obscured the role of Germans in political developments to which they had contributed mightily since 1933.

In Germany in 1945, there was a spate of suicides among those who could not bear defeat, but there was almost no vigilante justice like that in France, where approximately ten thousand alleged collaborationists were executed. Most Germans were literally *fahnenflüchtig*, an expression that commonly refers to the act of deserting king and country, sometimes an honorable action but, in this case, something less honorable: the Germans abandoned history itself and its responsibilities and judgments. In 1945 they had few explanations, little recourse to narrative, and only broken, hypocritical, and self-pitying phrases to make sense of the war that, as they saw it, had suddenly broken out on top of them. All at once, sometime between the onset of the Russian offensive on January 12, 1945, and the final capitulation of German armies on May 8, Germans from all walks of life reconfigured themselves into powerless and passive objects amid a gigantic catastrophe that completely overwhelmed them.

In many ways, crouching down against the winds of the Third Reich's disastrous final days reenacted the experience of the air raids that seized Germany's skies in the last years of the war. The air war that observers had alarmingly predicted for all of Europe in 1938 and 1939 came to Germany swiftly in 1942 and 1943 and reached its apogee in the winter of 1945. (Half of the 600,000 civilians who perished in air raids on Germany did so in the last four months of the war, just as half of the 5 million German soldiers who were killed in the war lost their lives in the nine months after the failed assassination plot on Hitler in July 1944. The narratives of Nazi history could not integrate these late losses.) Already during the Czechoslovak crisis of 1938, Europeans anticipated mostly passive parts for themselves in the coming conflict, dreading the aerial bombardments that would destroy their cities, their neighbors, and their families. Air raids were imagined from the perspective of the victim, not the invader. They were conceived of as catastrophes, not a war between people or states but a manifestation of the elemental forces of technological war itself.

As the Allied air assault on Germany began, Hitler enrolled the victims of aerial bombardment in the "avant-garde of hate" and enlisted them as front soldiers in Germany's war. British and American raids were described as "terror attacks." Many Germans gossiped about so-called wonder weapons; Germany's "revenge is sure to come." For their part, Britons, who had suffered the Luftwaffe's air attacks in the fall of 1941, cheered the reprisal raids that the Allies began to launch in 1942 and 1943. French prisoners in Krefeld watched the night sky "criss-crossed with blazing trails," lit up by "brilliant flashes of anti-aircraft fire," and "studded with explosive starbursts," enthralled by the "magical, barbaric extravaganza!" The Nazi "monster was all-powerful," Agnès Humbert reflected, "but now his enemies are strong, and they must kill, kill, kill." "Civilization has to use the weapons of barbarism in order to prevail." Yet remarkably, civilians under air attack often removed the assaults from the frame of the ongoing war. Skies that suddenly filled with bombers seemed a terrible meteorological event, like a powerful storm or onrushing comet or an exploding volcano. Referring to the attacks on Hamburg in July 1943, in which some 40,000 people perished, Wehrmacht officer and novelist Ernst Jünger reflected on the fact that "the victims died like fish or grasshoppers, in an elemental way, beyond history." The extreme heat formed a "heaving, ebbing tide of dead." Others took measure of the extraordinary force of events with Old Testament passages describing the pulverization of life into the dust and ash of death. Hans Erich Nossack referred to "unknowable forces" and eschewed all proper nouns in his narrative of "the end" in Hamburg. The firestorm was "the raging of the world against itself."[21]

"The whole German sky seemed to be stocked with the silver four-engined aircraft of the Americans," wrote psychologist Matthais Menzel about the frightful raid against Berlin on February 3, 1945: "The silver swarm" swept "hard over us," "undeterred, unimpeded by anyone or anything." There was no limit to the combustibility of the disaster. "What actually is the saturation level of a catastrophe?" Menzel asked. In these accounts, there are few references to the actual war that was taking place in 1943 or 1945, or to the belligerents. The bombed did not feel themselves as Germans or even victims of war, but as the puny casualties of a cosmic event. "We were completely defenseless": above in the sky, "the wings, quiet, majestic, purposeful," below in the ground, the "small group of people in this tiny basement."[22]

People who had been bombed struggled to find the right words to comprehend the "inferno" in which they found themselves trapped. The words they found tended to remove them from the war and to obscure their part in it; they instead saw a greater, more elemental power at work. Germans let the Allied air war bomb themselves out of World War II. Texts describing the bombing as a terrible catastrophe, and not as a consequence of the war that began with the German invasion of Poland in September 1939, were self-exculpatory.

The phenomenon of denationalizing the air war was not limited to Germany, however. It cannot be seen only as an attempt to balance Germany's moral ledger books of the war. In Italy, for example, Allied bombardment was "experienced as an uncontrollable natural catastrophe," as "a crack of lightning smashing into daily life"; the bombs were "not associated with the person who dropped them," one scholar writes. The disappearance of national borders in air war meant that local events were surprisingly interchangeable. "I just happened to be in Berlin," wrote Swiss journalist Konrad Warner, but "I could just as easily have experienced the same things in London or in Bucharest, in Sofia or in Leningrad. A metropolis dies!" Perhaps it was as city dwellers rather than as national citizens that Europeans contemplated aerial bombardment. And city dwellers exhibited strikingly little desire for revenge. Under the bombs, German civilians even evinced sympathy. Bombs on "Dortmund, Düsseldorf, Sardinia, Sicily"—the list was "atrocious," wrote Léon Werth, a French Jew. Allied air raids, in which "the earth is plowed up," allowed Anne Frank to move from the "terrible outside" of her streets in Amsterdam, where deportations separated Jewish families, to a far-reaching vision of "the whole globe" "waging war" on itself. It was no longer the case of "no German" spoken, as had been dictated by the "Secret Annex

Rules": "The whole earth waits," Anne wrote, "and there are many who wait for death."[23]

In "The Psychological Effects of Air Raids," a study published in 1941 in the *Journal of Abnormal and Social Psychology*, Philip Vernon of the University of Glasgow found that in an aerial bombardment, people tended to put themselves at the very center of a terrifying drama in which predators came closer and closer to their prey. Squadrons two or three miles away were said "to have been heard passing directly overhead." Typical also was "the statement: 'Bombs fell in an ever-narrowing circle round us from 10 pm to 4 am.'" People lowered their voices when planes flew overhead, "lest one attracts their attention." They scurried into the shadows of streets. The delusion of being the "single spectator" registered the complete helplessness of the individual, the reduction of the subject to an object, the player to a prop.[24]

It was with this sense of awe or awesomeness that Germans came to look at the Nazi leaders at the end of the war. If once they had cast themselves as lead players in National Socialism and in World War II, they now reduced their roles to very bit parts. Already in the summer of 1943, after survivors in Hamburg had crawled out of their shelters, they were counseled by their pastor not to look back, not to look at their own past: "For what should we look back? New tasks lie ahead of us. . . . After the destruction of the cities Sodom and Gomorrah, Lot's wife received the command: do not look back! She was turned into a pillar of salt when she did. . . . The command declares: 'do not look back, just forwards!' Whoever does not understand this and looks back anyway, will become paralyzed, unable to act, the dreadful events like a millstone around the neck."

The catastrophe of the bombings strengthened the new attitude that emphasized traveling light, traveling to a place where everyone else would meet up, postcatastrophe. The once sturdy Nazi narratives of German history had disintegrated, as more and more people no longer could see their lives unfolding in a meaningful way. They could not find the right words or take much solace in Germany's future or its past. One survivor of the 1943 bombing of Hamburg noted that "now Time sits down sadly in a corner and feels useless."[25] Perhaps all epics, overriding as they do so many complex and human features, are what the Nazi one turned out to be: dead ends.

The Patriotic Narrative

IN THE COUNTRIES THAT GERMANY OCCUPIED DURING THE WAR, residents drafted strong antifascist narratives. These powerful narratives cast the vast majority of the population as victims of the Germans and highlighted the heroic resistance of countless patriotic individuals who served and saved the nation. In many ways, this martyrological myth was as strong as it was because it was credible. By the end of the war, the unbending, cruel nature of German racism drastically diminished the ranks of those who for reasons of anticommunism or, in the case of the Ukrainians and the Baltic countries, ethnic self-determination, might have been willing to work with the occupation forces. In Poland, with its newspapers, courts, and schools, the underground secret state exerted an increasingly powerful and tangible influence on public opinion. The anti-German feeling that had coalesced in France by the middle of 1941 was only strengthened by the national spectacle that ensued when the Germans publicly threatened to kill imprisoned French civilians in retaliation for the assassination of a few Wehrmacht officials (and on many occasions did so) and when occupation authorities tightened the screws on labor conscription.

But this myth was also false. It glossed over important distinctions between those who had, for opportunistic or ideological reasons, cooperated with the German occupiers and those who did not. It did not distinguish between those who volunteered to work in Germany, if only for economic reasons, and those who were forced to do so. Most of the population did not actively join anti-German resistance movements, and those who did often enough terrorized the local population in order to survive by appropriating food and supplies. By commemorating the nation itself as a martyr, patriotic narratives also relied on renewed distinctions between "us" and "them," using the universalism of antifascism as a guise for exclusive, embattled, and sometimes anti-Semitic nationalisms.

By and large, the antifascist myth left out the Jews, for attention to their fate, when it became known, would have raised questions about complicity and choice, disrupting what one historian describes as "the 'mythical amalgamation' of very different categories of victims."[26]

Consider, for instance, a vignette from Sartre's "Paris Under the Occupation." Depicting the German enemy as "an octopus, which surreptitiously seized our best men and spirited them away," Sartre tries to re-create the feeling that "at any minute the door might open to admit a gust of cold, night air, and three soft-spoken Germans with revolvers." "One day," he recalled, "you might ring up a friend and the telephone bell would throb for a long time in an empty flat. You would go round and ring at the door, but no-one would open. When the porter finally forced the lock, there would be two chairs standing close together in the hall, and between them a few fag-ends of German cigarettes." Here, narrator, friend, and porter are all enrolled in a patriotic conspiracy, recognizing each other as fellow participants even if they play different roles. It is a small drama in the "Republic of Silence." Sartre does not contemplate the possibility that the "fag-ends" might have been from cigarettes smoked by French police, who often worked alongside the Germans in their counterinsurgency efforts. They could have been Gauloises instead of Junos. Resistance networks were easily infiltrated and, on account of the violence they incited, did not always enjoy the support even of friends, and as a result conversations, especially on the telephone, which could be tapped, were conducted with circumspection. Porters and concierges in apartment houses in occupied Paris also watched the coming and going of neighbors. Concierges joined the so-called Concierge Radio network to pass along news about the uprising against the German occupation in August 1944, a heroic moment. But they also routinely reported foreigners and other unknown individuals to the police, something refugees knew well.[27] For all these reasons, the French were on guard in their dealings with each other. Sartre's recollection of the occupation as a quiet conspiracy of resistance seems more like the prompt for a false recovered memory.

Traces of the mutual suspicion that divided rather than united the French were apparent in the faulty signals between the narrator and his niece who sit in mutual silence in Vercors's *The Silence of the Sea*. In that novel the German officer, whom the two French characters have to take in but try to ignore, admires the bookshelf stocked with the French classics: Balzac, Chateaubriand, Descartes, Flaubert. But Vercors is not so sure about their authority, since a few years later he called into question the identification of France and literature in his short story "Impotence." Vercors wrote the story immediately after the massacre of civilians at Oradour-sur-Glane on June 10, 1944, four days after the Allied *débarquement* in Normandy—450 women and children were burned to death in the local church. In Vercors's story, the extreme violence of the German SS only highlighted the powerlessness of even the French Resistance figure and bibliophile Renaud Houlade. Although he has not committed the crime, Houlade feels completely degraded by his incapacity to prevent it. He is humiliated by his humane tastes, his literary conversations with Balzac, Stendhal, and Valéry, so much so that he sets out to burn his library. Words have lost the capacity to console or inspire and now seem to conspire in a vast fraud about human nature. Houlade realizes that the literary sensibility of *le mot juste* is "shameless, a nastiness to vomit up! Man, what is he really? The bitchiest of creatures! The most vile and the most deceitful and the most cruel."[28]

If André Chamson in *The Well of Miracles* gradually sorted shades of gray into white and black, and if Sartre worked to build an integrated "Republic of Silence," other observers could not shake the anxiety that came from not being able to easily distinguish collaborators amid French society. Novelist Elsa Triolet ended the war on a clearly unheroic note, writing of Normandy, "'A poor sort of invasion,' somebody said." "Everything's in a terrible mess," she continued, "railways, the minds of men, and food supplies. . . . Will it be over tomorrow; will it last another winter, another month, or a century?" Everyone "had to start waiting again, in an ever-deepening bath of blood, surrounded by an heroic community now going rather to seed." A paralyzing apathy prevailed: "Housewives have ceased sweeping and making soup. Everyone eats cold food, drinks any sort of liquid. Writers no longer write." The "Boches," the Maquis, and the Milice all readied for some sort of action, creating a general state of alarm. "The danger lies not in doing this or that, but in happening to be on the spot where a raid occurs." It was dispiriting to see how cowardice, egoism, stupidity, graft, and ambition survived "on this storm-tossed raft." The closer the liberation approached, the more "the whole fabric was in tatters. In our impatience we had all begun tearing it apart."[29] Patriotic narratives were intended to clean up such messes; to cure the "disease of the occupation," in the words of Vercors; and to positively identify the German provenance of Sartre's "fag-ends" lying on the floor.

Like French patriotic narratives, Polish texts emphasized the suffering of Poles at the hands of the German occupiers. Observers were keenly aware of the arrests and executions taking place around them. Throughout the fall of 1943, the public address system in Warsaw, the so-called barking trumpets, provided the names of the unfortunate hostages threatened with execution. Day after day, the loudspeakers named doomed Poles: the sweeps through the city "don't mean a camp or forced labor any more: they are tomorrow's list of executed." Along the streets, "the lorries they call *budy* or the shiny blue *kostusie*, open ones with benches full of uniforms," sped by. Even in the suburbs, day trippers recognized "a trail of fresh drops of blood leading us all the way to the door of the shop." On another street, local "women had been mopping up" bloodstains with their handkerchiefs. "There were little shrines with flowers; men took off their hats as they passed, women knelt down and prayed." Among themselves, neighbors discussed the particulars, the "two boys, one seventeen, the other twenty," who had been arrested "yesterday," their mothers "mad with shock." Another victim was "that man who came here once with some poetry." "A stranger," but really not.[30] Relatives often knew the numbers assigned to prisoners sent to Auschwitz.

In Poland the violence was visible, intimate, and extensive, much more so than in France, where most people simply did not feel in danger when walking down the street. Reflecting on Poles who had been arrested, writer Zofia Nałkowska confessed, "It is sheer chance that they are not me." Her identification with the prisoners was strong. There they were, she imagined, "lined up, their eyes blindfolded, their hands tied behind their backs, their mouths *gagged with plaster*." As a result, the spirit of resistance was unmistakable, drawing on the traditions of the Polish underground under Russian occupation and on a strong feeling of beleaguered national identity. Poland regarded itself as the "Christ of nations."

When Stanisław Szefler arrived in Warsaw after fleeing German-annexed Pomerania in 1940, he cheered the robust sense of Polishness; people talked, joked, and sang patriotic songs on the train. There was a "specific dialect of the Warsaw occupation": a German was called a "temp," Pawiak would be avenged, and Poland would not go under. "Poland has not yet perished," averred the national anthem. One-third of all Poles reported knowing relatives active in the resistance.[31]

At first glance, the Polish patriotic narrative was characterized by its circumscribed, even tidy, features. It was virulently anti-German, exclusively nationalistic, and profoundly suspicious of strangers, including Polish Jews. Of course, Jews could hardly be avoided, at least before they were ghettoized, since they constituted about 10 percent of the population (and Polish Jews about one-third of all Jews in Europe), but they were marginal to Poles' accounts of Poland during the occupation. Nałkowska and other diarists such as Ludwik Landau referred to them in vague, abstract terms—"they" who were not encompassed in the Polish "we." Even after three hundred thousand Jews had been taken from the Warsaw Ghetto and killed, a Home Army leaflet could in the summer of 1943 portray the executions of one thousand Poles as "the largest mass murder in the capital."[32] In the underground press, Jews were either ignored or disparaged for their passivity in ways that reinforced anti-Semitism. The merry-go-round that began operating on the grounds of Krasinski Square at the very moment the Warsaw Ghetto went up in flames is only the most chilling image of the indifference of the Poles to the fate of the Jews.

But the idea that Poles during the war wholeheartedly embraced a blatantly chauvinistic narrative of Polish patriotism is, ultimately, too simple. Narratives of the occupation of Poland include reflections on the nature of Polish patriotism, indifference toward Jews, and the price of thinking in terms of "us" and "them." Nałlkowska herself was repelled by the violent rhetoric of the resistance and the way that rhetoric effaced human beings. After "dissenters" visited her apartment, Nałkowska wrote that their point of view "echoes with the horrific clash of new life-and-death" struggles, and "hatreds and orders to murder," presumably Germans, their Polish accomplices, and Ukrainians. "Love for another human being, the exhilaration of it, the unspoken happiness of discovering oneself through others, the proving of oneself by delight in them," all this "must be squashed flat with the very ground . . . turned into nothing." Nałlkowska was amazed and frightened at the "profound conviction" of the partisans. The same thing also frightened Milosz, who spoke of "the spirit of history," a murderous tempest in the minds of men.[33]

Nałkowska's suspicions about the blinding words of resistance represent broader, mostly inarticulated, dissatisfactions with the resistance and its ideology, its anti-Semitism, and its degeneration into banditry. Poles remembered the resistance, but also the sheer misery of the occupation, the privations of hunger, the forced labor, and the loss of their homes and possessions. The requirement just to survive overwhelmed people. "I am being devoured by my fucking life," complained writer Andrzej Trzebinski. Consumed with himself, with eating and keeping warm, and avoiding trouble in the streets, Trzebinski could not get a handle on events lying outside the precincts of today and tomorrow.[34]

When the long-postponed "Warsaw Uprising" against the Germans did come, it burned itself out in a calamitous forced evacuation of the city, since tens of thousands of heroic, lightly armed Warsaw citizens were no match for the German Wehrmacht and its artillery. The defeat snuffed out much of the life of Poland. Nałkowska was perhaps particularly unsympathetic to the "senseless uprising," but she had a good eye for the wreckage the inevitable German counteroffensive left behind. From a rural outpost she imagined the "empty spots" across Warsaw, "in place of those closed human homes, the countless little fortresses of life, spread and studded with its objects": "the drawers of letters and photographs," the "boxes of lace and ribbons," the "plates and cups," the "pots and pans," the "brooms and dusters." The history of those who had lived in Warsaw had been destroyed. It was now "one of the many dead cities of history." Its inhabitants constituted a homeless army of "new down-and-outs," "eating their way through dozens of square kilometers like caterpillars devouring the leaves of whole forests." This bitter end for Warsaw and its citizens was followed by the termination of Poland's claim for national self-determination after the victory of the Soviet army in January 1945. "At least," admitted Nałkowska, the "nightmare is finished."[35]

Accounts of the Polish patriotic narrative are also misleading with regard to Jews. However unevenly they were considered, Jews still figured more prominently in Polish texts than in French or German ones. The record of anti-Semitism in Poland is well known; according to Emanuel Ringelblum, talk about "getting rid of the Jews" could be "heard in the trains and in the market, in the trams and on the streets." Jews in Warsaw increasingly ghettoized themselves already in the spring of 1940, before the Germans did so formally that fall, in order to escape gangs of Polish looters and hooligans. But there also existed a "secret city" of Jews in hiding and their Catholic helpers. There were perhaps three to four thousand *szmalcowniks*, blackmailers and denouncers, whose terrifying gauntlet almost all Jews living outside the ghetto had to run, often several times during the period of occupation. After the "Great Action," the criminals would stand guard outside the ghetto walls to pounce on escaping Jews. Dozens of Jews could be imperiled by a single determined *szmalcownik*. Yet it took many Poles to save just one Jew, who usually moved from one safehouse, or *melina*, to another to escape danger. One historian estimates that at the very least between seventy and ninety thousand citizens of Warsaw worked to save the twenty-eight thousand Jews who were hiding at any one point in the months before the Warsaw Uprising in the summer of 1944.[36]

With this "secret city" in mind, consider again the merry-go-round in Krasinski Square. Historian Tomasz Szarota has definitively established that one merry-go-round was hurriedly set up in the park on April 20, 1943, a day after the beginning of the Warsaw Ghetto Uprising. It remained in operation until breaking down on April 26. Czeslaw Milosz saw it from a crosstown streetcar on Easter Sunday, April 25. Seeing the merry-go-round in the shadow of the uprising, the poem "Campo di Fiori" was "torn out of me," he recalled. One of the leaders of the Jewish underground, Marek Edelman, also remembered seeing the merry-go-round "spinning from the window, the barrel organ playing, girls' skirts, red and blue with white dots, swirling in the window." That was "our curse," the "Jewish road" to death alongside Polish merriment. Milosz's poem captured the same image: the wind that "blew open the skirts of the girls" would also "drift dark skies" of smoke above the burning ghetto.[37]

Just how many people actually lined up to ride the merry-go-round is unclear, but Jews in the ghetto could hear the good cheer in the park long before April 1943. In any case, the city filled with amusements and music piped through loudspeakers over the Easter weekend. "Huge crowds" gathered at the park. Some onlookers were there because "the people of Warsaw are eager to fight and just as eager to watch a fight." They did not necessarily pity the Jews, adds one of the characters in Jerzy Andrzejewski's story "Holy Week," but they certainly enjoyed the spectacle of the humiliation of the Germans. Milosz saw people identify a Jew in the ruins: "Oh, he's fallen." A few even pointed out "Jews! Jews!" to German gunners near the park. Most Poles watched in stunned silence. Ludwik Landau refers to "lively, even nervous interest": "The majority play the role of neutral observers," but sympathy for the Jews appeared to be growing. Observers saw that Poles wept. In the evening, neighbors climbed up onto the roofs of their apartment buildings to watch the smoke billow out of the ghetto. According to Landau, "They observed what was happening with dread and expressed the conviction that 'once they have finished with the Jews, they will start to deal with us.'"[30]

One particular story is mentioned in several diaries written during the war and memoirs recalling the events after war. It is probably a composite. It concerns commuters in a streetcar, one of whom makes the comment, "The kikes are being fried" or expresses joy at the fact that the Jews of Warsaw would soon be no more. The other passengers are silent, or silently indignant. The story admits the anti-Semitism of Poles, a feeling apparently deep enough to keep most people from saying anything to contradict the commentator. Yet the *single* anti-Semite contrasts with the general sympathy with the Jewish uprising. Yet again, it is an entirely passive sympathy; the story thematizes and thus criticizes the silence of most Poles. There is an undertone of shame, shame about the record of Polish anti-Semitism and shame about not doing anything for the Jews. Eyewitness accounts that repeat this story not only recognize the indifference of Poles but also themselves grapple with that indifference. One author after another gets to the merry-go-round in Krasinski Square and then moves to build the horrible contrast: "two steps away, behind the ghetto walls, the sounds of fighting"; "fifty steps further on are the ghetto walls . . .

clouds of flame, smoke, and dust." "We are all heartless," wrote Aurelia Wyleżyńska about the Easter merriment.[39]

To this day, there are indignant Polish patriots who blame Milosz's poem, which was first published in 1944, for inducing a false memory of the merry-go-round, but the merry-go-round was in fact spinning in Krasinski Square and commentaries on the indifference it revealed and the shame it induced circulated widely at the time of the Warsaw Ghetto Uprising. What makes the indifference more complicated is the real possibility, raised by Szarota, that the Germans deliberately assembled an amusement park in the square in order to enact and highlight Polish indifference to an audience of both Poles, on the one side of the ghetto wall, and Jews, on the other.

Witnessing the Warsaw Ghetto Uprising, Zofia Nałkowska found the reality of the "awesome processions of the resigned," the "leaps into the flames," and the "leaps into the pits" unbearable. But what made it unbearable was actually the realization that people were bearing it. "No one fathoms the phrase" "laying in ashes." What usually makes reality bearable, she commented, is that "it comes through to us in fragments of happenings, in scraps of accounts, in echoes of shots," and "in swirls of smoke." She could hardly imagine what was actually happening "over there" in the ghetto. Although "the only reason I write is to arrest, to halt life in its evanescent passage," she found it difficult to comprehend suffering in the ghetto. She found words much more easily when she described the prisoners transported in the truck because she could imagine being an arrested Pole but not an insurgent Jew. But even in "Aryan" Warsaw, "the width of the street, the thickness of a wall, the distance of a neighborhood" kept terror at a remove. Nałkowska was surprised that she was surprised, since "the things that are going on are in accordance with the rest of nature," "cats and birds," "birds and insects," "wolves and sheep." Why should she be appalled at what was happening among men? she wondered. Nałkowska was ashamed at being alive, and she was ashamed at how easily she got over that shame. Words did not come out right, nor was it clear to Nałkowska why she was making the effort, particularly when she saw that it did not really matter to her if she did. "Nearby," "far away," her deceased mother, Poles, Jews in the ghetto—the "dead, dead" were everywhere, were ghosts, phantoms because they were beyond words and comprehension. They were fragments, scraps, and echoes only.

After the war, Nałkowska tried one more time to represent the suffering she had seen, but this time she gave up the idea of perfecting her words and instead self-consciously passed along their inadequacy. In one of the first fictional representations of the Holocaust, in her short story collection *Medallions*, published in 1946, she explored how unfamiliar we are to ourselves in corners of death. The story "By the Railway Track" concerns a Jewish woman collapsed "by the railway track" after being shot while attempting to escape from a train taking her to a death camp. She lay there all day. "The day was white," Nałkowska writes, making plain to passersby the unacceptability of their behavior in not coming to the woman's aid. But the story also makes plain to readers that "it was a time of terror." The story continues, perhaps because the answer about terror was insufficient: at nightfall a "small-town guy" came to the woman "by the railway track," bringing not food or medicine, but vodka and cigarettes. He agreed to her request to kill her: "Why he shot her isn't clear. Maybe he felt sorry for her."

There were many questions left unasked by the railway track. Did the "small-town guy" kill the woman because he was an anti-Semite or because Jews were fair game or because he did feel sorry for her? And was such a mercy killing permissible for Catholics? The story recognizes the power of the Germans who ran the trains, but reveals as well the moral degradation of everyone who witnessed and recounted the action by the railway track. The scraps of description and conversation ultimately prevent comprehension and reproduce the ways people understood reality selectively in order to make it bearable. The story itself, like the image of the merry-go-round or the streetcar vignette, was passed around in postwar Poland; each "medallion" not only reveals that "people dealt this fate to people," the book's epigraph, but indicates that people circulated the hard-to-hold-onto medallions, they talked in a mishmash of sympathy and revulsion, cliché and horror.[40] Sturdy as it was, the patriotic Polish narrative about the German occupation revealed cracks in Polish behavior. It was sufficiently self-conscious about the relations between Poles and Jews not to be considered completely exclusionary or self-absorbed. "Between ourselves" admitted small but unmistakable feelings of both guilt and shame.

The Word in History

FROM THE PERSPECTIVE OF THOSE JEWS WHO WERE ABLE TO COMMENT on their fate from the ghettos, the power of the ability of the Germans to narrate postwar history seemed overwhelming. The destruction threatened to cast the vanished Jews into complete oblivion. As it was, Yiddish, the expressive language of the Jewish *folksmenschen*, was very nearly destroyed. The 7 million speakers of Yiddish in the 1920s had been reduced twenty years later to fewer than 700,000; a language and culture that were once as robust as Czech or Greek were now smaller than Estonian or Basque.[41] *Yiddishkeit* never recovered from the Nazi onslaught. The lives of Jews were at stake in the war, and so were the distinctive culture and long history of East European Jewry.

The terrible fear as the German assault advanced in the spring and summer of 1942 was the complete exit of the Jews from an indifferent, hostile world, one that threatened not only to bring the history of the Jews to an end but also to hollow out history and its commemorative functions altogether. In this view, there would be no point to history if the murdered Jews were simply forgotten, if the German version of history prevailed. Without "redress," "atonement," and judgment, history would have no meaning, insisted Oskar Rosenfeld.[42] That is why Jews, even in their precarious circumstances, put enormous faith in words and in the power of words to record injustice. The suffering and resilience of the Jews over the centuries had made history a vital part of Jewish identity, and its transcription and reception over time indicated how it reflected the survival of the people. For Jews, historians would always find readers. If this still applied, the fate of the Jews in the 1940s might not be subsumed within a voracious, triumphant National Socialist narrative of history. Instead, the history of humanity might heed the testimony of the ghettos.

Noted Jewish historian Isaac Schiper, who survived the "Great Action" in the Warsaw Ghetto, confided to a fellow inmate in the Majdanek concentration camp where he ultimately perished his fears about the forces that would shape postwar accounts of World War II. "History is usually written by the victor," he explained. "What we know about murdered peoples is only what their murderers vaingloriously cared to say about them. Should our murderers be victorious, should *they* write the history of this war, our destruction will be presented as one of the most beautiful pages of world history." Even in the case that the Germans did not narrate postwar accounts of the war's events, "they may wipe out our memory altogether, as if we had never existed, as if there had never been a Polish Jewry, a ghetto in Warsaw, a Majdanek." To the author of *The Economic History of the Jews in Poland During the Middle Ages*, it was vital for the Jews to prepare a counterhistory. Yet precisely because of their magnitude, German crimes could not be so easily uncovered, much less avenged. "Nobody will *want* to believe" recent Jewish history, worried Schiper, "because our disaster is the disaster of the entire civilized world." Shame rather than ignorance or complicity could well inhibit knowledge of the truth. Schiper was quite prescient regarding the patriotic histories written by the occupied in the twenty or thirty years after the end of the war and the way they failed to discuss the persecution of the Jews: "We'll have the thankless job of proving to a reluctant world that we are Abel, the murdered brother."[43] For decades, the emphasis of histories of the war fell on the resistors, not the victims. Oblivion threatened the history of the Jews.

Schiper's younger colleague historian Emanuel Ringelblum was less pessimistic. He was convinced that the evidence, if prepared with professional thoroughness and objectivity, would be believed by "future generations"; the key was to document and preserve the record of Jewish suffering, which was the premise of Ringelblum's Warsaw Ghetto Archive. However, for David Graber, a young assistant with the archive, the formal excellence of historical documentation was not enough: the documents had to "scream the truth at the world." In any case, without the archive there would be no scream. When he appended a postscript on August 4, 1942, at "4 pm," as he was hurriedly burying Ringelblum's archive during the "Great Action," he worried whether anyone would hear the scream:

"Neighboring street besieged. We are all feverish. . . . [W]e prepare for the worst. We hurry." Gustawa Jarecka, also a member of Oyneg Shabes and the author of the ghetto account "The Last Stage of Resettlement Is Death," argued that "the record must be hurled like a stone under history's wheel in order to stop it."[44] Cast in the right way, Jarecka hoped, words would have great power.

Young and old, professional and amateur, historians in the Warsaw Ghetto had different conceptions of how history worked. Ringelblum had faith in the established protocols of historical research and reception, while Graber and Jarecka believed that their documents needed to be composed intentionally to upset ordinary understandings of twentieth-century events. For his part, Schiper emphasized the power of the narrator, not simply the evidence in the documents, and he also paid attention to the willingness of the reader to understand the written evidence. For that reason, he thought it much more possible that German history could override Jewish testimony. Taken together, these perspectives on history suggested the range of political and aesthetic factors that determined the content of the histories written in the ghetto and the impact their authors imagined them having. Two strong if somewhat contradictory assumptions stand out in the prefatory remarks of ghetto diarists, chroniclers, and archivists. On the one hand, there was the power of the narrator to structure history for a relatively credulous audience: the history that might be written by the German victors. On the other hand, there was the basic humanitarian impulses of postwar readers who would recognize and understand the scale and horror of Jewish suffering as well as the terrorism committed by their persecutors. The second assumption, but not the first, was challenged by fears that the ghetto historian might not find the right words and that the postwar reader might not believe them.

Given the almost cinematographic speed of events with which events turned against the Jews when the Germans arrived in 1939 (the image is Ringelblum's), the excruciating slowness of developments once the Germans began to lose the war in 1943, and the terrible depredations meted out against the victims in their almost complete isolation, it is astonishing how much faith the chroniclers of the persecution had in the conscience of humanity. It was a conscience, they thought, that had to be shaken, perhaps, or screamed at, but there was nevertheless tremendous confidence that the postwar world would recognize the suffering of the Jews and exact vengeance on the perpetrators. Ghetto chroniclers repeatedly conjured up "future historians" who would know how to appreciate what had been written down. There were many reasons Jews wrote up personal and collective accounts of their wartime experience. Writing continued the tradition of handing down God's word, of witnessing the injustices that had befallen the Jewish people, and of destroying the memory or, at least, the historical claims of Amalek, the biblical enemy of the Jews. Words had always guaranteed the survival of the Jews as a people. Even so, the widespread expectation that the Jewish wartime experience would be assimilated into general secular history after the war is striking. Chroniclers wrote in anticipation that their suffering would be recognized and commemorated once the Germans had been vanquished and punished.

"Once the details of these events are . . . told in full," wrote Abraham Lewin in May 1942 about murders in the Warsaw Ghetto and deportations from Lwów, "the world's conscience will be taken by storm and that vile beast that is at the throat of the peoples of Europe and choking them to death will be bound and shackled once and for all." Marian Berland regarded Jewish diaries as providing "an invaluable historical document" that would aid "the public prosecutor who will . . . indict the criminals." "A History of a Jewish Family During the German Occupation," confirmed Calel Perechodnik, writing in Warsaw in 1943, "will persuade the democratic states to condemn ruthlessly all Germans, and avenge the innocent deaths of millions of small Jewish children and women."[45]

To bear witness presumed that the world would understand what had been witnessed by the Jews. The primary reason for establishing the Oyneg Shabes Archive was to preserve the records of the struggle of the Jewish people; the assumption that the rest of the world would know what to do with the archive after the war was not, at least at first, questioned. "Jewish suffering and Jewish liberation and redemption are part and parcel of the general calamity," averred Ringelblum. "Objective documentation" will "work for the good of mankind." A simple sentence, an aside commending mutual-aid networks in the Warsaw Ghetto, confidently predicted that there would be a time "when historians come to write the history of the courtyard committees during the days of the Nazi war against the Jews." Indeed, most diarists writing in the ghettos and in the underground saw themselves as chroniclers for a posterity in which humane and enlightened civilization had been restored. The last words in Chaim Kaplan's diary, "If my life ends—what will become of my diary," indicate the importance he put on future readers; the material survival of the diary itself is Kaplan's concern, not the question of whether readers will be able or willing to understand his account. Understanding became a more complicated issue as the German assault gained momentum, but the first impulse to write and to continue write, as expressed by Hélène Berr in Paris or Anne Frank in Amsterdam or Chaim Kaplan in Warsaw, rested on the conviction that postwar readers would share the moral and ethical values of the diarists themselves. Even when it was clear that crimes against the Jews had "no parallel" in "the whole of human history," Abraham Lewin appealed to history to keep "our blood" from being covered and make sure that empty silences would be filled with "our cries" "until the ends of time."[46] Jews might not survive, but their voices, written down and preserved, would be heard.

In this rendition of history, the Nazis stood outside as completely alien elements. Diarists often referred to their German tormentors as "beasts," "blond beasts," or "black beasts"; Jews described them as "butchers," "sadists," and "psychopaths." The Nazi was an "Angel of Death." These epithets emphasized the gratuitous cruelty of the Germans, but at the same time denied them any social-historical particularity. Jews generally did not contemplate the Nazis in a comprehensive historical framework in which concepts like the National Socialist "new authoritarian age" or the "new European order" had relevance. They were despots and tyrants, known from all time and to all time, and as such their days, like all the murderers' days, were numbered. This schema of beauty and the beast, of good and bad, was accepted so uncritically because its self-evidence promised to accelerate the end of the war and the end of the suffering of the Jews.

When Jews compared themselves to trapped miners or shipwrecked sailors, they emphasized the fact that their physical connection to the rest of the world had become broken, but affirmed their existential connection to the readers who would pore over their last words. "The scenes of panic" will "vanish with the sinking ship, or with a burning house from which nobody manages to escape, or from a coal pit at the time of an explosion, when the bodies of the miners are buried alive," wrote Rachel Auerbach, but "our descriptions may remain as our witness." Stuck in the Warsaw Ghetto, Władysław Szlengel also thought about trapped sailors in a submarine accident that had been the subject of a prewar Soviet film. There was no reason for him to be on the boat, remarked Szlengel; he was not a heroic Soviet sailor. Nonetheless, he believed that the future would be enriched "through my poems, sketches, and writings": "On the wall of my submarine I scrawl my poem-documents . . . I, a poet of AD 1943." The conventional nature of the disaster scenes hardly squares with the unique destitution of the ghetto, but these analogies, these references to modern disasters reported on by the prewar press, offered a way for Jewish writers to affirm their connections to the outside world. The rescue efforts failed, but the victims, like the shipwrecked sailors, would be remembered. Oskar Rosenfeld was more pessimistic when he wrote about ghetto diarists and their diaries: "They did not know where [their records] would be washed up nor by whom it would be read."[47] But the genre of the message in the bottle generally postponed rather than doomed communication between the shipwreck and the harbor.

Szlengel's submarine film, Rosenfeld's "Robinsonade on the continent," and also Klemperer's "Köpenickiade," as he titled a vignette recorded in his diary, with a nod to Carl Zuckmayer's satiric play *The Captain of Köpenick*, all were conventional literary models intended to make the catastrophe that had befallen the Jews seem legible to the outside world. Ghetto chroniclers relied on the feuilletonist style of prewar reportage, passed on conventional "literary and stylistic clichés," and used an array of Latin and French phrases, all practices that simultaneously registered the limits of language in expressing the accumulation of horrors and constituted a deliberate attempt to reaffirm the credibility of humanist ideals.[48] There was a tremendous desire for coherent narratives that would connect the terrible present to the past and the future. Indeed, captive Jews were often unable to recognize the systematic nature of the Nazi program of murder because they retained faith in the universality of

Judeo-Christian values. This desire could lead to trauma when individuals, during and after the war, could not integrate their experiences in history or autobiography. Holocaust narratives were cracked by loss and death, but the incentive and intention of those who wrote them were to create a meaningful and understandable text.

Of course, this faith in the means of expression and the inevitability of comprehension could produce complacency about the German onslaught; hope could blind victims, and it made them hesitant either to flee the ghetto or to resist. Even after renewed deportations, there was a tendency for people in the ghetto to breathe a sigh of relief if they were not among those selected and to return to "normal" rhythms. Writing in Lodz after the September 1942 deportations that took away those "under ten" and "over 65," one-fifth of the ghetto, Josef Zelkowicz observed the unwillingness of residents to fully absorb what had happened. Despite "everything that your eyes have seen, your ears have heard, and your human heart has felt," ultimately "you will grab yourself by the hand and cry out, 'It isn't true!' You will not believe it even though you have personally heard and sensed it, because your limited intellect cannot grasp it. The truth is universal, vast and surprising in both its beauty and its ugliness," he concluded, "in contrast to intellect and logic, which are personal and, perforce, limited." One of the reasons Samuel Golfard began to write a diary in Peremyshliany, in Galicia, was to compose memories "for those who will survive and who might quickly forget what they had lived through not so long ago." He wanted to tear open "wounds already healed."[49]

There were Jewish writers who resisted integrating their wartime experiences into a wider history of humanity. Their reflections and insights were premised on their extreme isolation. Writing in hiding in Brussels, sixteen-year-old diarist Moshe Flinker did not believe in the persistence of the European post office in which Jewish mail was delivered and letters read and answered. He felt like an "invisible man." "It is like being in a great hall," he wrote in a striking passage, "where many people are joyful and dancing and also where there are a few people who are not happy and who are not dancing. And from time to time a few people of this latter kind are taken away, led to another room, and strangled. The happy, dancing people in the hall do not feel this at all. Rather, it seems as if this adds to their joy and doubles their happiness."[50] Moshe Flinker was hardly alone in believing that German anti-Semitism had contaminated the whole of Europe. In his view, the imagined postwar world would offer no relief to the Jews. And this was in fact the case in Poland.

Other nations occupied by the Germans anticipated liberation as the war dragged on; they could see a new era of history taking shape. Running out of time, however, Jews became more and more doubtful about ever seeing an American, a British, or a Soviet soldier in the place of the German Wehrmacht and the SS. The Poles or the French did not have to confront the question that haunted Jews: their future existence as a people and the future existence of their history.

Flinker did not believe that a Russian victory or a British advance would benefit the Jews, but, at the same time, he continued to avidly follow war news about the Russians and the British in 1943. Jews such as Flinker were torn between despair and hope, between recognizing Jews as part of a common humanity and accepting the conclusion that they had been betrayed, between applying the precedents of secular history and biblical tradition and rejecting them as inadmissible. This gave narratives of Jewish history produced during the war a mottled, quarrelsome, and uncertain aspect that stands in stark contrast to the seamless authority and violent words of the German epic the National Socialists told. Jewish history was fragmented, while epic German history was merely unfinished. But given its longing for narrative form and the bitterness with which Jews contemplated their isolation, Jewish history continued to anticipate the possibility of assimilation and comprehension. After all, "had those in the ghettos been convinced," as some scholars are today, "that the war years stood outside history, that the Holocaust defied the literary imagination, and that all critical standards had therefore to be suspended, there would have been no Jewish response to speak of."[51]

In "The Last Stage of Resettlement Is Death," which was written between September 1942, at the end of the "Great Action," and January 1943, the beginning of active Jewish resistance in the Warsaw Ghetto, Gustawa Jarecka took note of the urgent "desire to write." It is astonishing how many people from all walks of life took up diaries and wrote chronicles. "Everyone wrote," remarked Ringelblum, "journalists, writers, social workers, teachers, young people and even children." Diarists themselves commented on the tendency to write diaries in the ghetto. Not surprisingly, *The Chronicle of the Lodz Ghetto* observed in June 1942 that "the price of waste paper is reaching unprecedented heights in the ghetto."[52]

At the same time, Jarecka felt "the repugnance of words." "We hate words," she continued, "because they too often have served as a cover for emptiness or meanness. We despise them for they pale in comparison with the emotion tormenting us." In the ghetto, Jewish texts no longer necessarily contained words of truth. "The word—well, you know," wrote Paul Celan after the war—

> *corpses. Let us wash them,*
> *Let us comb their hair,*
> *Let us turn their eye*
> *to the heavens.*

In the margins of a French novel entitled *Les vrais riches* (True Riches, published in 1892 by François Coppée, a popular Parisian writer), an unknown diarist in Lodz confessed, "Human speech is too impoverished to even describe the deficiency of words necessary to portray in an approximate way our suffering." For Yitzhak Katzenelson, rummaging through the debris left behind in the Warsaw Ghetto after the "Great Action," it was not the lines in the discarded books that gave him consolation or recollected a vanished world but the empty spaces between the lines that "filled me with terror," for they suggested what had not been recorded, what could not be said. Maybe the distance between the ghetto and the outside was too great: Szlengel in his poem "Four Sons" imagined one of his sons sitting in New York City, listening to a radio broadcast about the suffering of the Jews in Europe that is repeatedly interrupted by commercials reminding Jewish "listeners that when they need candles to mourn," "they should remember to use only the candles of Firm X." Commodification was not understanding. Referring to documents composed in the ghetto, one scholar suggests that "man struggles within the walls of speech as though in prison."[53]

Jarecka herself tacked back and forth. She could not completely give up hope that as "in the past," as in ancient times, as in the book of Lamentations, as on the occasion of Emile Zola's "J'accuse," as in the shock over the Kishinev pogrom, as after reading Werfel on the Armenians, when "the word meant human dignity and was man's best possession—an instrument of communication between people"—the cries of the ghetto would eventually "produce an echo."[54] In some ways, the suspicion that there were no words adequate to express the suffering of the Jews reflected an ongoing, stubbornly pursued struggle with language itself, but was not a sign of despair to give up the endeavor to record events and express the pain they had inflicted. Writers continued to gather up paper, to take time to write in terrible conditions, and to preserve the documents they produced.

The "final solution," the Holocaust, was written up by both Germans and Jews, but their histories took very different forms. The German epic remained unfinished and rested on a fundamental break with what the Germans took to be repudiated universal history. In its place, Germans drafted a new history, a new order to be imposed on the old world. In the end, the sheer violence of the Nazi racial project raised doubts about the assimilability of the "final solution" into this new German history. The "final solution" remained, somehow, "unthinkable." As the catastrophe unfolded, Jewish historians raised doubts about the expressability and comprehensibility of the terrible events, but most did not completely lose faith that Jewish suffering would find an echo. They were extremely concerned with integrating the Jewish experience in the war into the overall course of both Jewish and modern history. Their greatest fear was that the documents they prepared would be lost or misunderstood. There were many witnesses who contemplated the unfathomableness of mass murder, but Jews during World War II struggled against the forced isolation that the Nazis had imposed on them. They resisted becoming extraneous in any way—as "Jews," as victims of extreme, almost unknowable violence, as witnesses left with only a debased, incommunicative vocabulary.

For contemporaries, the integration of Jewish experience into universal narratives of history was the guarantee that Jewish voices would be heard, remembered, and commemorated. By contrast, today historians such as Saul Friedländer worry that such assimilation leads to a sense that the events could be settled into regular narratives about twentieth-century history, stripping them of their terror and of the unsettlement they might generate in subsequent generations of readers. There is what one scholar refers to as a "double paradox" in the confrontation of Jewish histories in the 1940s and present-day histories of the Holocaust. On the one hand, in the ghetto, chroniclers repeatedly insisted that words were not adequate to the demands of expression, even as they continued to search for suitable forms. It was as if they were saying to imagined readers, "You must understand, but at the same time you cannot." On the other hand, historians today sometimes take as the key to present-day understanding precisely what was not comprehensible at the time, emphasizing not so much the struggle to witness the events of the 1940s, but the overall inability to witness and to communicate. Instead of painful composition, it is the diary (as was in fact the case in Lodz) that ends in midsentence that provides the telling evidence of the limits to comprehension.[55]

Friedländer rightly insists on the inadequacy of any narrative of the Holocaust and World War II that attempts to "domesticate disbelief." An explanation that explains in a way that settles the question of mass murder becomes complicit in the crime it investigates. The victims themselves hardly invited the domestication of their unprecedented terror. They were all too aware of the scope of destruction that made it so difficult to accept historical precedent as relevant, whether that precedent concerned the example of the destruction of the First Temple in ancient times or the expulsion of Jews from Spain in the fifteenth century or the pogroms in Kishinev in 1903. And they were aware that the way these previous disasters had been written up as history undoubtedly robbed them of some of their terror. Jews understood that they were not simply shipwrecked sailors or trapped miners. They also understood the power of the records that castaways had left behind. The assimilation of present-day events in precedent remained a nagging question. At the time, however, the overriding fear was that the Holocaust's victims would be excluded from the history that had already registered those precedents and had over the centuries incorporated them. Domestication is unacceptable if it means settling for an explanation of past events, but, examining the testimony from the present of the 1940s, domestication also means recognizing the overwhelming desire among Jews in the ghettos and camps to be included in remembrance and not to be forgotten. It means acknowledging their demand that their experiences be written into a common history in which Jews were not a wild or extraneous part. The "common sense of mankind" to which Justice Jackson referred at the opening of the Nuremberg trials routinely resists the evidence of "incredible events," whose detail would induce shame and guilt, and history repeatedly smoothes over the terror of experience simply by using language, making analogies and comparisons, and composing stories. To break down our resistance to the evidence of the "incredible events," it is necessary to pass on not simply the records of those who experienced them but also the records of the struggle to witness and testify about them. It is necessary to reckon with the worry that Jews in the 1940s expressed about the adequacy of any story of Jewish suffering.

WORDS IN WARTIME WERE BROKEN OFF AND BROKEN. VICTIMIZATION, innocence, and guilt were consistently misattributed before and during World War II. From the beginning, the preoccupation with the technological capacities of modern warfare interfered with understanding Germany's racial aims. The actual threat war posed to human beings was not appreciated for a long time, because observers thought constantly about air war. During the war, horizons of empathy were limited, and patriotic narrators ignored the stories of suffering that they did not feel part of. Reliance on clichés in speech and precedents in history narrowed understanding. The categories in which people placed themselves and others prevented full comprehension of the disaster unfolding in German-occupied Europe. Growing suspicions that language was inadequate registered the unprecedented nature of the destruction taking place, but if testimony was to be provided, this suspicion had to be overcome, at least provisionally. The broken words that survive the war as a result are all we have to understand how contemporaries saw the war around them, failed to see its terrible violence, and attempted to translate the destruction into narratives. Unspeakability became everyone's language in the war. The perpetrator regarded the problem as a weakness of nerves, a general failure of ordinary Germans to accept responsibility for the mass murder carried out in their name, that in the end threatened to disable epic. The indifferent eyewitness expressed unspeakability whenever he or she refused to see what was happening to innocent victims. The national-ist stumbled onto it after realizing that the heroic record of the suffering, martyred nation under German occupation was itself a very selective rec-ollection of wartime events. Soldiers fell silent after no longer being able to explain the sacrifices they endured. Civilians themselves were silenced by the attention trained on the conventional military theater. Bulletins of the war also barely registered the screams and explosions that accompa-nied the destruction of Jewish communities across Europe. Condemned and bewildered Jews wavered between trusting and not trusting words. Almost all contemporaries in the war thought in terms of categories in order to contain the violence that was erupting around them. Looking back on the events, the historian feels slapped in the face.

To think about our affinity for words and for narratives in wartime, I want to recount a scene from Rebecca West's Yugoslavian travelogue, *Black Lamb and Grey Falcon*. The scene, depicting a warrior at a comrade's graveside, suggests the strong connections between the experience of loss and the attachment one feels to the nation and to the narrative be-hind the nation. On her visit to Sarajevo just before the start of World War II, West entered a cemetery. Not far from the gates she saw "a new grave, a raw wound in the grass." The deceased was likely the victim of a military skirmish, because "a young officer" stood at the grave's edge. "He rocked backwards in his grief, though very slightly," she reported. All at once, "he tore open his skirted coat as if he were about to strip," but just as quickly "his hand did up the buttons."[56] In this brief gesture, as the mourner avoided surrendering to private grief, West recognized the "dis-cipline" of the soldier who understood and accepted loss in the name of the nation. "His hand did up the buttons," although he had been tempted to cast off the uniform.

It is through the uniform of the narrative that we remember and judge, that we try to make sense of wars' graves, but it is the broken words, the undone buttons, the stripping of the coat, that incite the narratives we compose. The two gestures suggest that any story should give a full account, but also that it cannot. The hand wavers, the hand tears at the coat, the hand also buttons back up the buttons. There are too many graves for an encompassing narrative of World War II, yet there are too many graves not to read with care the narratives that survive, the arrangements they made and the order they sought to impose, and the broken words over which they stumbled.

NOTES

Chapter 1: Talk in Wartime

1. Leonard Woolf, *The Journey Not the Arrival Matters* (New York, 1969), 9–10.

2. Hermione Lee, *Virginia Woolf* (New York, 1997), 726.

3. Mary Favret, *War at a Distance: Romanticism and the Making of Modern Wartime* (Princeton, NJ, 2010), 10. On Virginia Woolf, see Marina MacKay, *Modernism and World War II* (Cambridge, 2007), 30.

4. Entry for 6 Oct. 1941, Léon Werth, *Déposition: Journal, 1940–1944* (Paris, 1992), 245–246.

5. Entry for 22 Sept. 1941, Victor Klemperer, *I Will Bear Witness, 1933–1941: A Diary of the Nazi Years* (New York, 1998), 435; entry for 15 July 1942, Hélène Berr, *The Journal of Hélène Berr* (New York, 2008), 97.

6. Norman Davies, *Europe at War, 1939–1945: No Simple Victory* (London, 2006), 32.

7. Wolfram Wette, "Zwischen Untergangspathos und Überlebenswillen: Die Deutschen im letzten halben Kriegsjahr, 1944/45," in *Das letzte halbe Jahr: Stimmungsberichte der Wehrmachtpropaganda, 1944/45*, edited by Wette, Ricarda Bremer, and Detlef Vogel (Essen, 2001), 23–24; Ronald C. Rosbottom, *When Paris Went Dark: The City of Light Under German Occupation, 1940–1944* (New York, 2014), 195.

8. Marcel Aymé, "While Waiting," in *The Man Who Walked Through Walls* (London, 2012), 295; Georg Kreis, *Zensur und Selbstzensur: Die schweizerische Pressepolitik im Zweiten Weltkrieg* (Frauenfeld, 1973), 260; Karl Barth, "Unsere Kirch und die Schweiz in der heutigen Zeit" (1940), in *Eine Schweizer Stimme, 1938–1945* (Zurich, 1948), 169.

9. Wilm Hosenfeld letter to his wife, 25 Mar. 1944, in Hosenfeld, *"Ich versuche jeden zu retten": Das Leben eines deutschen Offiziers in Briefen und Tagebüchern* (Munich, 2004), 800–801.

10. Entry for 21 Sept. 1939, Zygmunt Klukowski, *Diary of the Years of Occupation, 1939–44* (Urbana, 1993), 16.

11. Entry for 27 Jan. 1945, Matthais Menzel, *Die Stadt ohne Tod: Berliner Tagebuch, 1943/45* (Berlin, 1946), 116; Arthur Koestler quoted in Bernhard Wasserstein, *The Ambiguity of Virtue: Gertrude van Tijn and the Fate of the Dutch Jews* (Cambridge, 2014), 105.

12. René Schindler, *Ein Schweizer erlebt das geheime Deutschland* (Zurich, 1945), 7–8; entries for 3–7 Oct. 1941 and 10 Mar. 1943, Lisa de Boor, *Tagebuchblätter: Aus den Jahren, 1938–1945* (Munich, 1963), 86, 135.

13. On watching the Germans, Oskar Rosenfeld, "Little Ghetto Mirror, July 28, 1944: Apocalypse or Redemption?," in *In the Beginning Was the Ghetto: Notebooks from Lodz*, edited by Hanno Loewy (Evanston, IL, 2002), 280; Ruta Sakowska, *Menschen im Ghetto* (Osnabrück, 1999), 197; and Tomasz Szarota, *Warschau unter dem Hakenkreuz: Leben und Alltag in besetztem Warschau* (Paderborn, 1985), 246. On labor conscription,

entries for 3 Jan. and 11 Mar. 1943, Henri Drouot, *Notes d'un Dijonnais pendant l'occupation allemande, 1940–1944* (Dijon, 1998), 606, 632; entry for 22 Nov. 1942, Jeanne Oudot-Rodoz, *Les cahiers verts: Journal de l'esperance* (Besançon, 1995), 188; and entry for 2 Apr. 1943, Andre Sernin, *La remontée: Journal d'un etudiant parisien sous l'occupation, 1943–1944* (Paris, 2008), 13. On shoveling, entry for 10 Mar. 1942, Mihail Sebastian, *Journal, 1935–1944: The Fascist Years* (New York, 2000), 481. On Hitler, Ian Kershaw, *Hitler, 1936–1945: Nemesis* (New York, 2000), 565.

14. Ella to Erich Neuss, 31 Jan. 1941 and 10 Sept. 1943 in Kempowski-Archive, 6257, Akademie der Künste, Berlin; Elisabeth Gebensleben to Irmgard Brester, 6 Apr. and 26 Oct. 1933, in *Between Two Homelands: Letters Across the Borders of Nazi Germany*, edited by Hedda Kalshoven (Urbana, 2014), 76, 91; Irene to Ernst Guicking, 3 Oct. 1941, in Kempowski-Archive, 5962, Akademie der Künste, Berlin.

15. Franz Blättler, *Warschau, 1942: Tatsachenbericht eines Motorfahrers der zweiten schweizerischen Ärztemission 1942 in Polen* (Zurich, 1945), 35.

16. Entries for 26 Sept. 1938 and 13 Sept. 1939, Friedrich Kellner, *"Vernebelt, verdunkelt sind alle Hirne": Tagebücher, 1939–1945*, 2 vols. (Göttingen, 2011), 1:16, 21; entry for 5 June 1944, Werner Otto Müller-Hill, *The True German: The Diary of a World War II Military Judge* (New York, 2013), 44; entry for 23 Dec. 1944, Joachim Günther, *Das letzte Jahr: Mein Tagebuch, 1944–1945* (Hamburg, 1948), 395.

17. John Reed, *Ten Days That Shook the World* (New York, 1919), 14.

18. Celia Bertin, *Marie Bonaparte: A Life* (New York, 1982).

19. Marie Bonaparte, *Myths of War* (London, 1947), 13, 24, 41–42, 47.

20. Entry for 17 Dec. 1939, Klukowski, *Diary of the Years of Occupation*, 61; entry for 9 Feb. 1941, Drouot, *Notes d'un Dijonnais*, 98; Julian Jackson, *France: The Dark Years, 1940–1944* (Oxford, 2001), 281. See also Leonardo Blake, *The Last Year of War—and After* (London, 1940).

21. Bonaparte, *Myths of War*, 110–111. See also entries for 21 May and 23 Sept. 1940, Edith Thomas, *Pages de journal, 1939–1944* (Paris, 1995), 63, 97. On Göring, entry for 18 May 1941, Emmanuel Ringelblum, *Notes from the Warsaw Ghetto*, edited by Jacob Sloan (New York, 1958), 178. See also "late October" 1942, Agnès Humbert, *Resistance: A Woman's Journal of Struggle and Defiance in Occupied France* (New York, 2008), 167.

22. Bonaparte, *Myths of War*, 45; entry for 13 Dec. 1943, Kellner, *"Vernebelt, verdunkelt sind alle Hirne,"* 1:587.

23. Stephen Wittek, *The Media Players: Shakespeare, Middleton, Jonson, and the Idea of News* (Ann Arbor, 2015), chap. 2; entry for 5 Aug. 1941, Jacques Bielinky, *Un journaliste juif à Paris sous l'occupation: Journal, 1940–1942* (Cerf, 1992), 136; Daniel Blatman, "Presse, clandestinité et société: Une autre réalité s'exprime," in *En direct du ghetto: La presse clandestine juive dans le ghetto de Varsovie (1940–1943)*, edited by Blatman (Paris, 2004), 23–24.

24. Jean-Marie Guillon, "Talk Which Was Not Idle: Rumours in Wartime France," in *Vichy, Resistance, Liberation: New Perspectives on Wartime France*, edited by Hanna Diamond and Simon Kitson (Oxford, 2005), 74, 82; entries for 2 Dec. 1939 and 1 Sept. 1940, Oudot-Rodoz, *Les cahiers verts*, 23, 85; entry for 14 Oct. 1940, Liliane Schroeder, *Journal d'occupation: Paris, 1940–1944* (Paris, 2000), 54.

25. Szarota, *Warschau unter dem Hakenkreuz*, 169; Jacob Gerstenfeld-Maltiel, *My Private War: One Man's Struggle to Survive the Soviets and the Nazis* (London, 1993), 84; Shimon Huberband, *Kiddush Hashem: Jewish Religious and Cultural Life in Poland During the Holocaust* (New York, 1987), 43.

26. Rosbottom, *When Paris Went Dark*, 296; KP, 1 Aug. 1943, in Christel Beilmann, *Eine katholische Jugend in Gottes und dem Dritten Reich: Briefe, Berichte, Gedrucktes, 1930–1945* (Wuppertal, 1989), 29.

27. Lizzie Collingham, *The Taste of War: World War Two and the Battle for Food* (New York, 2012), 340; Ian Ousby, *Occupation: The Ordeal of France, 1940–1944* (London, 1997), 49.

28. Jean-Louis Curtis, *The Forests of the Night* (London, [1947] 1948), 224; entry for 3 Feb. 1944, Anne Frank, *The Diary of a Young Girl* (New York, 1995), 182; entry for 27 Oct. 1940, Oudot-Rodoz, *Les cahiers verts*, 99.

29. Entry for 11 June 1942, Abraham Lewin, *A Cup of Tears: A Diary of the Warsaw Ghetto* (Oxford, 1988), 131; entries for 14 and 27 Mar. 1944, Frank, *Diary of a Young Girl*, 217, 239–241; entries for 22 June and 1–2 July 1941, Dawid Sierakowiak, *The Diary of Dawid Sierakowiak: Five Notebooks from the Lodz Ghetto*, edited by Alan Adelson (New York, 1996), 105–108.

30. Favret, *War at a Distance*, 64; entries for 3 and 10 Oct. 1940 and 27 July 1942, Werth, *Déposition: Journal, 1940–1944*, 51, 56, 327.

31. Maurice Rajsfus, *Paris, 1942: Chroniques d'un survivant* (Paris, 2002), 13, 49.

32. Entries for 18 and 22 Sept. and 13 and 15 Dec. 1940, Bielinky, *Journaliste juif à Paris*, 52, 54, 81; entry for 13 Mar. 1943, Micheline Bood, *Les années doubles: Journal d'une lycéene sous l'occupation* (Paris, 1974), 187.

33. Entries for 28 June 1942 and 4 June and 13 Aug. 1941, Bielinky, *Journaliste juif à Paris*, 228, 118–119, 138. Bielinky was not the only one who overheard a preference for "la dictature judéo-maçonnique"; see entry for 13 Dec. 1941, Thomas, *Pages de journal*, 162.

34. Aymé, "While Waiting." See also Paul Achard, *La queue: Ce qui s'y disait ce qu'on y pensait* (Paris, 1945); and Vladimir Sorokin, *The Queue* (London, 1988).

35. Bernward Dörner, *Die Deutschen und der Holocaust: Was niemand wissen wollte, aber jeder wissen konnte* (Berlin, 2007), 94; Sönke Neitzel and Harald Welzer, *Soldaten: Protokolle von Kämpfen, Töten und Sterben* (Frankfurt, 2011), 119, 157.

36. Entry for 22 Mar. 1942, Gerhard Nebel, *Bei den nördlichen Hesperiden: Tagebuch aus dem Jahre 1942* (Wuppertal, 1948), 73; entry for 23 Mar. 1944, Günther, *Das letzte Jahr*, 11–12; Heinz Döll to his parents, 4 Sept. 1944, Kempowski-Archive, 5910/1, Akademie der Künste, Berlin.

37. Heinrich to Annemarie Böll, 27 July 1944, in his *Briefe aus dem Krieg, 1939–1945*, edited by Jochen Schubert (Cologne, 2001), 1099; Böll, "Reunion on the Avenue," in *The Stories of Heinrich Böll* (New York, 1986), 21–22.

38. Alya Aglan, *Le remps de la Résistance* (Arles, 2008), 47; Arlette Farge and Michel Chaumont, *Les mots pour résister: Voyage de notre vocabulaire politique de la Résistance à aujourd'hui* (Paris, 2005), 9, 30; Asa Briggs, *The War of Words: The History of Broadcasting in the United Kingdom* (London, 1970), 3:367–368.

Chapter 2: Hitler Means War!

1. Heinrich Böll, *What's to Become of the Boy?* (Brooklyn, 2011), 9–10; entry for 11 Dec. 1947, Tagebuch no. 10, Nachloss Franz von Göll, Landesarchiv Berlin, E Rep. 200-43, Acc. 3221, no. 10.

2. Entries for 2, 24, and 29 May and 1 June 1933, Karl Dürkefälden, *"Schreiben wie es wirklich war . . . ": Aufzeichungen Karl Duerkefaeldens aus den Jahren, 1933–1945*, edited by Herbert and Sibylle Obenaus (Hannover, 1985), 46, 53–54.

3. Entry for 17 July 1933, Erich Ebermayer, *Denn heute gehört uns Deutschland . . .* (Hamburg, 1959), 155; Elisabeth Gebensleben to Irmgard Brester, 9 Nov. 1933, in *Between Two Homelands: Letters Across the Borders of Nazi Germany*, edited by Hedda Kalshoven (Urbana, 2014), 92.

4. *New York Times*, 8 Mar. and 18 May 1934. Seabury's translations from *Mein Kampf* are his own and do not conform to the available 1933 abridged translation by Dugdale.

5. Wolfgang König, *Volkswagen, Volksempfänger, Volksgemeinschaft: "Volksprodukte" im Dritten Reich; Vom Scheitern einer nationalsozialistischen Konsumgesellschaft* (Paderborn, 2004), 82–85; Asa Briggs, *The War of Words: The History of Broadcasting in the United Kingdom* (London, 1970), 3:70.

6. See entry for 26 Sept. 1938, Charles Lindbergh, *The Wartime Journals of Charles A. Lindbergh* (New York, 1970), 76; Alexander Werth, *France and Munich: Before and After the Surrender* (New York, 1939), 224; "Radio-Reviews: Adolf Hitler," *Variety*, 14 Sept. 1938.

7. See entry for 26 Sept. 1938, C. Lindbergh, *Wartime Journals*, 76; *New York Times*, 14 July 1934; "Radio-Reviews: Adolf Hitler."

8. Entry for 8 Mar. 1936, Victor Klemperer, *I Will Bear Witness, 1933–1941: A Diary of the Nazi Years* (New York, 1998), 155; *New York Times*, 12 Sept. 1938.

9. Robert Brasillach, *A Translation of "Notre avant-guerre/Before the War,"* translated by Peter Tame (Lewiston, NY, 2002), 58, 110, 143–144.

10. Ibid., 247–248, 250, 291, 300.

11. Richard W. Steele, "The Great Debate: Roosevelt, the Media, and the Coming of the War, 1940–1941," *Journal of American History* 71 (June 1984): 69–92.

12. Pierre Laborie, *L'opinion francaise sous Vichy* (Paris, 1990), 89.

13. Ibid., 89–90; Irène Némirovsky, *Suite Française*, translated by Sandra Smith (New York, 2006), 47, 91, 205, 220.

14. Laborie, *L'opinion francaise*, 89–90.

15. Erich Maria Remarque, *All Quiet on the Western Front* (New York, 1982), 13, 35, 84–85, 123, 225.

16. Robert Dinse, *Das Freizeitleben der Grossstadtjugend* (Eberswalde, 1932), 49. See also entry for 25–26 July 1931, Victor Klemperer, *Leben sammlen, nicht fragen wozu und warum: Tagebücher, 1925–1932* (Berlin, 1996), 726–727. On popularity, see Modris Eksteins, *Rites of Spring: The Great War and the Birth of the Modern Age* (Boston, 1989), 276.

17. Martin Ceadel, *Pacifism in Britain, 1914–1945: The Defining of a Faith* (Oxford, 1980), 129, 131.

18. Laborie, *L'opinion francaise*, 93; Julian Jackson, *France: The Dark Years, 1940–1944* (Oxford, 2001), 87; Jean Giono, *To the Slaughterhouse* (London, [1931] 1969), 7, 37;

Richard Goslan, "Jean Giono: From Pacifism to Collaboration," *Telos* 193 (2007): 109–122; Jean Giono, "The Triumph of Life" (1942), in *Defeat and Beyond: An Anthology of French Wartime Writing, 1940–1945*, edited by Germaine Brée and George Bernauer (New York, 1970), 39–40.

19. Giono, *To the Slaughterhouse*, 56.

20. Bertrand Russell, *Which Way to Peace?* (London, 1936), 221–222; Goslan, "Jean Giono," 115, 121.

21. Maginot quoted in Ian Ousby, *Occupation: The Ordeal of France, 1940–1944* (London, 1997), 21. On overall defense, see Karl Ferdinand Werner, "Deutschland und Frankreich, 1936–1939," in *Deutschland und Frankreich, 1936–1939*, edited by Klaus Hildebrand and Werner (Munich, 1981), xvi. On peasants, see Laborie, *L'opinion francaise*, 157. French statesman quoted in Werth, *France and Munich*, 249.

22. Laborie, *L'opinion francaise*, 202.

23. Remarque, *All Quiet on the Western Front*, 94.

24. Georg Hensel, "Der Sack überm Kopf," in *Meine Schulzeit im Dritten Reich: Erinnerungen deutscher Schriftsteller*, edited by Marcel Reich-Ranicki (Munich, 1984), 129; Heinrich to Annemarie Böll, 3 Apr. 1943, in Böll, *Briefe aus dem Krieg, 1939–1945*, edited by Jochen Schubert (Cologne, 2001), 682–683. On the lingering influence of Remarque, see Joachim Dollwet, "Menschen im Krieg, Bejahung—und Widerstand?," *Jahrbuch für Westdeutsche Landesgeschichte* 13 (1987): 279–322, quoting a letter dated 27 Dec. 1942 (302). On socialization going back into the Weimar Republic, see Christoph Rass, *"Menschenmaterial": Deutsche Soldaten an der Ostfront; Innenansichten einer Infanteriedivision, 1939–1945* (Paderborn, 2003).

25. Langdon-Davies quoted in Mark Rawlinson, *British Writing of the Second World War* (Oxford, 2000), 73; Jean-Paul Sartre, *The Reprieve* (New York, 1947), 86.

26. Robert Young, "The Use and Abuse of Fear: France and the Air Menace in the 1930s," *Intelligence and National Security* 2, no. 4 (1987): 93, 96, 99; Rawlinson, *British Writing of the Second World War*, 73; H. G. Wells, *The Outline of History* (New York, 1920), 1084–1085, quoting the Royal United Service Institution's Sir Louis Jackson, and *Things to Come* (New York, 1935). On airpower in general, see Edward Warner, "Douhet, Mitchell, Seversky: Theories of Air Warfare," in *Makers of Modern Strategy*, edited by Edward Mead Earle (Princeton, NJ, 1944); as well as Michael Sherry, *The Rise of American Air Power: The Creation of Armageddon* (New Haven, CT, 1987). Baldwin quoted in *House of Commons Debates*, vol. 270, cols. 631–632, 10 Nov. 1932. According to historians of airpower, only a very few individuals questioned the devastation of air war, although strategists disagreed about the proper deployment of bombers. See Lee Kennett, *A History of Strategic Bombing* (New York, 1982); and R. J. Overy, *The Air War, 1939–1945* (New York, 1980).

27. Helena Swanwick in 1935 quoted in Susan Grayzel, *At Home and Under Fire: Air Raids and Culture in Britain from the Great War to the Blitz* (Cambridge, 2012), 152; Huxley quoted in Ceadel, *Pacifism in Britain*, 183.

28. Young, "Use and Abuse of Fear," 98, 100; Telford Taylor, *Munich: The Price of Peace* (New York, 1979), 247.

29. Rawlinson, *British Writing of the Second World War*, 70–71; A. C. Grayling, *Among the Dead Cities: The History and Moral Legacy of the WWII Bombings of Civilians in Germany and Japan* (New York, 2006), 134; Ceadel, *Pacifism in Britain*, 216.

30. Ritchie Calder quoted in Rawlinson, *British Writing of the Second World War*, 71.

31. Young, "Use and Abuse of Fear," 97, 99; Urs Bialer, *The Shadow of the Bomber: The Fear of Air Attack and British Politics, 1932–1939* (London, 1980).

32. Grayzel, *At Home and Under Fire*, 227, 234–246.

33. Young, "Use and Abuse of Fear," 101, 103; Ernst Denckler, *Deutschland!! Schläfst du?? Luftgefahr droht! In 1 Stunde! Flieger! Bomben! Giftgas! Ueber Berlin! Deinen Städten! Deinen Industriegebieten! Was tut dein Volk? Wie schützt es sich? Handle! Eine Aufklärungsschrift für Alle!!* (Berlin, 1932). On maps, see "Deutschlands Bedrohung aus der Luft," *Der Flieger* 5 (Mar. 1932); Freiherr von Bülow, "Luftrüstungen des Auslandes und Wirkungsmöglichkeiten der Bombenflugzeuge auf Deutschland," *Gasschutz und Luftschutz* 1 (Aug. 1931): 5; and *Illustrirte Zeitung*, no. 4523 (19 Nov. 1931).

34. Young, "Use and Abuse of Fear," 103.

35. Diary entry for 21 Sept. 1938, Anne Morrow Lindbergh, *The Flower and the Nettle: Diaries and Letters of Anne Morrow Lindbergh, 1936–1939* (New York, 1976), 409; Grayzel, *At Home and Under Fire*, 266–267.

36. Laurence Goldstein, *The Flying Machine and Modern Literature* (Bloomington, IN, 1986), 39. On Germany, see *Die Sirene*, no. 6 (Mar. 1936); on Kiel, *Internationales Luftfahrt Archiv*, 6 Oct. 1933; and on gas masks, *Die Gasmaske* 3 (Feb. 1931) and Otto Alfred Teetzmann, *Luftschutz: Die deutsche Schicksalsfrage* (Stuttgart, 1934), 268. Gilles's self-portrait can be seen in Aachen's Suermondt-Ludwig Museum.

37. Norman Ingram, *The Politics of Dissent: Pacifism in France, 1919–1939* (Oxford, 1991), 183.

38. Entry for 28 Sept. 1938, Irmgard Brester's notebook, in *Between Two Homelands*, edited by Kalshoven, 124.

39. "Ovation in London," *Times* (London), 1 Oct. 1938, 12.

40. Diary entry for 29 Apr. 1939, Anne Morrow Lindbergh, *War Within and Without: Diaries and Letters of Anne Morrow Lindbergh, 1939–1945* (New York, 1980), 4; Susan Hertog, *Anne Morrow Lindbergh: Her Life* (New York, 1999), 381, 395.

41. Diary entries for 2 and 3 Sept. 1939, A. M. Lindbergh, *War Within and Without*, 44, 47–48; entry for 31 Mar. 1939, C. Lindbergh, *Wartime Journals*, 172.

42. Diary entries for 3 Sept. 1939 and 29 Apr. 1940, A. M. Lindbergh, *War Within and Without*, 47–48, 80.

43. Entries for 10 Oct. 1940 and 31 May 1941, C. Lindbergh, *Wartime Journals*, 403, 499; Wayne S. Cole, *Charles A. Lindbergh and the Battle Against American Intervention in World War II* (New York, 1974), 28.

44. Cole, *Charles A. Lindbergh*, 34; Anne to her mother, 5 Aug. 1936, A. M. Lindbergh, *Flower and the Nettle*, 100–101.

45. Taylor, *Munich*, 761–762.

46. Entries for 23 June and 21 Sept. 1938, C. Lindbergh, *Wartime Journals*, 23, 72.

47. Entries for 9 Sept. and 1 Oct. 1938, ibid., 70–85; Taylor, *Munich*, 759–760.

48. Diary entry for 21 Sept. 1938, A. M. Lindbergh, *Flower and the Nettle*, 409; entry for 26 Sept. 1938, C. Lindbergh, *Wartime Journals*, 76; Hertog, *Anne Morrow Lindbergh*, 331–332.

49. Daniel Hucker, *Public Opinion and the End of Appeasement in Britain and France* (Farnham, 2011), 36, 249; Keith Feiling, *The Life of Neville Chamberlain* (London, 1946), 320–321.

50. Anne to her mother, 24 Sept. 1938, A. M. Lindbergh, *Flower and the Nettle*, 413; Grayzel, *At Home and Under Fire*, 256–259; David Faber, *Munich: The 1938 Appeasement Crisis* (New York, 2008), 358; entry for 28 Sept. 1938, C. Lindbergh, *Wartime Journals*, 79.

51. Journalist Alexander Werth quoted in Taylor, *Munich*; Werth, *France and Munich*, 279; *Daily Mail*, 27 Sept. 1938.

52. *Time*, 26 Sept. 1938; Faber, *Munich*, 266; *New York Times*, 12 Sept. 1938; "Radio-Reviews: Adolf Hitler"; "Market Seesaws to Hitler's Speech" and "France Sees Issue Drawn for Hitler," *New York Times*, 27 Sept. 1938.

53. Diary entries for 26 and 27 Sept. 1938, A. M. Lindbergh, *Flower and the Nettle*, 415–418; entry for 28 Sept. 1938, C. Lindbergh, *Wartime Journals*, 78.

54. Taylor, *Munich*, 875; entry for 27 Sept. 1938, C. Lindbergh, *Wartime Journals*, 77–78; *Daily Mail*, 27 Sept. 1938.

55. Faber, *Munich*, 1.

56. Hucker, *Public Opinion*, 59, 71; "With Honor," *Daily Mail*, 1 Oct. 1940; entry for 9 Sept. 1940, Jeanne Oudot-Rodoz, *Les cahiers verts: Journal de l'esperance* (Besançon, 1995), 89; Faber, *Munich*, 421; Jackson, *France*, 93.

57. Hucker, *Public Opinion*, 111.

58. See, for example, William D. Irvine, "Domestic Politics and the Fall of France in 1940," in *The French Defeat of 1940: Reassessments*, edited by Joel Blatt (Providence, 1998), 95–99.

59. Simon Garfield, *We Are at War: The Diaries of Five Ordinary People in Extraordinary Times* (London, 2006), 24; Antony Beevor, *The Second World War* (New York, 2012), 27.

60. Garfield, *We Are at War*, 20, 41, 59, 61, 87; Edmund Dubois, *Paris sans lumière* (Lausanne, 1946), 28.

61. Rulka Langer, *The Mermaid and the Messerschmidt* (New York, 1942), 65–66; entries for 1 and 3 Sept. 1939, Dawid Sierakowiak, *The Diary of Dawid Sierakowiak: Five Notebooks from the Lodz Ghetto*, edited by Alan Adelson (New York, 1996), 31, 33.

62. Entry for 10 Oct. 1940, C. Lindbergh, *Wartime Journals*, 402; Cole, *Charles A. Lindbergh*, 37.

Chapter 3: A New Authoritarian Age?

1. Yvonne Poulle, "La France à l'heure allemande," *Bibliothèque de l'école des chartes* 157, no. 2 (1999): 494–495; Renée Poznanski, *Jews in France During World War II* (Hanover, NH, 2001), 206; entry for 10 Dec. 1941, Liliane Schroeder, *Journal d'occupation: Paris, 1940–1944* (Paris, 2000), 107, 118.

2. Jean-Louis Bory, *Mon village à l'heure allemande* (Paris, 1945). See also Thomas Kernan, *France on Berlin Time* (Philadelphia, 1941).

3. Colette, *Paris durch mein Fenster* (Zurich, 1946), 32, 36–37, 90.

4. Entry for 11 June 1940, Roger Langeron, *Paris: Juin 40* (Paris, 1946), 16.

5. Saint-Exupery quoted in Ian Ousby, *Occupation: The Ordeal of France, 1940–1944* (London, 1997), 43; Colette quoted in Olivier Philipponnat and Patrick Lienhardt, *The Life of Irène Némirovsky, 1903–1942* (New York, 2010); Benoîte's entry for 9 June 1940 in Benoîte and Flora Groult, *Diary in Duo* (New York, 1965), 22.

6. On maps, see Hanna Diamond, *Fleeing Hitler: France, 1940* (Oxford, 2007), 66; on "rouler," see Edmund Dubois, *Paris sans lumière* (Lausanne, 1946), 63; on vehicles, see Irène Némirovsky, *Suite Française*, translated by Sandra Smith (New York, 2006), 75; Julian Jackson, *France: The Dark Years, 1940–1944* (Oxford, 2001), 121.

7. Stanley Hoffmann, "The Trauma of 1940: A Disaster and Its Traces," in *The French Defeat of 1940: Reassessments*, edited by Joel Blatt (Providence, 1998), 355.

8. On miracles, see Ronald C. Rosbottom, *When Paris Went Dark: The City of Light Under German Occupation, 1940–1944* (New York, 2014), 26; on Sablon, see Robert Brasillach, *Grüsse für Marie-Ange* (Munich, 1954), 88.

9. Benoîte's entry for 9 June 1940 in Benoîte and Groult, *Diary in Duo*, 22.

10. Philippe Burrin, *Living with Defeat: France Under the German Occupation, 1940–1944* (London, 1996), 299–301; entry for 23 Sept. 1940, Léon Werth, *Déposition: Journal, 1940–1944* (Paris, 1992), 45; Jackson, *France*, 442, discussing Jean Cassou and Vercors.

11. Némirovsky, *Suite Française*, 196; entry for 1 Aug. 1940, Schroeder, *Journal d'occupation*, 40.

12. Entry for 17 June 1940, Lore Walb, *Ich die Alte, ich, die junge: Konfrontation mit meinen Tagebüchern, 1933–1945* (Berlin, 1997), 184.

13. T. Sakmyster, "Nazi Documentaries of Intimidation," *Historical Journal of Film, Radio, and Television* 16, no. 4 (1996): 485–514; Olivia Manning, *The Balkan Trilogy* (New York, 2010), 255–256; entry for 1 May 1941, Ernst Jünger, *Strahlungen* (Munich, 1955), 33. On diplomats, entry for 17 Mar. 1941, Markus Feldmann, *Tagebuch, 1939–1941* (Basel, 2001), 439.

14. Gideon Botsch, *"Politische Wissenschaft" im Zweiten Weltkrieg: Die "Deutschen Auslandswissenschaften" im Einsatz, 1940–1945* (Paderborn, 2006), 159–164; "Deutsches Kriegführung und Kriegsziel," *Neue Zürcher Zeitung*, no. 1654 (14 Nov. 1940).

15. Edgar Bonjour, *Geschichte der schweizerischen Neutralität: Vier Jahrhunderte eidgenössische Aussenpolitik* (Basel, 1971), 4:77, 79, 169; Ernst Schürch quoted in Willi Gautsch, *General Henri Guisan: Commander-in-Chief of the Swiss Army in World War II* (Rockville Centre, NY, 2003), 168.

16. Walter Wolf, *Faschismus in der Schweiz: Die Geschichte der Frontenbewegung in der deutschen Schweiz, 1930–1945* (Zurich, 1969), 15; Kurt Guggenheim, *Wir waren unser vier* (Zurich, 1949), 97–98.

17. Markus Heiniger, *Dreizehn Gründe: Warum die Schweiz im Zweiten Weltkrieg nicht erobert wurde* (Zurich, 1989), 213.

18. Bonjour, *Geschichte der schweizerischen Neutralität*, 4:129.

19. Jost Adam, *Die Haltung der Schweiz gegen das Nationalsozialistische Deutschland im Jahre, 1940* (Mainz, 1972), 132–133; "Pilet-Golaz's Appell," *Volksrecht*, no. 148 (6 June 1940); "Ein Sieg für die Rhetorik," *Die Weltwoche* 32 (2004).

20. *Berner Tagewacht*, 15 and 20 June 1940, quoted in Adam, *Haltung der Schweiz*, 145; "Eine Revolution spricht uns an . . . ," *Neue Zürcher Zeitung* (hereafter cited as *NZZ*), no. 1056 (23 July 1940).

21. Gautsch, *General Henri Guisan*, 170–171, 173; Jacques Meurant, *La presse et l'opinion publique de la Suisse romande face a l'Europe en guerre* (Neuchatel, 1976), 381–384.

22. Gautsch, *General Henri Guisan*, 171; entry for 26 June 1940, Denis de Rougemont, *Journal d'une époque, 1926–1946* (Paris, 1968), 429–430; entry for 25 June

1940, Feldmann, *Tagebuch, 1939–1941*, 230; *Basler Nachrichten*, no. 173 (26 June 1940); Bonjour, *Geschichte der schweizerischen Neutralität*, 4:127.

23. Bonjour, *Geschichte der schweizerischen Neutralität*, 4:131; entries for 13 Dec. 1940 and 23 Apr. 1941, Feldmann, *Tagebuch, 1939–1941*, 380, 464.

24. Gautsch, *General Henri Guisan*, 54–55, 171; entry for 7–8 Aug. 1940, Bernard Barbey, *Fünf Jahre auf dem Kommandoposten des Generals: Tagebuch des Chefs des Persönlichen Stabes General Guisans, 1940–1945* (Bern, 1948), 37. On Pilet-Golaz, see 23 Apr. 1941, Feldmann, *Tagebuch, 1939–1941*, 464.

25. Entries for 9 and 16 July 1940, Barbey, *Fünf Jahre auf dem Kommandoposten des Generals*, 29–30.

26. Gautsch, *General Henri Guisan*, 220, 239–240; entry for 25 July 1940, Barbey, *Fünf Jahre auf dem Kommandoposten des Generals*, 31–32; *New York Times*, 29 July 1940.

27. Entry for 7–8 Aug. 1940, Barbey, *Fünf Jahre auf dem Kommandoposten des Generals*, 35; Bonjour, *Geschichte der schweizerischen Neutralität*, 4:157, 166; Gautsch, *General Henri Guisan*, 174, 235.

28. Gautsch, *General Henri Guisan*, 225; Oscar Gauye, "Au Rütli, 25 juillet 1940: Le discours du Général Guisan; Nouveaux aspects," *Studien und Quellen* 10 (1984): 5–55; entry for 27–28 Aug. 1940, Barbey, *Fünf Jahre auf dem Kommandoposten des Generals*, 39.

29. "Politisches Erwachen," *NZZ*, no. 1656 (14 Nov. 1940); Gottfried Guggenbühl, "Unbeschauliche Bermerkungen," *NZZ*, no. 1062 (24 July 1940).

30. Hans Mahler, "Gedanken eines Unternehmers über unsere Zukunft," *NZZ*, no. 1051 (22 July 1940); F. Zimmermann-Locher, "Diskussion über schweizeriche Zeitfragen: Gedanken eines Soldaten," *NZZ*, no. 219 (8 Aug. 1940); Jules Düblin, "Diskussion über schweizersiche Zeitfragen: 'Körpergefühl—Lebensgefühl—Staatsgefühl,'" *NZZ*, no. 1415 (1 Oct. 1940); C. L., "Diskussion über schweizerische Zeitfragen: Ruf nach 'Neuordnung,'" *NZZ*, no. 233 (22 Aug. 1940).

31. K. Haettenschwiller, "Diskussion über schweizerische Zeitfragen: Ein junger Angestellter spricht," *NZZ*, no. 1231 (27 Aug. 1940); Robert Eibel, "Die Idee des Gotthard-Bundes," *NZZ*, no. 1229 (27 Aug. 1940); H. A., "Unsere Wehrmänner schreiben: Ein Jahr im Felde," *NZZ*, no. 1243 (29 Aug. 1940); Werner Weber, "Diskussion über schweizerische Zeitfragen: Gedanken eines Eidgenossen," *NZZ*, no. 1627 (9 Nov. 1940).

32. Adam, *Haltung der Schweiz*, 145, 173; André Lasserre, *Schweiz: Die dunkeln Jahre: Oeffentliche Meinung, 1939–1945* (Zurich, 1992), 21, 200; Ernst von Weizsäcker in June 1940 quoted in Jürg Fink, *Die Schweiz aus der Sicht des Dritten Reiches, 1933–1945: Einschätzung und Bewertung durch die oberste Führung seit der Machtergreifung* (Zurich, 1985), 151.

33. "In belagerter Festung," *NZZ*, no. 1629 (10 Nov. 1940); Kurt Guggenheim, *Alles in Allem* (Zurich, 1957), 942, 961–962.

34. C. L., "Diskussion über schweizerische Zeitfragen." See also Christian Gruber, *Die politischen Parteien der Schweiz im Zweiten Weltkrieg* (Vienna, 1966), 48.

35. Adam, *Haltung der Schweiz*, 198; Gruber, *Die politischen Parteien der Schweiz*, 17, 31; Lasserre, *Schweiz*, 221.

36. Guggenheim, *Alles in Allem*, 844; Ernst von Schenk, "Staat und Wirtschaft der Schweiz," *NZZ*, no. 214 (4 Aug. 1940); "Vom Umlernen, Umstellen und Umfallen," *NZZ*, no. 966 (5 July 1940).

37. *NZZ*, 6 Aug. 1940; Guggenheim, *Wir waren unser vier*, 48.

38. Adam, *Haltung der Schweiz*, 9; Pierre Laborie, *Resistants, vichyssois et autres: L'evolution de l'opinion et des comportements dans le Lot de 1939 à 1944* (Paris, 1980), 171; entries for 7 and 12 Sept. 1940, Jean Guéhenno, *Diary of the Dark Years, 1940–1944: Collaboration, Resistance, and Daily Life in Occupied Paris*, translated by David Bell (Oxford, [1947] 2014), 18–19; "Erneuerung," *NZZ*, no. 1479 (13 Oct. 1940).

39. Werner Möckli, *Das schweizerische Selbstverständnis beim Ausbruch des Zweiten Weltkrieges* (Zurich, 1973), 97; Ernst Schürch, "Einheit oder Einigkeit?" (7 Aug. 1940), republished in *Bemerkungen zum Tage* (Bern, 1942), 113; "Das Kernstück der Erneuerung," *NZZ*, no. 253 (11 Sept. 1940); Willi Bretscher, "Jahreswende" (1 Jan. 1941), in *Im Sturm von Krise und Krieg: "Neue Zürcher Zeitung," 1933–1944, Siebzig Leitartikel* (Zurich, 1987), 276; "Eine Revolution spricht uns an." In general, Jakob Messerli, *Gleichmässig, Pünklich, Schnell: Zeiteinteilung und Zeitgebrauch in der Schweiz im 19. Jahrhundert* (Zurich, 1995).

40. Möckli, *Das schweizerische Selbstverständnis*, 1; Yves-Alain Morel, *Aufklärung oder Indoktriantion? Truppeninformation in der Schweizer Armee, 1914–1945* (Zurich, 1996), 67; "Erneuerung"; Albert Oeri in *Basler Nachrichten*, 2 July 1940, quoted in Alice Meyer, *Anpassung oder Widerstand: Die Schweiz zur Zeit des deutschen Nationalsozialismus* (Frauenfeld, 1965), 115–116.

41. Eugen Th. Rimli, "Die Schweizerische Landesausstellung: Eine Dokumentation schweizerischer Zusammenarbeit und Zusammengehörigkeit," in *Das Goldene Buch der LA, 1939*, edited by Julius Wagner (Zurich, 1939), 6; Lasserre, *Schweiz*, 26.

42. Frisch quoted in Andre Lasserre, "Political and Humanitarian Resistance in Switzerland, 1939–45," in *Switzerland and the Second World War*, edited by Georg Kreis (London, 2000), 214; Julius Wagner, ed., *Festliche Landi: Die festliche Veranstaltungen der schweizerische Landesausstellung 1939 in Wort und Bild* (Zurich, n.d. [1939]); Arthur Mojonnier, "Heimat und Volk," in *Das Goldene Buch*, edited by Wagner, 14.

43. Walter Schauffelberger, "Das 'Réduit national' 1940, ein militärhistorischer Sonderfall," in *Erfundene Schweiz: Konstruktion nationaler Identität*, edited by G. P. Marchal and A. Mattioli (Zurich, 1992), 208.

44. Möckli, *Das schweizerische Selbstverständnis*, 9; Max Frisch, *Dienstbüchlein* (Frankfurt, 1974), 72–73; Otto Philipp Häfner, "Herbst in der Schweiz," *Das Reich*, no. 27 (24 Nov. 1940), quoted in Fink, *Die Schweiz aus der Sicht*, 201.

45. Diary entry for 3 May 1943, quoted in Paul Widmer, *Minister Paul Frölicher: Der umstrittenste Schweizer Diplomat* (Zurich, 2012), 155; Gaston Haas, *"Wenn man gewusst hätte, was sich drüben im Reich abspielte . . . ," 1941–1943: Was man in der Schweiz von der Judenvernichtung wusste* (Basel, 1997). Joke cited in Heiniger, *Dreizehn Gründe*, 67.

46. Pierre Laborie, *L'opinion francaise sous Vichy* (Paris, 1990), 236.

Chapter 4: Living with the Germans

1. Entry for 4 Mar. 1941, Liliane Schroeder, *Journal d'occupation: Paris, 1940–1944* (Paris, 2000), 69; entry for 8 Mar. 1941, Micheline Bood, *Les années doubles: Journal d'une lycéene sous l'occupation* (Paris, 1974), 87.

2. Ian Ousby, *Occupation: The Ordeal of France, 1940–1944* (London, 1997), 121; Jean-Paul Sartre, "Paris Under the Occupation," quoted in *French Writing on English Soil: A Choice of French Writing Published in London Between November 1940 and June*

1944, edited by J. G. Weightman (London, 1945), 126; Colette, *Paris durch mein Fenster* (Zurich, 1946), 90.

3. Guéhenno quoted in Julian Jackson, *France: The Dark Years, 1940–1944* (Oxford, 2001), 273; Bood, *Les années doubles*.

4. Richard Vinen, *The Unfree French: Life Under the Occupation* (New Haven, CT, 2006), 368–369; John Sweets, *Choices in Vichy France* (Oxford, 1986), 84; Pierre Laborie, *L'opinion française sous Vichy* (Paris, 1990) and *Resistants, vichyssois et autres: L'evolution de l'opinion et des comportements dans le Lot de 1939 à 1944* (Paris, 1980).

5. "Photo Exhibit Shows Paris Under Nazi Occupation, Minus the Misery," *New York Times*, 25 Apr. 2008. Some of these photographs had already been published in David Pryce-Jones, *Paris in the Third Reich: A History of the German Occupation, 1940–1944* (New York, 1981), 150–151. On Schroeder, see entries for 16 July and 14 Oct. 1940 and 16 May, 30 Apr., and 28 Oct. 1941, Schroeder, *Journal d'occupation*, 31, 54, 81, 77, 106. See also "La fête de la Groupement corporatif de la presse au Vélodrome d'Hiver," *Le Petit Parisien*, 27 Oct. 1941.

6. "Marianne est remplacée à Versailles par le maréchal Pétain," *Le Petit Parisien*, 16 July 1942; entry for 27 Nov. 1940, Roger Langeron, *Paris: Juin 40* (Paris, 1946), 198; entry for 5 Aug. 1941, Jacques Bielinky, *Un journaliste juif à Paris sous l'occupation: Journal, 1940–1942* (Cerf, 1992), 136. On *Signal*, see Rainer Rutz, *Signal: Eine deutsche Auslandsillustrierte als Propagandainstrument im Zweiten Weltkrieg* (Essen, 2007), 163.

7. Pierre Sorlin, "The Struggle for Control of French Minds, 1940–1944," in *Film and Radio Propaganda in World War II*, edited by K. R. M. Short (Knoxville, TN, 1983), 254–266; Hélène Eck, "La radiodiffusion national et la 'culture française,'" in *Les intellectuels et l'occuaption, 1940–1944: Collaborer, partier, résister*, edited by Albrecht Betz and Stefan Martens (Paris, 2004), 236–237.

8. Françoise Taliano–des Garets, ed., introduction to *Villes et culture sous l'occupation* (Paris, 2012), 19; Elizabeth Strebel, "Vichy Cinema and Propaganda," in *Film and Radio Propaganda*, edited by Short, 287.

9. Entries for 14, 17, and 23 June 1940, Langeron, *Paris: Juin 40*, 41–44, 66, 99.

10. Gilles Perrault, *Paris Under the Occupation* (London, 1989), 38; Ronald C. Rosbottom, *When Paris Went Dark: The City of Light Under German Occupation, 1940–1944* (New York, 2014), 52.

11. Edmund Dubois, *Paris sans lumière* (Lausanne, 1946), 112–113; Sartre, "Paris Under the Occupation," 123–124.

12. Jean Texcier, "Conseils à l'occupé," in *Ecrire dans la nuit* (Paris, 1945); entries for 1 Sept. and "late December" 1940, Agnès Humbert, *Resistance: A Woman's Journal of Struggle and Defiance in Occupied France* (New York, 2008), 17, 28.

13. Dubois, *Paris sans lumière*, 113.

14. Entry for 12 Jan. 1943, Maurice Toesca, *Cinq ans de patience, 1939–1945* (Paris, 1975), 147–150.

15. Entries for 21 and 30 June, Benoîte and Flora Groult, *Diary in Duo* (New York, 1965), 31, 33–34.

16. Ousby, *Occupation*, 168, 170.

17. Entry for 1 Mar. 1941, Jean Guéhenno, *Diary of the Dark Years, 1940–1944: Collaboration, Resistance, and Daily Life in Occupied Paris*, translated by David Bell (Oxford, [1947] 2014), 64.

18. Entry for 23 Nov. 1940, Charles Rist, *Une saison gâtée: Journal de la guerre et de l'occupation, 1939–1945* (Paris, 1983), 107; entry for 1 Mar. 1941 and 12 Feb. 1943, Guéhenno, *Diary of the Dark Years*, 64, 196; Jackson, *France*, 285; entry for 21 Nov. 1940, Edith Thomas, *Pages de journal, 1939–1944* (Paris, 1995), 109; Sartre, "Paris Under the Occupation," 124. On Germans, see Felix Hartlaub, "Rubrik: Tout seul oder le civil equivoque; Metro," "Autre Impression: Metro," and "Blitzmädchen," in *Tagebuch aus dem Kriege*, in *Das Gesamtwerk*, by Hartlaub (Frankfurt, 1955), 67, 74, 91; "Auf der Metro," no. 29 (1–15 Oct. 1941) and "Die Metro," 83 (6–20 Nov. 1943), in *Der deutsche Wegleiter*, republished in *Où sortir à Paris? Le guide du soldat allemand* (Paris, 2013).

19. Entry for 3 Dec. 1943, Guéhenno, *Diary of the Dark Years*, 229.

20. James W. Brown and Lawrence D. Stokes, eds., *The Silence of the Sea—Le Silence de la mer: A Novel of French Resistance During World War II by "Vercors"* (New York, 1991), 80, 96.

21. Ibid., 81, 83.

22. Irène Némirovsky, *Suite Française*, translated by Sandra Smith (New York, 2006), 265; Claude Morgan, *They Live Again* (London, [1944] 1950); Jean-Louis Curtis, *The Forests of the Night* (London, [1947] 1948).

23. Entry for 28 Mar. 1941, Henri Drouot, *Notes d'un Dijonnais pendant l'occupation allemande, 1940–1944* (Dijon, 1998), 143; entry for 7 Feb. 1944, Andre Sernin, *La remontée: Journal d'un etudiant parisien sous l'occupation, 1943–1944* (Paris, 2008), 186; Gesine Heddrich, *Deutschland und Frankreich als Hetero- und Auto-Image während der Zeit der Occupation im Zweiten Weltkrieg am Beispiel der Schriftsteller Vercors (Jean Bruller) und Robert Brasillach* (Frankfurt, 1997), 116.

24. Entry for 5 Sept. 1940, Toesca, *Cinq ans de patience*, 84–85; "March 1941," Anne Somerhausen, *Written in Darkness: A Belgian Woman's Record of the Occupation, 1940–1945* (New York, 1946), 51.

25. Entry for 21 July 1940, Schroeder, *Journal d'occupation*, 32–33; entry for 10 July 1941, Somerhausen, *Written in Darkness*, 69; entry for 17 Nov. 1942, Anne Frank, *The Diary of a Young Girl* (New York, 1995), 51; entry for 17 June 1942, "Notebook D," Oskar Rosenfeld, *In the Beginning Was the Ghetto* (Evanston, IL, 2002), 72.

26. Entries for 16, 24, and 31 Dec. 1940 and 1 and 27 Jan. 1941, Bood, *Les années doubles*, 54, 60, 62–63, 77; Pryce-Jones, *Paris in the Third Reich*.

27. Entries for 7 and 12 Sept. 1940, Guéhenno, *Diary of the Dark Years*, 18–19; entry for 16 Nov. 1940, Drouot, *Notes d'un Dijonnais*, 37.

28. Entries for 31 Dec. 1940 and 1 Jan. 1941, Jeanne Oudot-Rodoz, *Les cahiers verts: Journal de l'esperance* (Besançon, 1995), 109–112; entry for 16 May 1941, Schroeder, *Journal d'occupation*, 81–84.

29. Entry for 24 Mar. 1941, Guéhenno, *Diary of the Dark Years*, 71; Asa Briggs, *The War of Words: The History of Broadcasting in the United Kingdom* (London, 1970), 3:368; entry for 26 Mar. 1941, Bood, *Les années doubles*, 92. On the German response, see entries for 29 Mar. and 3 Apr. 1941, Drouot, *Notes d'un Dijonnais*, 144, 154; Charles Rolo, *Radio Goes to War: The "Fourth Front"* (New York, 1942), 175–176.

30. Entry for 11 Dec. 1940, Schroeder, *Journal d'occupation*, 60.

31. Entries for 5 and 9 June and 24 Aug. 1941, Bood, *Les années doubles*, 105, 106, 117.

32. Entries for 12 and 15 Apr. and 1 Aug. 1941, ibid., 98, 101, 112; Joseph Kessel, *Army of Shadows*, translated by Haakon Chevalier (New York, 1944), 69.

33. Tomasz Szarota, *Warschau unter dem Hakenkreuz: Leben und Alltag in besetzten Warschau* (Paderborn, 1985), 41; entry for 8 May 1940, William L. Shirer, *Berlin Diary, 1934–1941* (New York, 1942), 265; "Meldungen aus dem Reich," 14 May 1940, in *Meldungen aus dem Reich, 1938–1945*, edited by Heinz Boberach (Herrsching, 1984), 4:1131–1132; Brandys quoted in Yisrael Gutman, *The Jews of Warsaw, 1939–1943: Ghetto, Underground, Revolt* (Bloomington, IN, 1982), xiii.

34. Lilka Trzcinska-Croydon, *The Labyrinth of Dangerous Hours: A Memoir of the Second World War* (Toronto, 2004), 29; "Visitor Finds Life Easier; Squalor and Wealth Contrast in City," *New York Times*, 14 Jan. 1940. In general, Szarota, *Warschau unter dem Hakenkreuz*, 15–16; Hania Warfield and Gaither Warfield, *Call Us to Witness: A Polish Chronicle* (New York, 1945), 126, 167.

35. Wladyslaw Bartoszewski, *Warsaw Death Ring, 1939–1944* (Kraków, 1968), 21.

36. Rulka Langer, *The Mermaid and the Messerschmidt* (New York, 1942), 326. See also Bartoszewski, *Warsaw Death Ring*, 24–25; and "Vatican Adds Data on Nazi Executions: 53 Jews Taken in a Warsaw Raid Are Slain," *New York Times*, 8 Mar. 1940. On Nalewki Street in the Ghetto, Emanuel Ringelblum, "O.S." (Dec. 1942), in *To Live with Honor and Die with Honor! Selected Documents from the Warsaw Ghetto Underground Archives "O.S.,"* edited by Joseph Kermish (Jerusalem, 1986), 10.

37. Bartoszewski, *Warsaw Death Ring*, 28–33; entry for 2 Jan. 1940, Zygmunt Klukowski, *Diary of the Years of Occupation, 1939–44* (Urbana, 1993), 67; Wladyslaw Szpilman, "Meines Vaters Verbeugungen," in *Hiob, 1943: Ein Requiem für das Waschauer Getto*, edited by Karin Wolff (Neukirchen, 1983), 58; Szarota, *Warschau unter dem Hakenkreuz*, 18.

38. Jochen Böhler, *Auftakt zum Vernichtungskrieg: Die Wehrmacht in Polen, 1939* (Frankfurt, 2006), 60, 189; Alexander Rossino, *Hitler Strikes Poland: Blitzkrieg, Ideology und Atrocity* (Lawrence, KS, 2003), 72, 154–169; Christopher Browning, *The Origins of the Final Solution: The Evolution of Nazi Jewish Policy, September 1939–March 1942* (Lincoln, NE, 2004), 17. Widely used as a training manual, Edwin Erich Dwinger's *Der Tod in Polen: Eine volksdeutsche Passion* (Jena, 1940) is the key example of the propaganda.

39. Wolfgang Jacobmeyer, *Heimat und Exil: Die Anfänge der polnischen Untergrundbewegung im Zweiten Weltkrieg* (Hamburg, 1973), 198; entry for 29 May 1940, Klukowski, *Diary of the Years of Occupation*, 88.

40. Warfield and Warfield, *Call Us to Witness*, 163–167; Langer, *Mermaid and the Messerschmidt*, 324.

41. Eberhard Gebensleben to his grandmother Minna von Alten, 13 Sept. 1939, in *Between Two Homelands: Letters Across the Borders of Nazi Germany*, edited by Hedda Kalshoven (Urbana, 2014), 133. Bromberg was central to the vernacular German memory of the war. See Dwinger, *Der Tod in Polen*; Erhard Wittek, *Ein Becher Wasser und andere Begebenheiten aus Polen* (Dresden, 1940); and Wittek, *Der Marsch nach Lowitsch* (Berlin, 1942). Together these books sold hundreds of thousands of copies.

42. "Deaths in Poland Put at 5,000,000," *New York Times*, 3 Feb. 1940. This figure is a wild exaggeration.

43. Hans-Jürgen Bömelburg, "Die deutsche Besatzungspolitik in Polen, 1939 bis 1945," in *Die polnische Heimatarmee: Geschichte und Mythos der Armia Krajowa seit dem Zweiten Weltkrieg*, edited by Bernhard Chiari (Munich, 2003), 57; Böhler, *Auftakt zum Vernichtungskrieg*, 202–203; Wolfgang Jacobmeyer, "Der Überfall auf Polen und der

neue Charakter des Krieges," in *September 1939: Krieg, Besatzung, Widerstand in Pole*, edited by Christoph Klessmann (Göttingen, 1989), 23.

44. Bömelburg, "Deutsche Besatzungspolitik in Polen," 61.

45. "2000 Intellectuals Disappear in Warsaw," *New York Times*, 26 Mar. 1940; Jacobmeyer, "Überfall auf Polen," 28.

46. "Abteilungsleitersitzung," 2 Dec. 1939; "Polizeisitzung," 30 May 1940; and "Abteilungsleitersitzung," 6 Nov. 1940, in Hans Frank, *Das Diensttagebuch des deutschen Generalgouverneurs in Polen, 1939–1945*, edited by Werner Präg and Wolfgang Jacobmeyer (Stuttgart, 1975), 73, 210, 304.

47. *Warschauer Zeitung* quoted in "'German Master Race' to Dominate Poland," *New York Times*, 26 Nov. 1939; Sitzung des Reichsverteidigungsausschusses, 2 Mar. 1940, Frank, *Diensttagebuch des deutschen Generalgouverneurs*, edited by Präg and Jacobmeyer, 128.

48. "Abteilungsleitersitzung," 12 Sept. 1940, Frank, *Diensttagebuch des deutschen Generalgouverneurs*, edited by Präg and Jacobmeyer, 264; Polish Ministry of Information, *The Nazi Kultur in Poland* (London, 1945), 183.

49. "Polizeisitzung," 30 May 1940, quoted in *Die faschistische Okkupationspolitik in Polen (1939–1945)*, edited by Werner Röhr (Berlin, 1989), 173; Bartoszewski, *Warsaw Death Ring*, 37–38.

50. Bartoszewski, *Warsaw Death Ring*, 88–90.

51. Stefan Korbonski, *The Polish Underground State: A Guide to the Underground, 1939–1945* (New York, 1978), 11.

52. "Polizeibesprechung," 25 Jan. 1943, and "Abteilungsleitersitzung," 2 Dec. 1939, Frank, *Diensttagebuch des deutschen Generalgouverneurs*, edited by Präg and Jacobmeyer, 611–612, 72–73; the German city governor of Lublin, Dr. Fritz Cuhorst, quoted in Thomas Kühne, *Belonging and Genocide: Hitler's Community, 1918–1945* (New Haven, CT, 2010), 92; Melita Maschmann, *Account Rendered: A Dossier on My Former Self*, edited by Geoffrey Strachan (London, 1964), 71.

53. "Plans 'Jim Crow' Cars: Warsaw Will Isolate Poles and Jews from German Riders," *New York Times*, 17 Jan. 1940; Anatoli Kuznetzov, *Babi Yar: A Document in the Form of a Novel* (New York, 1970), 226; Warfield and Warfield, *Call Us to Witness*, 159–161. See also Czeslaw Madajczyk, *Die Okkupationspolitik Nazideutschlands in Polen, 1939–1945* (Cologne, 1988), 167n4.

54. Warfield and Warfield, *Call Us to Witness*, 162; "Merkblatt für den Aufenthalt Wehrmachtangehöriger in Warschau," Sept. 1941, in NL Zahn–von Wurstemberger, 15, Archiv für Zeitgeschichte, Zurich; entries for 20 Sept. and 11 Nov. 1940, Klukowski, *Diary of the Years of Occupation*, 117, 124–125.

55. Langer, *Mermaid and the Messerschmidt*, 273, 276; Tomasz Szarota, "Alltag in Warschau und anderen besetzten Hauptstaedten," in *September 1939*, edited by Klessmann, 88; Madajczyk, *Okkupationspolitik Nazideutschlands*, 185; *Biuletyn Informacyjny*, 28 Oct. 1943, quoted in Bartoszewski, *Warsaw Death Ring*, 202. The teacher is cited in Georg Hansen, "'Damit wurde der Warthegau zum Exerzierplatz des praktischen Nationalsozialismus': Eine Fallstudie zur Politik der Einverleibung," in *September 1939*, edited by Klessmann, 67.

56. Sitzung des Reichsverteidigungsausschusses, 2 Mar. 1940, and entry for 3 Aug. 1943, Frank, *Diensttagebuch des deutschen Generalgouverneurs*, edited by Präg and Jacobmeyer, 128, 717.

57. Entry for 12 Jan. 1944, Frank, *Diensttagebuch des deutschen Generalgouverneurs*, edited by Präg and Jacobmeyer, 772; Madajczyk, *Okkupationspolitik Nazideutschlands*, 77, 106.

58. Alexandre Wolowski, *La vie quotidienne a Warsovie sous l'occupation nazie, 1939–1945* (Paris, 1977), 94, 163–164; entry for 5 Aug. 1940, quoted in Lucjan Dobroszycki, *Reptile Journalism: The Official Polish-Language Press Under the Nazis, 1939–1945* (New Haven, CT, 1994), 121; Jan Karski, *Story of a Secret State* (Boston, 1944), 73.

59. Karski, *Story of a Secret State*, 73; entries for 1 Sept. 1940 and 10 Mar. 1941, Klukowski, *Diary of the Years of Occupation*, 113–114, 140.

60. Wolowski, *Vie quotidienne*, 261–262, 272; Stefan Korbonski, *Fighting Warsaw: The Story of the Polish Underground State, 1939–1945* (London, 1956), 245–249.

61. *Pobudka*, 16 Nov. 1939, and *Biuletyn Informacyjny*, 7 May 1942, quoted in Piotr Majewski, "Konzept und Organisation des 'zivilen Kampfes,'" in *Polnische Heimatarmee*, edited by Chiari; entries for 14, 19, and 29 Feb. 1940, Klukowski, *Diary of the Years of Occupation*, 76–78; J. Gorecki, *Stories for the Rampart: The Story of Two Lads in the Polish Underground Movement* (London, 1945), 23. On the press, see Dobroszycki, *Reptile Journalism*, 75.

62. Sitzung des Reichsverteidigungsausschusses, 2 Mar. 1940, Frank, *Diensttagebuch des deutschen Generalgouverneurs*, edited by Präg and Jacobmeyer, 136; Marek Jan Chodakiewicz, *Between Nazis and Soviets: A Case Study of Occupation Politics in Poland* (Lanham, MD, 2004), 119. See also Barbara Engelking, "'Sehr geehrter Herr Gestapo': Denunziationen im deutsch besetzten Polen, 1940/41," in *Genesis des Genozids: Polen, 1939–1941*, edited by Klaus-Michael Mallmann and Bogdan Musial (Darmstadt, 2004).

63. Madajczyk, *Okkupationspolitik Nazideutschlands*, 148, 152; Sitzung des Reichsverteidigungsausschusses, 2 Mar. 1940, Frank, *Diensttagebuch des deutschen Generalgouverneurs*, edited by Präg and Jacobmeyer, 136; Wolowski, *Vie quotidienne*, 260.

64. Entries for 8 Jan. 9 June, and 24 Nov. 1940, Klukowski, *Diary of the Years of Occupation*, 68, 90, 126.

65. Chodakiewicz, *Between Nazis and Soviets*, 81, 111–112.

66. Entry for 12 Jan. 1944, Frank, *Diensttagebuch des deutschen Generalgouverneurs*, edited by Präg and Jacobmeyer, 772; Chodakiewicz, *Between Nazis and Soviets*, 47, 49, 120, 183–184, 187, 191; Wolowski, *Vie quotidienne*, 172.

67. Entries for 11 Sept., 29 Oct., 23 Nov., and 14 Dec. 1939, 13, 46–47, 54, 60, Christoph Klessmann, *Die Selbstbehauptung einer Nation: NS-Kulturpolitik und polnische Widerstandsbewegung* (Düsseldorf, 1971), 19.

68. Klaus-Peter Friedrich, *Nationalsozialistische Judenmord und das polnisch-jüdische Verhältnis im Diskurs der polnische Untergrundpresse (1942–1944)* (Marburg, 2006), 47–48.

69. Jacobmeyer, *Heimat und Exil*, 71.

70. Smolar and Jozef Cyrankiewicz quoted in Antony Polonsky, "Beyond Condemnation, Apologetics and Apologies: On the Complexity of Polish Behavior Toward the Jews During the Second World War," in "The Fate of the European Jews, 1939–1945: Continuity or Contingency?," special issue, *Studies in Contemporary Jewry* 13 (1997): 204.

71. Jan Gross, *Polish Society Under German Occupation: The Generalgouvernement, 1939–1944* (Princeton, NJ, 1979), 171–172; Jozef Chalasinksi, *Vergangenheit und Zukunft der polnischen Intelligenz* (Marburg, 1965).

Chapter 5: Journey to Russia

1. James W. Brown and Lawrence D. Stokes, eds., *The Silence of the Sea—Le Silence de la mer: A Novel of French Resistance During World War II by "Vercors"* (New York, 1991), 96–97; Jean-Louis Bory, *French Village* (London, [1945] 1948), 66; Jean-Louis Curtis, *The Forests of the Night* (London, [1947] 1948), 186; Irène Némirovsky, *Suite Française*, translated by Sandra Smith (New York, 2006), 338.

2. Némirovsky, *Suite Française*, 350.

3. Entry for 8 Jan. 1941, Jean Guéhenno, *Diary of the Dark Years, 1940–1944: Collaboration, Resistance, and Daily Life in Occupied Paris*, translated by David Bell (Oxford, [1947] 2014), 52; entry for 2 Nov. 1942, Charles Rist, *Une saison gâtée: Journal de la guerre et de l'occupation, 1939–1945* (Paris, 1983), 287; entries for 20 July and 14 Sept. 1941, Mihail Sebastian, *Journal, 1935–1944: The Fascist Years* (New York, 2000), 381, 410.

4. "'L'histoire ne se répète pas': Un parallèle difficile à établir; Le sort de Napoleon n'attend pas Adolf Hitler," *Signal*, nos. 23–24 (Dec. 1941); "Tolstois 'Krieg und Frieden,'" *Neue Zürcher Zeitung*, nos. 211 and 250 (8 and 15 Feb. 1942); René Juvet, *Ich war dabei . . . 20 Jahre Nationalsozialismus: Tatsachenbericht eines Schweizers* (Zurich, 1944), 120; David G. Roskies, *Against the Apocalypse: Responses to Catastrophe in Modern Jewish Culture* (Cambridge, 1984), 205; Herman Kruk, "Library and Reading Room in the Vilna Ghetto, Strashun Street 6," in *The Holocaust and the Book: Destruction and Preservation*, edited by Jonathan Rose (Amherst, MA, 2001), 194.

5. Alexandra Epstein, July 1942, quoted in Olivier Philipponnat and Patrick Lienhardt, *The Life of Irène Némirovsky, 1903–1942* (New York, 2010), 425n6.

6. Werner Hütter, letters dated 14 July and 10 Dec. 1941, Kempowski-Archive, 4627, Akademie der Künste, Berlin; entry for 2 Nov. 1942, Rist, *Une saison gâtée*, 287; Kurt to Rudolf Erichson, 27 Jan. 1943, Kurt Erichson, *Abschied ist Immer: Briefe an den Bruder im Zweiten Weltkrieg* (Frankfurt, 1994), 96; "June 1942," Emmanuel Ringelblum, *Notes from the Warsaw Ghetto*, edited by Jacob Sloan (New York, 1958), 299–300.

7. Churchill quoted in Asa Briggs, *The War of Words: The History of Broadcasting in the United Kingdom* (London, 1970), 3:9. On events, see Jeff Love, "The Great Man in War and Peace," in *Tolstoy on War: Narrative Art and Historical Truth in "War and Peace,"* edited by Rick McPeak and Donna Tussing Orwin (Ithaca, NY, 2012), 92. See also Jochen Hellbeck, "*War and Peace* for the Twentieth Century," *Raritan* (2007).

8. "Im Kessel von 'Viborg,'" *Neue Zürcher Zeitung*, no. 1478 (21 Sept. 1941).

9. Czeslaw Milosz, "The Experience of War," in *Legends of Modernity: Essays and Letters from Occupied Poland, 1942–1943* (New York, 2005), 76–87.

10. Ryncki, "Reglement," Komitee für Hilfsaktionen unter dem Patronat des Schweiz. Roten Kreuzes, 8.12.41, NL Zahn–von Wurstemberger / 15, Archiv für Zeitgeschichte, Zurich.

11. Entry for 28 Sept. 1940, Markus Feldmann, *Tagebuch, 1939–1941* (Basel, 2001), 315; Rudolf Bucher, *Zwischen Verrat und Menschlichkeit: Erlebnisse eines Schweizer Arztes an der deutsch-russischen Front, 1941/42* (Frauenfeld, 1967), 29; entry for 18 Oct. 1941, Elsi Eichenberger, *Als Rotkreuzschwester in Lazaretten der Ostfront*, edited by Reinhold Busch (Berlin, 2004), 24; scrapbook in NL Zahn–von Wurstemberger, 18, Archiv für Zeitgeschichte, Zurich.

12. Entries for 17 and 18 Oct. 1941, Ernst Gerber, *Im Dienst des roten Kreuzes*, edited by Reinhold Busch (Berlin, 2002), 34–35; "Einführung," Ernst Baumann and Hubert de Reynier, *Leiden und Sterben in Kriegslazaretten: Kriegstagebücher aus den Lazaretten von Smolensk, Winter, 1941/42*, edited by Reinhold Busch (Berlin, 2009), 27; Eichenberger, *Rotkreuzschwester*, 82.

13. Entry for 22 Oct. 1941, Hubert de Reynier, "Ärztemission unter dem Patronat des schweizerischen Roten Kreuzes, 13.10.1941–29.1.1942," in Baumann and de Reynier, *Leiden und Sterben*, edited by Busch, 174; "Einführung," in Baumann and de Reynier, *Leiden und Sterben*, edited by Busch, 26–27; Bucher, *Zwischen Verrat*, 29.

14. Entries for 22 and 24 Oct. 1941, de Reynier, "Ärztemission unter dem Patronat," in Baumann and de Reynier, *Leiden und Sterben*, edited by Busch, 173, 177; Eichenberger, *Rotkreuzschwester*, 27; entry for 23 Oct. 1941, Gerber, *Im Dienst des roten Kreuzes*, 46.

15. Eichenberger, *Rotkreuzschwester*, 27, 37; entry for 20 Oct. 1941, de Reynier, "Ärztemission unter dem Patronat," in Baumann and de Reynier, *Leiden und Sterben*, edited by Busch, 171; entries for 21 and 22 Oct. 1941, Gerber, *Im Dienst des roten Kreuzes*, 37, 42.

16. Eichenberger, *Rotkreuzschwester*, 35.

17. See, for example, Klara Löffler, *Aufgehoben: Soldatenbriefe aus dem Zweiten Weltkrieg; Eine Studie zur subjektiven Wirklichkeit des Krieges* (Bamberg, 1992); Klaus Latzel, *Deutsche Soldaten—nationalsozialistischer Krieg? Kriegserlebnis—Kriegserfahrung, 1939–1945* (Paderborn, 1998); Sönke Neitzel and Harald Welzer, *Soldaten: Protokolle von Kämpfen, Töten und Sterben* (Frankfurt, 2011). Oeri quoted in Paul Widmer, *Minister Paul Frölicher: Der umstrittenste Schweizer Diplomat* (Zurich, 2012), 124.

18. Eichenberger, *Rotkreuzschwester*, 34.

19. Bucher, *Zwischen Verrat*, 142. In the following missions, the Swiss continued to encounter frank and detailed references to the murder of thousands of Jews. For Riga, see entry for 12 Aug. 1942, Christoph Mörgeli, "Die dritte Ärztemission von 1942 an die deutsche Ostfront im Tagebuch des Zürcher Arztes Robert Hegglin," *Zürcher Taschenbuch 2015* 135 (2014): 300–304, and entries for 2–3 July and 29 Aug. 1942, "3. Ostfront Mission des Schweizerischen Rotes Kreuzes," NL Gerhard Weber; for Charkov, see entry for 14 Feb. 1943, "Tagebuch Oberleutnant Bircher, 24.11.42–5.3.43," NL Eugen Bircher, 11.3.6.1, both in Archiv für Zeitgeschichte, Zurich.

20. Eichenberger, *Rotkreuzschwester*, 60, 125. See also Karel Berkhoff, *Harvest of Despair: Life and Death in Ukraine Under Nazi Rule* (Cambridge, 2004), 147.

21. Entries for 28 Oct. and 4 Dec. 1941, Gerber, *Im Dienst des roten Kreuzes*, 92–95, 165. See also Mark Mazower, *Hitler's Empire: How the Nazis Ruled Europe* (New York, 2008), 161.

22. Eichenberger, *Rotkreuzschwester*, 97–99.

23. Ibid., 143–144.

24. Ibid., 114–116.

25. Bucher, *Zwischen Verrat*, 140–141.

26. Informal questionnaire, "Personelles," date stamped 16 Feb. 1942 in NL Ernst Gerber, 3, Archiv für Zeitgeschichte, Zurich; undated letter (1942) probably from Fritz Thönen to Eugen Bircher in NL Eugen Bircher, 11.3.5.3, Archiv für Zeitgeschichte, Zurich; entry for 23 Oct. 1941, de Reynier, "Ärztemission unter dem

Patronat," in Baumann and de Reynier, *Leiden und Sterben*, edited by Busch, 175; entry for 1 Dec. 1941, Ernst Baumann, "Kriegstagebuch," ibid., 142; and Eichenberger, *Rotkreuzschwester*, 99–100, 272–273.

27. Eichenberger, *Rotkreuzschwester*, 221–222.

28. Ibid., 232–233.

29. Ibid., 294.

30. Franz Blättler, *Warschau, 1942: Tatsachenbericht eines Motorfahrers der zweiten schweizerischen Ärztemission 1942 in Polen* (Zurich, 1945), 10–11, 40–41. On the killing of French African prisoners of war, see Raphael Scheck, *Hitler's African Victims: The German Army Massacres of Black French Soldiers in 1940* (Cambridge, 2006).

31. Entry for 22 Jan. 1942, de Reynier, "Ärztemission unter dem Patronat," in Baumann and de Reynier, *Leiden und Sterben*, edited by Busch, 339.

32. Undated letter (1942) probably from Thönen to Bircher; Tomasz Szarota, *Warschau unter dem Hakenkreuz: Leben und Alltag in besetzten Warschau* (Paderborn, 1985), 46; Stephan Lehnsteadt, *Okkupation im Osten: Besatzeralltag in Warschau und Minsk, 1939–1944* (Munich, 2009), 278–283; Jacek Leociak, *Text in the Face of Destruction: Accounts from the Warsaw Ghetto Reconsidered* (Warsaw, 2004), 186–187.

33. Wilhelm Schepping, "'Lili Marleen': Eine denkwürdige Liedbiographie," in *Good-Bye Memories: Lieder im Generationengedächtnis des 20. Jahrhunderts*, edited by Barbara Stambolis and Jürgen Reulecke (Essen, 2007), 218–219.

34. Eichenberger, *Rotkreuzschwester*, 298–299; Bucher, *Zwischen Verrat*, 235–236; Edgar Bonjour, *Geschichte der schweizerischen Neutralität: Vier Jahrhunderte eidgenössische Aussenpolitik* (Basel, 1971), 4:458–459; Gaston Haas, *"Wenn man gewusst hätte, was sich drüben im Reich abspielte . . . ," 1941–1943: Was man in der Schweiz von der Judenvernichtung wusste* (Basel, 1997), 151.

35. Blättler, *Warschau, 1942*, 41–42; Neitzel and Welzer, *Soldaten*, 8, 393–394.

36. Eichenberger, *Rotkreuzschwester*, 22, 34, 133; Bucher, *Zwischen Verrat*, 62, 64, 79; Bonjour, *Geschichte der schweizerischen Neutralität*, 4:458–459.

37. Letters dated 21 Oct. and 13 Nov. 1941, Helmuth James von Moltke, *Briefe an Freya, 1939–1945*, edited by Beate Ruhm von Oppen (Munich, 1988), 307–308, 318.

38. Diary entry for 6 Nov. 1941 and letter dated 4 Dec. 1941, Johannes Hürter, ed., *Ein deutscher General an der Ostfront: Briefe und Tagebücher des Gotthard Heinrici, 1941/42* (Erfurt, 2001), 103, 117; *Das Schwarze Korps*, 22 Feb. 1945.

39. Andreas Jasper, *Zweierlei Weltkriege? Kreigserfahrungen deutscher Soldaten in Ost und West, 1939–1945* (Paderborn, 2011), 158–161; letters dated 19 and 20 Dec. 1941 and 2, 11, and 21 Jan. 1942, Hürter, *Ein deutscher General an der Ostfront*, 130–131, 136–139.

40. Entry for 30 June 1941, Henri Drouot, *Notes d'un Dijonnais pendant l'occupation allemande, 1940–1944* (Dijon, 1998), 217; entry for 21 Dec. 1941, Rist, *Une saison gâtée*, 217.

41. Tomasz Szarota, "Alltag in Warschau und anderen besetzten Hauptstaedten," in *September 1939: Krieg, Besatzung, Widerstand in Polen*, edited by Christoph Klessmann (Göttingen, 1989), 74, 78.

42. Blättler, *Warschau, 1942*, 19–20. See also entry for 10 Dec. 1942, "Tagebuch Oberleutnant Bircher, 24.11.42–5.3.43," NL Eugen Bircher, 11.3.6.1, Archiv für Zeitgeschichte, Zurich.

43. Jacob Gerstenfeld-Maltiel, *My Private War: One Man's Struggle to Survive the Soviets and the Nazis* (London, 1993), 73; entry for 31 Dec. 1941, Zygmunt Klukowski, *Diary of the Years of Occupation, 1939–44* (Urbana, 1993), 179; entry for 17 Sept. 1942, Yitskhok Rudashevski, *The Diary of the Vilna Ghetto: June 1941–April 1943* (Tel Aviv, 1973), 53–54; entry for 31 Aug. 1941, Léon Werth, *Déposition: Journal, 1940–1944* (Paris, 1992), 343; entries for 12, 25, and 28 Sept. and 11 and 14 Oct. 1942, Rist, *Une saison gâtée*, 272–280.

44. Entry for 22 Nov. 1942, Jeanne Oudot-Rodoz, *Les cahiers verts: Journal de l'esperance* (Besançon, 1995), 187; entry for 29 Nov. 1942, Drouot, *Notes d'un Dijonnais*, 582; entry for 2 Jan. 1943, Rudashevski, *Diary of the Vilna Ghetto*, 116; Jan Nowak, *Courier from Warsaw* (Detroit, 1982), 33; letters to Annemarie, 14 Dec. 1942 and 29 Jan. 1943 in Heinrich Böll, *Briefe aus dem Krieg, 1939–1945*, edited by Jochen Schubert (Cologne, 2001), 1:573, 599.

45. Norman Davies, *Europe at War, 1939–1945: No Simple Victory* (London, 2006), 116.

Chapter 6: The Fate of the Jews

1. Vejas Gabriel Liulevicius, *War Land on the Eastern Front: Culture, National Identity, and German Occupation in World War I* (Cambridge, 2000), 8.

2. "Hitler Demands Colonies, 'Riches' for Japan and Italy; Tells U.S. Not to Meddle," *New York Times*, 31 Jan. 1939; Herr Hitler's Speech, *Times*, 31 Jan. 1939; "Hitler Talk Indicates Nazi Leaders Remain Thoroughly Anti-Semitic," Jewish Telegraphic Agency, 1 Feb. 1939, www.jta.org/1939/02/01/archive/hitler-talk-indicates-nazi-leaders-remain-thoroughly-anti-semitic.

3. Jeffrey Herf, *The Jewish Enemy: Nazi Propaganda During World War II and the Holocaust* (Cambridge, 2006), 14; "Die Vernichtung der jüdischen Rasse," *Der Kampf*, no. 92 (3 Dec. 1941).

4. Elisabeth Freund, "Zwangsarbeit Berlin 1941" [ms. dated Havana, Dec. 1941], in *Jüdisches Leben in Deutschland: Selbstzeugnisse zur Sozialgeschichte, 1918–1945*, edited by Monika Richarz (Stuttgart, 1982), 381; Howard K. Smith, *Last Train from Berlin* (New York, 1942), 197; Karl Dürkefälden, *"Schreiben wie es wirklich war . . .": Aufzeichnungen Karl Duerkefaeldens aus den Jahren, 1933–1945*, edited by Herbert and Sibylle Obenaus (Hannover, 1985), 108; Gaston Haas, *"Wenn man gewusst hätte, was sich drüben im Reich abspielte . . . ," 1941–1943: Was man in der Schweiz von der Judenvernichtung wusste* (Basel, 1997), 250.

5. Entry for 17 July 1941, Klaus Budzinski diary, Kempowski Archive, 3585, Akademie der Künste, Berlin; Joseph Goebbels, "Die Juden sind schuld!," *Das Reich*, 16 Nov. 1941; Helmut Schubert (of the Rassenpolitisches Amt der NSDAP), "Wie die Judenfrage gelöst wird," *Die Front: Feldzeitung einer Armee*, no. 414 (18 July 1942).

6. A newspaper cited in the entry for 3 Oct. 1941, Anna Haag, *Leben und gelebt werden* (Tübingen, 2003), 245.

7. Isa to Fritz Kuchenbuch, 19 Apr., 16 and 22 June, 2 and 8 July, and 14 Aug. 1941, Kempowski Archive, 5483, Akademie der Künste, Berlin; entry for 22 June 1941, Victor Klemperer, *I Will Bear Witness, 1933–1941: A Diary of the Nazi Years* (New York, 1998), 390.

8. Isa to Fritz Kuchenbuch, 23 July 1941 and 4 Feb. 1942, Kempowski Archive, 5483, Akademie der Künste, Berlin.

9. Ibid., 23 Nov. 1941; Alfred Gottwaldt and Diana Schulle, *Die Judendeportationen aus dem Deutschen Reich, 1941–1945* (Wiesbaden, 1995), 95.

10. Peter Longerich, *"Davon haben wir nichts gewusst!": Die Deutschen und die Juden-verfolgung, 1933–1945* (Berlin, 2006), 219–220; Heinrich Himmler, "Rede in Posen," 4 Oct. 1943, NS19/4010, Bundesarchiv Berlin.

11. Entry for 26 Nov. 1941, "Kriegstagebuch," in *Leben und gelebt werden*, by Haag, 252–253.

12. Hannah Arendt, *The Human Condition* (Chicago, 1958); Gordon Craig, *Europe Since 1815* (New York, 1961); Leon L. Jick, "The Holocaust: Its Uses and Abuses in the American Public," *Yad Vashem Studies* 14 (1981): 14; Ana Douglass and Thomas A. Vogler, eds., introduction to *Witness and Memory: The Discourse of Trauma* (New York, 2003), 21.

13. Gunnar S. Paulsson, *Secret City: The Hidden Jews of Warsaw, 1940–1945* (New Haven, CT, 2002), 1; Jean Amery, *At the Limits of the Mind: Compilations by a Survivor on Auschwitz and its Realities* (Bloomington, IN, 1980).

14. Susan Zuccotti, *The Holocaust, the French, and the Jews* (New York, 1993), 109; Dorothy Kaufmann, *Edith Thomas: A Passion for Resistance* (Ithaca, NY, 2004), 88; entry for 24 July 1942, Charles Rist, *Une saison gâtée: Journal de la guerre et de l'occupation, 1939–1945* (Paris, 1983), 262.

15. Vercors, *The Battle of Silence* (New York, 1968), 124–125.

16. Entry for 8 Jan. 1943, Albert Grunberg, *Journal d'un coiffeur juif a Paris sous l'occupation* (Paris, 2001), 75; entry for 10 July 1942, Jean Guéhenno, *Diary of the Dark Years, 1940–1944: Collaboration, Resistance, and Daily Life in Occupied Paris*, translated by David Bell (Oxford, [1947] 2014), 164.

17. Entry for 16 July 1942, Liliane Schroeder, *Journal d'occupation: Paris, 1940–1944* (Paris, 2000), 146–147; entries for 20 Dec. 1941 and 24 July 1942, Rist, *Une saison gâtée*, 215, 262; entry for 22 Feb. 1943, Denise Domenach-Lallich, *Une jeune fille libre: Journal (1939–1944)* (Paris, 2005), 215–217; entry for 25 July 1942, Jeanne Oudot-Rodoz, *Les cahiers verts: Journal de l'esperance* (Besançon, 1995), 177; entries for 14 and 19 July 1942, Henri Drouot, *Notes d'un Dijonnais pendant l'occupation allemande, 1940–1944* (Dijon, 1998), 492, 494.

18. Entry for 15 Dec. 1941, Benoîte and Flora Groult, *Diary in Duo* (New York, 1965), 197.

19. Edith Thomas, "Crier la vérité!," *Les Lettres Françaises* (Oct. 1942), quoted in Kaufmann, *Edith Thomas*, 88.

20. Edmund Dubois, *Paris sans lumière* (Lausanne, 1946), 111–118.

21. Entry for 22 Jan. 1944, Hélène Berr, *The Journal of Hélène Berr* (New York, 2008), 245. The scene in the Berr household is set in Ronald C. Rosbottom, *When Paris Went Dark: The City of Light Under German Occupation, 1940–1944* (New York, 2014), 256.

22. Quoted in Samuel D. Kassow, *Who Will Write Our History? Emanuel Ringel-blum, the Warsaw Ghetto, and the Oyneg Shabes Archive* (Bloomington, IN, 2007), 320–321.

23. Entries for 27 Oct., 22 May, 17 July, and 11 Apr. 1942, Zygmunt Klukowski, *Diary of the Years of Occupation, 1939–44* (Urbana, 1993), 222, 199, 205, 191.

24. Entries for 26 Oct. 1942, 22 Mar. 1943, 23 and 26 Oct. and 26 Nov. 1942, ibid., 221, 247, 220, 222, 227.

25. Entries for 29 Sept. and 11, 14, 16, and 22 Oct. 1939, 29 Aug. 1940, 4 Aug. 1941, and 20 Jan. 1942, ibid., 33, 39–40, 42, 45, 113, 166, 182.

26. Entries for 26 Mar., 8 Apr., and 8 and 10 Aug. 1942, ibid., 189, 191, 208–210.

27. Entries for 8 Aug. and 21, 24 and 26 Oct., 1942, 26 Mar., 8 Apr., and 8 and 10 Aug. 1942, ibid., 210, 219–220, 222.

28. Entries for 21 Oct. 1942 and 2 July 1943, ibid., 219, 265.

29. Klaus-Peter Friedrich, *Nationalsozialistische Judenmord und das polnisch-jüdische Verhältnis im Diskurs der polnische Untergrundpresse (1942–1944)* (Marburg, 2006), 97–98; Yisrael Gutman and Shmuel Krakowski, *Unequal Victims: Poles and Jews During World War Two* (New York, 1986), 72–73.

30. Diary entry for 18 June 1943, Hans Frank, *Das Diensttagebuch des deutschen Generalgouverneurs in Polen, 1939–1945*, edited by Werner Präg and Wolfgang Jacobmeyer (Stuttgart, 1975), 690.

31. Friedrich, *Nationalsozialistische Judenmord*, 115; Wladyslaw Bartoszewski, *Warsaw Death Ring, 1939–1944* (Kraków, 1968), 162; Vladka Meed, *On Both Sides of the Wall: Memoirs from the Warsaw Ghetto* (New York, [1948] 1973), 139; Jonathan Huener, *Auschwitz, Poland, and the Politics of Commemoration, 1945–1979* (Athens, OH, 2003).

32. Friedrich, *Nationalsozialistische Judenmord*, 99, 122–123.

33. *Prawda*, no. 9 (1942), quoted in ibid., 99; entry for 22 May 1942, Klukowski, *Diary of the Years of Occupation*, 199.

34. On Szlengel and Milosz, see www.yadvashem.org/yv/en/education/newsletter /30/two_poets.asp; Meed, *On Both Sides of the Wall*, 111–113; entry for 17 June 1942, Chaim A. Kaplan, *The Scroll of Agony: The Warsaw Diary of Chaim A. Kaplan*, edited and translated by Abraham I. Katsh (New York, 1965), 293; Timothy Snyder, *Bloodlands: Europe Between Hitler and Stalin* (New York, 2012), 290.

35. Jaroslaw Rymkiewicz, *The Final Station: Umschlagplatz* (New York, 1994), 290–291. See also Calel Perechodnik, *Am I a Murderer? Testament of a Jewish Ghetto Policeman* (Boulder, CO, 1996), 36.

36. Entry for 9 May 1942, Klukowski, *Diary of the Years of Occupation*, 197; Roman Knoll, describing the situation in the summer of 1943 and *Mloda Polska* (Young Poland), 13 Oct. 1943, both quoted in Gutman and Krakowski, *Unequal Victims*, 118, 110–111.

37. Jacob Gerstenfeld-Maltiel, *My Private War: One Man's Struggle to Survive the Soviets and the Nazis* (London, 1993), 82–83; Perechodnik, *Am I a Murderer?*, 72, 90.

38. Roman Knoll quoted in David Engel, *In the Shadow of Auschwitz: The Polish Government-in-Exile and the Jews, 1939–1942* (Chapel Hill, NC, 1987), 63, 80; Antony Polonsky, "Beyond Condemnation, Apologetics and Apologies: On the Complexity of Polish Behavior Toward the Jews During the Second World War," in "The Fate of the European Jews, 1939–1945: Continuity or Contingency?," special issue, *Studies in Contemporary Jewry* 13 (1997): 203.

39. Engel, *In the Shadow of Auschwitz*, 10, 175–176; Ruta Sakowska, *Menschen im Ghetto* (Osnabrück, 1999), 231–232; "June 1942," Emmanuel Ringelblum, *Notes from the Warsaw Ghetto*, edited by Jacob Sloan (New York, 1958), 293; Edward Raczynski, *The Mass Extermination of Jews in German Occupied Poland* (London, 1942).

40. Entry for 1 July 1942, Etty Hillesum, *Etty: The Letters and Diaries of Etty Hillesum, 1941–1943*, edited by Klaas A. D. Smelik, translated by Arnold J. Pomerans (Grand Rapids, MI, 2002), 460; entry for 9 Oct. 1942, Anne Frank, *Anne Frank: The Diary of a Young Girl*, edited by Otto H. Frank and Mirjam Pressler (New York, 1991), 54–55. Other alert Jews in Amsterdam did not know about the news until much later. See Rita Goldberg, *Motherland: Growing Up with the Holocaust* (New York, 2015), 126.

41. Richard Evans, *The Third Reich in History and Memory* (Oxford, 2015), 128.

42. Entries for 6 and 14 Nov. 1943, Berr, *Journal of Hélène Berr*, 196, 214.

43. Entries for 1 Nov. and 6 and 7 Dec. 1943 and 15 Feb. 1944, ibid., 194, 226–228, 258.

44. Haïm Guri, "Face au mal absolu," in *Littérature et résistance*, edited by Ruth Reichelberg and Judith Kaufmann (Reims, 2000), 22; entries for 28 Oct. and 12 Nov. 1943, Berr, *Journal of Hélène Berr*, 185, 204.

45. Nahman Blumenthal quoted in Amos Goldberg, "The History of the Jews in the Ghettos: A Cultural Perspective," in *The Holocaust and Historical Methodology*, edited by Dan Stone (New York, 2012), 190; Raul Hilberg, "The Judenrat: Conscious or Unconscious 'Tool,'" in *Patterns of Jewish Leadership in Nazi Europe, 1933–1945*, edited by Yisrael Gutman and Cynthia Haft (Jerusalem, 1979), 39–40.

46. Entries for 25 Oct. 1939, 16 and 31 May, and 3 June 1942, Kaplan, *Scroll of Agony*, edited and translated by Katsh (New York, 1965), 57, 274, 285–286.

47. Sakowska, *Menschen im Ghetto*, 217; entries for 3, 7, 9, 16, and 27 June 1942, Kaplan, *Scroll of Agony*, edited and translated by Katsh, 286, 287, 289, 292, 302–303.

48. Entries for 22, 23, and 26 July 1942, Kaplan, *Scroll of Agony*, edited and translated by Katsh, 319, 322, 325; Meed, *On Both Sides of the Wall*, 20.

49. Entries for 2 and 4 Aug. 1942, Kaplan, *Scroll of Agony*, edited and translated by Katsh, 336, 338–339; Ruta Sakowska, *Die zweite Etappe ist der Tod: NS-Ausrottungspolitik gegen die polnischen Juden, gesehen mit den Augen der Opfer* (Berlin, 1993), 44.

50. Entries for 5 and 15 Sept. 1942, Herman Kruk, *Last Days of the Jerusalem of Lithuania* (New Haven, CT, 2002), 350; entry for 27 July 1942, Dawid Sierakowiak, *The Diary of Dawid Sierakowiak: Five Notebooks from the Lodz Ghetto*, edited by Alan Adelson (New York, 1996), 200.

51. Alfred Kaufmann quoted in Monica Kingreen, "'Wir werden darüber hinweg kommen': Letzte Lebenszeichen deportierter hessischer Juden; Eine dokumentarische Annäherung," in *Deportation der Juden aus Deutschland: Pläne, Praxis, Reaktionen, 1938–1945*, edited by Birthe Kundrus and Beate Meyer (Göttingen, 2004), 99.

52. Entry for 11 July 1942, Hillesum, *Etty*, 485.

53. Entry for 17 Feb. 1942, "About Moods to Keep in Memory—Public," Oskar Rosenfeld, *In the Beginning Was the Ghetto: Notebooks from Lodz*, edited by Hanno Loewy (Evanston, IL, 2002), 7–8; Angelika Eder, "Die Deportationen im Spiegel lebensgeschichtlicher Interviews," in *Die Deportationen der Hamburger Juden, 1941–1945*, edited by Forschungsstelle fur Zeitgeschichte (Hamburg, 2002), 48.

54. Bernhard Wasserstein, *The Ambiguity of Virtue: Gertrude van Tijn and the Fate of the Dutch Jews* (Cambridge, 2014), 147–148, 255; entry for 22 Sept. 1942, Hillesum, *Etty*, 527–528.

55. Sakowska, *Zweite Etappe ist der Tod*, 57; Yisrael Gutman, "The Concept of Labor in Judenrat Policy," in *Patterns of Jewish Leadership*, edited by Gutman and Haft,

169; Göran Rosenberg, *A Brief Stop on the Road from Auschwitz* (New York, 2015), 56; Gustavo Corni, *Hitler's Ghettos: Voices from a Beleaguered Society, 1939–1944* (London, 2002), 187.

56. Entry for 14 Nov. 1942, Abraham Lewin, *Cup of Tears: A Diary of the Warsaw Ghetto* (Oxford, 1988), 208–209; Andrea Löw, *Juden im Getto Litzmannstadt: Lebensbedingungen, Selbstwahrnehmung, Verhalten* (Göttingen, 2006), 284, 321; Gerstenfeld-Maltiel, *My Private War*, 98.

57. Gerstenfeld-Maltiel, *My Private War*, 48.

58. Entry for 26 May 1942, "Notebook C," Rosenfeld, *In the Beginning*, edited by Loewy, 62.

59. Entry for 8 Mar. 1942, Kruk, *Last Days*, 226; Gerstenfeld-Maltiel, *My Private War*, 65; entry for 29 Jan. 1943, Wendy Lower, ed., *The Diary of Samuel Golfard and the Holocaust in Galicia* (Lanham, MD, 2011), 62; Sakowska, *Zweite Etappe ist der Tod*, 49.

60. "Little Ghetto Mirror, July 28, 1944, Apocalypse or Redemption," in Rosenfeld, *In the Beginning*, edited by Loewy, 280–281; entries for 31 Jan. and 5 Sept. 1941 and 27 June 1942, Kaplan, *Scroll of Agony*, edited and translated by Katsh, 111, 192, 302–303.

61. Entry for 11 Nov. 1942, Sierakowiak, *Diary of Dawid Sierakowiak*, edited by Adelson, 229.

62. Perechodnik, *Am I a Murderer?*, 150–154.

63. Ibid., 40–50. See also Yitzhak Katzenelson, *The Song of the Murdered Jewish People*, translated by Noah H. Rosenbloom (Hakibuutz Hameuchad, 1980).

64. Perechodnik, *Am I a Murderer?*, 90; entries for 13 and 16 Sept. 1943, Yitzhak Katzenelson, *Vittel Diary (22.5.43–16.9.43)* (Beit Lohamei Haghetaot, 1972), 221–222, 229; Sakowska, *Zweite Etappe ist der Tod*, 244.

Chapter 7: The Life and Death of God

1. Richard Schweitzer, *The Cross and the Trenches: Religious Faith and Doubt Among British and American Great War Soldiers* (New York, 2003), xxi, 6.

2. Vesna Drapac, *War and Religion: Catholics in the Churches of Occupied Paris* (Washington, DC, 1998), 244.

3. Patrick Montague, *Chelmno and the Holocaust: The History of Hitler's First Death Camp* (Chapel Hill, NC, 2012), 104–111; Samuel D. Kassow, *Who Will Write Our History? Emanuel Ringelblum, the Warsaw Ghetto, and the Oyneg Shabes Archive* (Bloomington, IN, 2007), 287–292; *The Ghetto Speaks*, no. 2 (5 Aug. 1942).

4. C. Fred Alford, *After the Holocaust: The Book of Job, Primo Levi, and the Path to Affliction* (Cambridge, 2009), 6; Jean Améry, *At the Limits of the Mind: Compilations by a Survivor on Auschwitz and its Realities* (Bloomington, IN, 1980), 13.

5. Philip Friedman, *Martyrs and Fighters: The Epic of the Warsaw Ghetto* (New York, 1954), 103–104.

6. David G. Roskies and Naomi Diamant, *Holocaust Literature: A History and Guide* (Lebanon, NH, 2012), 61; Peter Schindler, "Responses of Hassidic Leaders and Hassidim During the Holocaust in Europe, 1939–1945" (Ph.D diss., New York University, 1972), 139.

7. "Why," dated 15 Oct. 1942, in Emmanuel Ringelblum, *Notes from the Warsaw Ghetto*, edited by Jacob Sloan (New York, 1958), 310.

8. Entry for 4 Sept. 1941, Herman Kruk, *Last Days of the Jerusalem of Lithuania* (New Haven, CT, 2002), 92–93.

9. André Neher, *The Exile of the Word: From the Silence of the Bible to the Silence of Auschwitz* (Philadelphia, 1981), 207; Steven Kepnes, "Job and Post-Holocaust Theodicy," in *Strange Fire: Reading the Bible After the Holocaust*, edited by Tod Linafelt (New York, 2000), 260.

10. Anson Laytner, *Arguing with God: A Jewish Tradition* (Northvale, NJ, 1990), 31; Gershon Greenberg, introduction to *Wrestling with God: Jewish Theological Responses During and After the Holocaust*, edited by Steven T. Katz, Schlomo Biderman, and Gershon Greenberg (New York, 2007), 35; David G. Roskies, *Against the Apocalypse: Responses to Catastrophe in Modern Jewish Culture* (Cambridge, 1984), 202.

11. Nehemia Polen, *The Holy Fire: The Teachings of Rabbi Kalonymus Kalman Shapira, the Rebbe of the Warsaw Ghetto* (Northvale, NJ, 1994), 19, 109; Alan Mintz, *Hurban: Responses to Catastrophe in Hebrew Literature* (New York, 1984), 4, 52. See also Sarah Katherine Pinnock, *Beyond Theodicy: Jewish and Christian Thinkers Respond to the Holocaust* (Albany, 2002), 53, and Greenberg, introduction to *Wrestling with God*, edited by Katz, Biderman, and Greenberg, 45. On the bombing, Schindler, "Responses of Hassidic Leaders," 44.

12. Polen, *Holy Fire*, 30, 34–35.

13. Ibid., 119.

14. Entries for 12 and 28 Dec. 1942 and 19 Jan. 1943, Moshe Flinker, *Auch wenn ich hoffe: Das Tagebuch des Mosche Flinker* (Berlin, 2008), 39, 64–65, 74; Elhanan Wasserman, "Tractate: The Onset of the Messiah" (1938), in *Wrestling with God*, edited by Katz, Biderman, and Greenberg, 37.

15. Entry for 19 Jan. 1943, Flinker, *Auch wenn ich hoffe*, 74.

16. Moshe Flinker, "Ein Ereignis," in ibid., 152–153.

17. Moshe Flinker, "Am Nachmittag vor dem Mittagsgebet," in ibid., 160–162; Shapira in Polen, *Holy Fire*, 35.

18. Kassow, *Who Will Write Our History?*, 287–288; entry for 30 Nov. 1942, Flinker, *Auch wenn ich hoffe*, 20–21; Henry Abramson, "Metaphysical Nationality in the Warsaw Ghetto: Non-Jews in the Wartime Writings of Rabbi Kalonimus Kalmish Shapiro," in *Contested Memories: Poles and Jews During the Holocaust and Its Aftermath*, edited by Joshua D. Zimmerman (New Brunswick, NJ, 2003), 161.

19. Yitzhak Katzenelson, *Vittel Diary (22.5.43–16.9.43)* (Beit Lohamei Haghetaot, 1972), 161; Emanuel Ringelblum, "Fragmentary Memoirs of the Work in 'Shops'" (1942?), in *To Live with Honor and Die with Honor! Selected Documents from the Warsaw Ghetto Underground Archives "O.S.,"* edited by Joseph Kermish (Jerusalem, 1986), 276–277.

20. Polen, *Holy Fire*, 103; Roskies, *Against the Apocalypse*, 233.

21. "June 1942," Ringelblum, *Notes from the Warsaw Ghetto*, edited by Sloan, 293; entry for 16 Aug. 1942, Abraham Lewin, *A Cup of Tears: A Diary of the Warsaw Ghetto* (Oxford, 1988), 157; and entry for 9 Aug. 1943, Katzenelson, *Vittel Diary (22.5.43–16.9.43)*, 102.

22. Simcha Bunem Shayevitch, "Slaughter Town," in *The Golden Peacock: A Worldwide Treasury of Yiddish Poetry*, edited by Joseph Leftwich (New York, 1961), 524–525; Wladyslaw Szlengel, "An Account with God," www.zchor.org/szlengel/account.htm;

Eliezier Berkovits, *With God in Hell: Judaism in the Ghettos and Deathcamps* (New York, 1979), 128; Neher, *Exile of the Word*, 220; Itzik Manger, "The Lovers of Israel in the Death Camp of Belshitz," in *Golden Peacock*, edited by Leftwich, 570.

23. Wladyslaw Szlengel, "It's About Time," www.zwoje-scrolls.com/shoah /szlengel.html.

24. Yitzhak Katzenelson, *The Song of the Murdered Jewish People*, translated by Noah H. Rosenbloom (Hakibuutz Hameuchad, 1980), 1:3 (p. 12), 15:13 (p. 85); entry for 24 Aug. 1943, Katzenelson, *Vittel Diary (22.5.43–16.9.43)*, 182.

25. Rachel Brenner, *Writing as Resistance: Four Women Confronting the Holocaust: Edith Stein, Simone Weil, Anne Frank, Etty Hillesum* (University Park, PA, 1997), 112; entries for 22 Nov. 1941 and 12 July 1942, Etty Hillesum, *Etty: The Letters and Diaries of Etty Hillesum, 1941–1943*, edited by Klaas A. D. Smelik, translated by Arnold J. Pomerans (Grand Rapids, MI, 2002), 148, 488–489.

26. Reeve Robert Brenner, *The Faith and Doubt of Holocaust Survivors* (New York, 1980); Alford, *After the Holocaust*, 78; Richard L. Rubenstein, "Job and Auschwitz," in *Strange Fire*, edited by Linafelt, 250.

27. Jochen-Christoph Kaiser, "Der Zweite Weltkrieg und der deutsche Protestantismus. Einige Anmerkungen," in *Kirchen im Krieg: Europa, 1939–1945*, edited by Karl-Joseph Hummel and Christoph Kösters (Paderborn, 2007), 228–229.

28. Wolfgang Müller, ed., *"Sternbriefe" es Grafen Kanitz, 1939–1944: Briefe christliche Soldaten aus dem II; Weltkrieg. Dokumentation* (Pocking, 1989) (privately published); Erika Dinkler-von Schubert, ed., *Feldpost: Zeugnis und Vermächtnis; Briefe und Texte aus dem Kreis der evangelischen Studentengemeinde Marburg, 1939–1945* (Göttingen, 1993).

29. Jäger, "März 1940 Sternbrief", von Kanitz, 10 Apr. 1940, "April 1940 Sternbrief"; and Laugs, 24 Oct. 1940, "November 1940 Sternbrief," in *"Sternbriefe" es Grafen Kanitz*, edited by Müller, 23–24, 39, 81.

30. Brick, 10 Feb. 1943, "März 1943 Sternbrief," and Winkelmann, 20 Mar. 1943, "April 1943 Sternbrief," in ibid., 349, 365; entry for 24 Dec. 1942, "Tagebuch Oberleutnant Bircher, 24.11.42–5.3.43," NL Eugen Bircher, 11.3.6.1, Archiv für Zeitgeschichte, Zurich. See also John Eckard, "'Es geht alles vorüber, es geht alles vorbei': Geschichte eines 'Durchhalteschlagers,'" *Jahrbuch des deutschen Volksliedarchivs: Lied und populäre Kultur—Song and Popular Culture* 50–51 (2005–2006): 163–222.

31. Laugs, 24 Feb. 1941, "März 1941 Sternbrief," and Walsdorff, 15 Mar. 1942, "Juni 1942 Sternbrief," in *"Sternbriefe" es Grafen Kanitz*, edited by Müller, 112, 223.

32. Boesenberg, 26 June 1940, and Fligge, 23 June 1940, "Juli 1940 Sternbrief"; and Loetsch, 23 Aug. 1941, "Oktober 1941 Sternbrief," in ibid., 43, 45, 162.

33. Dietlein, 24 Oct. 1942, "November 1942 Sternbrief," and 18 Nov. 1941, "Dezember 1941 Sternbrief," in ibid., 270–271, 213.

34. Dietlein, 16 Sept. 1943, "Oktober 1943 Sternbrief"; Loetsch, 24 Oct. 1943, "Dezember 1943 Sternbrief"; von Lupin, 22 June 1944, "Juli 1944 Sternbrief"; and von Kanitz, 1 Dec. 1941, "Dezember 1941 Sternbrief," in ibid., 460–461, 482–483, 553, 216.

35. Schröter, 23 Oct. 1942, "November 1942 Sternbrief"; Sturm, 1 July 1943, "August 1943 Sternbrief"; and Bösenberg, 21 Feb. 1943, "März 1943 Sternbrief," in ibid., 268–269, 432, 352.

36. Dinkler, 16 July 1943, Dinkler–von Schubert, *Feldpost*, 88.

37. Dinkler, 1 Dec. 1940; Rosing, 10 Oct. 1939; Günther Dehn, 17 Oct. 1942; and Dinkler, 6 Feb. 1942, in ibid., 46, 22, 75, 72.

38. Heinrich Giesen, "Mai 1940 Rundbrief"; Kurt Onnasch, "Rundbrief," Feb. 1940; Günther Dehn, 19 Jan. 1941; Reiner Mumm, "Rundbrief," July 1940; Dinkler, 11 June 1940; and Heinz Becker, 1 Sept. 1941, in ibid., 32, 36–37, 49, 62.

39. Gerhard Wackerbarth, 1 Dec. 1941; Dinkler, 6 Feb. 1942; Gerhard Arning, 16 Oct. 1942; Dinkler, diary entry, Nov. 1942 and the spring of 1944, in ibid., 67, 72, 80, 101, 98.

40. Hermann Bousset, 22 June 1942, ibid., 79.

41. Gerd Wicke, New Year's 1945; and Erika Dinkler, "Rundbrief," Jan. 1945, in ibid., 108–109.

42. Letter dated 23 Oct. 1941, Konrad Jarausch, ed., *Reluctant Accomplice: A Wehrmacht Soldier's Letters from the Eastern Front* (Princeton, NJ, 2011), 308; Christoph Holzapfel, "Das Kreuz der Weltkriege: Junge christliche Generation und Kriegserfahrungen," in *Kirchen im Krieg*, edited by Hummel and Kösters, 437.

Chapter 8: The Destruction of Humanity

1. Hubert G. Locke, *Searching for God in Godforsaken Times and Places: Reflections on the Holocaust, Racism, and Death* (Grand Rapids, MI, 2003), 29; entry for 17 Aug. 1942, Léon Werth, *Déposition: Journal, 1940–1944* (Paris, 1992), 338. On Algeria, Jean-Paul Sartre, introduction to *The Question*, by Henri Alleg (New York, 1958), 14–15.

2. Entry for 3 Apr. 1942, Werth, *Déposition: Journal, 1940–1944*, 276; Czeslaw Milosz, *Legends of Modernity: Essays and Letters from Occupied Poland, 1942–1943* (New York, 2005), 80, 175–177, 182–183, 185, 247–248; Sarah Kofman, *Smothered Words* (Evanston, IL, 1998), xx; Maurice Blanchot, *The Writing of the Disaster* (Lincoln, NE, 1986), 41.

3. Oskar Rosenfeld, "Remembrances," 9 June 1942, and "Off to Czarnickiego," 8 July 1944, in Oskar Rosenfeld, *In the Beginning Was the Ghetto: Notebooks from Lodz*, edited by Hanno Loewy (Evanston, IL, 2002), 68, 278; Joseph Frank, *Dostoevsky: A Writer in His Time* (Princeton, NJ, 2010), 199.

4. "Notebook K," 12 Feb.–7 June 1944, Rosenfeld, *In the Beginning*, edited by Loewy, 251; entry for 16 Oct. 1943, Ernst Jünger, *Strahlungen* (Munich, 1955), 332–333; Allan Mitchell, *The Devil's Captain: Ernst Jünger in Nazi Paris, 1941–1944* (New York, 2011), 48.

5. Entry for 11 Oct. 1943, Hélène Berr, *The Journal of Hélène Berr* (New York, 2008), 161.

6. Mark Mazower, *Hitler's Empire: How the Nazis Ruled Europe* (New York, 2008), 11. See also Claudia Koonz, *The Nazi Conscience* (Cambridge, 2003).

7. Moishe Postone, "Anti-Semitism and National Socialism," in *The Holocaust: Theoretical Readings*, edited by Neil Levi and Michael Rothberg (New Brunswick, NJ, 2003), 138.

8. Rita Goldberg, *Motherland: Growing Up with the Holocaust* (New York, 2015), 68. See also Berel Lang, "On the 'the' in 'the Jews'; or, From Grammar to Anti-Semitism," *Midstream* 49 (2003): 9–11.

9. Entry for 19 May 1940, Hans Frank, *Das Diensttagebuch des deutschen Generalgouverneurs in Polen, 1939–1945*, edited by Werner Präg and Wolfgang Jacobmeyer (Stuttgart, 1975), 200; Christopher Browning, *The Origins of the Final Solution: The Evolution of Nazi Jewish Policy, September 1939–March 1942* (Lincoln, NE, 2004), 69; Walther Föhl, "Die Bevölkerung des Generalgouvernments," in *Das General-Gouvernment*, edited by Max du Prel (Würzburg, 1942), 31–43.

10. Robert Zaretsky, *Nîmes at War: Religion, Politics, and Public Opinion in the Gard, 1938–1944* (University Park, PA, 1995), 158–159; Georg Kreis, "Swiss Refugee Policy, 1933–45," in *Switzerland and the Second World War*, edited by Kreis (London, 2000), 119.

11. Entry for 9 Oct. 1941, Jacques Bielinky, *Un journaliste juif à Paris sous l'occupation: Journal, 1940–1942* (Cerf, 1992), 155. On "good looks," that is, non-Jewish looks, Gunnar S. Paulsson, *Secret City: The Hidden Jews of Warsaw, 1940–1945* (New Haven, CT, 2002), 90.

12. Yitzhak Arad, "The Judenräte in the Lithuanian Ghettos of Kovno and Vilna," in *Patterns of Jewish Leadership in Nazi Europe, 1933–1945*, edited by Yisrael Gutman and Cynthia Haft (Jerusalem, 1979), 110; Oskar Rosenfeld, "Atmosphere à la outsettlement," 25 Mar. 1943, in Rosenfeld, *In the Beginning*, edited by Loewy, 208; Oskar Singer, "Epilog" (1942), in *"Im Eilschritt durch den Gettotag": Reportagen und Essays aus dem Getto Lodz*, edited by Sascha Feuchert (Berlin, 2002), 67.

13. Jacob Boas, *Boulevard des Misères: The Story of Transit Camp Westerbork* (Hamden, CT, 1985), 93; Samuel D. Kassow, *Who Will Write Our History? Emanuel Ringelblum, the Warsaw Ghetto, and the Oyneg Shabes Archive* (Bloomington, IN, 2007), 262; on Levi, C. Fred Alford, *After the Holocaust: The Book of Job, Primo Levi, and the Path to Affliction* (Cambridge, 2009), 112.

14. Chad Bryant, *Prague in Black: Nazi Rule and Czech Nationalism* (Cambridge, 2007), 63–64.

15. Ian Ousby, *Occupation: The Ordeal of France, 1940–1944* (London, 1997), 125; Sandra Ziegler, *Gedächtnis und Identität der KZ-Erfahrung: Niederländische und deutsche Augenzeugenberichte des Holocaust* (Würzburg, 2006), 183.

16. André Chamson, *Der Wunderbrunnen* (Potsdam, 1950), 12, 143, 145. See also Chamson, *Le Puits des miracles* (Paris, 1945).

17. Chamson, *Der Wunderbrunnen*, 7, 33–34; Colette, *Paris durch mein Fenster* (Zurich, 1946), 207.

18. Entry for 10 Jan. 1941, Denise Domenach-Lallich, *Une jeune fille libre: Journal (1939–1944)* (Paris, 2005), 46; Ousby, *Occupation*, 119; entry for 21 Jan. 1942, Liliane Schroeder, *Journal d'occupation: Paris, 1940–1944* (Paris, 2000), 126; Colette, *Paris durch mein Fenster*, 207. On "national," Jean Dutourd, *The Best Butter*, translated by Robin Chancellor (New York, 1955), 115.

19. Entry for 25 Feb. 1942, Charles Rist, *Une saison gâtée: Journal de la guerre et de l'occupation, 1939–1945* (Paris, 1983), 234; entry for 21 Aug. 1941, Valentin Feldman, *Journal de guerre, 1940–41* (Tours, 2006), 304–305; Janet Teissier du Cros, *Divided Loyalties: A Scotswoman in Occupied France* (London, 1962), 261.

20. Entry for 15 Oct. 1941, Werth, *Déposition: Journal, 1940–1944*, 249.

21. "Le Corbeau," *Der deutsche Wegleiter*, no. 80 (25 Sept.–9 Oct. 1943), republished in *Où sortir à Paris? Le guide du soldat allemand* (Paris, 2013), 119; John Sweets,

Choices in Vichy France (Oxford, 1986), 23; André Halimi, *La délation sous l'occupation* (Paris, 2010), 7.

22. Richard Vinen, *The Unfree French: Life Under the Occupation* (New Haven, CT, 2006), 216; Peter Tame, "André Chamson's Novel *Le Puits des miracles*: France at War?," *Forum of Modern Language Studies* 41 (2005): 229.

23. Chamson, *Le Puits des miracles*, 72–73.

24. Chamson, *Wunderbrunnen*, 256–266.

25. Pierre Laborie, *L'opinion francaise sous Vichy* (Paris, 1990); Laborie, *Resistants, vichyssois et autres: L'evolution de l'opinion et des comportements dans le Lot de 1939 à 1944* (Paris, 1980).

26. Jean-Paul Sartre, "The Republic of Silence," in *Defeat and Beyond: An Anthology of French Wartime Writing, 1940–1945*, edited by Germaine Brée and George Bernauer (New York, 1970).

27. Sweets, *Choices in Vichy France*, 84.

28. Bernard Wasserstein, *On the Eve: The Jews of Europe Before the Second World War* (New York, 2012), 436.

29. Wladyslaw Szlengel, "Things," *Chicago Review* (Autumn 2006): 283–286. On Veronal, Marion Kaplan, *Between Dignity and Despair: Jewish Life in Nazi Germany* (New York, 1998), 184. See also Barbara Engelking and Jacek Leociak, eds., *The Warsaw Ghetto: A Guide to the Perished City* (New Haven, CT, 2009), 84–85. In "Warsaw Ghetto Is 'Hell on Earth' Says Eye-witness Report," 13 May 1942, the *Jewish Telegraphic Agency* reported that Śliska Street also had to be abandoned.

30. Oskar Singer, "Litzmannstadt Getto, den 3. Mai 1942," in *"Im Eilschritt durch den Gettotag,"* edited by Feuchert, 38, 40; Oskar Rosenfeld, "Face of the Ghetto" (7 May 1942) and "Night Work in the Ghetto—Lecture for the Archive," in Rosenfeld, *In the Beginning*, edited by Loewy, 48, 212.

31. David Engel, *In the Shadow of Auschwitz: The Polish Government-in-Exile and the Jews, 1939–1942* (Chapel Hill, NC, 1987), 163. On fairies, see Harriet Beecher Stowe, *House and Home Papers* (Boston, [1864] 1890), 22, 60, 120–121.

32. Entries for 10 and 20 May 1942, Rosenfeld, *In the Beginning*, edited by Loewy, 50–51, 58; Singer, "Litzmannstadt Getto, den 3. Mai 1942," in *"Im Eilschritt durch den Gettotag,"* edited by Feuchert, 38.

33. Oskar Rosenfeld, "Remembrances for the Future" (Spring 1942), in Rosenfeld, *In the Beginning*, edited by Loewy, 35; Yisrael Gutman, *The Jews of Warsaw, 1939–1943: Ghetto, Underground, Revolt* (Bloomington, IN, 1982), 66–67; Hauser, *Tagebuch von Irene Hauser*, 3–4, 7, 9. See also Irene Hauser's diary in ZIH Jewish Memoir Collection 302, File 299, Reel 42, RG 02.208M, United States Holocaust Memorial Museum, Washington, DC.

34. Leyb Goldin, "Chronicle of a Single Day," in *The Literature of Destruction: Jewish Responses to Catastrophe*, edited by David G. Roskies (Philadelphia, 1988), 424–434. See also "Eine 24-Stunden-Chronik," misattributed to Gordin, in *Hiob 1943: Ein Requiem für das Waschauer Getto*, edited by Karin Wolff (Neukirchen, 1983), 124–134.

35. Oskar Rosenfeld, "Uncleanliness (Medical Questions)," in Rosenfeld, *In the Beginning*, edited by Loewy, 23–25; Andrea Löw, *Juden im Getto Litzmannstadt: Lebensbedingungen, Selbstwahrnehmung, Verhalten* (Göttingen, 2006), 127; Josef Zelkowicz, "Hold the Pot for Me," in *In Those Terrible Days: Notes from the Lodz Ghetto, 1941–1944*, by Zelkowicz (Jerusalem, 2002), 192.

36. Oskar Rosenfeld, "Painting in the Ghetto, December 25, 1943," "Face of the Ghetto (Early April [1942])," and "Mood," 20 Feb. 1942, in Rosenfeld, *In the Beginning*, edited by Loewy, 238–240, 36–37, 85; Ian Frazier, "On the Prison Highway," *New Yorker*, 30 Aug. 2010.

37. Zelkowicz, "Themis, You Hold People's Fate in Your Hands! (the Thirteenth Apartment)," in *In Those Terrible Days*, by Zelkowicz, 85; entry for 1 Aug. 1943, Sascha Feuchert, Erwin Liebfried, and Jörg Riecke, eds., *Die Chronik des Gettos Lodz/Litzmannstadt* (Göttingen, 2007), 3:360.

38. Gustavo Corni, *Hitler's Ghettos: Voices from a Beleaguered Society, 1939–1944* (London, 2002), 169.

39. "Tidbit" in "Notebook H, Notes, Recollections," 2 May 1943, in Rosenfeld, *In the Beginning*, edited by Loewy, 188.

40. Entry for 5 Oct. 1940, Emmanuel Ringelblum, *Notes from the Warsaw Ghetto*, edited by Jacob Sloan (New York, 1958), 68; entry for 31 Dec. 1942, Dawid Sierakowiak, *The Diary of Dawid Sierakowiak: Five Notebooks from the Lodz Ghetto*, edited by Alan Adelson (New York, 1996), 244; Emmanuel Ringelblum, "The Era of High Boots," 14 Dec. 1942, in Philip Friedman, *Martyrs and Fighters: The Epic of the Warsaw Ghetto* (New York, 1954), 81–82; Yitzhak Katzenelson, *The Song of the Murdered Jewish People*, translated by Noah H. Rosenbloom (Hakibuutz Hameuchad, 1980), 3:6–7 (p. 23).

41. Yitzhak Katzenelson, *Vittel Diary (22.5.43–16.9.43)* (Beit Lohamei Haghetaot, 1972), 104; Singer, "Litzmannstadt-Getto, den 24. Mai 1942," and "Notzeiten—Verbrecherzeiten," 27 May 1942, in *"Im Eilschritt durch den Gettotag,"* edited by Feuchert, 52, 54; "Dura Lex, Sed Lex (the Twenty-Third Apartment)," in *In Those Terrible Days*, by Zelkowicz, 133.

42. Entries for 5 and 19 Apr. and 30 May 1942 and 6 Mar. 1943, Sierakowiak, *Diary of Dawid Sierakowiak*, edited by Adelson, 151, 156, 176–177, 252; entries for 15 July and 1 Aug. 1942, Hauser, *Tagebuch von Irene Hauser*, 4, 7. On cigarettes, Singer, "Litzmannstadt-Getto, den 20. Mai 1942" and "Eldorado der Raucher," Oct. 1942, in *"Im Eilschritt durch den Gettotag,"* edited by Feuchert, 48, 50, 155–156.

43. Löw, *Juden im Getto Litzmannstadt*, 385; Zelkowicz, "Themis, You Hold People's Fate in Your Hands!" and "The Mosquito Gets Used to Hammer Blows (the Seventeenth Apartment)," in *In Those Terrible Days*, by Zelkowicz, 85, 100.

44. Entry for 29 Nov. 1940, quoted in Kassow, *Who Will Write Our History?*, 121.

45. Kassow, *Who Will Write Our History?*, 124; Ruta Sakowska, *Menschen im Ghetto* (Osnabrück, 1999), 87.

46. Jacek Leociak, *Text in the Face of Destruction: Accounts from the Warsaw Ghetto Reconsidered* (Warsaw, 2004), 175; Helena Szereszewska, *Memoirs from Occupied Warsaw, 1940–1945* (London, 1997), 165.

47. Entry for 12 July 1942 in Hauser, *Tagebuch von Irene Hauser*, 4; entries for 3 and 9 June 1942, "Notebook C," in Rosenfeld, *In the Beginning*, edited by Loewy, 65, 67; Adina Blady-Szwajger, *I więcej nic nie paniętam* (Warsaw, 1994), 40, quoted in Leociak, *Text in the Face of Destruction*, 151n36. See also entry for 28 Apr. 1943, in Zofia Nałkowska, "A Wartime Journal," *Polish Perspectives* 14 (Mar. 1970): 32.

48. June 1942 in Ringelblum, *Notes from the Warsaw Ghetto*, edited by Sloan, 293; Jan Karski, *Story of a Secret State* (Boston, 1944), 326.

49. "Idleness," Notebook A, in Rosenfeld, *In the Beginning*, edited by Loewy, 18–19; Barbara Engelking, *Holocaust and Memory: The Experience of the Holocaust and Its Consequences: An Investigation Based on Personal Narratives*, translated by Emma Harris (London, 2001), 67; entry for 6 May 1942, Sierakowiak, *Diary of Dawid Sierakowiak*, edited by Adelson, 163.

50. Entry for 14 Apr. 1943, Wendy Lower, ed., *The Diary of Samuel Golfard and the Holocaust in Galicia* (Lanham, MD, 2011), 95.

51. Zelkowicz, *In Those Terrible Days*, 35, 38, 116.

52. Ibid., 35–38, 60, 75.

53. Notebook E and "Face of the Ghetto," Notebook 13, Rosenfeld, *In the Beginning*, edited by Loewy, 77, 105–106.

54. Notebook 22, ibid., xxx, 98.

55. Bertrand Perz, "Das Ghetto in Lodz: Die Grenzen des Ghettos als Grenzen der Erklärung," in *Walled Cities und die Konstruktion von Communities: Das europäische Ghetto als urbaner Raum*, edited by Gerhard Milchram (Vienna, 2001), 113.

56. "Hunger," Notebook 13; and Notebook 22, Rosenfeld, *In the Beginning*, edited by Loewy, 89–90, 96.

57. Entry for 4 Sept. 1942, "In Those Terrible Days," in *In Those Terrible Days*, Zelkowicz, 289; entry for 2 Oct. 1942, "Notebook E," Rosenfeld, *In the Beginning*, edited by Loewy, 138.

58. Singer, "Mieten auf" (1942/43), in *"Im Eilschritt durch den Gettotag,"* edited by Feuchert, 161; entry for 3 Mar. 1944, "Notebook K," Rosenfeld, *In the Beginning*, edited by Loewy, 258; "Face of the Ghetto" (1942), Notebook 13, in ibid., 77.

59. Entry for 6 Sept. 1942, "In Those Terrible Days," in *In Those Terrible Days*, by Zelkowicz, 366; "A Bruise and a Welt in Every Dwelling," in ibid., 36, 70.

60. Entry for 5 Sept. 1942, "In Those Terrible Days," in ibid., 332–338.

61. Entry for 10 Aug. 1942, Abraham Lewin, *A Cup of Tears: A Diary of the Warsaw Ghetto* (Oxford, 1988), 151.

62. Katzenelson, *Song of the Murdered Jewish People*, 2:7 (p. 18), 2:15 (p. 20), 3:6 (p. 21), 5:8 (p. 34), 14:10 (p. 84), 15:13, 15 (p. 85).

Chapter 9: Broken Words

1. www.roberthjackson.org/speech-and-writing/opening-statement-before-the-international-military-tribunal.

2. Richard Raskin, *A Child at Gunpoint: A Case Study in the Life of a Photo* (Aarhus, 2004), 21; Peter Longerich, *Heinrich Himmler: Biographie* (Munich, 2008), 715.

3. iconicphotos.wordpress.com/2010/07/23/fall-of-france; A. E. Johann, "'Freedom Is Not Easy': *Reflexions au sujet d'une photo*," *Signal*, no. 5 (Mar. 1942); "1918 = 1943," *Signal*, no. 1 (Jan. 1944); Himmler at Posen on 4 Oct. 1943, quoted in Ian Kersaw, *Hitler, 1936–1945: Nemesis* (New York, 2000), 605.

4. Jewish historian Isaac Schiper quoted in Samuel D. Kassow, *Who Will Write Our History? Emanuel Ringelblum, the Warsaw Ghetto, and the Oyneg Shabes Archive* (Bloomington, IN, 2007), 210. Figures of arrested and deported Jews cited in Andrzej Wirth, introduction to *The Stroop Report: The Jewish Quarter of Warsaw Is No More!* (New York, 1979), pt. 3.

5. Raskin, *Child at Gunpoint*, 26.

6. White in Norbert Frei and Wulf Kansteiner, eds., *Den Holocaust erzählen: Historiographie zwischen wissenschaftlicher Empirie und narrativer Kreativität* (Jena, 2013), 60.

7. Christian Gerlach, *Kalkulierte Morde: Die deutsche Wirtschafts- und Vernichtungspolitik in Weissrussland, 1941 bis 1944* (Hamburg, 2000), 573–574; Klaus Hesse, " . . . Gefangenenlager, Exekution, . . . Irrenanstalt . . . : Walter Frentz' Reise nach Minsk im Gefolge Heinrich Himmlers im August 1941," in *Die Auge des Dritten Reiches: Hitlers Kameramann und Fotograph Walter Frentz*, edited by Hans Georg Hiller von Gaertringen (Berlin, 2007), 180–186; Longerich, *Heinrich Himmler: Biographie*, 552.

8. Dwinger to Ullmann, 14 Aug. 1941 in Berlin Document Center, SSO 166/1241, National Archives and Records Administration, College Park, MD. See also Peter Fritzsche, "Return to Soviet Russia: Edwin Erich Dwinger and the Narratives of Barbarossa," *Kritika* 10 (Summer 2009): 557–570. On Bach-Zelewski, Robert Jay Lifton, *The Nazi Doctors: Medical Killing and the Psychology of Genocide* (New York, 1986), 159, 437.

9. Rolf Düsterberg, *Hanns Johst: "Der Barde der SS"; Karrieren eiens deutschen Dichters* (Paderborn, 2004), 302–310.

10. Ibid., 303.

11. Entry for 2 Apr. 1942, Elke Fröhlich, ed., *Die Tagebücher von Joseph Goebbels: Sämtliche Fragmente* (Munich, 1994), pt. 2, 4:40–41; Alan E. Steinweis, "The Trials of Herschel Grynszpan: Anti-Jewish Policy and German Propaganda, 1938–1942," *German Studies Review* 31 (2008): 479.

12. David Bankier, "Signaling the Final Solution to the German People," in *Nazi Europe and the Final Solution*, edited by Bankier and Israel Gutman (New York, 2009), 19.

13. Albert to Agnes Neuhaus, 25 Sept.–9 Oct. and 30 Nov. 1941 and 1 Mar. 1942, in *Zwischen Front und Heimat: Der Briefwechsel des Münsterischen Ehepaares Agnes und Albert Neuhaus, 1940–1944*, edited by Karl Reddemann (Münster, 1996), 323, 362–363, 433.

14. Broadcast from France on 17 June 1940 in William L. Shirer, *"This Is Berlin": Radio Broadcasts from Nazi Germany, 1938–40* (New York, 1999), 328. See also Gustave Flocher, *Marching to Captivity: The War Diaries of a French Peasant, 1939–45*, edited by Christopher Hill (London, 1996), 128; entry for 20 Sept. 1941, Herman Kruk, *Last Days of the Jerusalem of Lithuania* (New Haven, CT, 2002), 103. See also *True to Type: A Selection from Letters and Diaries of German Soldiers and Civilians Collected on the Soviet-German Front* (London, n.d. [1943]); Michael Burleigh, *The Third Reich: A New History* (New York, 2000), 561; Gudrun Schwarz, *Eine Frau an seiner Seite: Ehefrauen in der "SS-Sippengemeinschaft"* (Hamburg, 1997), 227–228; and Fritzsche, "The Holocaust," in *Imagining the Twentieth Century*, edited by Fritzsche and Charles Stewart (Urbana, 1997), 66.

15. Janina Struk, *Photographing the Holocaust: Interpretations of the Evidence* (London, 2004), 59–60, 66; Sönke Neitzel and Harald Welzer, *Soldaten: Protokolle von Kämpfen, Töten und Sterben* (Frankfurt, 2011), 48. See also Alexander B. Rossino, "Eastern Europe Through German Eyes: Soldiers' Photographs 1939–1942," *History of Photography* 23, no. 4 (1999): 314, 317.

16. Alain Finkielkraut, *Verlust der Menschlichkeit: Versuch über das 20. Jahrhundert* (Stuttgart, 1998), 83–84.

17. Entries for 13 and 16 Sept. 1941, Konrad Jarausch, ed., *Reluctant Accomplice: A Wehrmacht Soldier's Letter from the Eastern Front* (Princeton, NJ, 2011), 283, 287–288; "Krieg bis in alle Ewigkeit?," *Die Front: Feldzeitung einer Armee*, no. 187 (22 Oct. 1941).

18. Finkielkraut, *Verlust der Menschlichkeit*, 83–84; Albert Camus, "Letters to a German Friend," in *Resistance, Rebellion, and Death*, translated by Justin O'Brien (New York, 1961), 9, 28, 30.

19. Saul Friedlander, "The 'Final Solution': On the Unease in Historical Interpretation," in *The Holocaust: Theoretical Readings*, edited by Neil Levi and Michael Rothberg (New Brunswick, NJ, 2003), 70–71; entries for 27 and 7 Mar. and 27 Apr. 1942 in Goebbels, *Tagebücher von Goebbels*, pt. 2, 3:561, 431–432, 4:184. See also Christian T. Barth, *Goebbels und die Juden* (Paderborn, 2003), 199n233.

20. Heinrich Döll to Heinz, 20 Sept. 1939 and 14/15 Oct. 1944, Döll correspondence, Kempowski Archive, 5940/1, Akademie der Künste, Berlin.

21. Entry for 13 Dec. 1943, Friedrich Kellner, *"Vernebelt, verdunkelt sind alle Hirne": Tagebücher, 1939–1945*, 2 vols. (Göttingen, 2011), 1:587; entries for Aug. 1942 and 21 June 1943, Agnès Humbert, *Résistance: A Woman's Journal of Struggle and Defiance in Occupied France* (New York, 2008), 158–159, 194; entry for 17 Aug. 1943, Ernst Jünger, *Strahlungen* (Munich, 1955), 296; Hans Erich Nossack, *The End: Hamburg, 1943* (Chicago, 2004), 5, 34.

22. Entries for 3 Feb. 1945 and 24 Aug. 1943, Matthais Menzel, *Die Stadt ohne Tod: Berliner Tagebuch, 1943/45* (Berlin, 1946), 119–120, 16; entry for 15 May 1943, Léon Werth, *Déposition: Journal, 1940–1944* (Paris, 1992), 475.

23. Gabriella Gribaudi, "Bombing and the Land War in Italy: Military Strategy, Reactions, and Collective Memory," in *Experience and Memory: The Second World War in Europe*, edited by Jörg Echternkamp and Stefan Martens (New York, 2010), 125; Konrad Warner, *Schicksalswende Europas*, quoted in *Travels in the Reich, 1933–1945: Foreign Authors Report from Germany*, edited by Oliver Lubrich (Chicago, 2010), 299–300; entry for 27 May 1943, Werth, *Déposition: Journal, 1940–1944*, 478–479; entries for 13 Jan. 1943 and 17 Nov. 1942, Anne Frank, *The Diary of a Young Girl* (New York, 1995), 63–64, 51–52.

24. Daniel Swift, *Bomber County: The Poetry of a Lost Pilot's War* (New York, 2010), 154.

25. Michael Reiter," "Christliche Existenz und sozialer Wandel in der ersten Hälfte des 20. Jahrhunderts: Eine Hamburger Kirchengemeinde in den politischen Auseinandersetzungen der Weimrarer Republik und des Dritten Reiches" (Ph.D. diss., University of Hamburg, 1992), 202; Nossack, *The End: Hamburg, 1943*, 63. On traveling light, see also Christel Beilmann to J. K., 25 Jan. 1945, in *Eine katholische Jugend in Gottes und dem Dritten Reich: Briefe, Berichte, Gedrucktes, 1930–1945*, by Beilmann (Wuppertal, 1989), 158.

26. Pieter Lagrou, *The Legacy of Nazi Occupation: Patriotic Memory and National Recovery in Western Europe, 1945–1965* (Cambridge, 2000), 253.

27. Jean-Paul Sartre, "Paris Under the Occupation," in *French Writing on English Soil: A Choice of French Writing Published in London Between November 1940 and June 1944*, edited by J. G. Weightman (London, 1945), 124–125. On concierges, see Ronald C. Rosbottom, *When Paris Went Dark: The City of Light Under German Occupation, 1940–1944* (New York, 2014), 329; Ivan Heilbut, *Birds of Passage* (New York, 1943), 3; Robert Brasillach, *Six heures à perdre* (Paris, 1944).

28. Versors, "L'impuissance," in *Le silence de la mer* (Paris, 1951), 126–127.

29. Elsa Triolet, *A Fine of Two Hundred Francs* (London, 1986), 262–263, 287.

30. Entries for 20 and 22 Oct. and 10 Nov. 1943 and 15 Jan. 1944, Zofia Nałkowska, "A Wartime Journal," *Polish Perspectives* 14 (Mar. 1971): 34–37.

31. Entries for 15 Oct. 1943 and 15 Jan. 1944, ibid.; Stanisław Szefler, *Okupacyjne drogi* (Warsaw, 1967), 185, 191. See also entry for 10 Dec. 1940, Stanisław Rembek, *Dziennik okupacyjny* (Warsaw, 2000), 139. On resistance, see Piotr Madajczyk, "Experience and Memory: The Second World War in Poland," in *Experience and Memory*, edited by Echternkamp and Martens, 72.

32. Quoted in Yisrael Gutman and Shmuel Krakowski, *Unequal Victims: Poles and Jews During World War Two* (New York, 1986), 117.

33. Entry for 10 Nov. 1943, 15 Jan. 1944, Nałkowska, "A Wartime Journal," 36; Czeslaw Milosz, "The Spirit of History," in *A Treatise on Poetry* (New York, 2001), 27.

34. Pawel Rodak, "Attitudes des écrivains polonais pendant la guerre," in *Ecrire sous l'occupation: Du non sonsentment à la Résistance France-Belgique-Pologne, 1940–1945*, edited by Bruno Curatolo and François Marcot (Rennes, 2011), 282–283. See also Piotr Madajczyk, "Experience and Memory: The Second World War in Poland," in *Experience and Memory*, edited by Echternkamp and Martens, 72.

35. Entries for 11 Aug. and 17 and 10 Oct. 1944 and 10 Feb. 1945, Nałkowska, "A Wartime Journal," 40–41, 43.

36. Emanuel Ringelblum, *Polish-Jewish Relations During the Second World War*, edited by Joseph Kermish and Shmuel Krakowski (Evanston, IL, 1974), 308; Gunnar S. Paulsson, *Secret City: The Hidden Jews of Warsaw, 1940–1945* (New Haven, CT, 2002), 5.

37. Tomasz Szarota, "The Merry-Go-Round on Krasinski Square: Did the 'Happy Throngs Laugh'? The Debate Regarding the Attitude of Warsaw's Inhabitants Towards the Ghetto Uprising," *Polin: Studies in Polish Jewry* 26 (2014): 493–515; Jan Błoński et al., "'Campo di Fiori' Fifty Years Later: The People Who Remain; A Discussion That Took Place on the Fiftieth Anniversary of the Warsaw Ghetto Uprising," *Polin: Studies Polish Jewry* 24 (2012): 418.

38. Szarota, "Merry-Go-Round on Krasinski Square," 496–497, 508, 510–511, 513.

39. Ibid., 506, 508, 513. Wyleżyńska cited in Rachel Feldhay Brenner, *The Ethics of Witnessing: The Holocaust in Polish Writers' Diaries from Warsaw, 1939–1945* (Evanston, IL, 2014), 79.

40. Zofia Nałkowska, *Medallions*, translated by Diana Kuprel (Evanston, IL, 2000). See also Zofia Lesinska, "Disgrace and Torment: The Holocaust in Zofia Nałkowska's *Medallions*," in *National Responses to the Holocaust: National Identity and Public Memory*, edited by Jennifer Taylor (Lanham, MD, 2014).

41. Peter Steinberg, *Journey to Oblivion: The End of the East European Yiddish and German Worlds in the Mirror of Literature* (Toronto, 1991), 9–10.

42. "About the Study 'Hunger'!," 16 Apr. 1944, Oskar Rosenfeld, *In the Beginning Was the Ghetto: Notebooks from Lodz*, edited by Hanno Loewy (Evanston, IL, 2002), 266.

43. Kassow, *Who Will Write Our History?*, 210.

44. Ibid., 210, 3, 6.

45. Entry for 30 May 1942, Abraham Lewin, *A Cup of Tears: A Diary of the Warsaw Ghetto*, edited by Antony Polonsky (Oxford, 1988), 108; Jacek Leociak, *Text in the Face of Destruction: Accounts from the Warsaw Ghetto Reconsidered* (Warsaw, 2004), 87, 89.

46. Ringelblum quoted in Kassow, *Who Will Write Our History?*, 387; entries for 29 Nov. 1940 and 4 Aug. 1942, Chaim Kaplan, *The Scroll of Agony: The Warsaw Diary of Chaim A. Kaplan*, edited and translated by Abraham I. Katsh (New York, 1965), 229, 340; entry for 11 Nov. 1942, Lewin, *Cup of Tears: A Diary of the Warsaw Ghetto*, 207.

47. Auerbach quoted in Philip Friedman, *Martyrs and Fighters: The Epic of the Warsaw Ghetto* (New York, 1954), 136; Szlengel in Kassow, *Who Will Write Our History?*, 316–317; Rosenfeld in Gustavo Corni, *Hitler's Ghettos: Voices from a Beleaguered Society, 1939–1944* (London, 2002), 6.

48. Leociak, *Text in the Face of Destruction*, 103–104; Jörg Riecke, "Notizen zur Sprache der Reportagen und Essays," in *"Im Eilschritt durch den Gettotag": Reportagen und Essays aus dem Getto Lodz*, edited by Sascha Feuchert (Berlin, 2002), 239–240.

49. Entry for 6 Sept. 1942, "In Those Terrible Days," in *In Those Terrible Days: Notes from the Lodz Ghetto, 1941–1944*, by Josef Zelkowicz (Jerusalem, 2002), 355; entry for 25 Jan. 1943, Wendy Lower, ed., *The Diary of Samuel Golfard and the Holocaust in Galicia* (Lanham, MD, 2011), 49.

50. Entry for 22 Jan. 1943, Moshe Flinker, *Auch wenn ich hoffe: Das Tagebuch des Moshe Flinker* (Berlin, 2008), 86. Translation from *Young Moshe's Diary: The Spiritual Torment of a Jewish Boy in Nazi Europe* (Jerusalem, 1963), 71.

51. David G. Roskies, *Against the Apocalypse: Responses to Catastrophe in Modern Jewish Culture* (Cambridge, 1984), 200.

52. Jarecka quoted in Kassow, *Who Will Write Our History?*, 6; Emanuel Ringelblum, "Oyneg Shabbes," in *The Literature of Destruction: Jewish Responses to Catastrophe*, edited by David G. Roskies (Philadelphia, 1988), 386; Sem Dresden, *Holocaust und Literatur* (Frankfurt, 1997), 33–34; entry for 11 June 1942, Lucjan Dobroszycki, ed., *The Chronicle of the Lodz Ghetto, 1941–1944* (New Haven, CT, 1984), 204.

53. Celan quoted in Leociak, *Text in the Face of Destruction*, 101; diarist quoted in Andrea Löw, *Juden im Getto Litzmannstadt: Lebensbedingungen, Selbstwahrnehmung, Verhalten* (Göttingen, 2006), 7; entry for 13 Sept. 1943, Yitzhak Katzenelson, *Vittel Diary (22.5.43–16.9.43)* (Beit Lohamei Haghetaot, 1972), 224; Ringelblum quoted in Kassow, *Who Will Write Our History?*, 319; Leociak, *Text in the Face of Destruction*, 101.

54. Gustawa Jarecka, "The Last Stage of Resettlement Is Death" (1942), quoted in Ruta Sakowska, *Die zweite Etappe ist der Tod: NS-Ausrottungspolitik gegen die polnischen Juden, gesehen mit den Augen der Opfer* (Berlin, 1993), 228–232.

55. Saul Friedländer, *The Years of Extermination: Nazi Germany and the Jews, 1939–1945* (New York, 2007), xxvi; Leociak, *Text in the Face of Destruction*, 103–104.

56. Rebecca West, *Black Lamb and Grey Falcon: The Record of a Journey Through Yugoslavia in 1937* (London, 1943), 1:390.

INDEX

Peter Fritzsche is the W. D. and Sarah E. Trowbridge Professor of History at the University of Illinois. The author of nine books, including the award-winning *Life and Death in the Third Reich*, he lives in Urbana, Illinois.